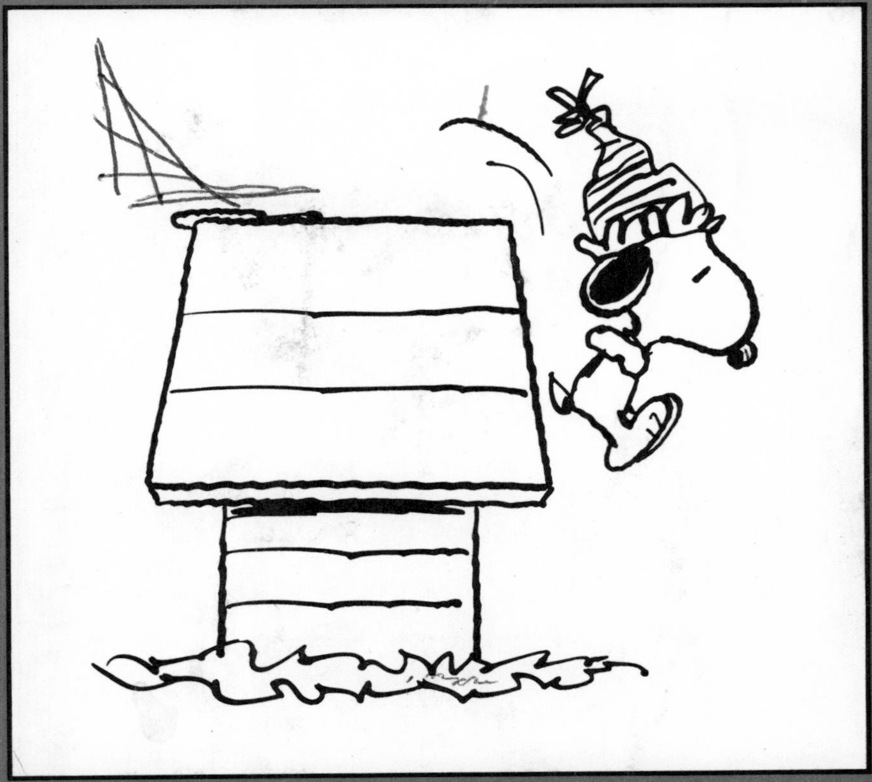

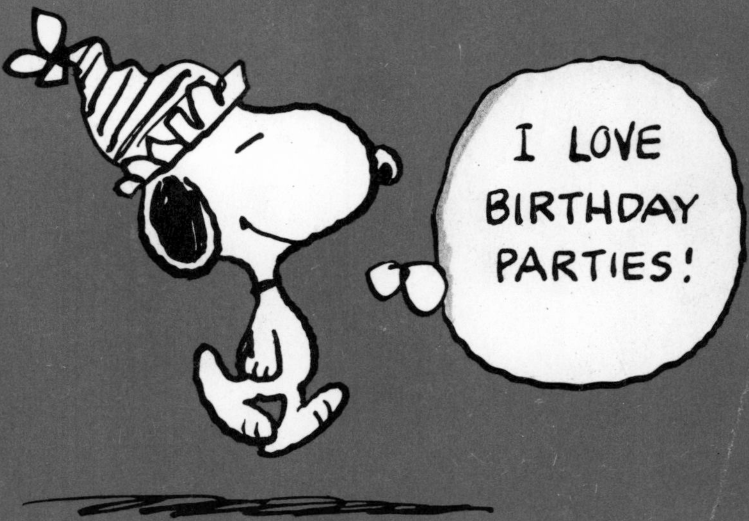
I LOVE
BIRTHDAY
PARTIES!

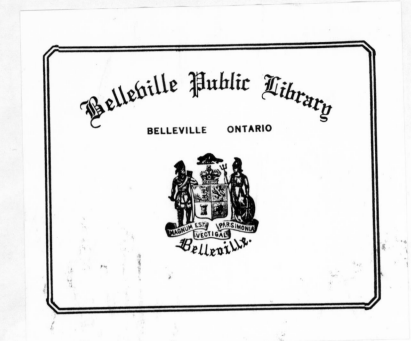

HAPPY BIRTHDAY, CHARLIE BROWN

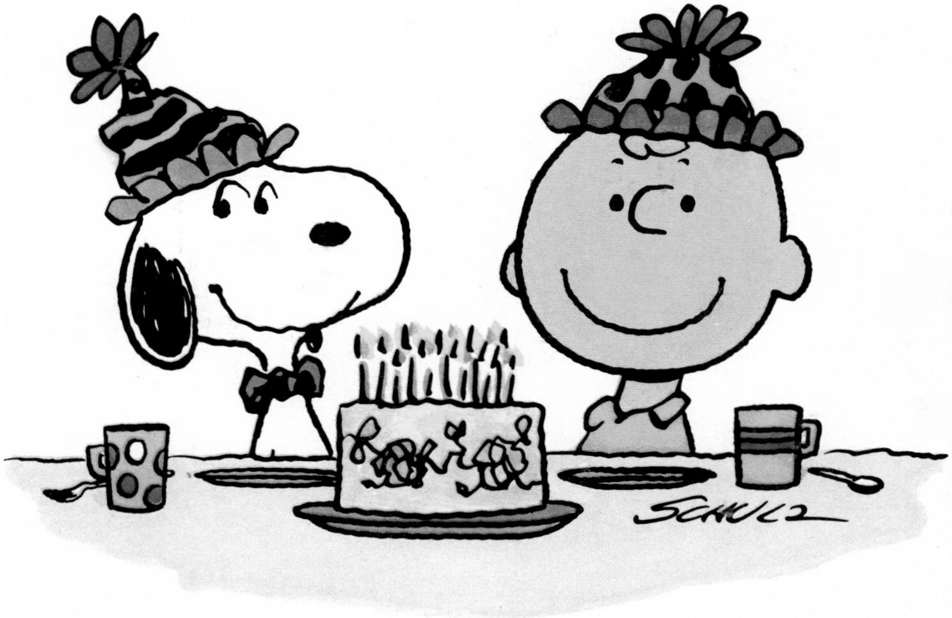
SCHULZ

For Debbie and Jeannie . . .

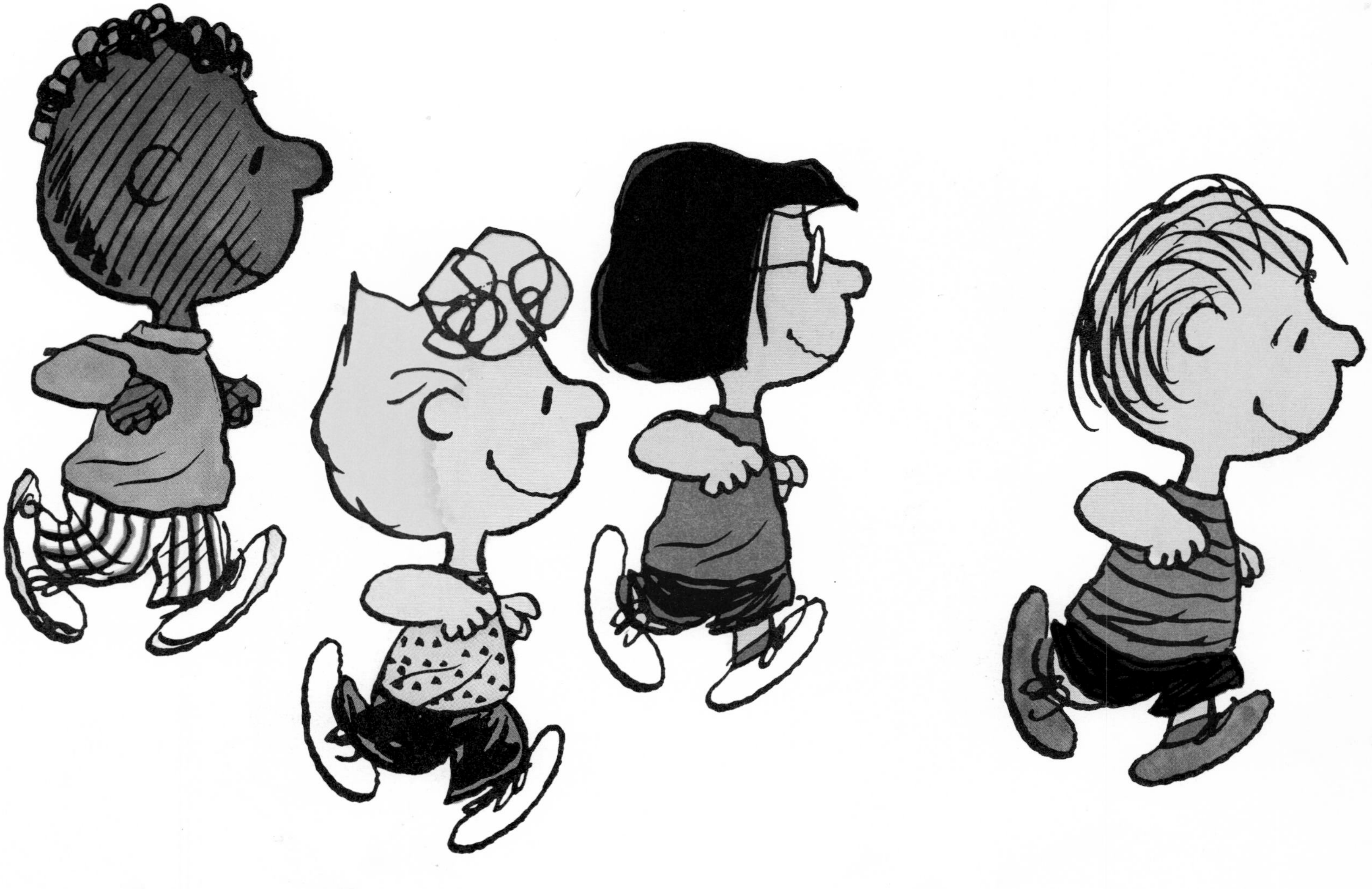

HAPPY BIRTHDAY,

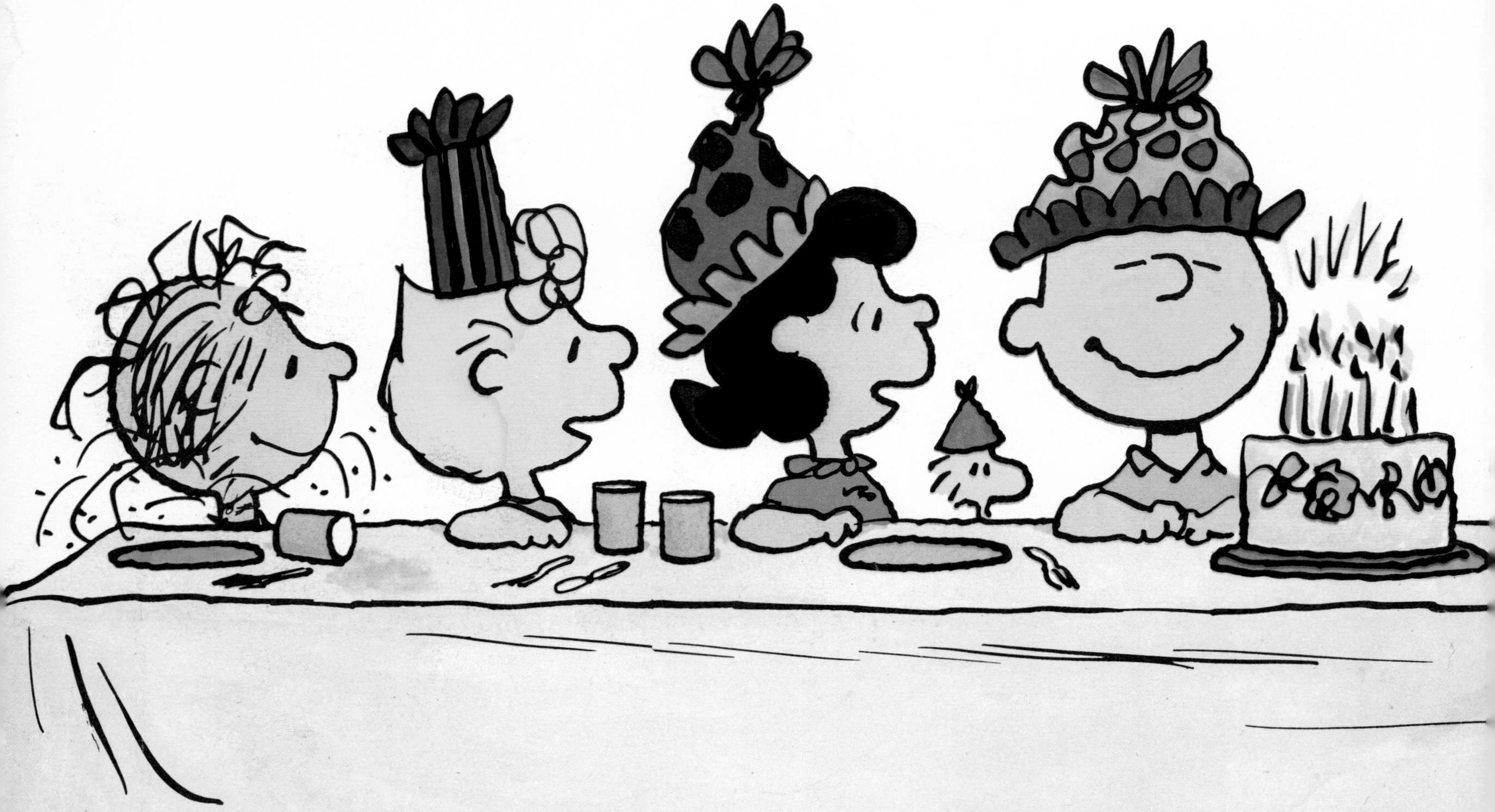

CHARLIE BROWN

Lee Mendelson in association with Charles Schulz

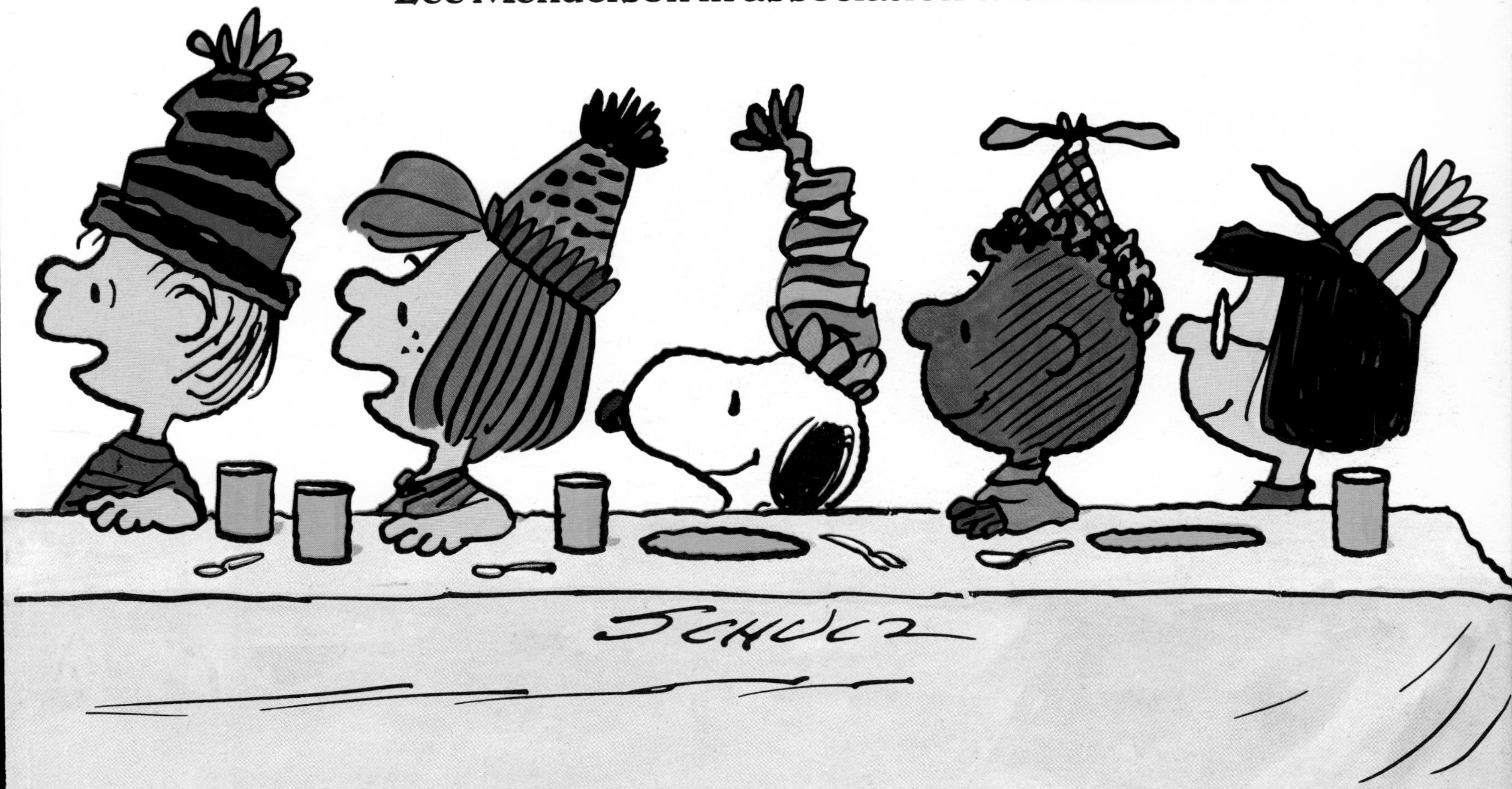
SCHULZ

Random House New York

Published in the United States by Random House, Inc., New York and simultaneously in Canada by Random House of Canada Limited, Toronto.

Library of Congress Cataloging in Publication Data

Mendelson, Lee.
Happy birthday, Charlie Brown.

SUMMARY: Highlights 30 years of the Peanuts comic strip, with reproductions of cartoons and anecdotes from its creator.
1. Schulz, Charles M. Peanuts. [1. Schulz, Charles M. Peanuts. 2. Cartoons and comics]
I. Schulz, Charles, M., joint author. II. Title.
PN6728.P4M46 741.5'973 79-4797
ISBN 0-394-50746-0

Manufactured in the United States of America

98765432

First Edition

FOREWORD

1979–1980 marks the thirtieth anniversary of Charles Schulz's *Peanuts*. It also marks our fifteenth year on network television with Charlie Brown and Snoopy.

This book celebrates those years, and also says "thank you" to the tens of millions of readers of the comic strip and the viewers of the television shows without whom none of this would have been possible.

Lee Mendelson
Executive Producer
Peanuts Movies and TV

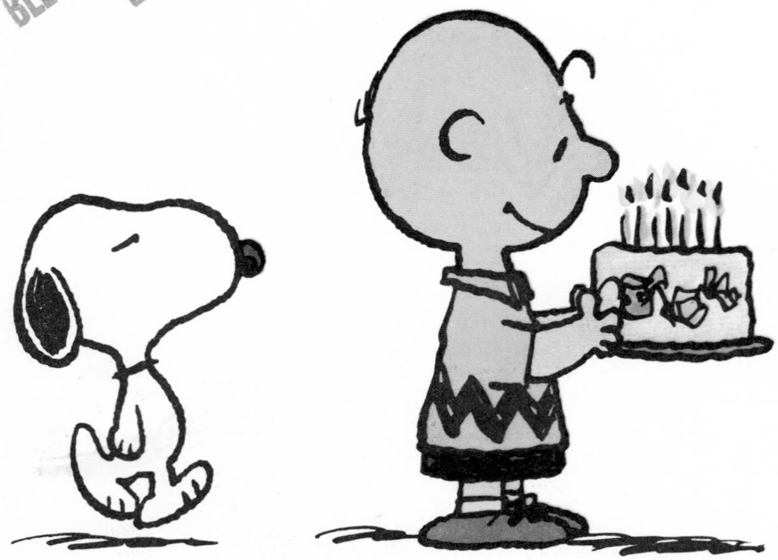

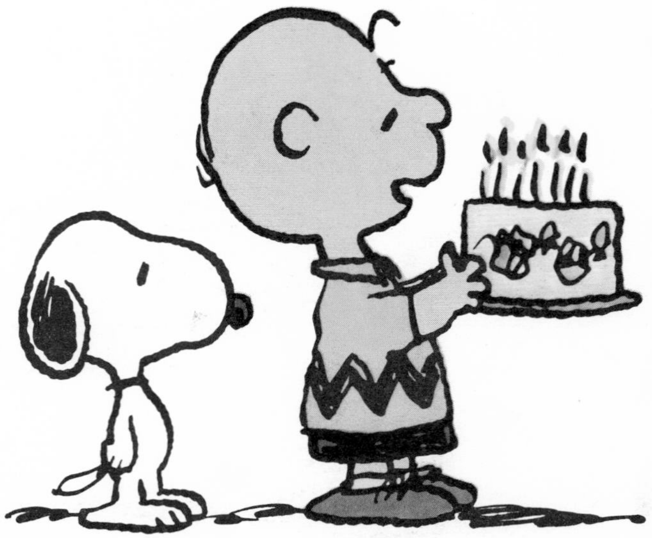

CONTENTS

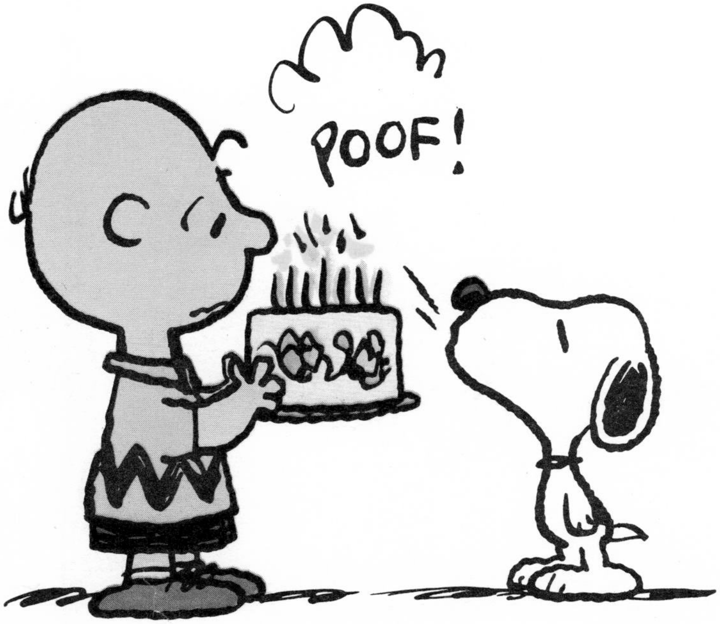

POOF!

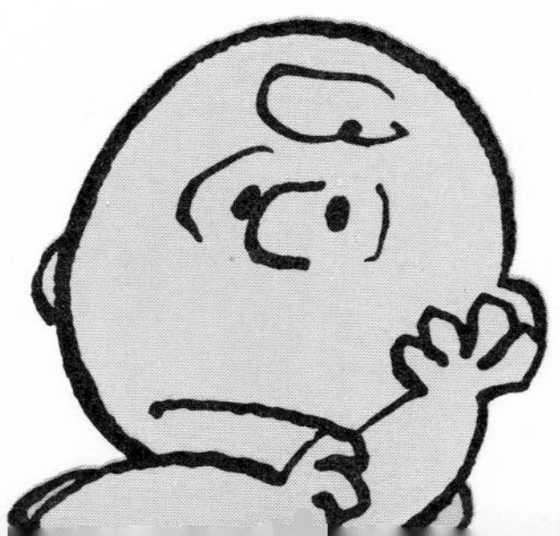

Thirty years . . . over ten thousand comic strips . . . over fifty thousand sketches . . . by one man with no assistants . . . *good grief!!!*

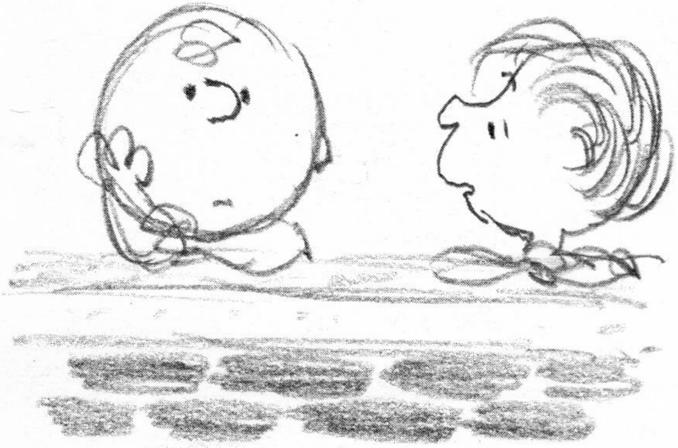
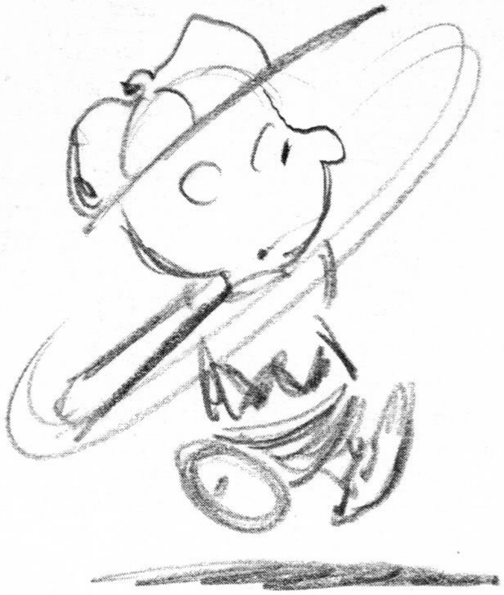
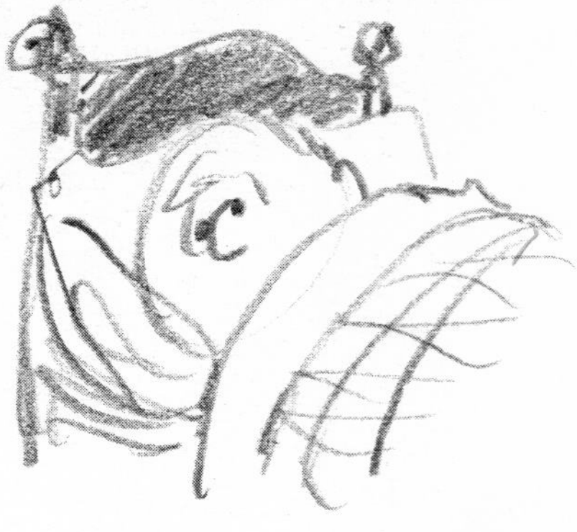
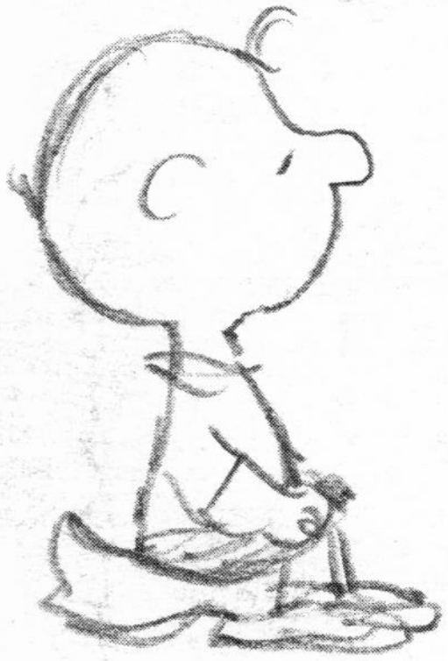
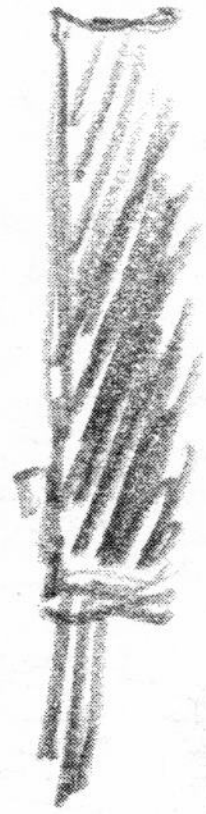
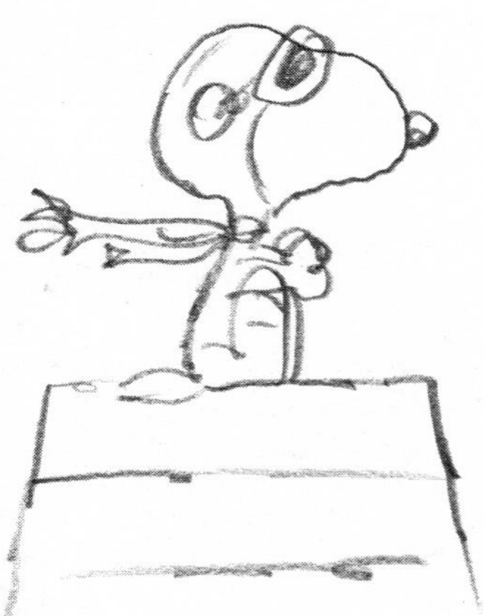
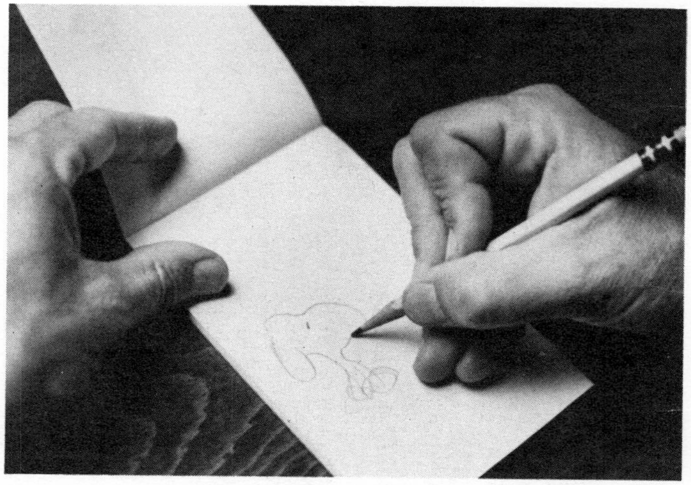
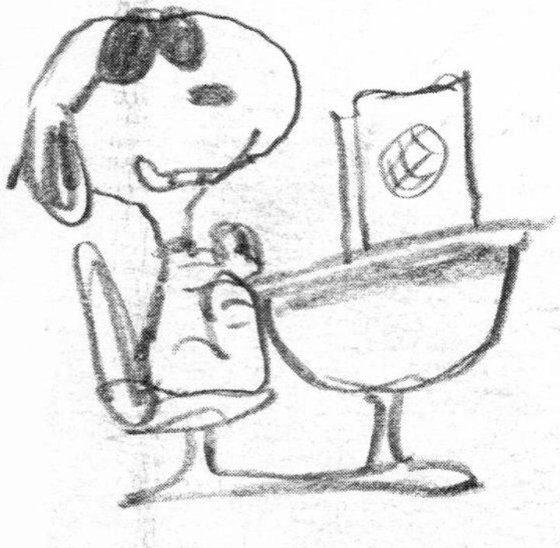
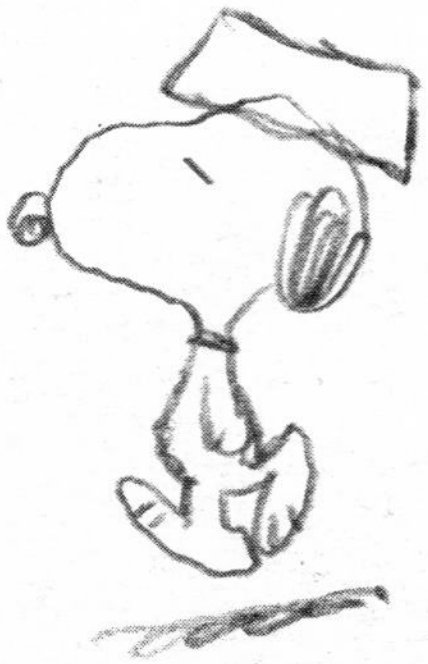
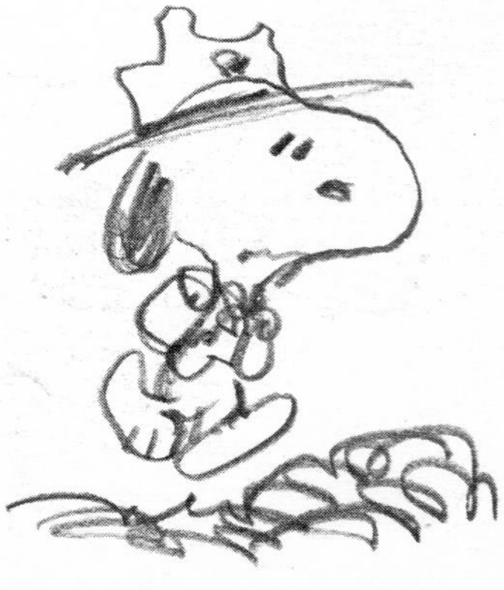
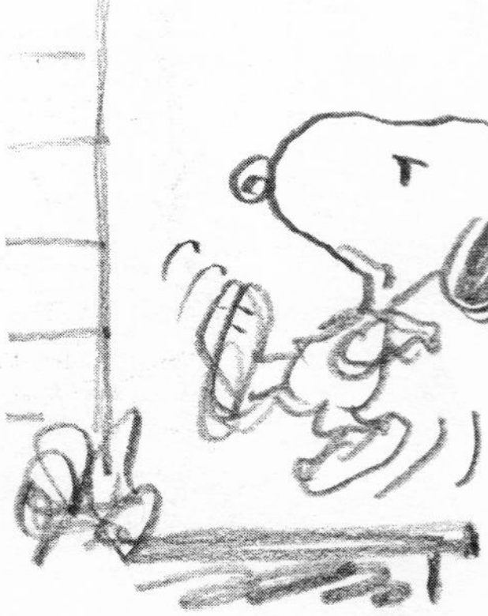

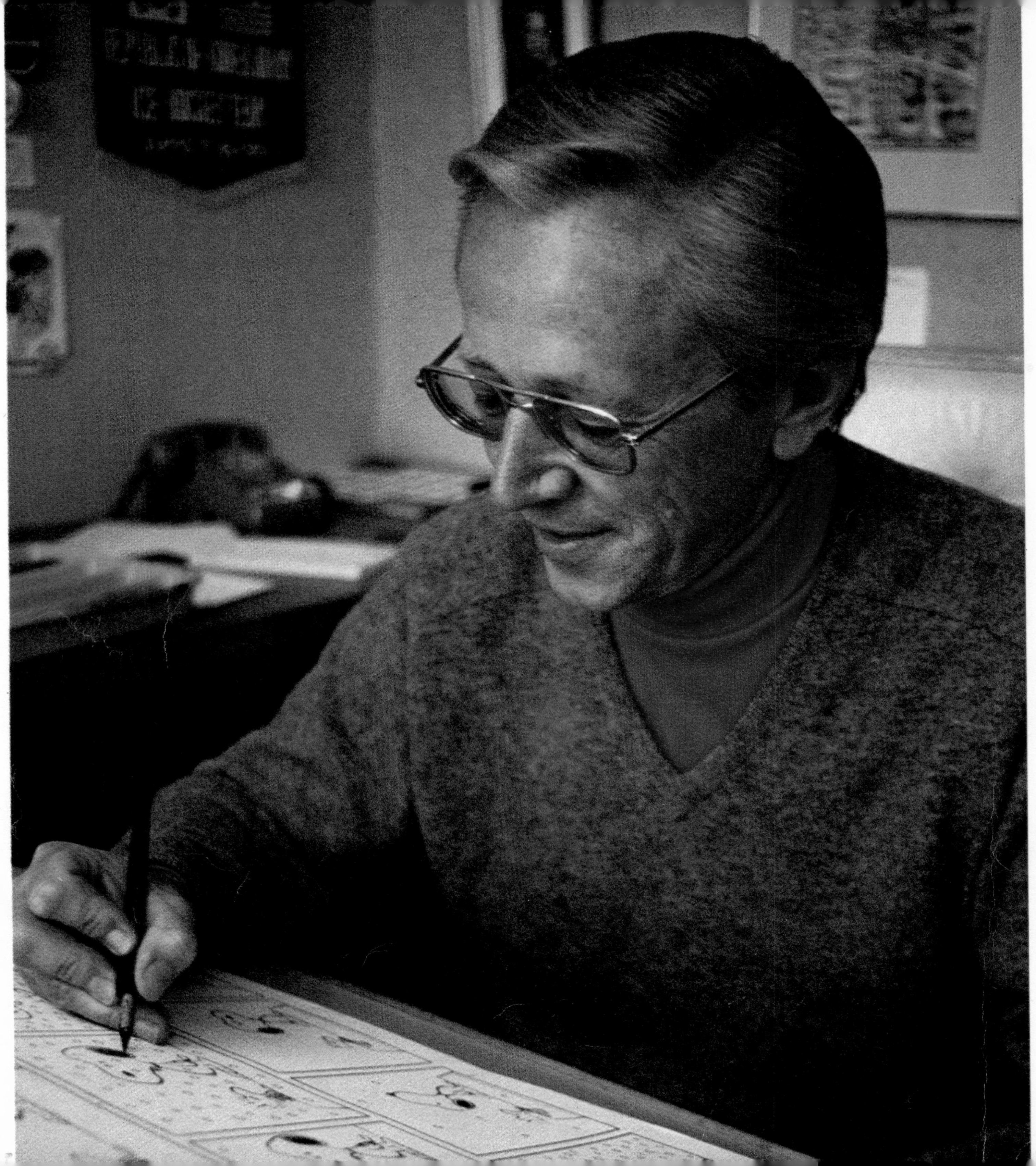

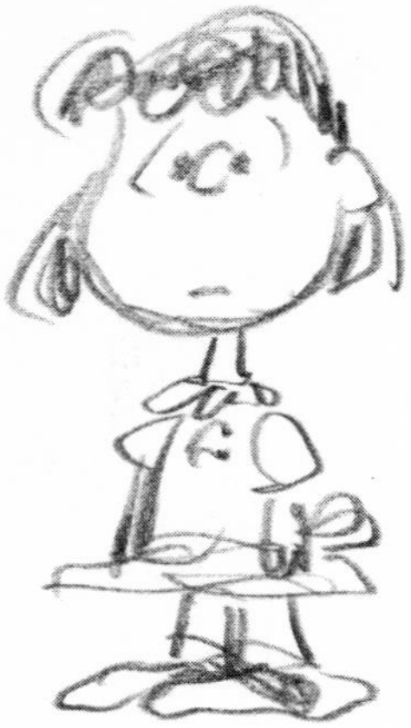

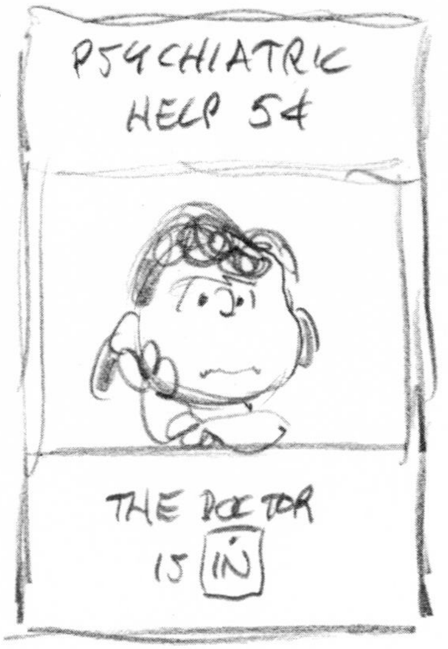
PSYCHIATRIC
HELP 5¢
THE DOCTOR
IS IN

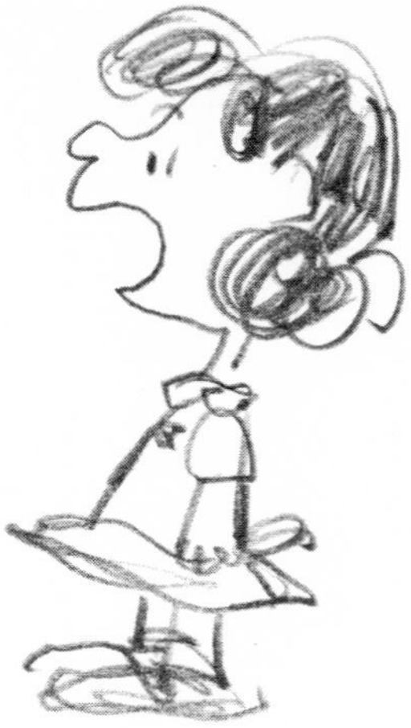

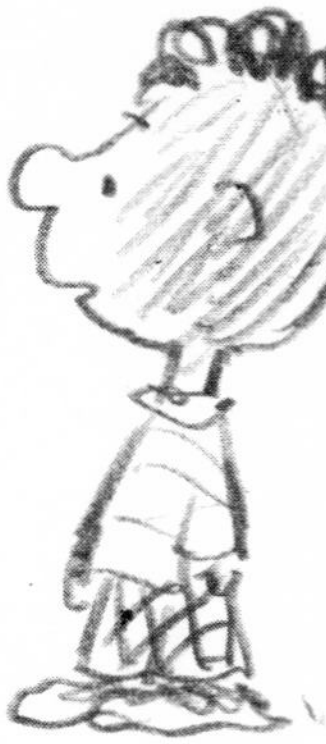

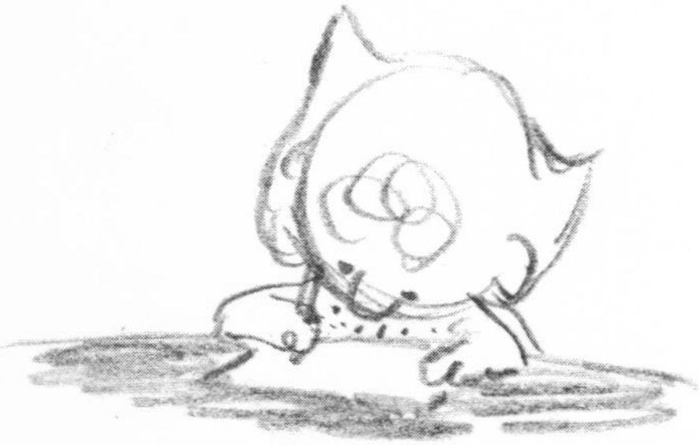

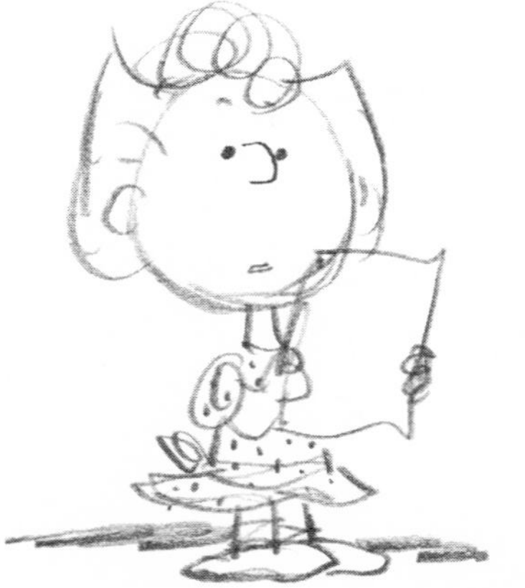

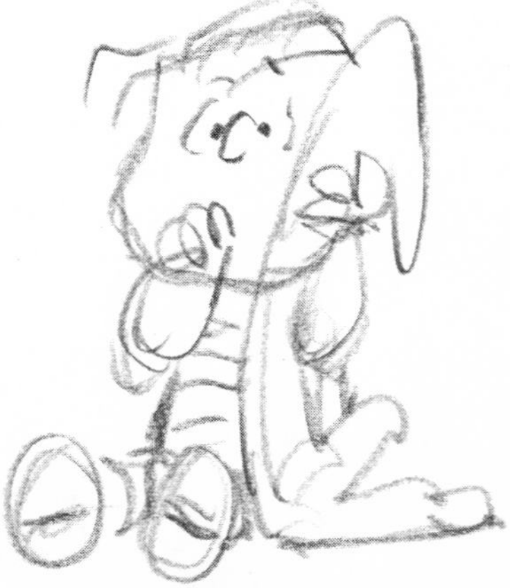

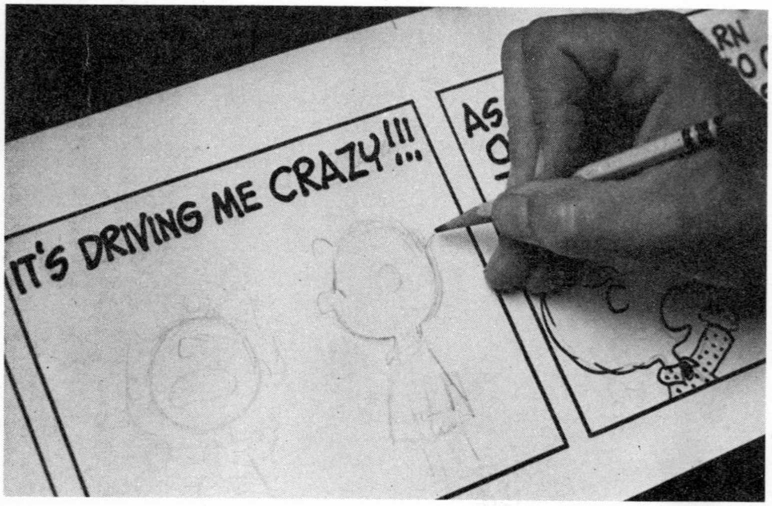
IT'S DRIVING ME CRAZY!!!

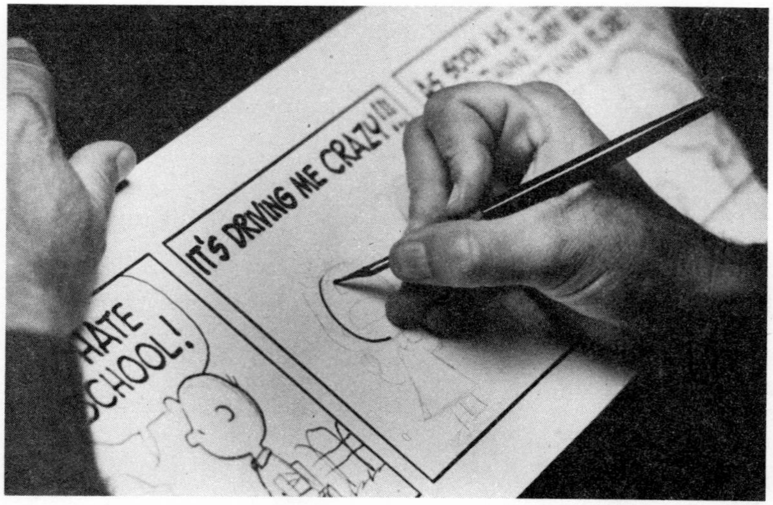
HATE
SCHOOL!
IT'S DRIVING ME CRAZY!!!

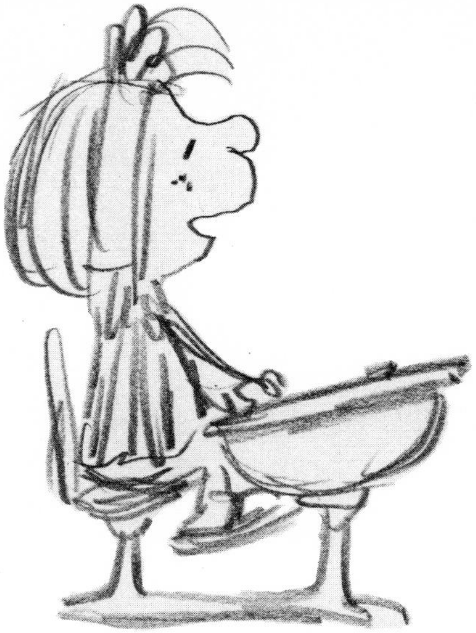

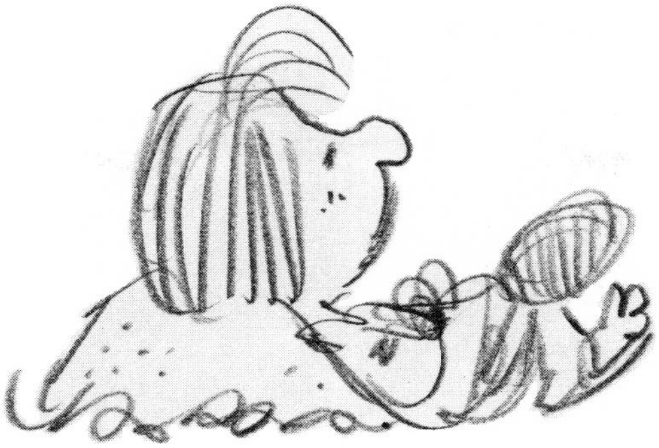

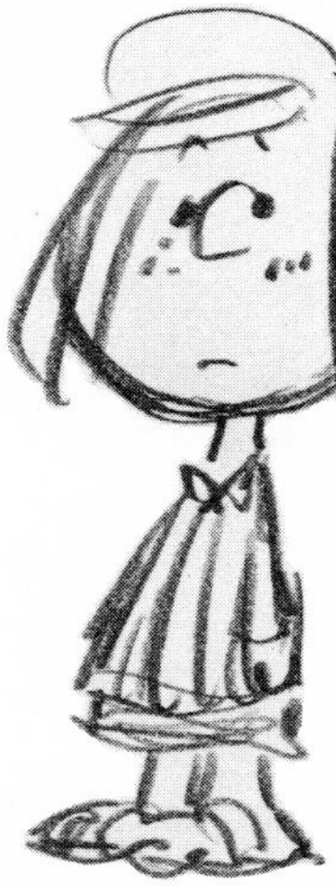

Says Schulz: "I just must do the inking and lettering myself. I take great pride in what I do, and when each strip is finished, I want to be able to say 'That's mine' . . . and after all these years I'd still rather sit down at the drawing board and try to create these funny sketches and ideas than do anything else . . . . with the possible exception of hitting a good overhead . . ."

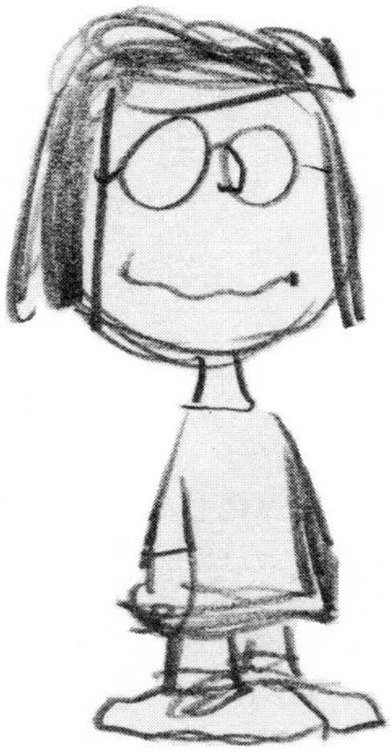

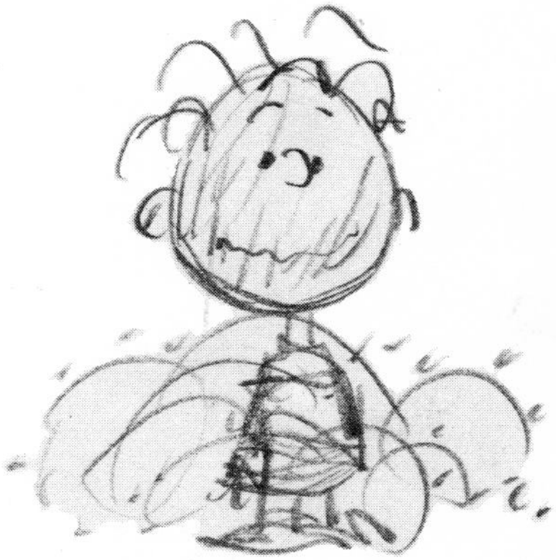

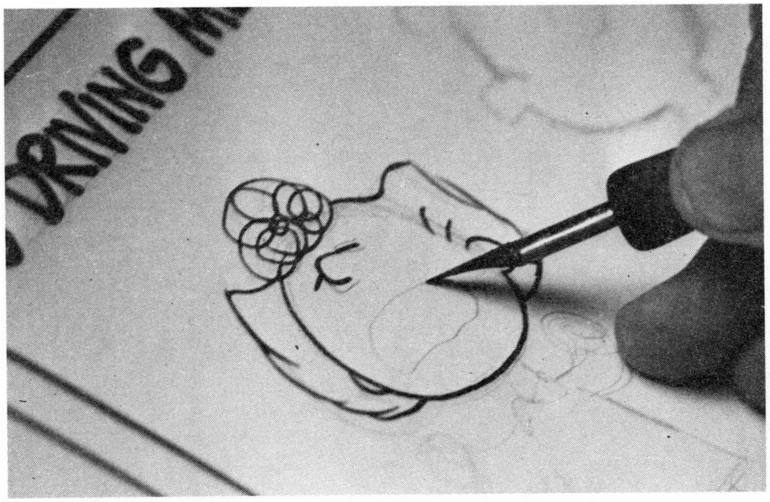
DRIVING

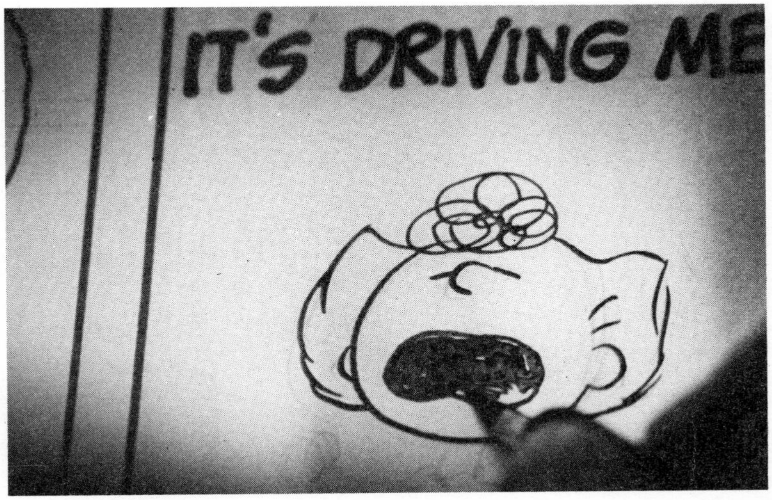
IT'S DRIVING ME

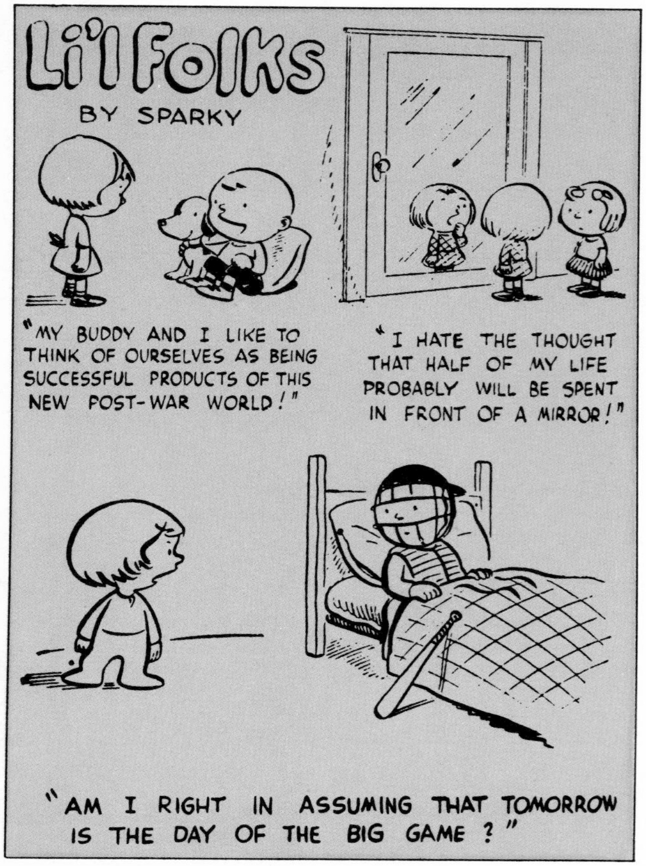
Li'l Folks
BY SPARKY
"MY BUDDY AND I LIKE TO THINK OF OURSELVES AS BEING SUCCESSFUL PRODUCTS OF THIS NEW POST-WAR WORLD!"
"I HATE THE THOUGHT THAT HALF OF MY LIFE PROBABLY WILL BE SPENT IN FRONT OF A MIRROR!"
"AM I RIGHT IN ASSUMING THAT TOMORROW IS THE DAY OF THE BIG GAME?"

It all started with a boy named Charlie Brown...

Charlie Brown made his first public appearance in 1947 in a feature called *Li'l Folks* in a St. Paul, Minnesota, newspaper. Charles Schulz signed the work as "Sparky," which was the nickname he had acquired, as a baby, after the horse "Sparkplug" in *Gasoline Alley.*

In October 1950 the characters from *Li'l Folks* became the characters in *Peanuts*, when United Feature Syndicate decided to distribute Schulz's work nationally. There were four characters in the original comic strip, but Charlie Brown quickly became the star.

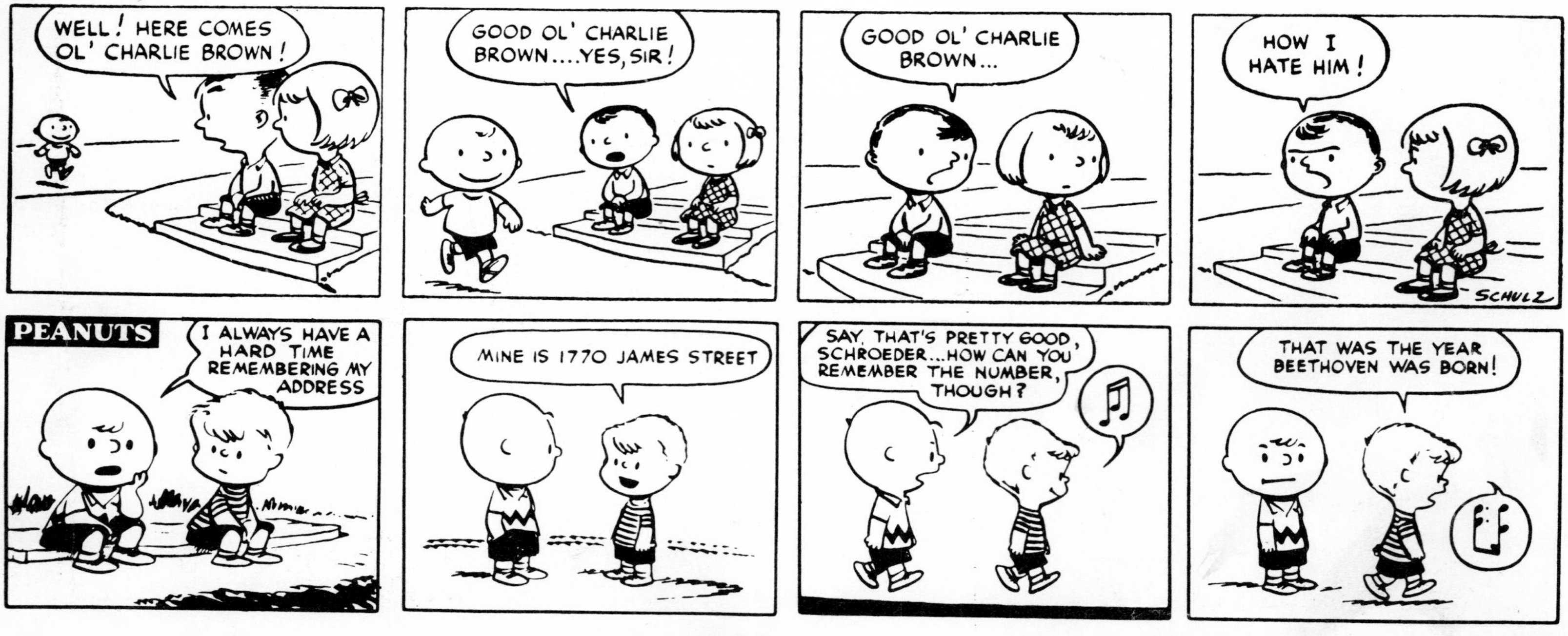
WELL! HERE COMES OL' CHARLIE BROWN!
GOOD OL' CHARLIE BROWN....YES, SIR!
GOOD OL' CHARLIE BROWN...
HOW I HATE HIM!
SCHULZ
PEANUTS
I ALWAYS HAVE A HARD TIME REMEMBERING MY ADDRESS
MINE IS 1770 JAMES STREET
SAY, THAT'S PRETTY GOOD, SCHROEDER...HOW CAN YOU REMEMBER THE NUMBER, THOUGH?
THAT WAS THE YEAR BEETHOVEN WAS BORN!

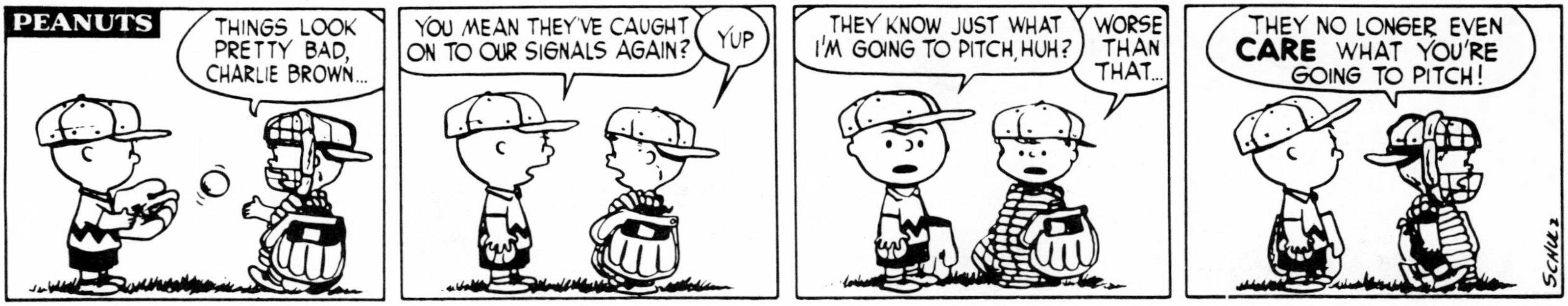
PEANUTS
THINGS LOOK PRETTY BAD, CHARLIE BROWN...
YOU MEAN THEY'VE CAUGHT ON TO OUR SIGNALS AGAIN?
YUP
THEY KNOW JUST WHAT I'M GOING TO PITCH, HUH?
WORSE THAN THAT...
THEY NO LONGER EVEN CARE WHAT YOU'RE GOING TO PITCH!
SCHULZ

By the mid-1950's, Charlie Brown's appearance was beginning to change: he looked a bit older, with a more mature face.

After ten more years, by the mid-1960's, Charlie Brown had changed a bit more and began to look much as he does today.

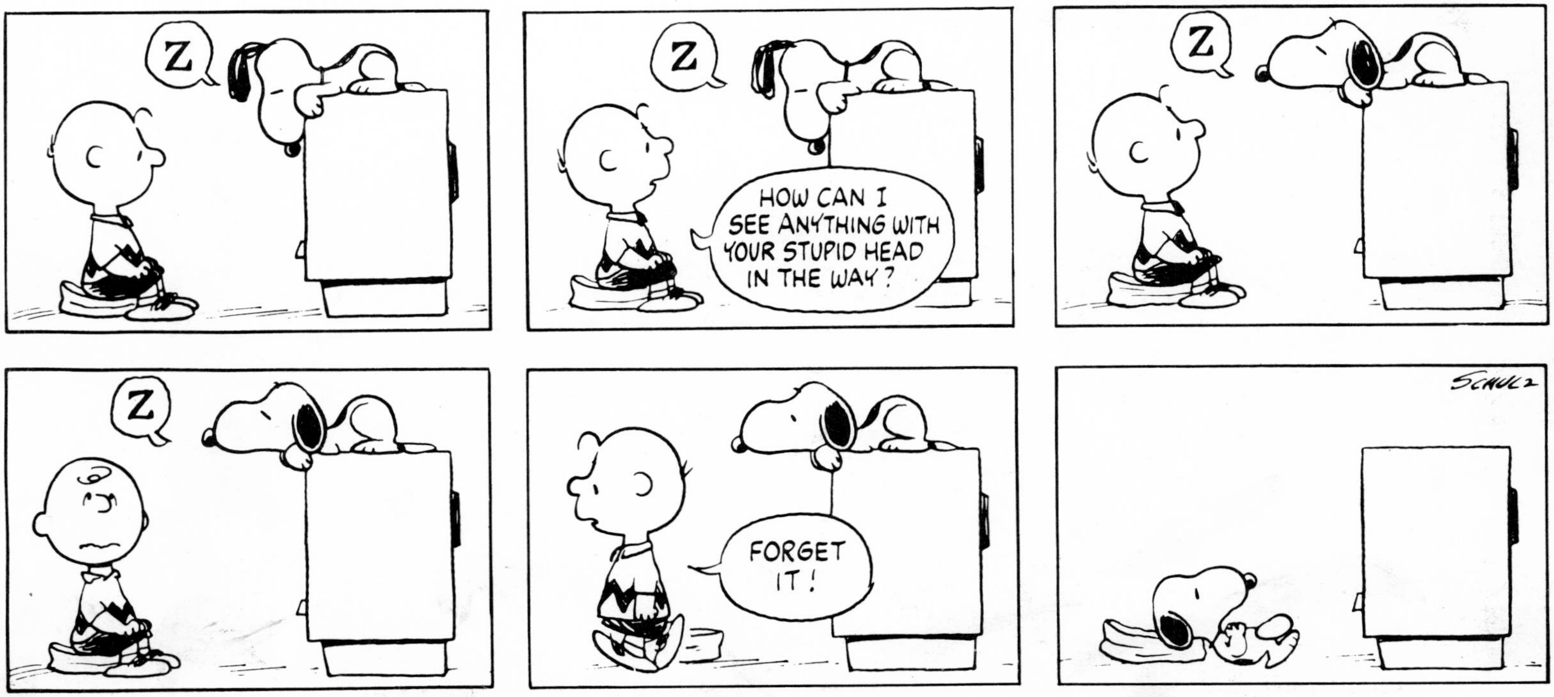
Z
Z
HOW CAN I SEE ANYTHING WITH YOUR STUPID HEAD IN THE WAY?
Z
Z
FORGET IT!
SCHULZ

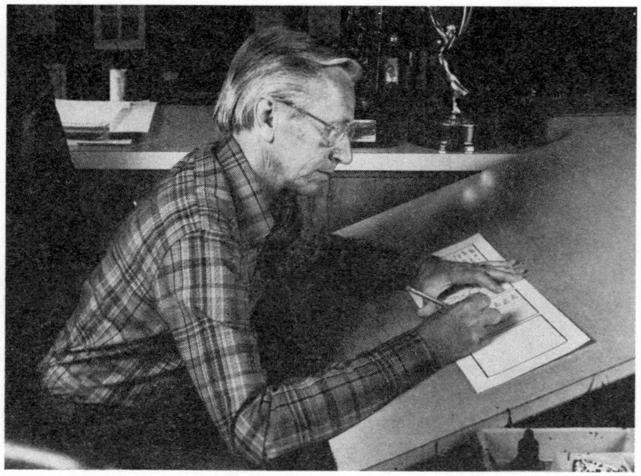

Why has Charlie Brown, with all his failures, become such a worldwide success? For one thing, if the very basis of comedy is, as some have written, watching *someone else* slip on a banana peel, then Charlie Brown is surely the greatest "slipper" of all time. In addition, his fans must also identify with his doubts, his anxieties, and his searchings — simply because his daily struggles often reflect our own daily struggles.

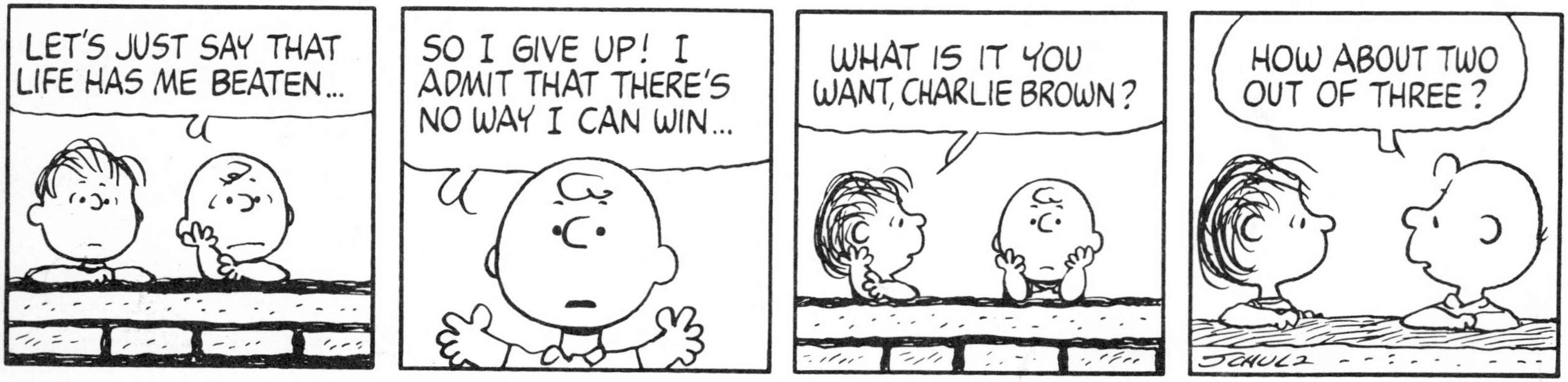

LET'S JUST SAY THAT LIFE HAS ME BEATEN...
SO I GIVE UP! I ADMIT THAT THERE'S NO WAY I CAN WIN...
WHAT IS IT YOU WANT, CHARLIE BROWN?
HOW ABOUT TWO OUT OF THREE?
SCHULZ

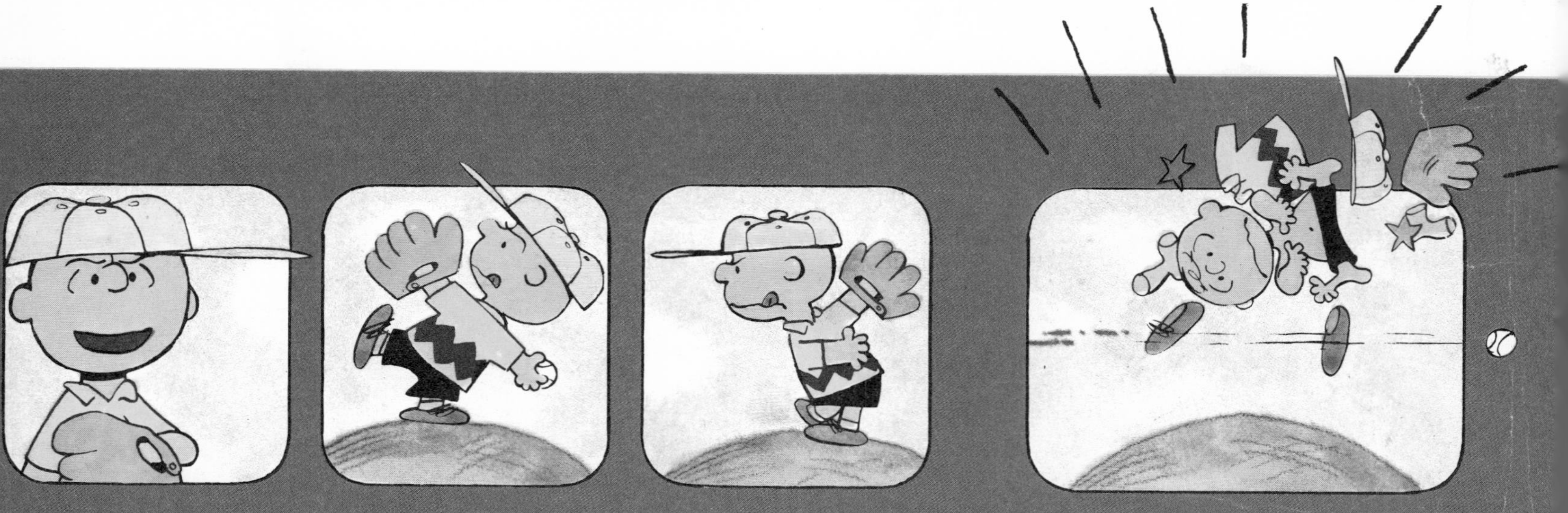

After 980 straight defeats, we're finally going to win our first baseball game!

I've got the winning spirit, now. I'll just wind up and burn it right by this guy. Here I go . . .

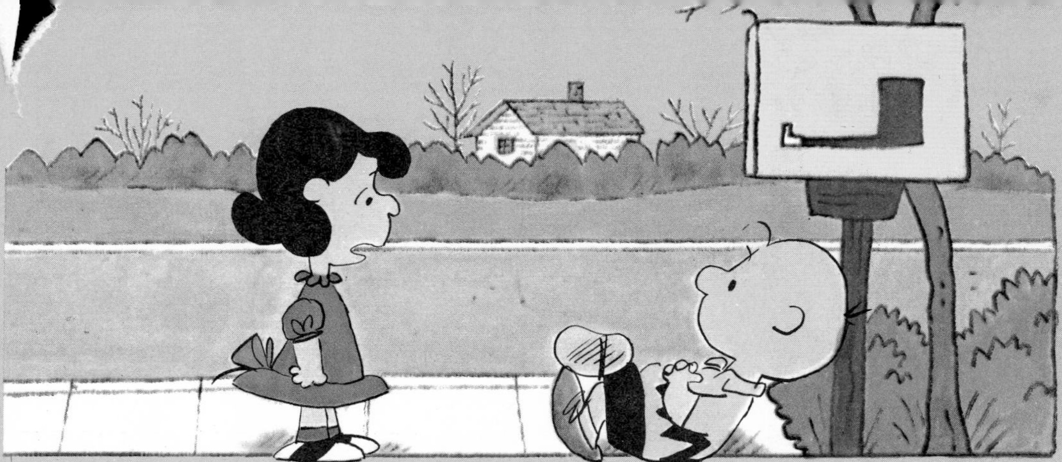

What are you doing, Charlie Brown?

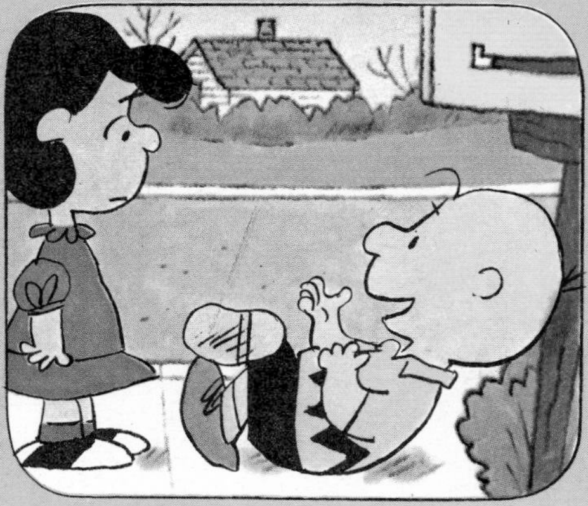

I'm waiting for valentines.

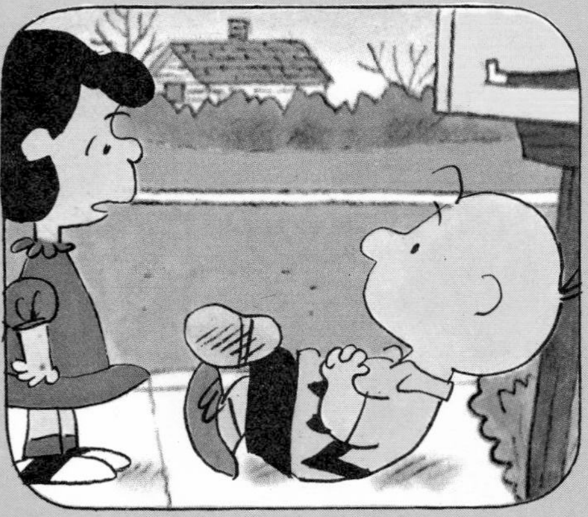

Oh. Well, good luck.

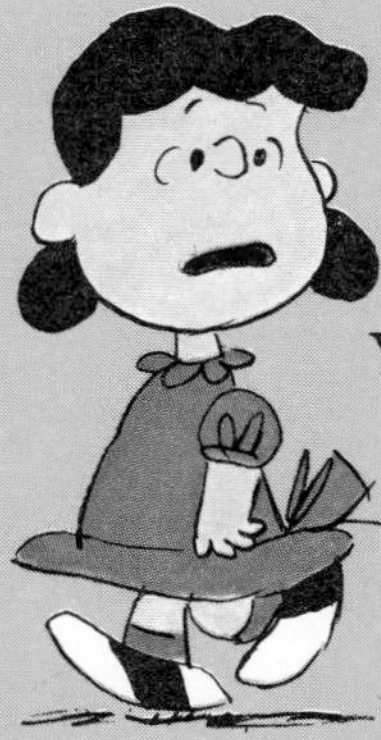

You'll need it!

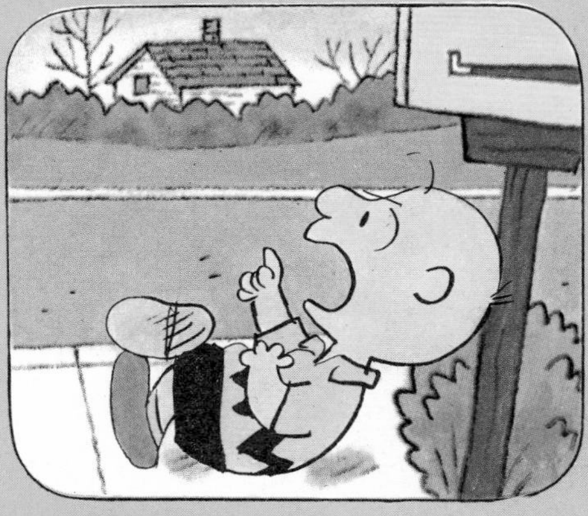

You didn't have to say that!

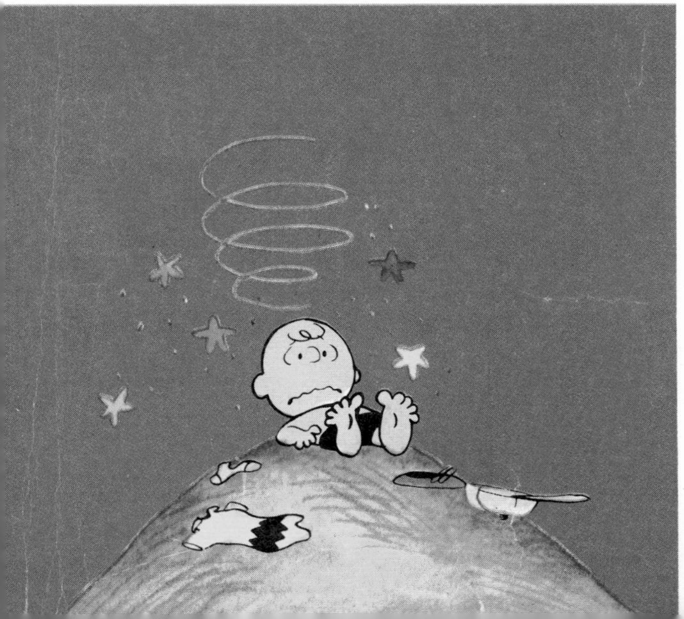

On the positive side, Charlie Brown is a very likable kid, someone with whom you'd like to play ball (if you don't mind losing) or join on a hike (if you don't mind getting lost). He never purposely offends any of the other kids, and I believe his basic decency is one of his main attractions to readers and viewers. Finally, he never gives up . . . never stops trying.

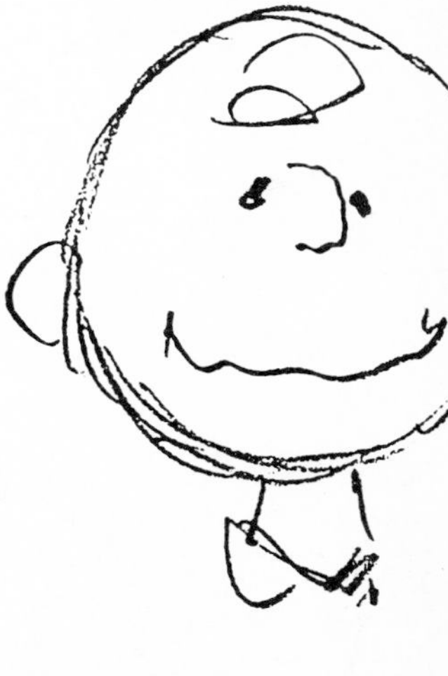

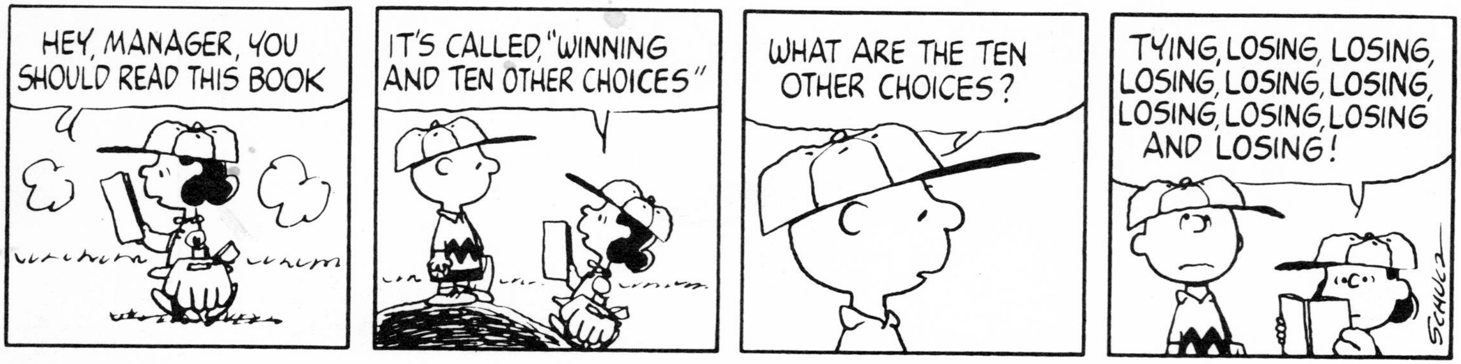
HEY, MANAGER, YOU SHOULD READ THIS BOOK
IT'S CALLED, "WINNING AND TEN OTHER CHOICES"
WHAT ARE THE TEN OTHER CHOICES?
TYING, LOSING, LOSING, LOSING, LOSING, LOSING, LOSING, LOSING, LOSING AND LOSING!
SCHULZ

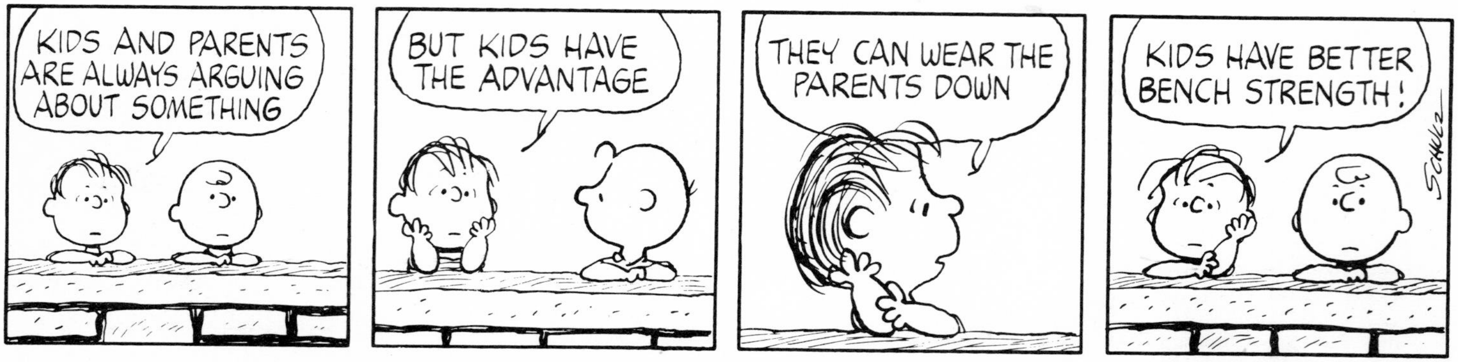
KIDS AND PARENTS ARE ALWAYS ARGUING ABOUT SOMETHING
BUT KIDS HAVE THE ADVANTAGE
THEY CAN WEAR THE PARENTS DOWN
KIDS HAVE BETTER BENCH STRENGTH!
SCHULZ

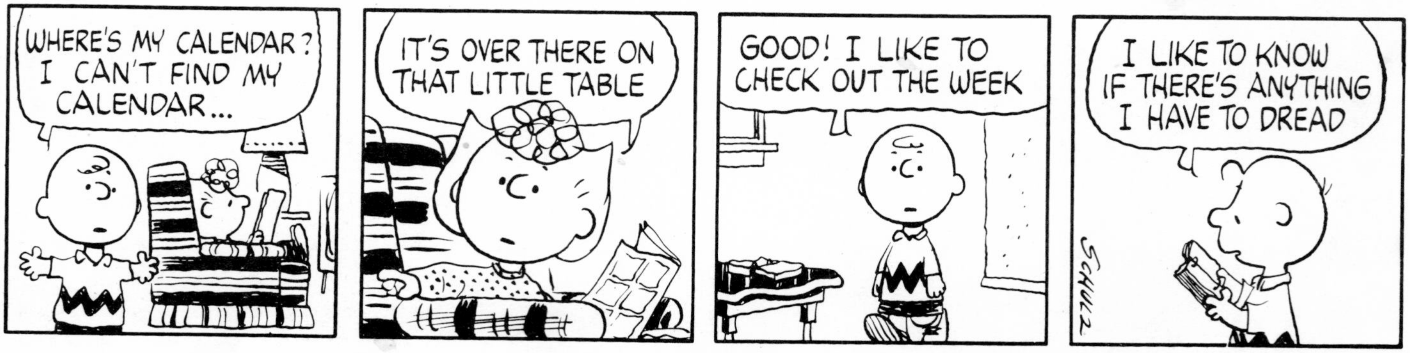
WHERE'S MY CALENDAR? I CAN'T FIND MY CALENDAR...
IT'S OVER THERE ON THAT LITTLE TABLE
GOOD! I LIKE TO CHECK OUT THE WEEK
I LIKE TO KNOW IF THERE'S ANYTHING I HAVE TO DREAD
SCHULZ

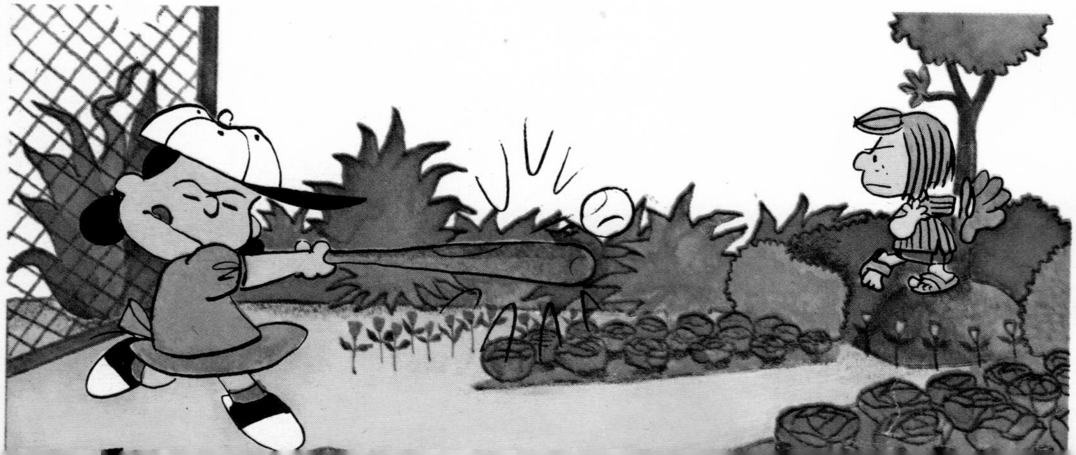

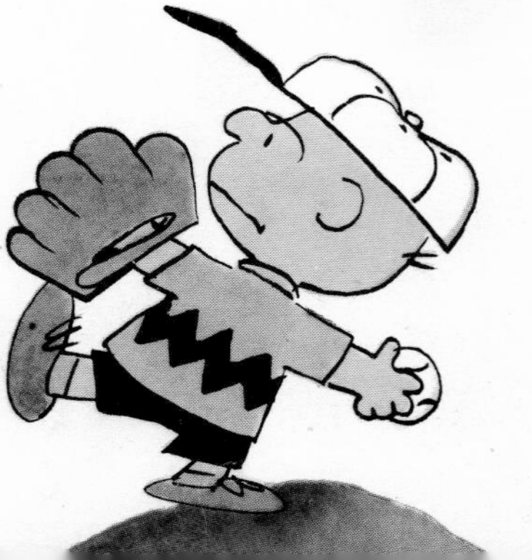

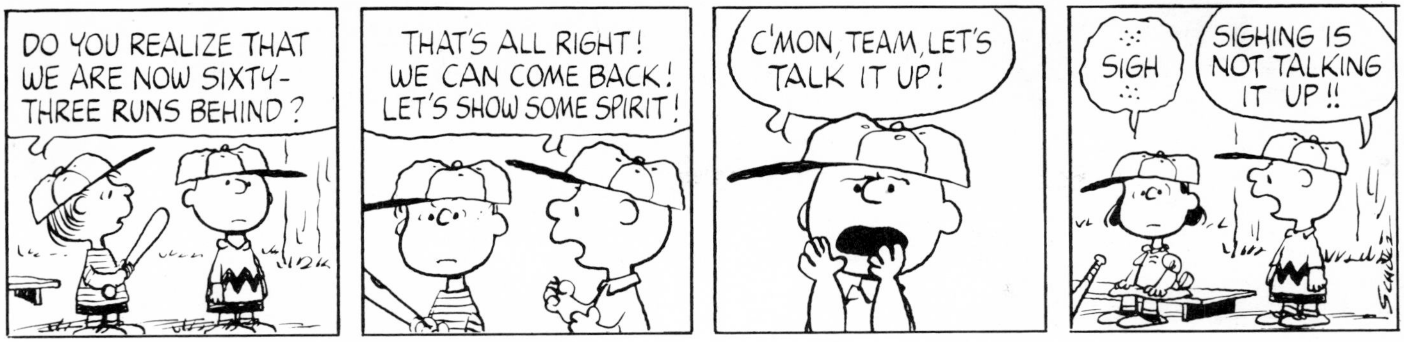
DO YOU REALIZE THAT WE ARE NOW SIXTY-THREE RUNS BEHIND?
THAT'S ALL RIGHT! WE CAN COME BACK! LET'S SHOW SOME SPIRIT!
C'MON, TEAM, LET'S TALK IT UP!
SIGH
SIGHING IS NOT TALKING IT UP!!
SCHULZ

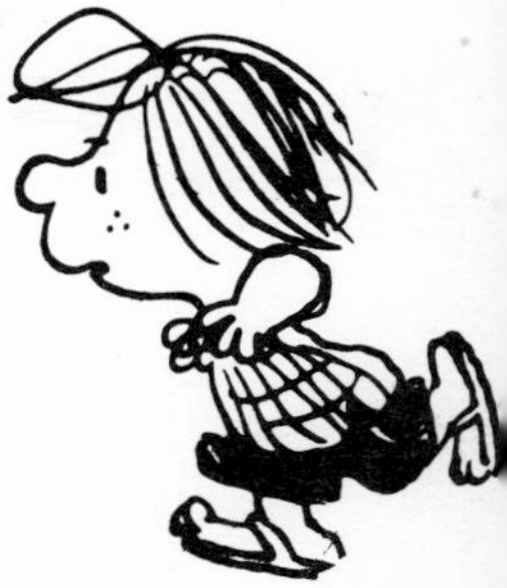

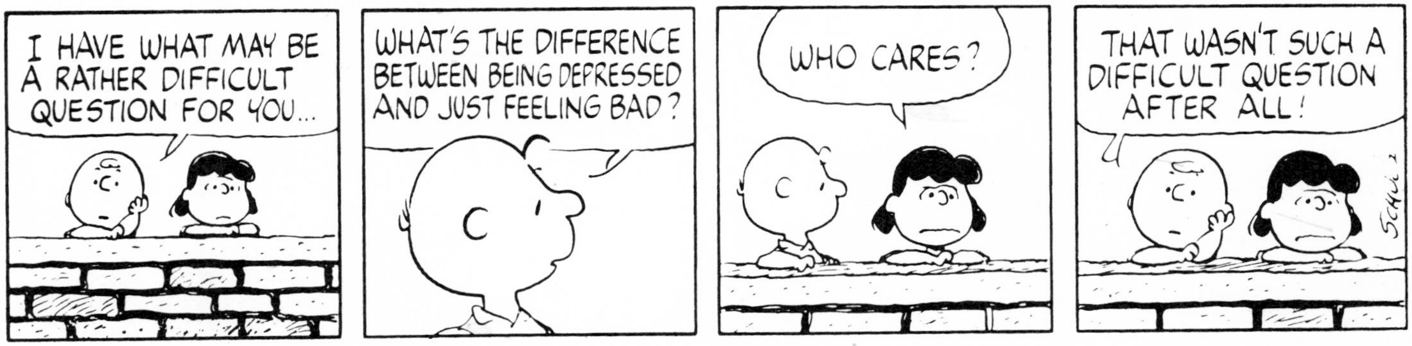
I HAVE WHAT MAY BE A RATHER DIFFICULT QUESTION FOR YOU...
WHAT'S THE DIFFERENCE BETWEEN BEING DEPRESSED AND JUST FEELING BAD?
WHO CARES?
THAT WASN'T SUCH A DIFFICULT QUESTION AFTER ALL!
SCHULZ

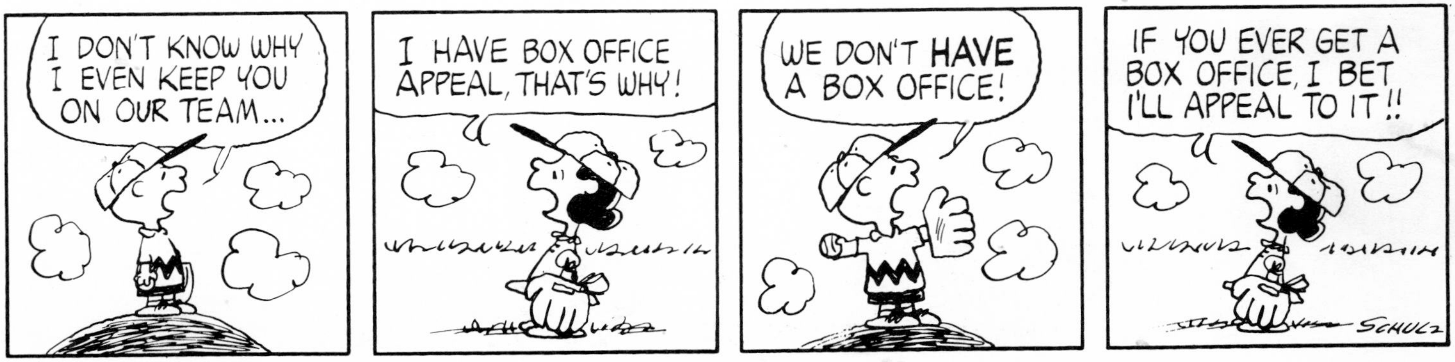
I DON'T KNOW WHY I EVEN KEEP YOU ON OUR TEAM...
I HAVE BOX OFFICE APPEAL, THAT'S WHY!
WE DON'T HAVE A BOX OFFICE!
IF YOU EVER GET A BOX OFFICE, I BET I'LL APPEAL TO IT!!
SCHULZ

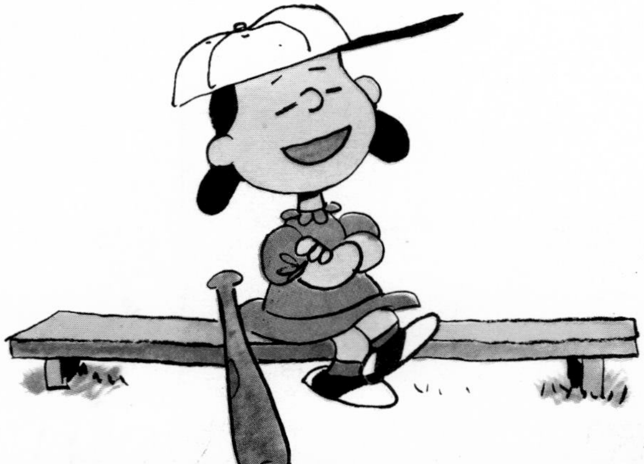

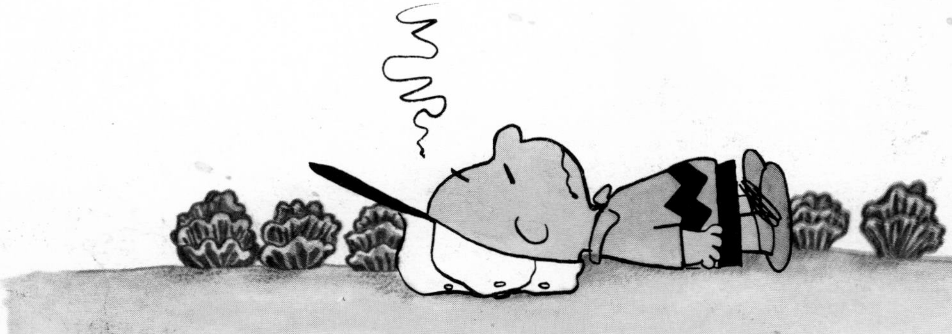

Charles Schulz recently said, "For all these years, I never could really pin down what Charlie Brown was all about. Then, one day recently, my associate, Evelyn Delgado, told me that on the previous night her son stormed into the house after a bad day at school, threw his jacket down, and said, 'Mom, I feel just like Charlie Brown.' Evelyn said she immediately knew how he felt, and she could deal with his frustrations . . .

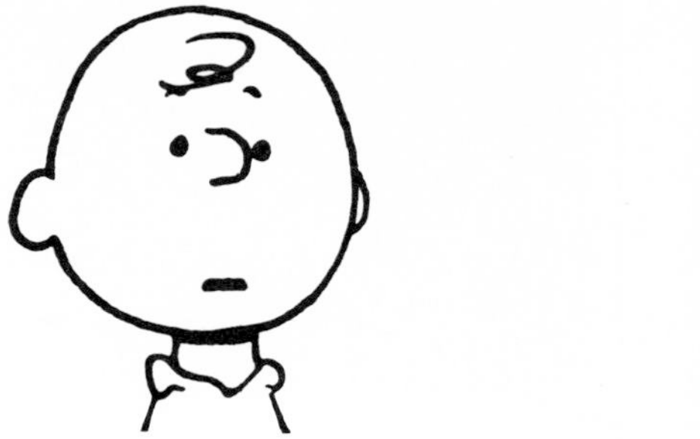

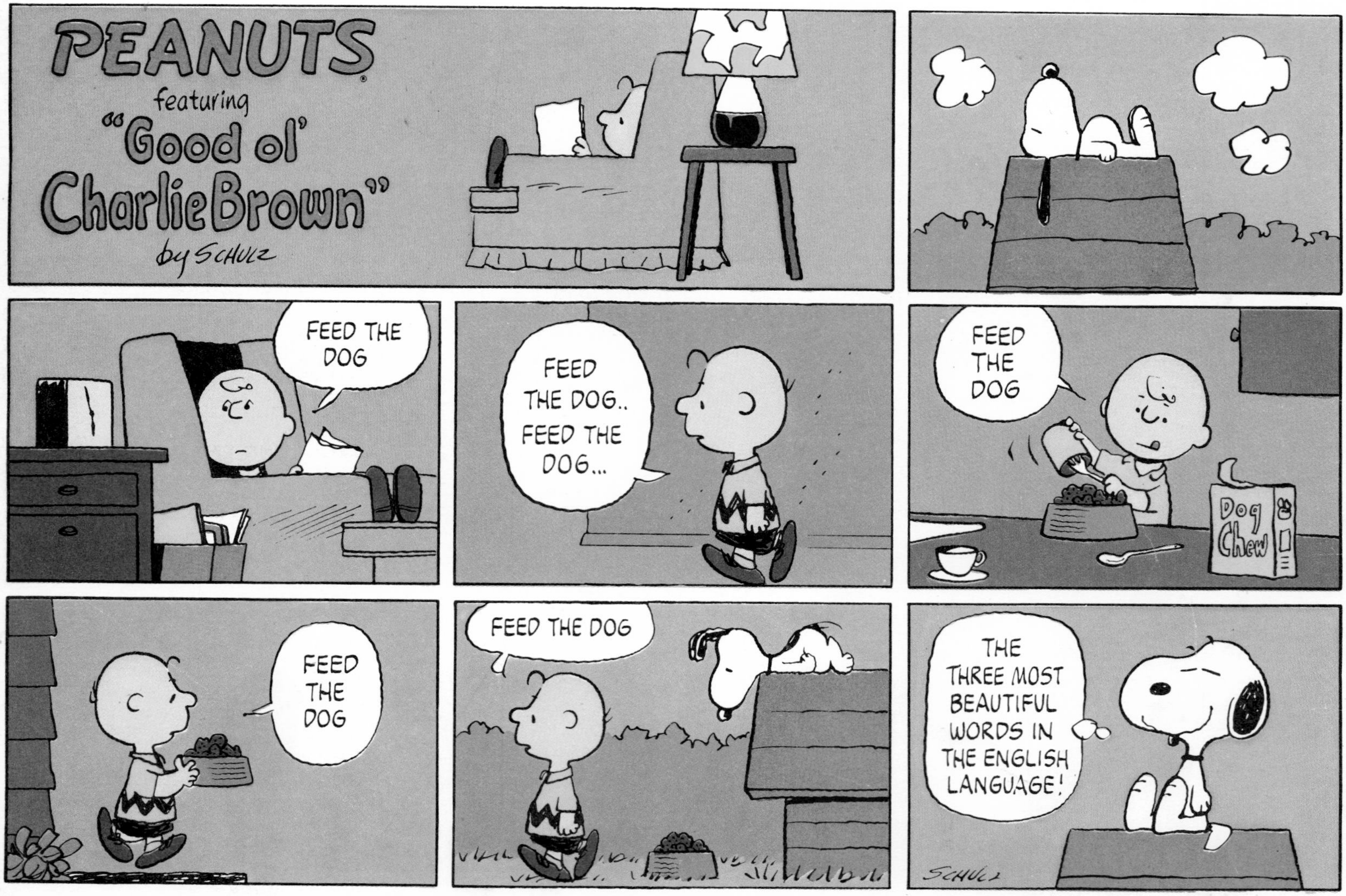
PEANUTS®
featuring "Good ol' CharlieBrown"
by SCHULZ
FEED THE DOG
FEED THE DOG.. FEED THE DOG...
FEED THE DOG
Dog Chew
FEED THE DOG
FEED THE DOG
THE THREE MOST BEAUTIFUL WORDS IN THE ENGLISH LANGUAGE!
SCHULZ

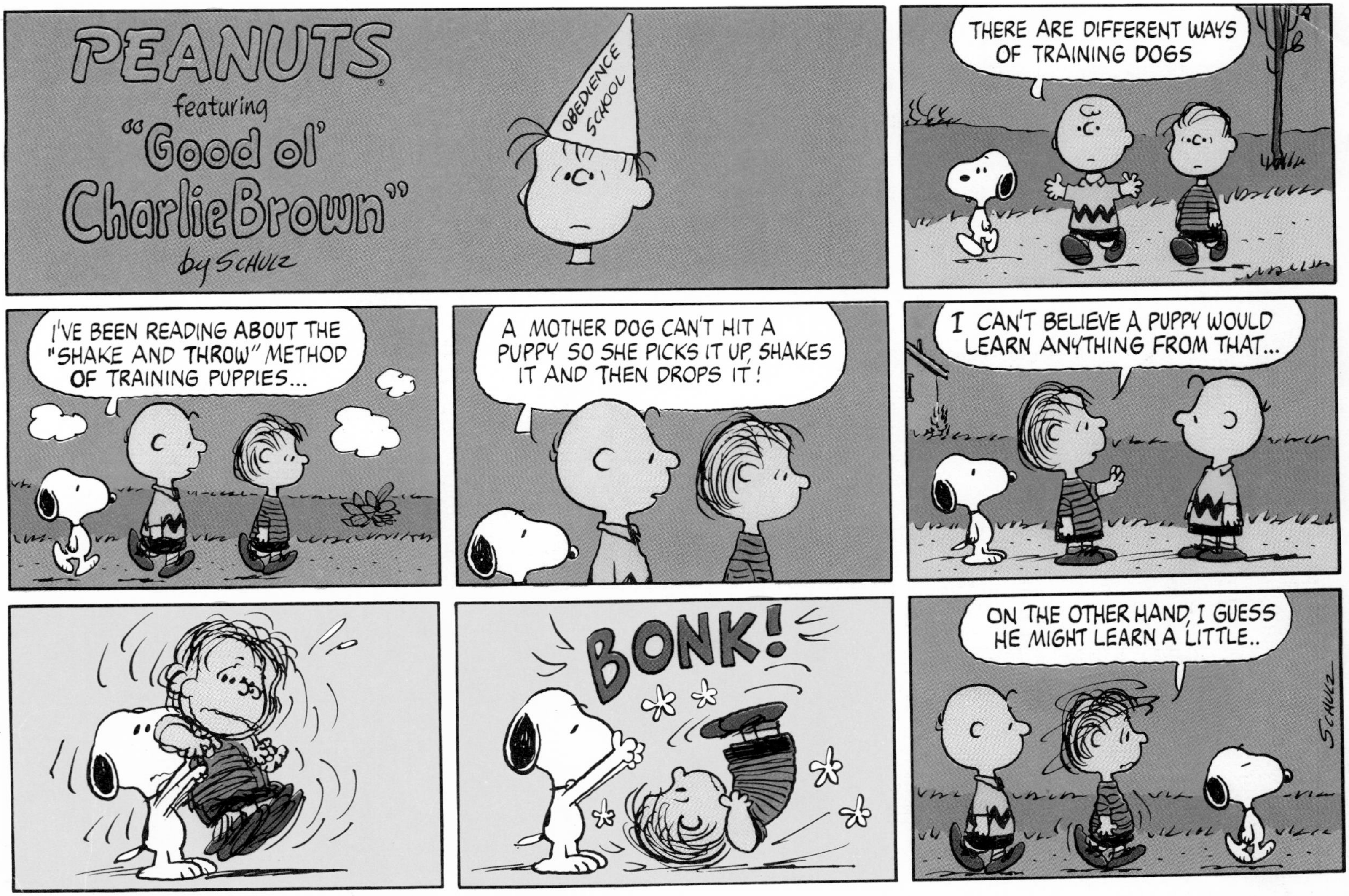
PEANUTS
featuring
"Good ol' Charlie Brown"
by SCHULZ
OBEDIENCE SCHOOL
THERE ARE DIFFERENT WAYS OF TRAINING DOGS
I'VE BEEN READING ABOUT THE "SHAKE AND THROW" METHOD OF TRAINING PUPPIES...
A MOTHER DOG CAN'T HIT A PUPPY SO SHE PICKS IT UP, SHAKES IT AND THEN DROPS IT!
I CAN'T BELIEVE A PUPPY WOULD LEARN ANYTHING FROM THAT...
BONK!
ON THE OTHER HAND, I GUESS HE MIGHT LEARN A LITTLE..
SCHULZ

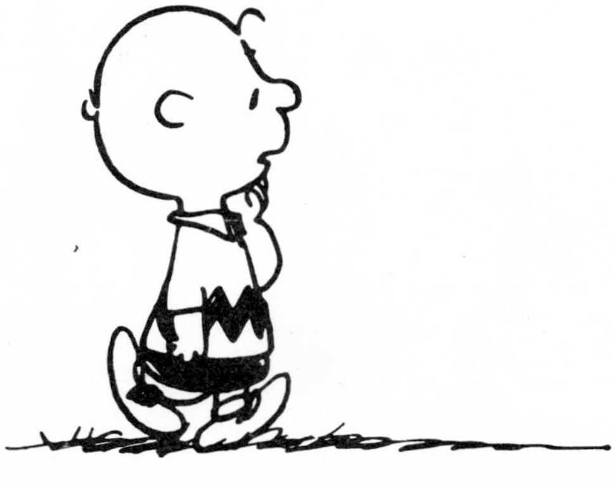

". . . and as she was telling me this, I suddenly realized, after thirty years, what Charlie Brown was all about. He defines certain basic feelings that we all share, and I guess people of all ages can thus identify with him."

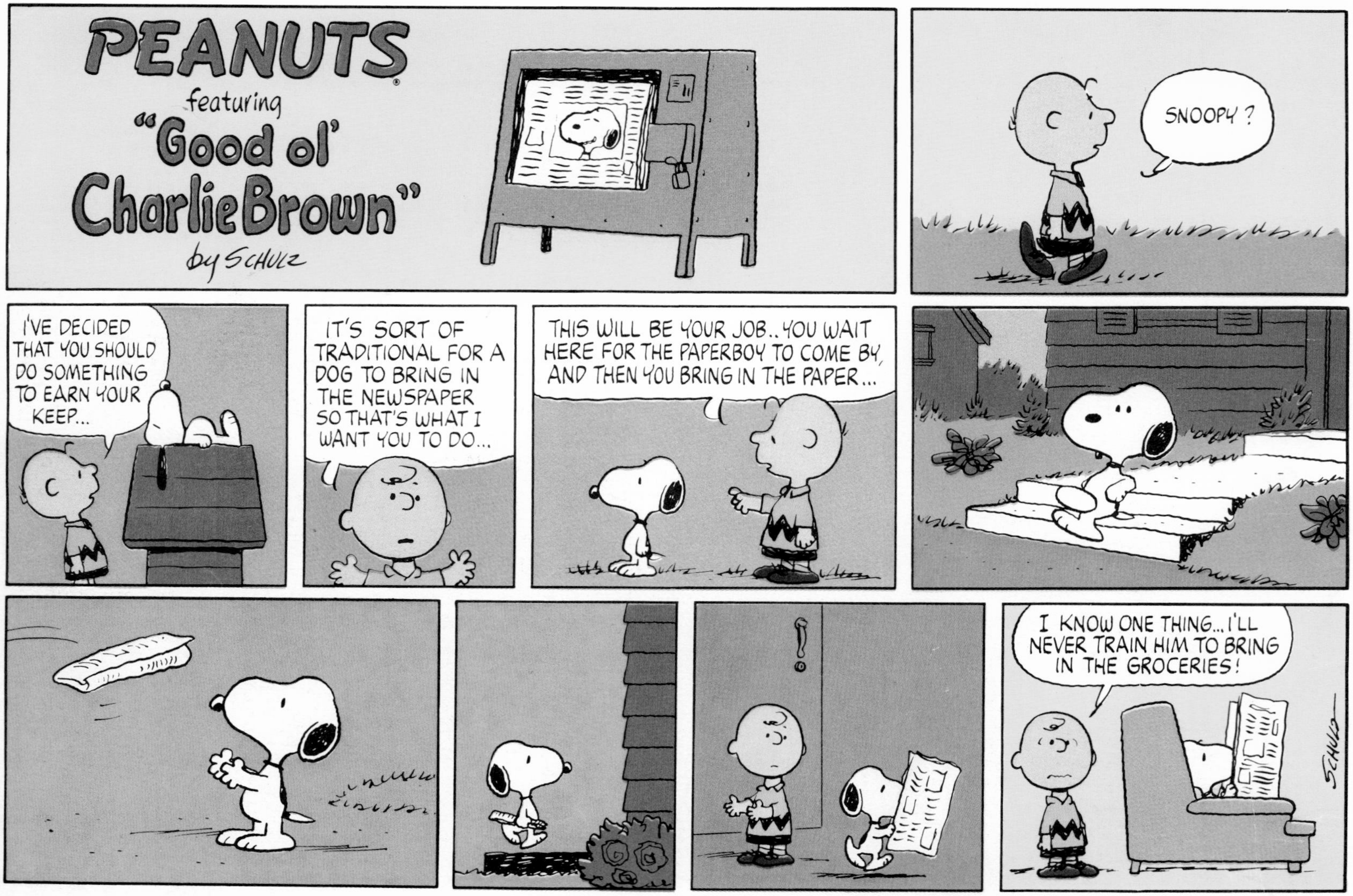
PEANUTS
featuring
"Good ol' Charlie Brown"
by SCHULZ
SNOOPY ?
I'VE DECIDED THAT YOU SHOULD DO SOMETHING TO EARN YOUR KEEP...
IT'S SORT OF TRADITIONAL FOR A DOG TO BRING IN THE NEWSPAPER SO THAT'S WHAT I WANT YOU TO DO...
THIS WILL BE YOUR JOB..YOU WAIT HERE FOR THE PAPERBOY TO COME BY, AND THEN YOU BRING IN THE PAPER...
I KNOW ONE THING...I'LL NEVER TRAIN HIM TO BRING IN THE GROCERIES!
SCHULZ

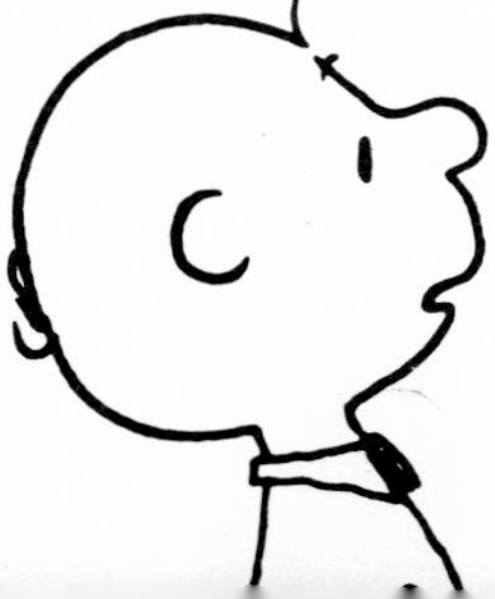

PEANUTS
featuring
"Good ol' CharlieBrown"
by SCHULZ
Deer
THAT SHOULD BE "DEAR"
IN THE SALUTATION OF A LETTER, THE PROPER WORD AND SPELLING OF THAT WORD IS "DEAR"
Deer are beautiful animals found in most parts of the world.
I'M SORRY... I DIDN'T REALIZE YOU WERE WRITING ABOUT DEER... I APOLOGIZE...
WELL, I SHOULD HOPE SO! IT SEEMS TO ME THAT A LOT OF THE PROBLEMS IN THIS WORLD ARE CAUSED BY PEOPLE WHO CRITICIZE OTHER PEOPLE BEFORE THEY KNOW WHAT THEY'RE TALKING ABOUT!
Dear Grandma,
SCHULZ

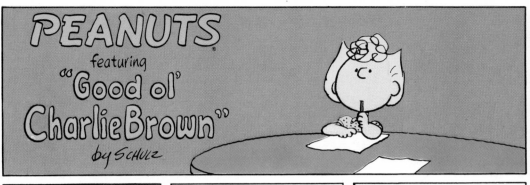

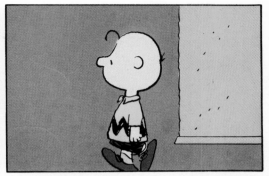

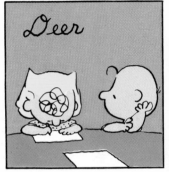

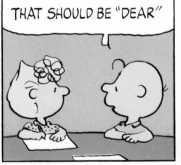

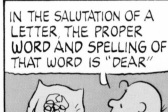

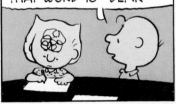

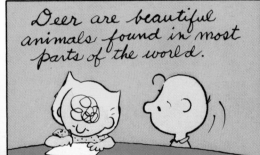

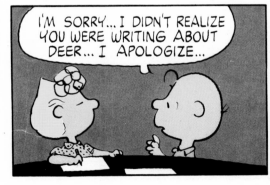

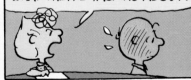

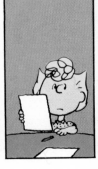

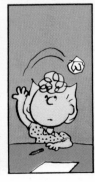

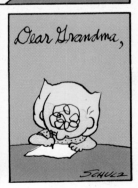

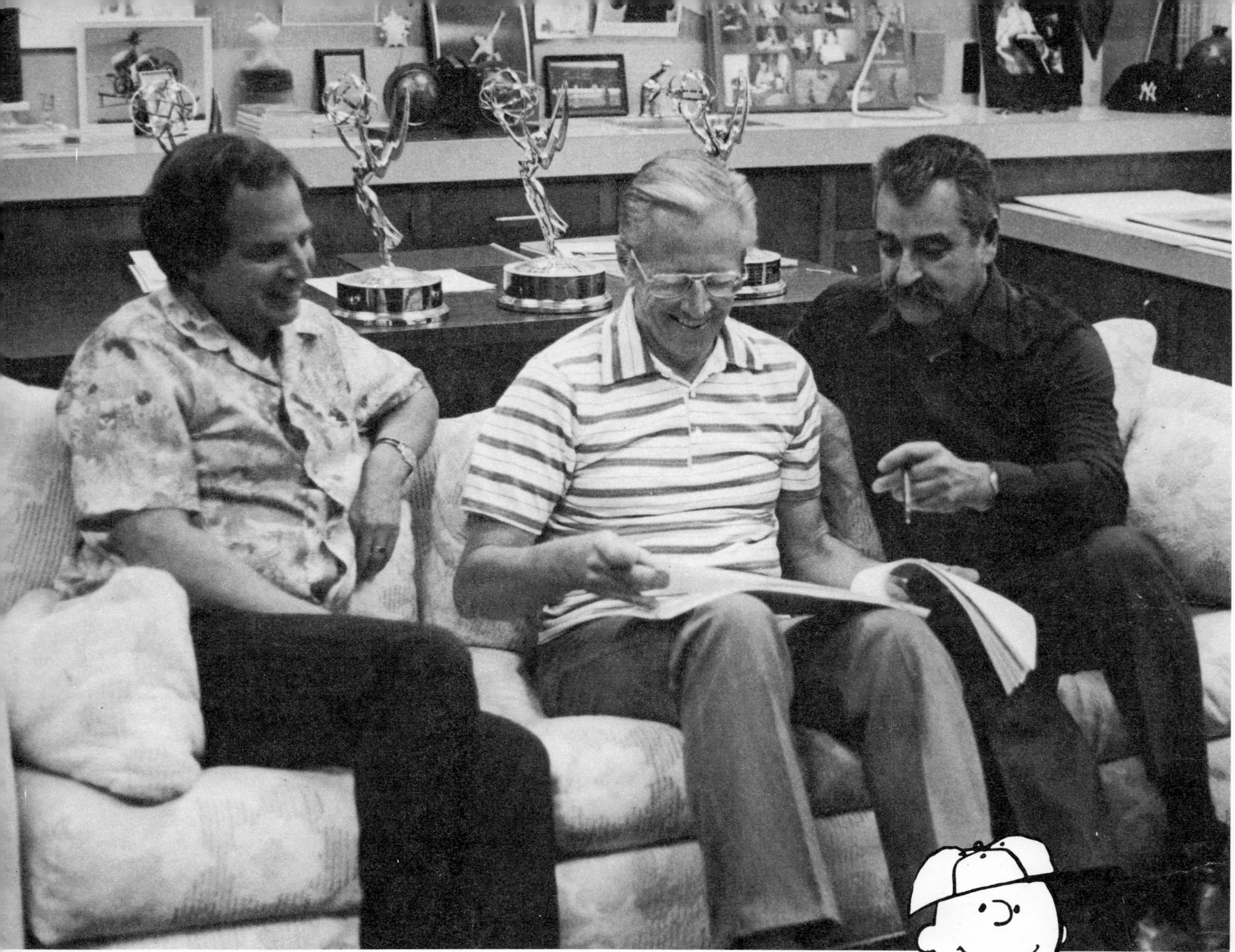

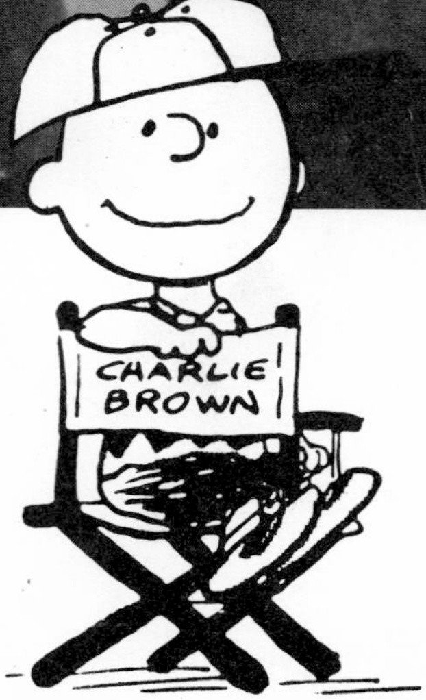
CHARLIE
BROWN

Who are these three men and what are they doing? We thought you'd never ask. That's me on the left, Sparky in the center, and animator Bill Melendez on the right. We're looking over the storyboard of our twentieth TV special. At least *we* think it's funny. Recently we were asked which of the TV specials seemed to have the most impact on viewers . . .

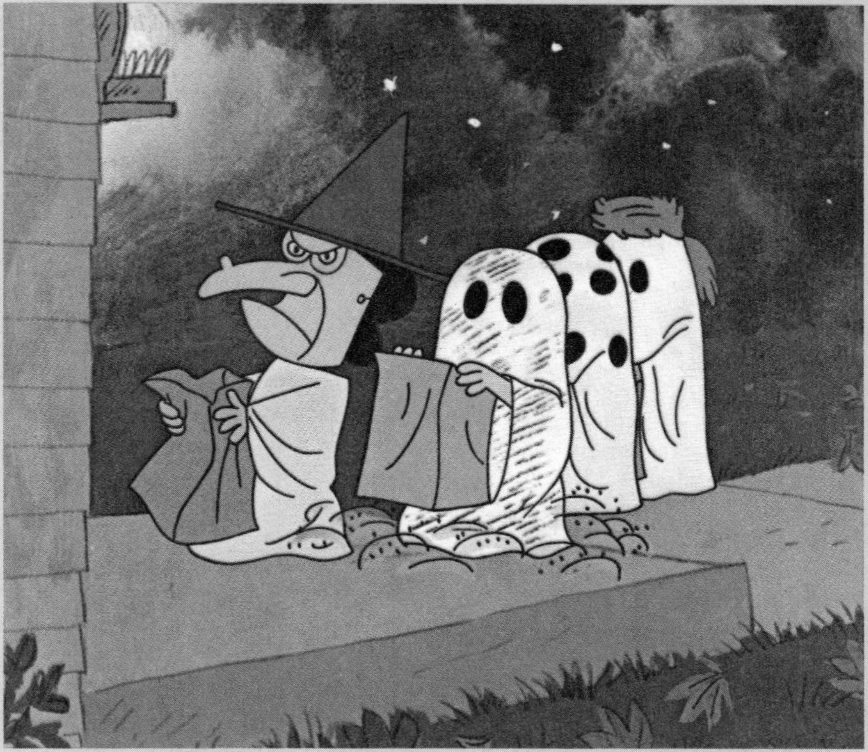

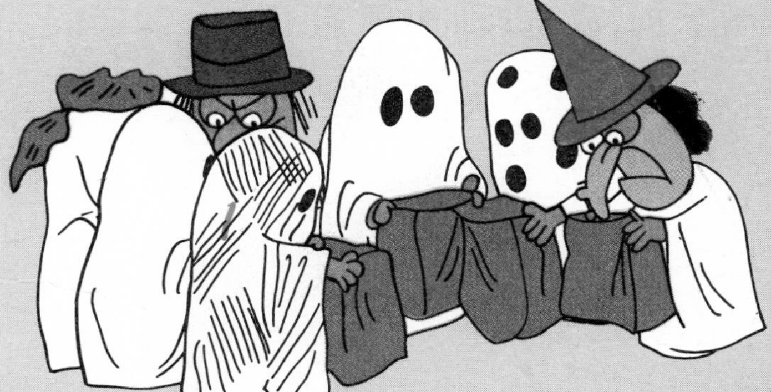

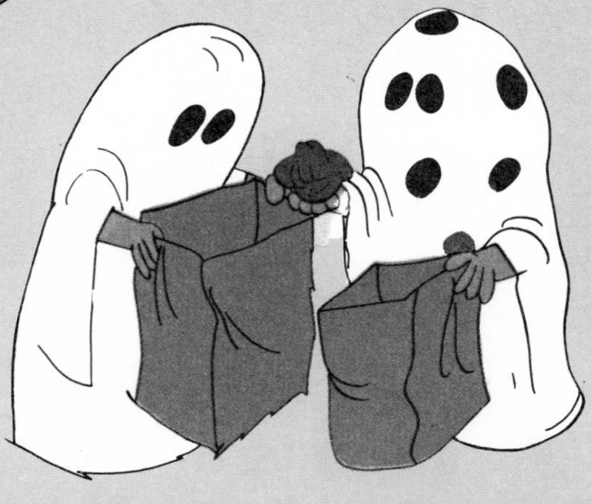

You're on TV now, Charlie Brown!

It's the Great Pumpkin, Charlie Brown seems to be one of the all-time favorites for viewers. It's been broadcast nine times to date. When viewers see poor Charlie Brown receiving only rocks in his trick-or-treat bag, they never fail to send bags of candy to Sparky's studio, from all across the country, for Charlie Brown.

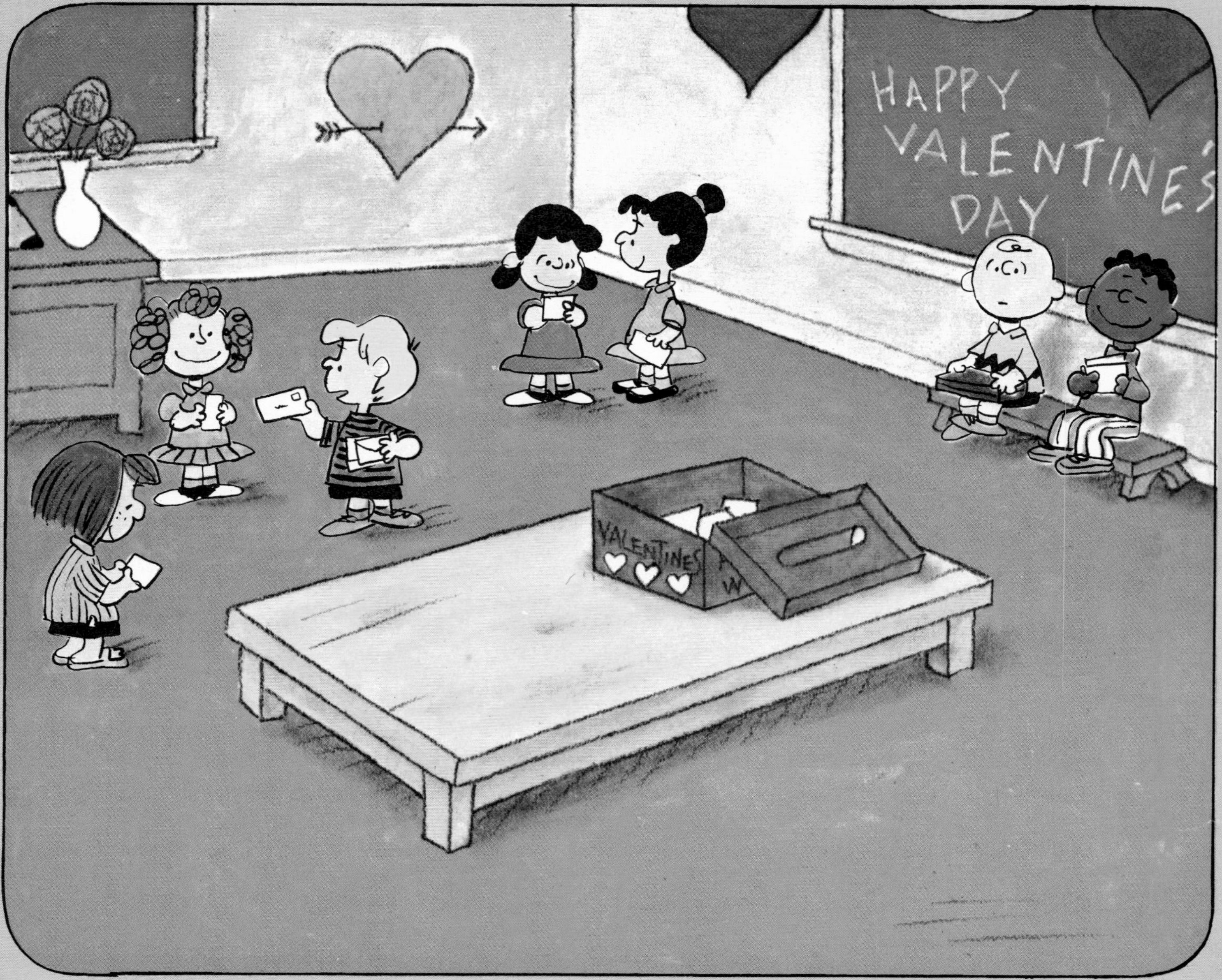
HAPPY
VALENTINE'S
DAY
VALENTINES

Here's one for Sally. And one for Frieda. One for Monte. One for Lucy. And one for Violet. One big one for Tom. One for Peppermint Patty. One for Franklin. And one for Linus. One for Pig-Pen. One for Amie. Another one for Frieda. Here's one for Jill. And here's one . . .

Hey! Maybe she *did* send me one. Maybe she sent me a valentine and it didn't get here till today! Maybe it's in our mailbox right now.

I'm afraid to look. If I look and there's nothing there, I'll be crushed. On the other hand, if she did send me a valentine . . . I've *got* to look.

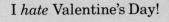

SMACK!

With *Be My Valentine, Charlie Brown* there was another national response when Charlie Brown was the only one in class *not* to receive a valentine. Viewers by the hundreds sent valentines to poor Charlie Brown.

I *hate* Valentine's Day!

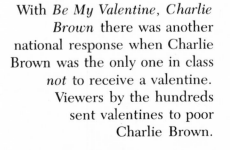

25

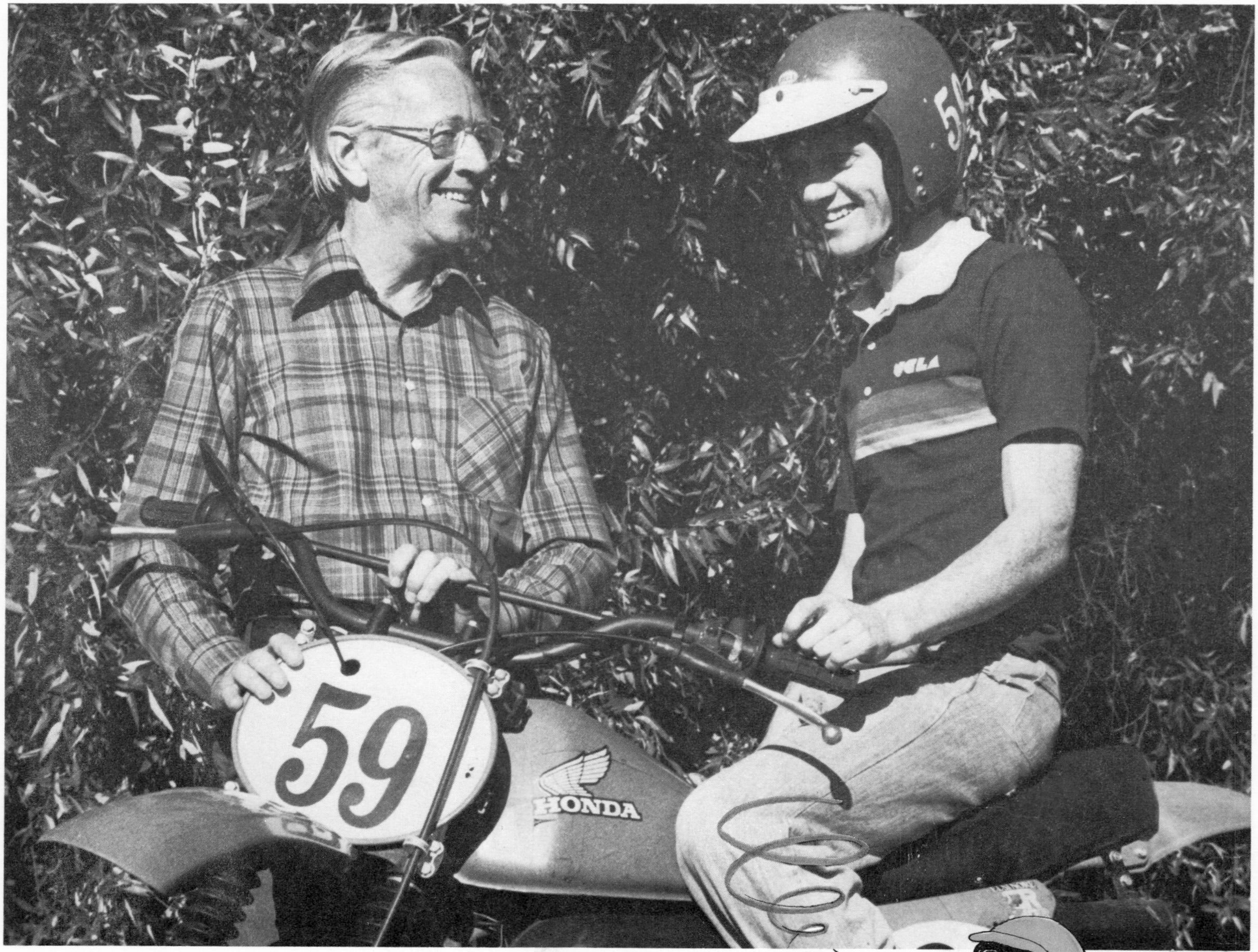
59
HONDA
UCLA

The *Peanuts* television shows, like the comic strip itself, are often inspired by events in Sparky's daily life. For example, son Monte Schulz's interest in World War I airplane models was the inspiration for the Red Baron strips and animation. And son Craig (pictured above with Sparky) got into motorcycles, which led eventually to the Emmy-winning TV special *You're a Good Sport, Charlie Brown*.

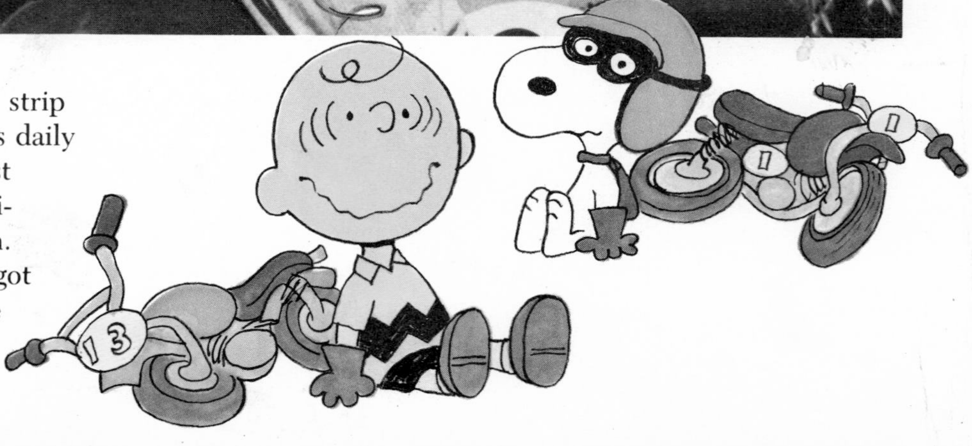

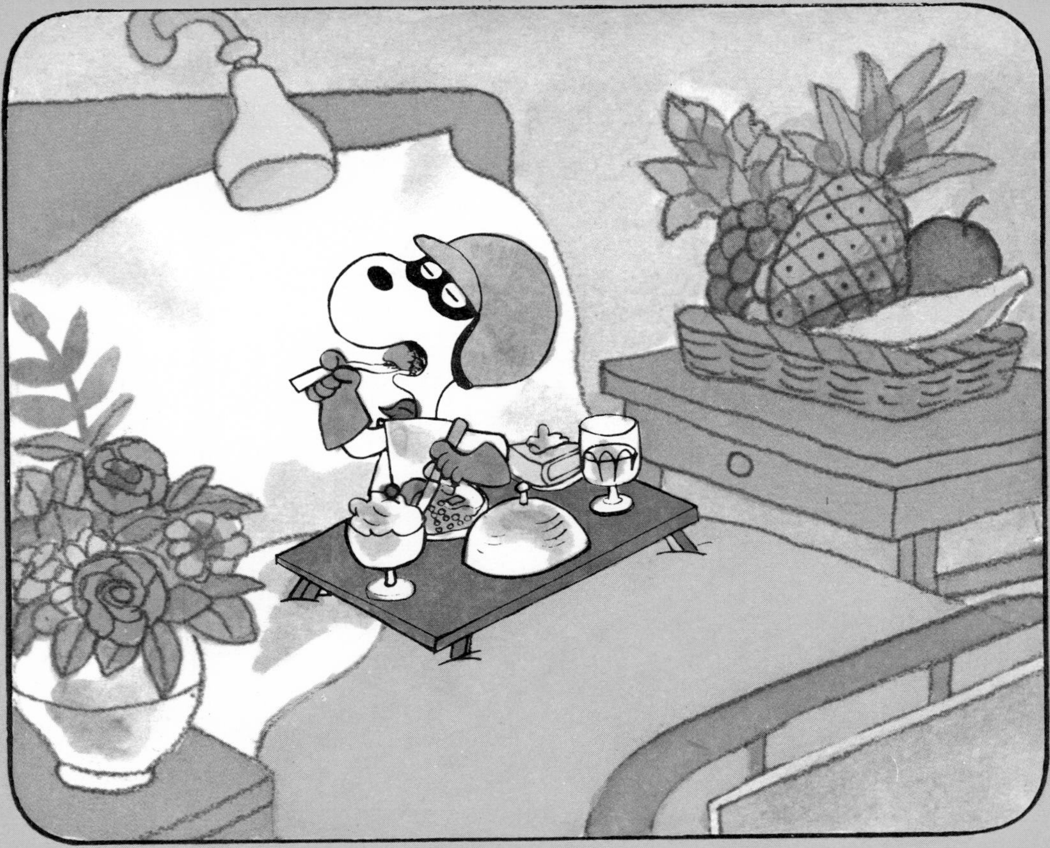

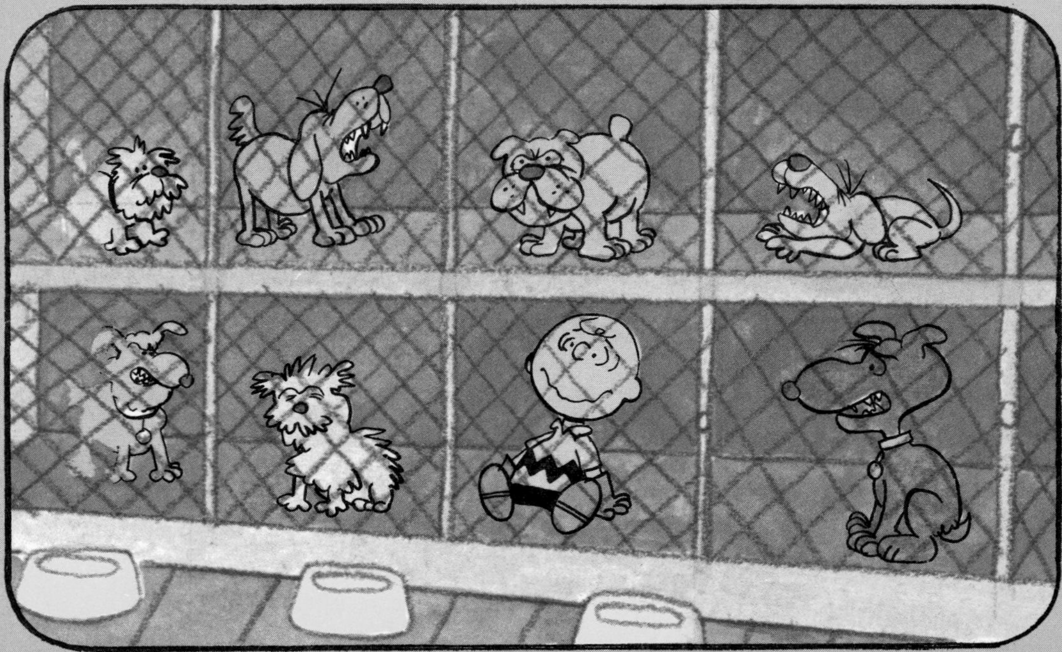

During the Moto-Cross motorcycle race, Snoopy and Charlie Brown collide and are rushed to the hospital. In the ambulance, however, things get mixed up, so Snoopy ends up in a plush hospital while Charlie Brown finds himself at the vet's.

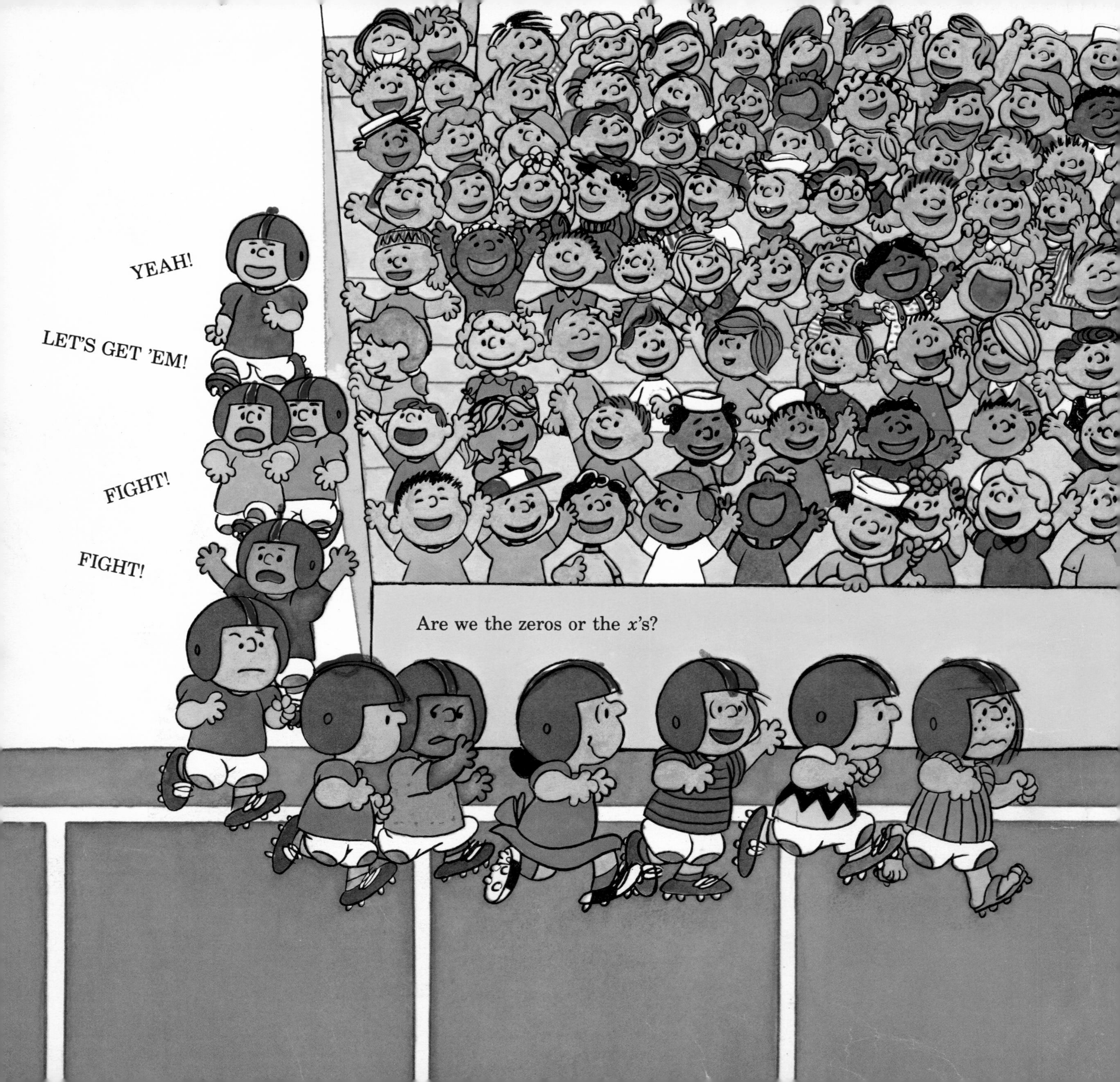
YEAH!
LET'S GET 'EM!
FIGHT!
FIGHT!
Are we the zeros or the *x*'s?

One of the highest-rated and most popular shows was *It's Your First Kiss, Charlie Brown,* but the original version created a small controversy. Every time Charlie Brown went to kick the football, Lucy, naturally, pulled it away. Viewers could accept this expected, well-known behavior, but each time he failed to kick the ball, Charlie Brown was criticized by his teammates for "goofing up." Many viewers wrote letters saying that this was simply more than they could take — Charlie Brown was *not* at fault, period. Sparky, Bill Melendez, and I agreed, so for the repeat broadcast we dubbed out the "goofing-up" references. So this was one incident where the public was indeed "heard from" and heeded.

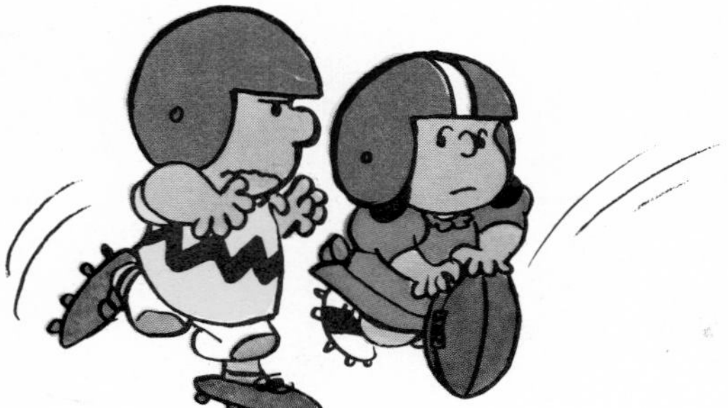

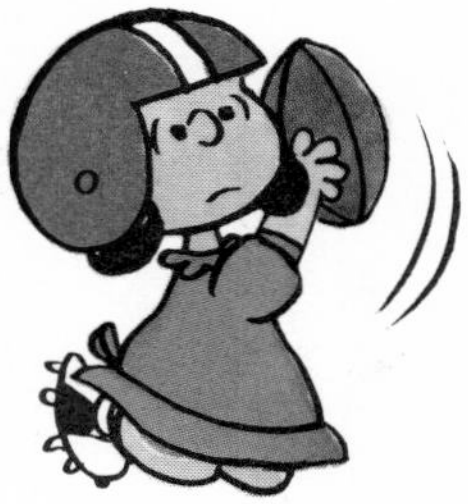

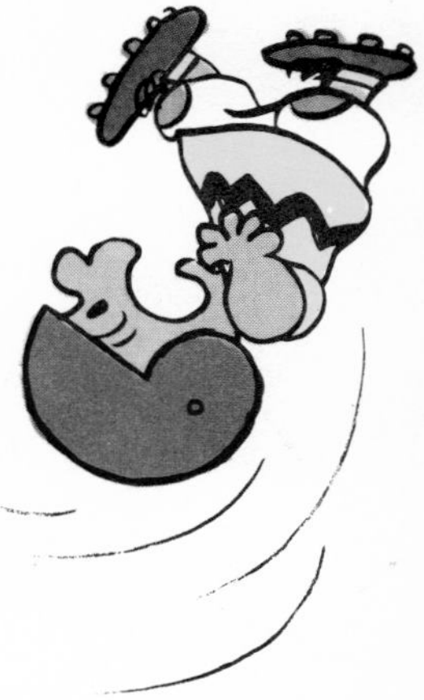

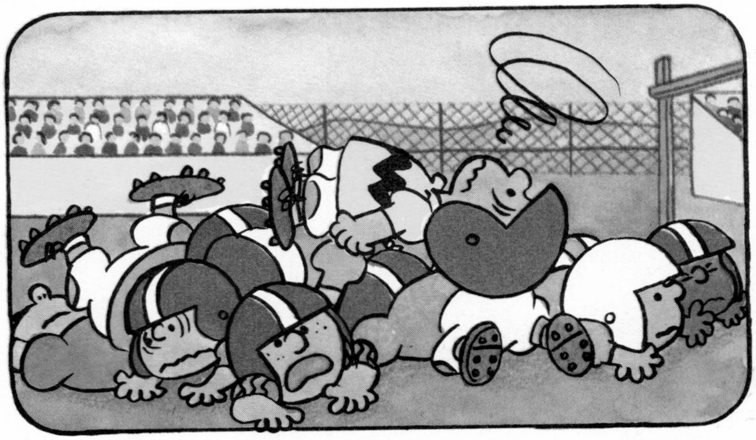

Chuck, you really goofed up on that play!

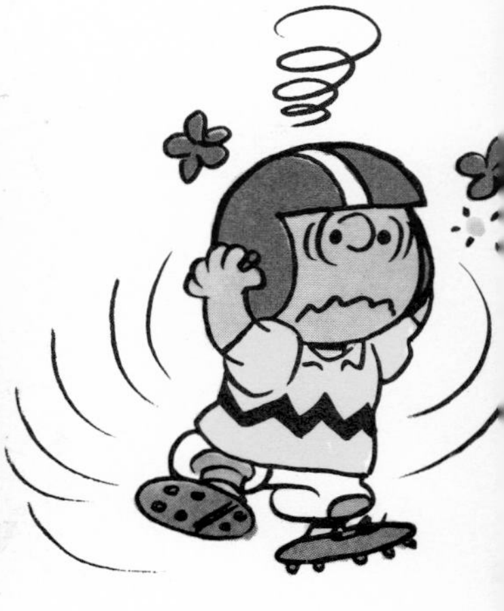

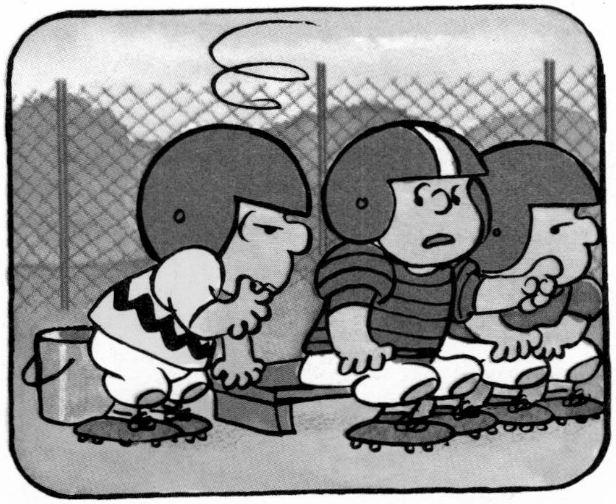

Too bad, Charlie Brown. That leaves them ahead. Now you have to go back for the kickoff.

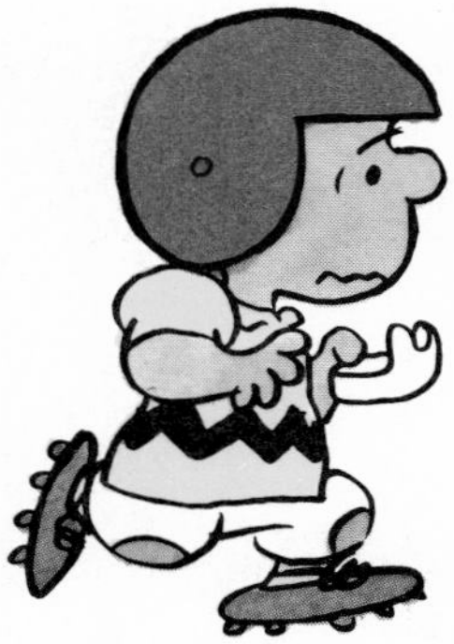

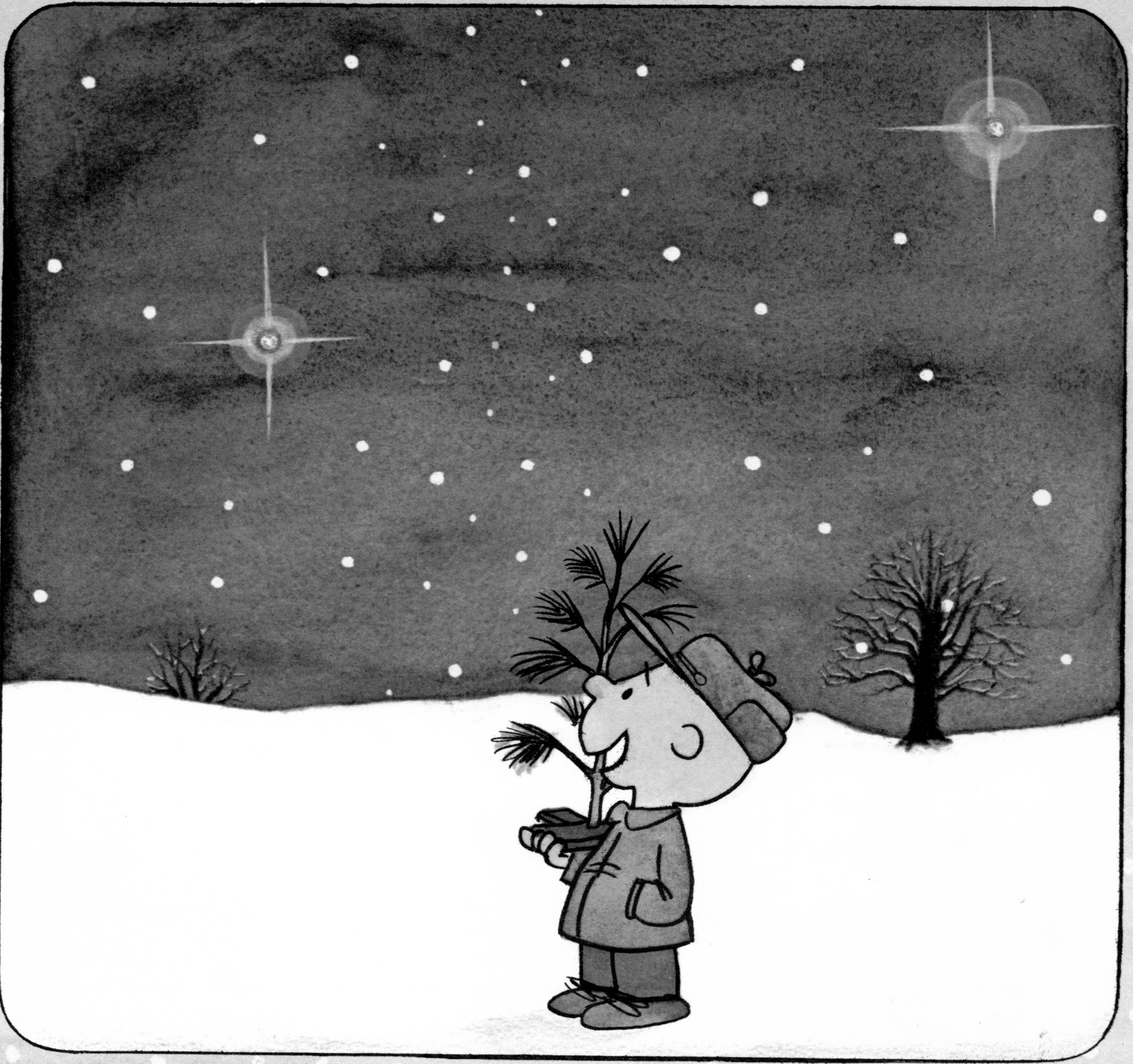

Linus is right. I won't let all this commercialism ruin my Christmas. I'll take this little tree home and decorate it. I'll show them it really *will* work in our play.

Augh! I've killed it! Everything I touch gets ruined!!

But it was our first show, produced back in 1965, that still seems to have the greatest impact on viewers. *A Charlie Brown Christmas* won an Emmy and a Peabody award and has been broadcast fourteen consecutive years.

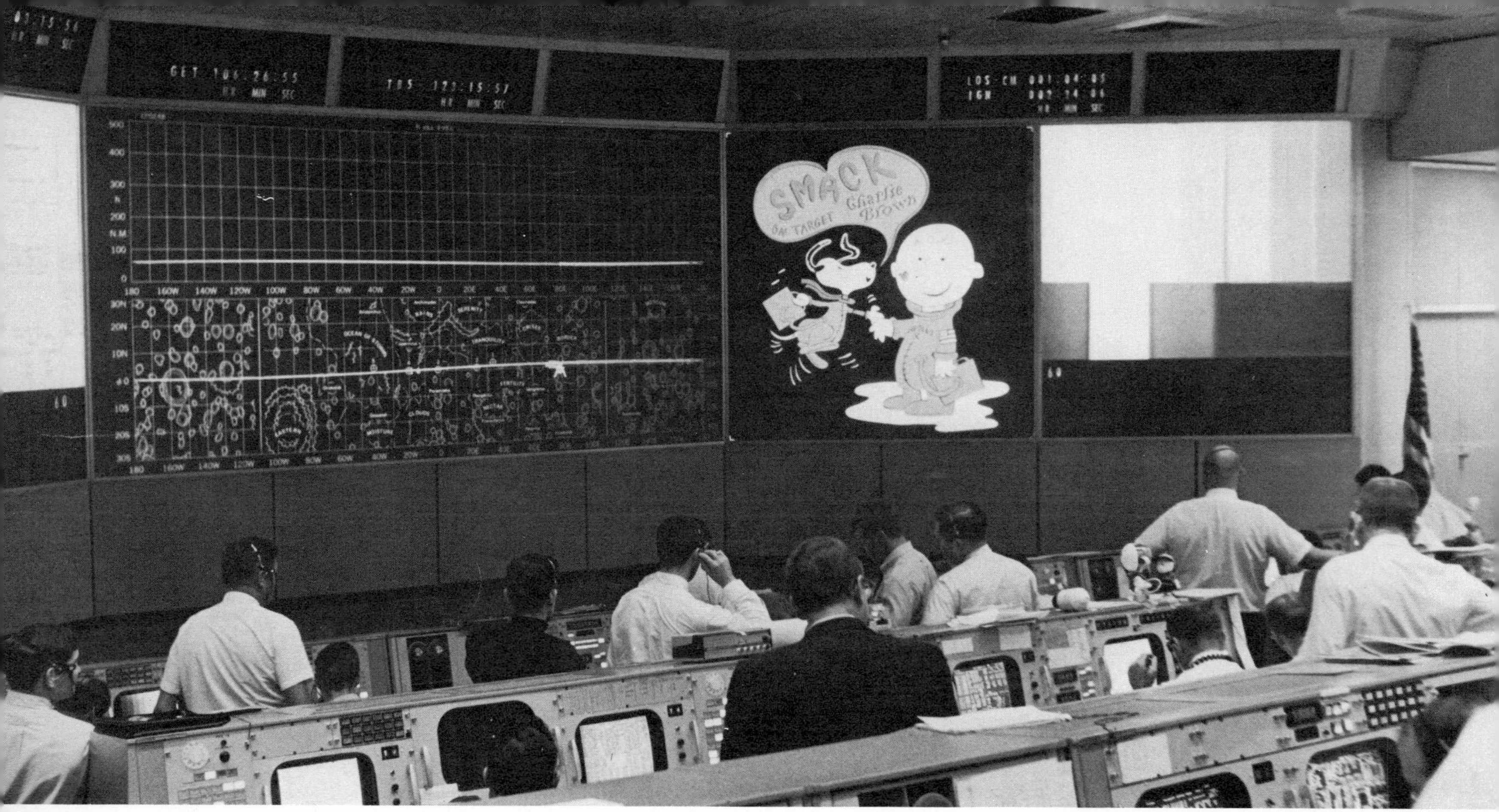
SMACK
ON TARGET
Charlie Brown

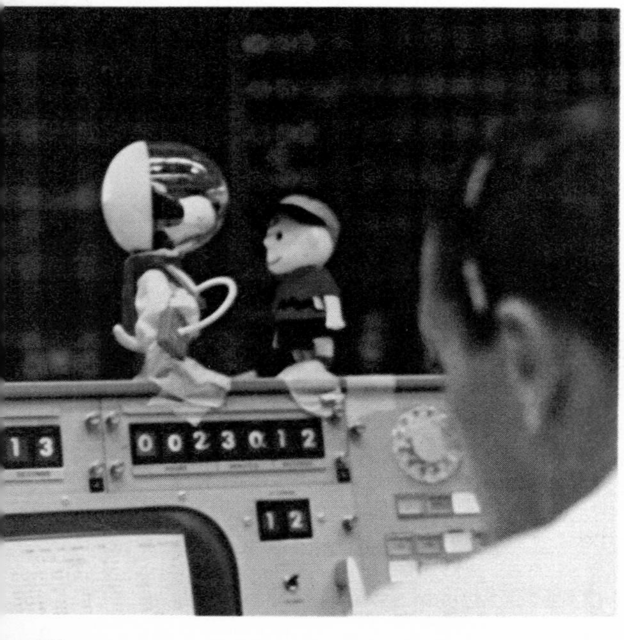

But for all his phenomenal success in newspapers and on television, Charlie Brown's finest hour actually came from outer space. In May of 1969, the Apollo 10 crew named their command module *Charlie Brown* and their lunar module *Snoopy*. For days, people around the world heard the code names crackle back and forth between NASA officials in Houston and the craft in space.

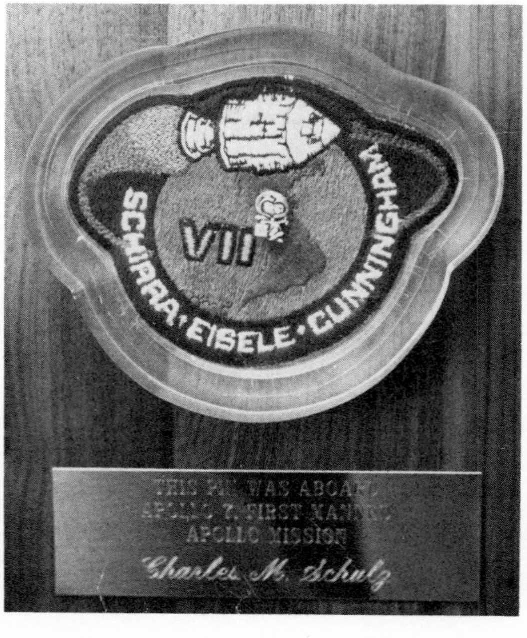
SCHIRRA • EISELE • CUNNINGHAM
VII
Charles M. Schulz

On the fourth international telecast made from the color-television camera aboard the Apollo 10 spacecraft, astronaut John Young held up a drawing of Charlie Brown (*see right*). When this picture was transmitted to earth, Apollo 10 was halfway to the moon. For an old Buck Rogers fan like Sparky, this was a momentous occasion!

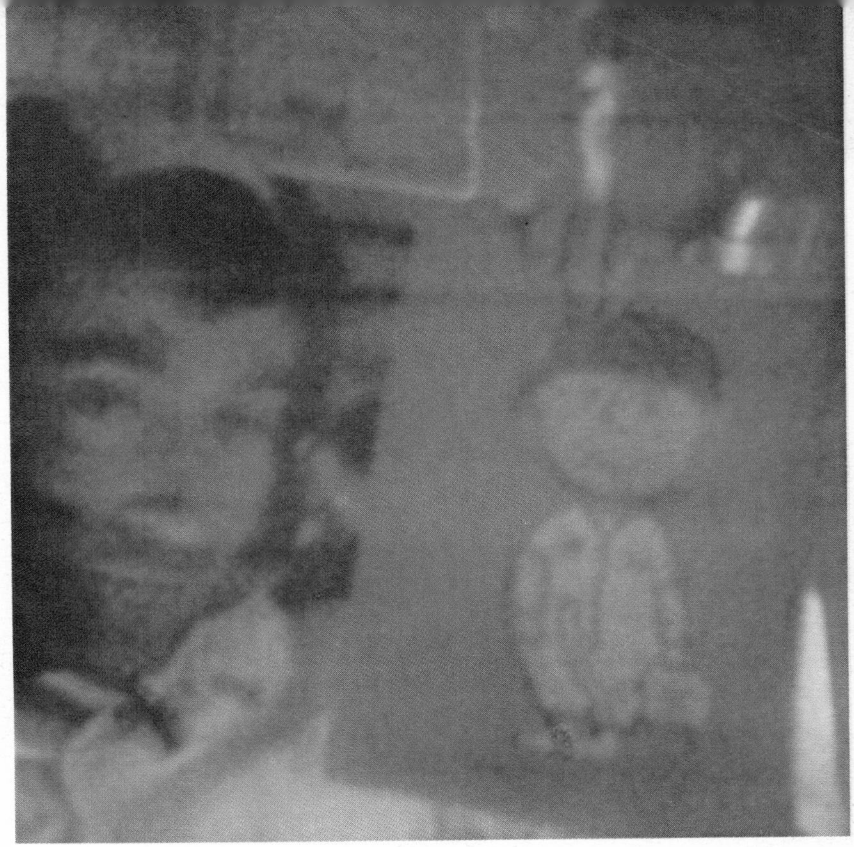

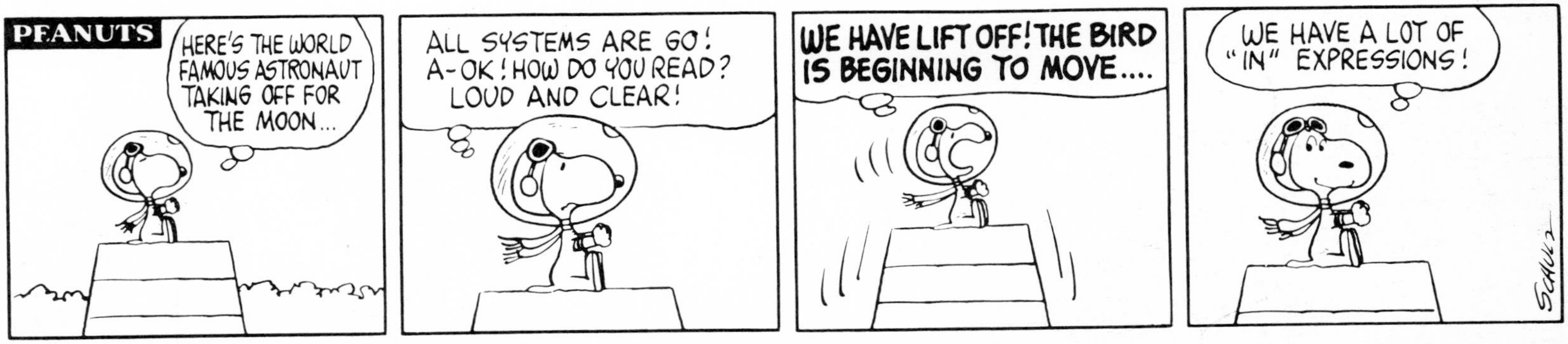
PEANUTS
HERE'S THE WORLD FAMOUS ASTRONAUT TAKING OFF FOR THE MOON...
ALL SYSTEMS ARE GO! A-OK! HOW DO YOU READ? LOUD AND CLEAR!
WE HAVE LIFT OFF! THE BIRD IS BEGINNING TO MOVE....
WE HAVE A LOT OF "IN" EXPRESSIONS!
SCHULZ

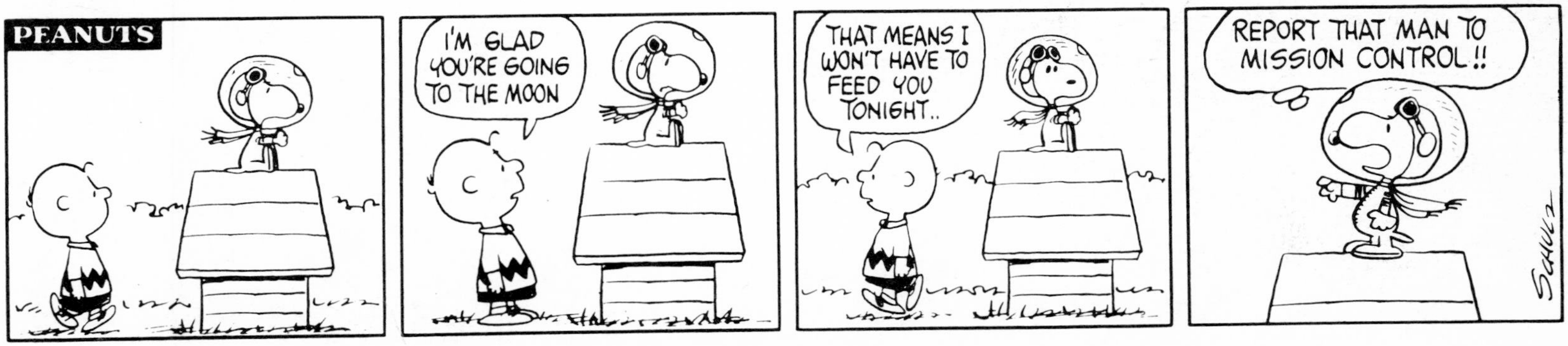
PEANUTS
I'M GLAD YOU'RE GOING TO THE MOON
THAT MEANS I WON'T HAVE TO FEED YOU TONIGHT..
REPORT THAT MAN TO MISSION CONTROL!!
SCHULZ

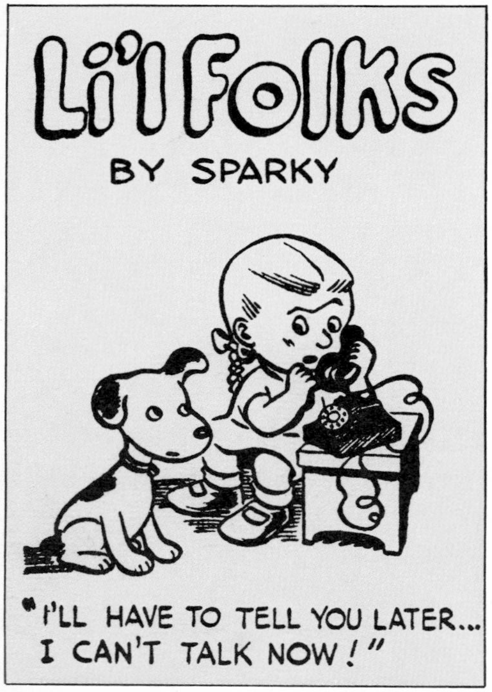
Li'l Folks
BY SPARKY
"I'LL HAVE TO TELL YOU LATER... I CAN'T TALK NOW!"

He's your dog, Charlie Brown

Snoopy, like his master Charlie Brown, was first seen in the late 1940's in Sparky's *Li'l Folks* feature, although he didn't look like the Snoopy we know today. In the 1950's Snoopy started to look a little more like his final self, but his thoughts were limited to reactions like "gulp" (*see below*). By the 1960's, however, Snoopy (*see right*) started to look and to think the way we know him today.

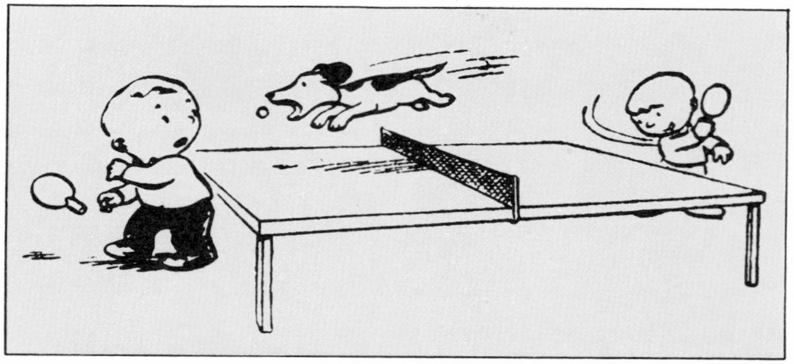

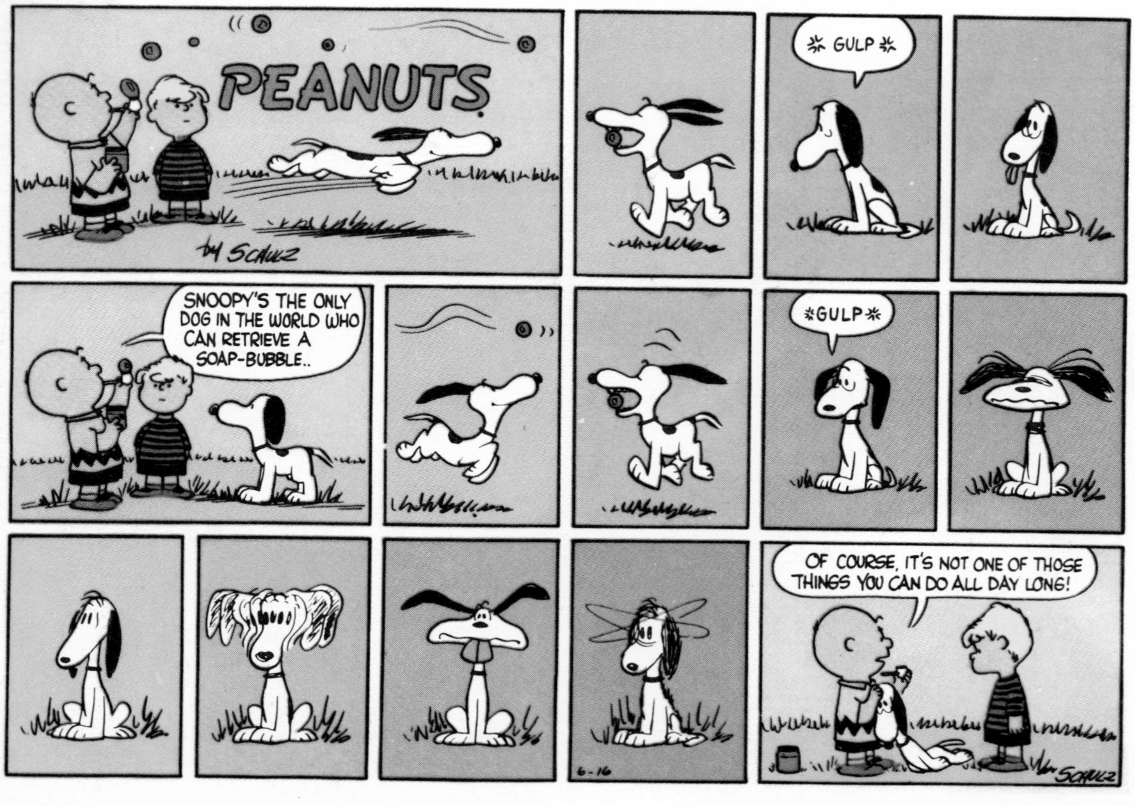
PEANUTS
GULP
SNOOPY'S THE ONLY DOG IN THE WORLD WHO CAN RETRIEVE A SOAP-BUBBLE..
GULP
OF COURSE, IT'S NOT ONE OF THOSE THINGS YOU CAN DO ALL DAY LONG!

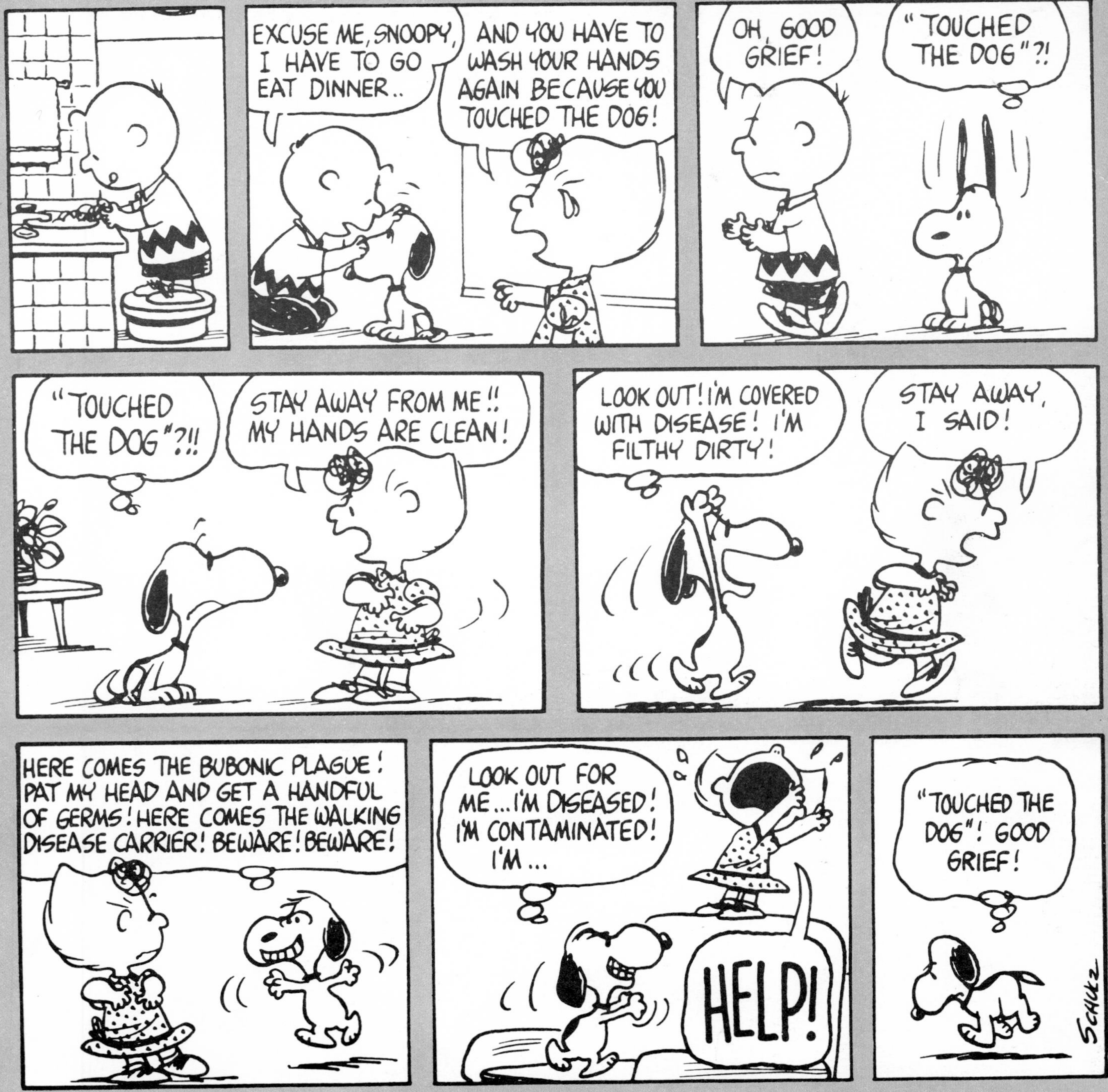
EXCUSE ME, SNOOPY, I HAVE TO GO EAT DINNER..
AND YOU HAVE TO WASH YOUR HANDS AGAIN BECAUSE YOU TOUCHED THE DOG!
OH, GOOD GRIEF!
"TOUCHED THE DOG"?!
"TOUCHED THE DOG"?!!
STAY AWAY FROM ME!! MY HANDS ARE CLEAN!
LOOK OUT! I'M COVERED WITH DISEASE! I'M FILTHY DIRTY!
STAY AWAY, I SAID!
HERE COMES THE BUBONIC PLAGUE! PAT MY HEAD AND GET A HANDFUL OF GERMS! HERE COMES THE WALKING DISEASE CARRIER! BEWARE! BEWARE!
LOOK OUT FOR ME...I'M DISEASED! I'M CONTAMINATED! I'M...
HELP!
"TOUCHED THE DOG"! GOOD GRIEF!
SCHULZ

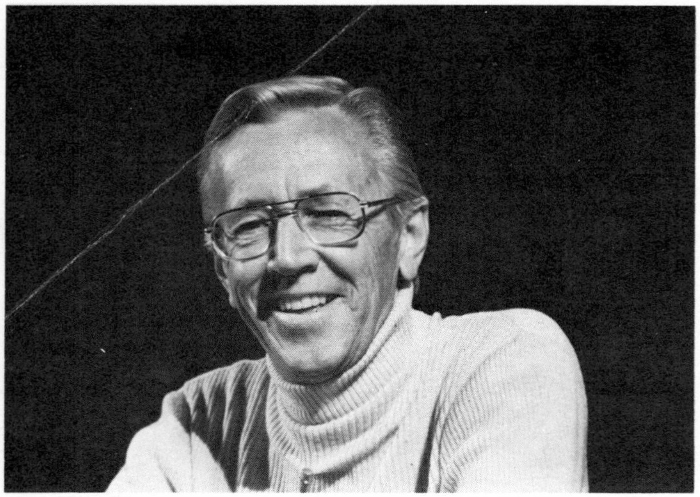

We asked Sparky his thoughts about this beagle, who is such a Walter Mitty character. "I think Snoopy is the easiest of the characters to draw and probably the most fun. Snoopy represents the dream of a lot of people who would like to be a club champion or to be a world-famous flying ace. But there's another quality about Snoopy that I think makes the whole thing work. This is a quality of innocence combined with a little bit of egotism. You put those two qualities together, and I think you have trouble, especially with Snoopy."

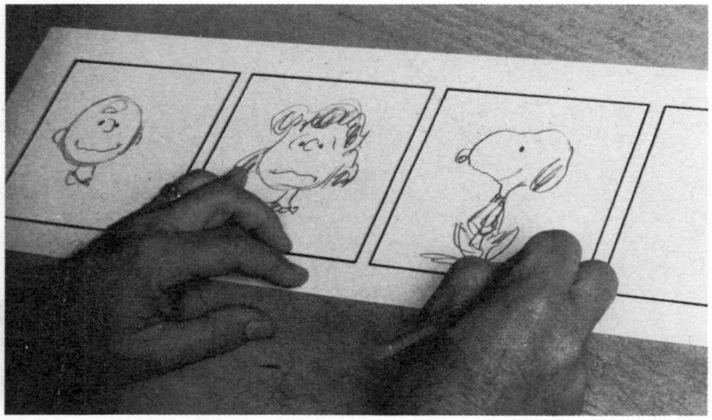

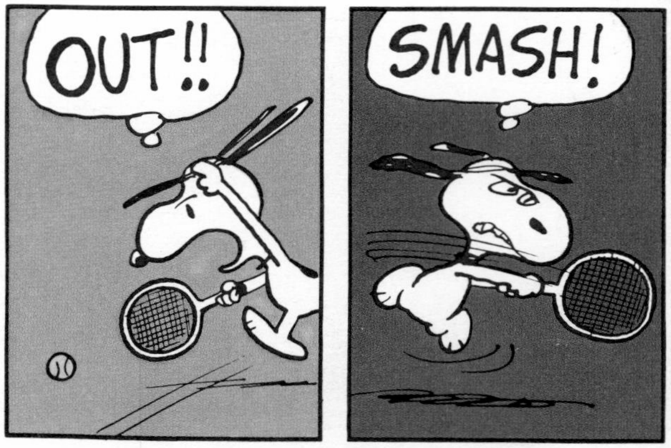
OUT!!
SMASH!

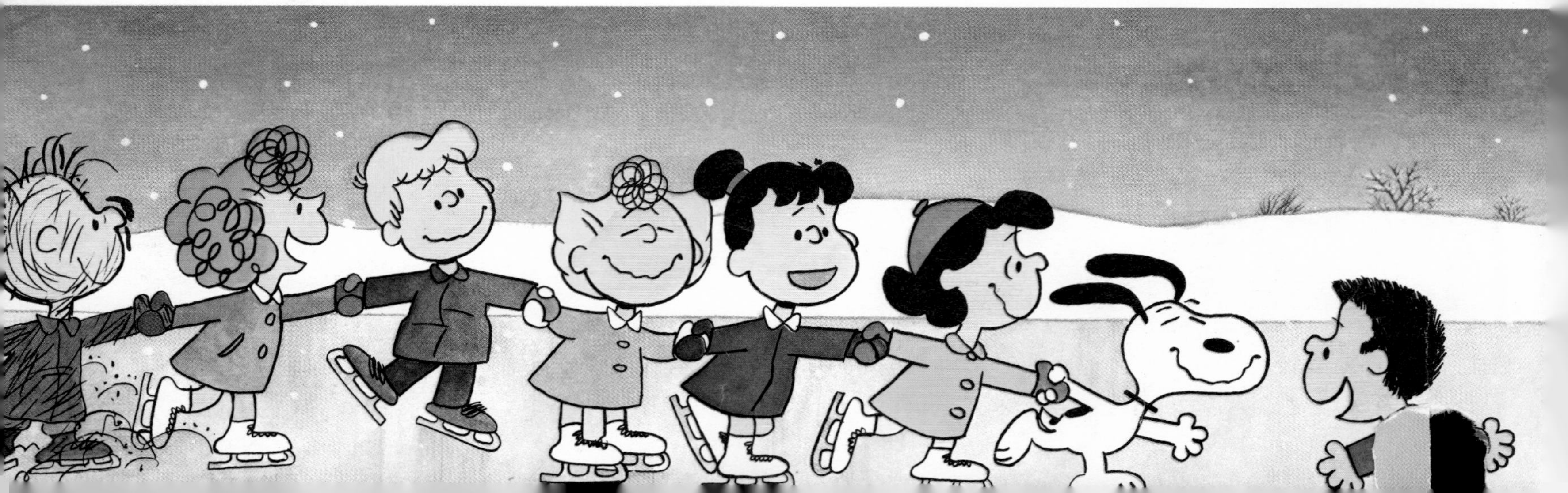

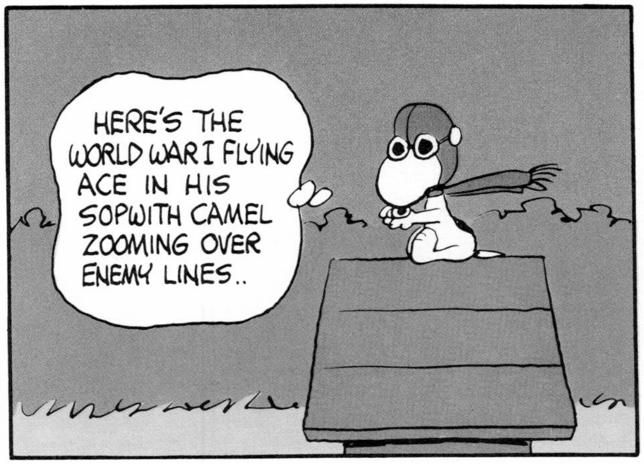
HERE'S THE WORLD WAR I FLYING ACE IN HIS SOPWITH CAMEL ZOOMING OVER ENEMY LINES..

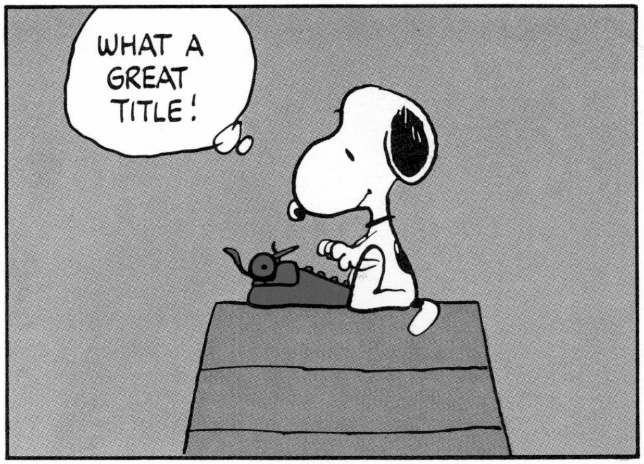
WHAT A GREAT TITLE!

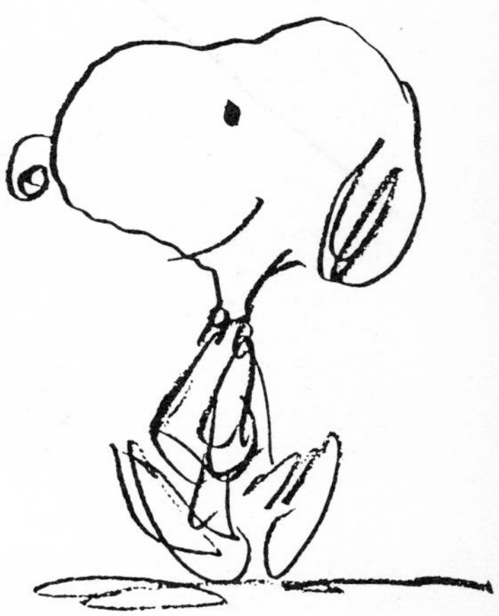

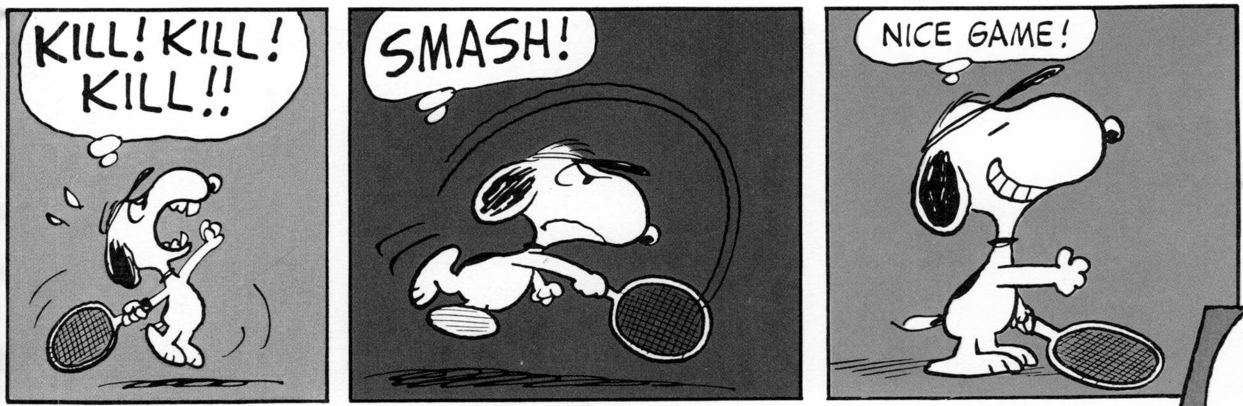
KILL! KILL! KILL!!
SMASH!
NICE GAME!

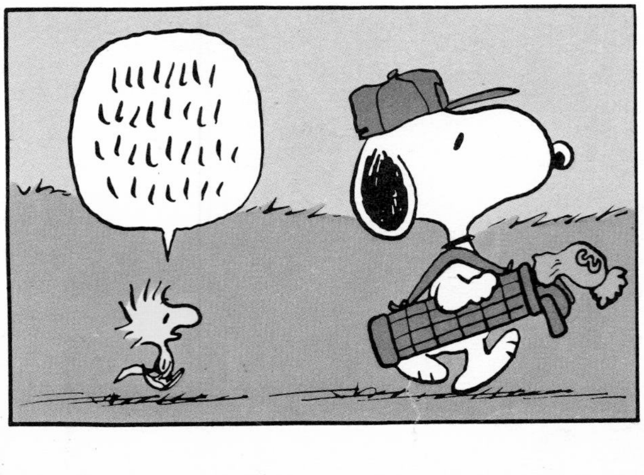

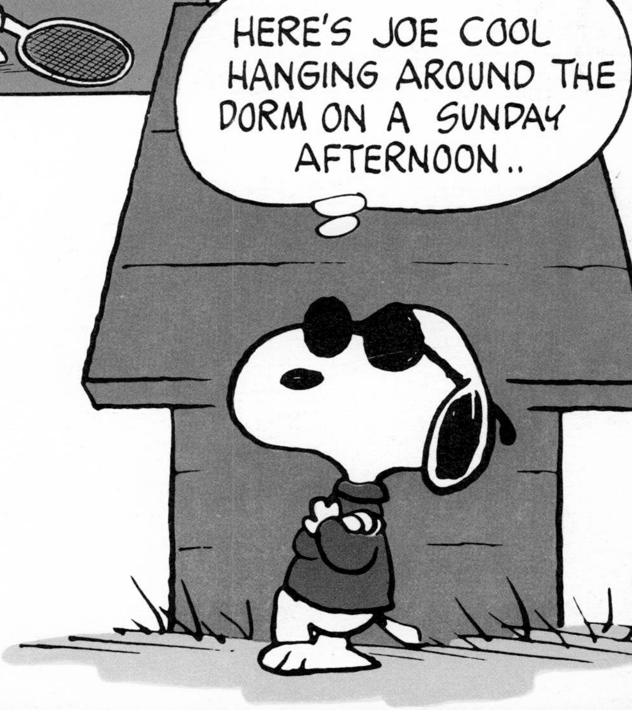
HERE'S JOE COOL HANGING AROUND THE DORM ON A SUNDAY AFTERNOON..

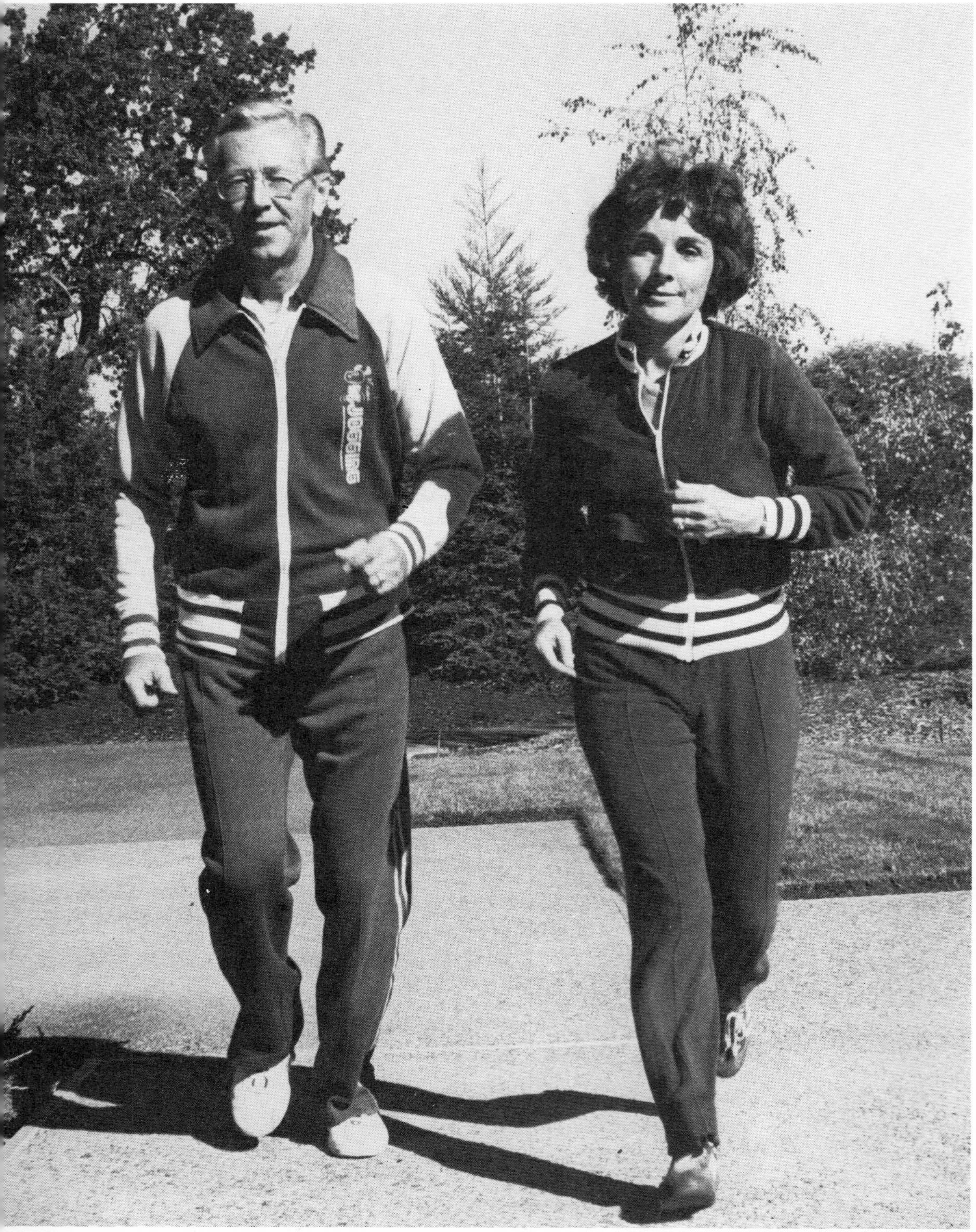

Snoopy in the comic strip often ends up doing what Sparky does in his own daily routine. Sparky and his wife, Jeannie, jog two miles at least three times a week, and the thoughts of Sparky as he runs usually become the thoughts of Snoopy as *he* runs (*see right*).

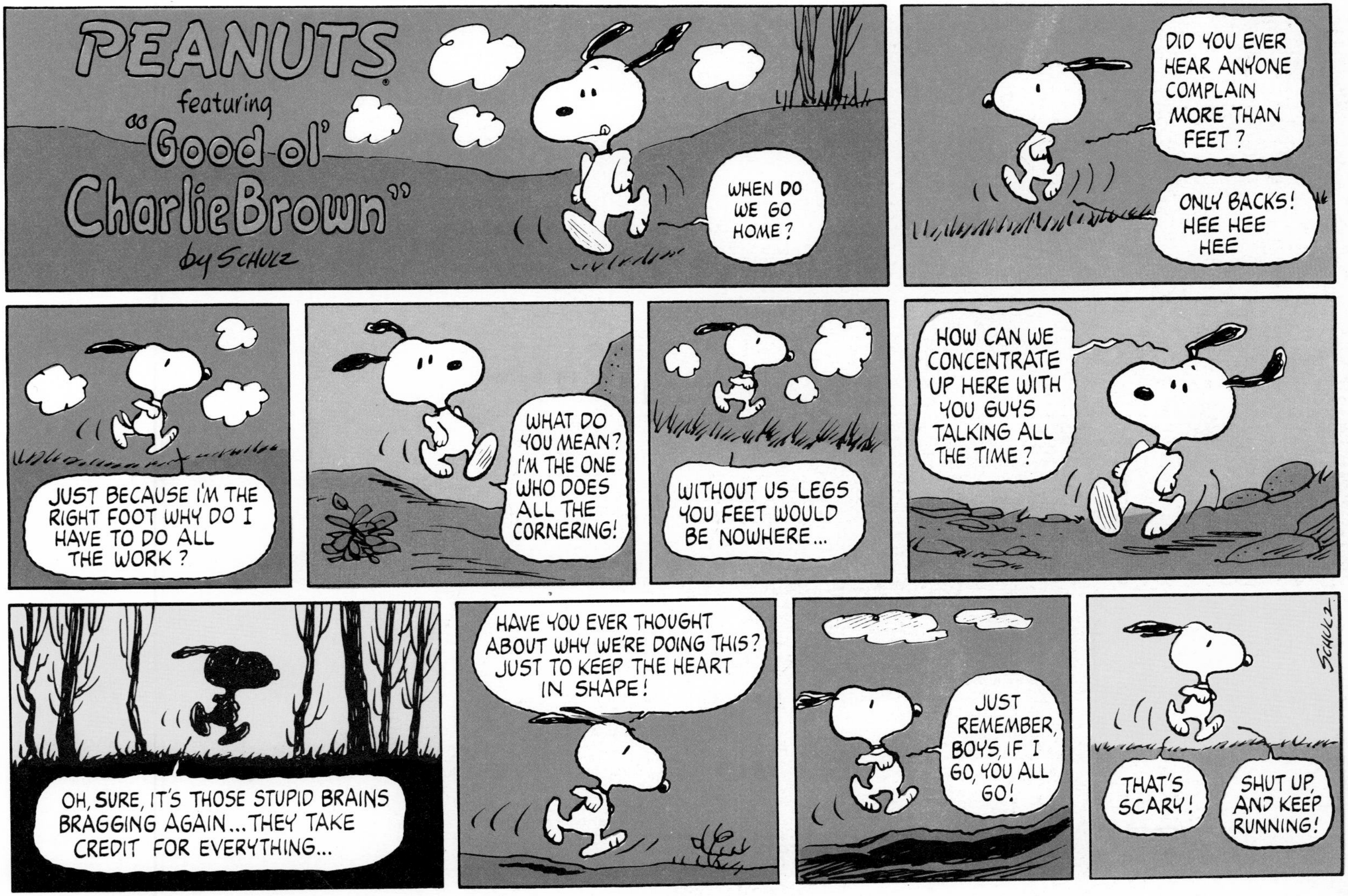
PEANUTS
featuring
"Good ol' Charlie Brown"
by SCHULZ
WHEN DO WE GO HOME?
DID YOU EVER HEAR ANYONE COMPLAIN MORE THAN FEET?
ONLY BACKS! HEE HEE HEE
JUST BECAUSE I'M THE RIGHT FOOT WHY DO I HAVE TO DO ALL THE WORK?
WHAT DO YOU MEAN? I'M THE ONE WHO DOES ALL THE CORNERING!
WITHOUT US LEGS YOU FEET WOULD BE NOWHERE...
HOW CAN WE CONCENTRATE UP HERE WITH YOU GUYS TALKING ALL THE TIME?
OH, SURE, IT'S THOSE STUPID BRAINS BRAGGING AGAIN... THEY TAKE CREDIT FOR EVERYTHING...
HAVE YOU EVER THOUGHT ABOUT WHY WE'RE DOING THIS? JUST TO KEEP THE HEART IN SHAPE!
JUST REMEMBER, BOYS, IF I GO, YOU ALL GO!
SCHULZ
THAT'S SCARY!
SHUT UP, AND KEEP RUNNING!

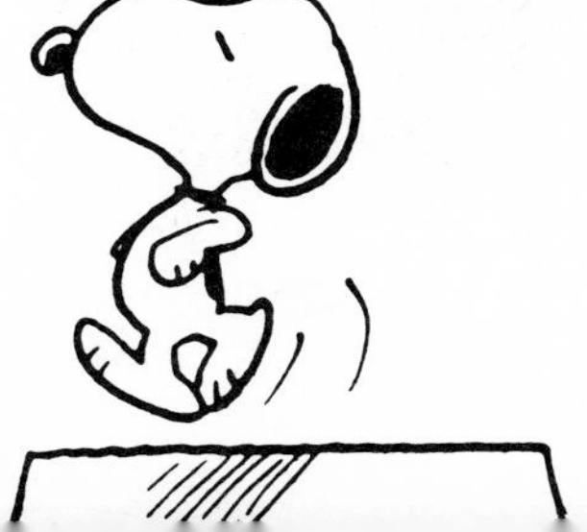

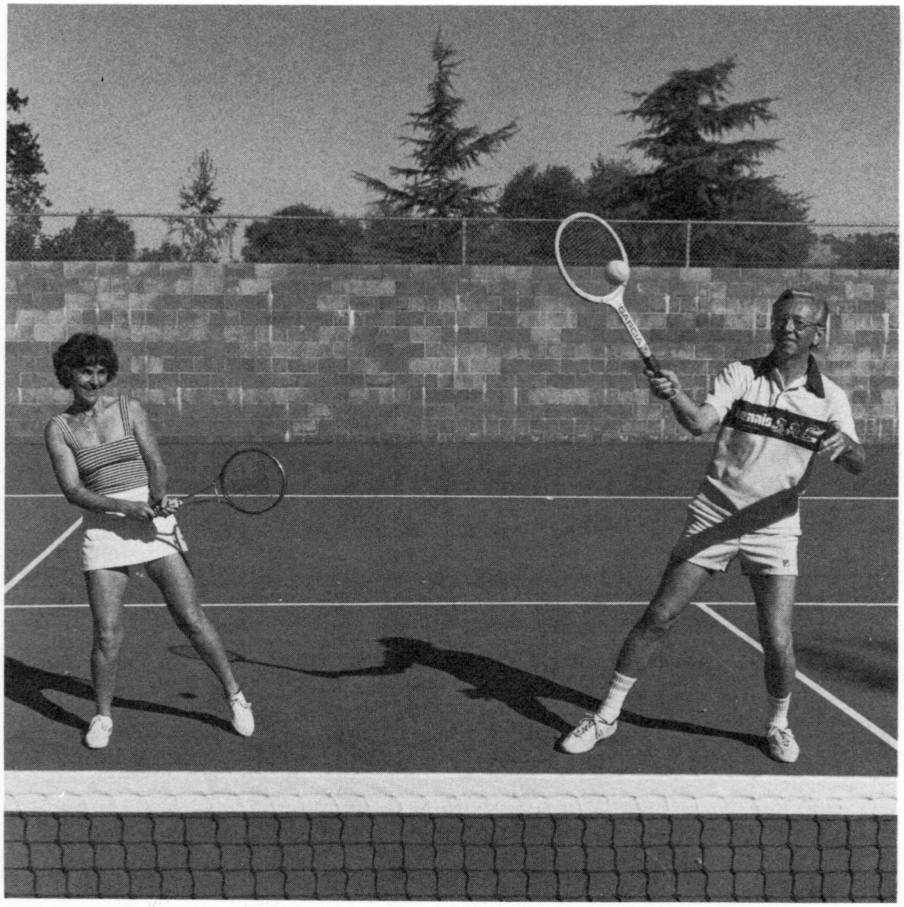

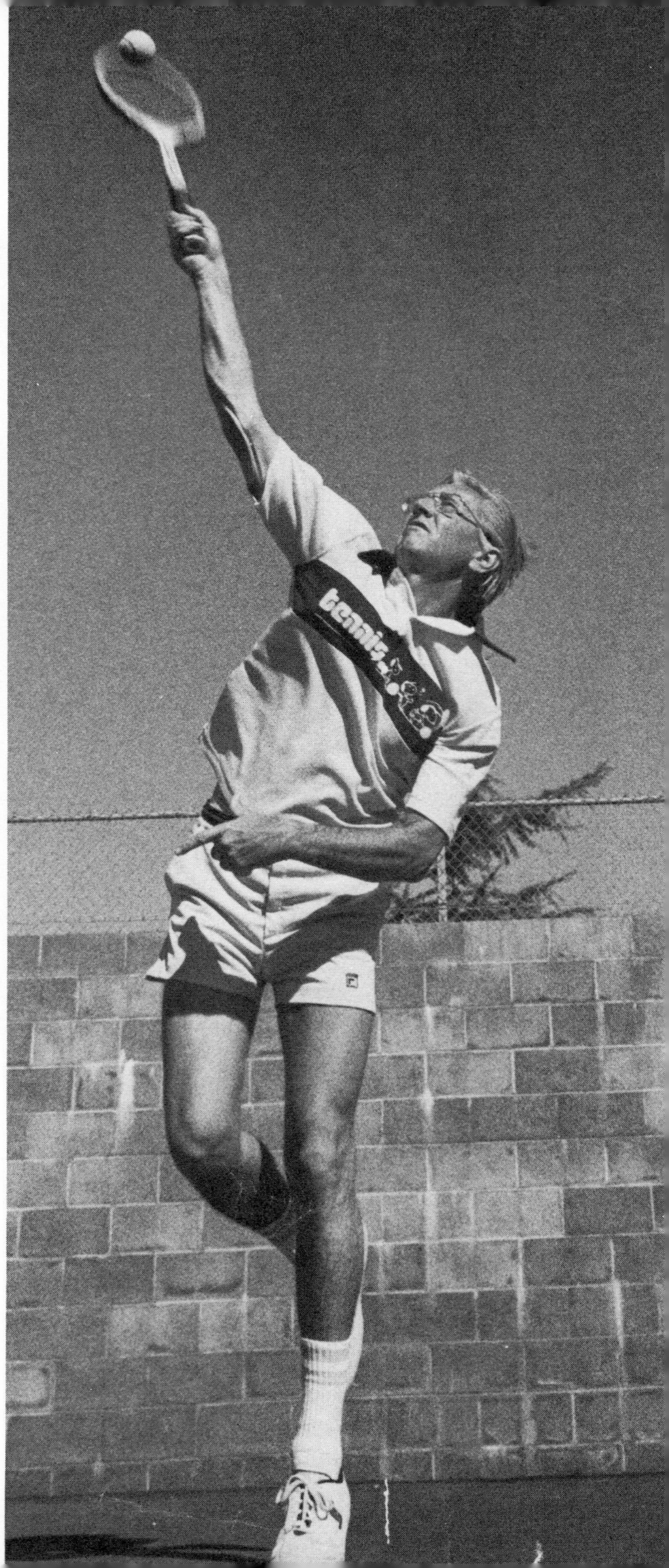

During the past six years, Sparky and Jeannie have become avid tennis players. With an indoor and outdoor court built right next to the studio, they manage to play a few sets of tennis almost every day the full year round. Consequently, Snoopy too has become a tennis player.

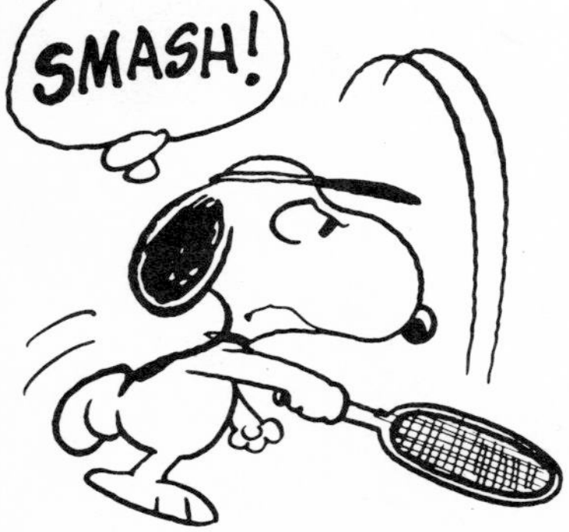
SMASH!

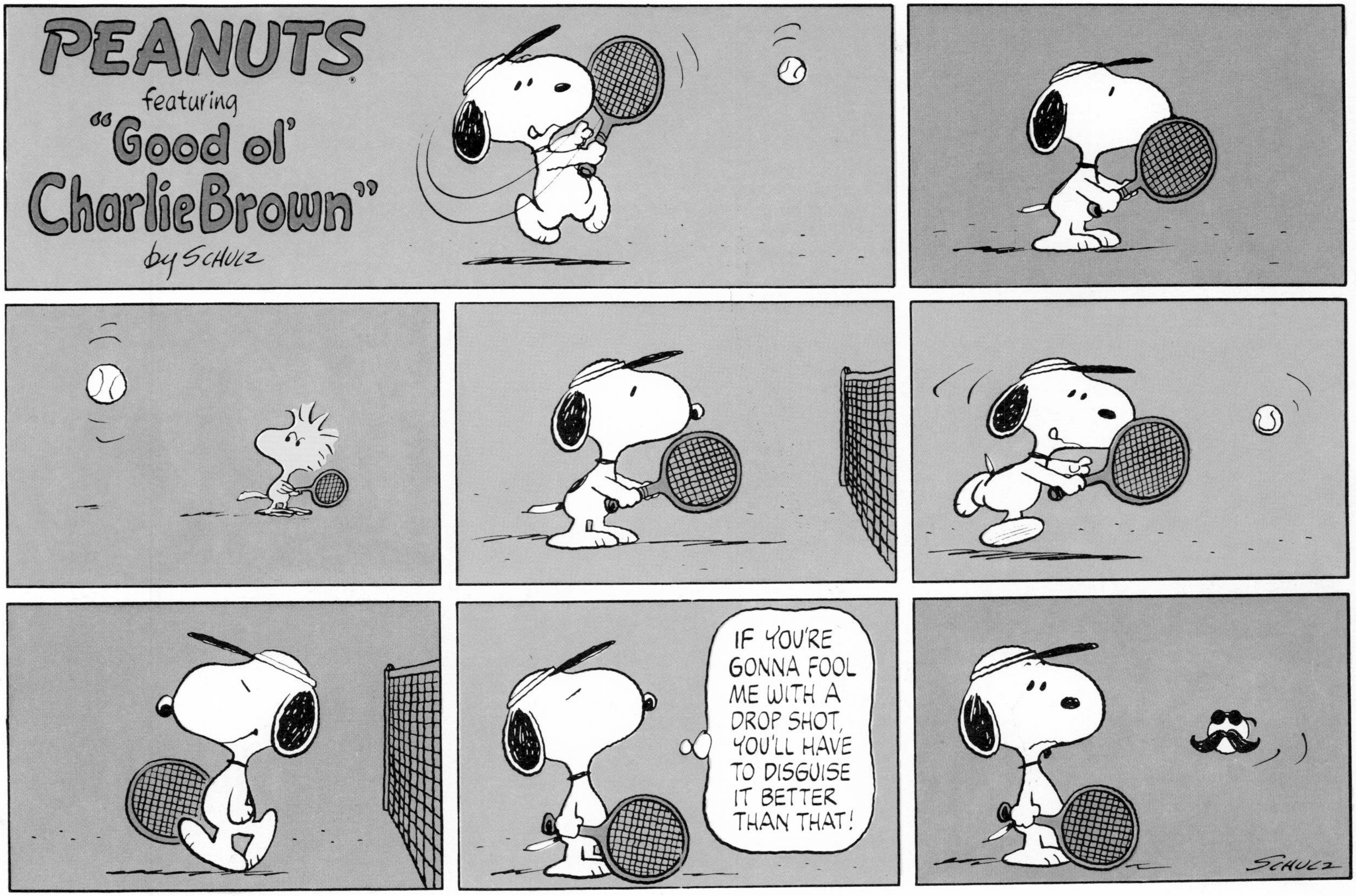
PEANUTS
featuring
"Good ol' Charlie Brown"
by SCHULZ
IF YOU'RE GONNA FOOL ME WITH A DROP SHOT, YOU'LL HAVE TO DISGUISE IT BETTER THAN THAT!
SCHULZ

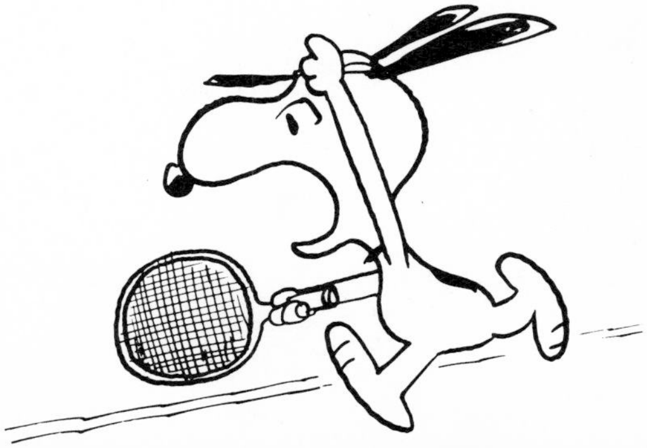

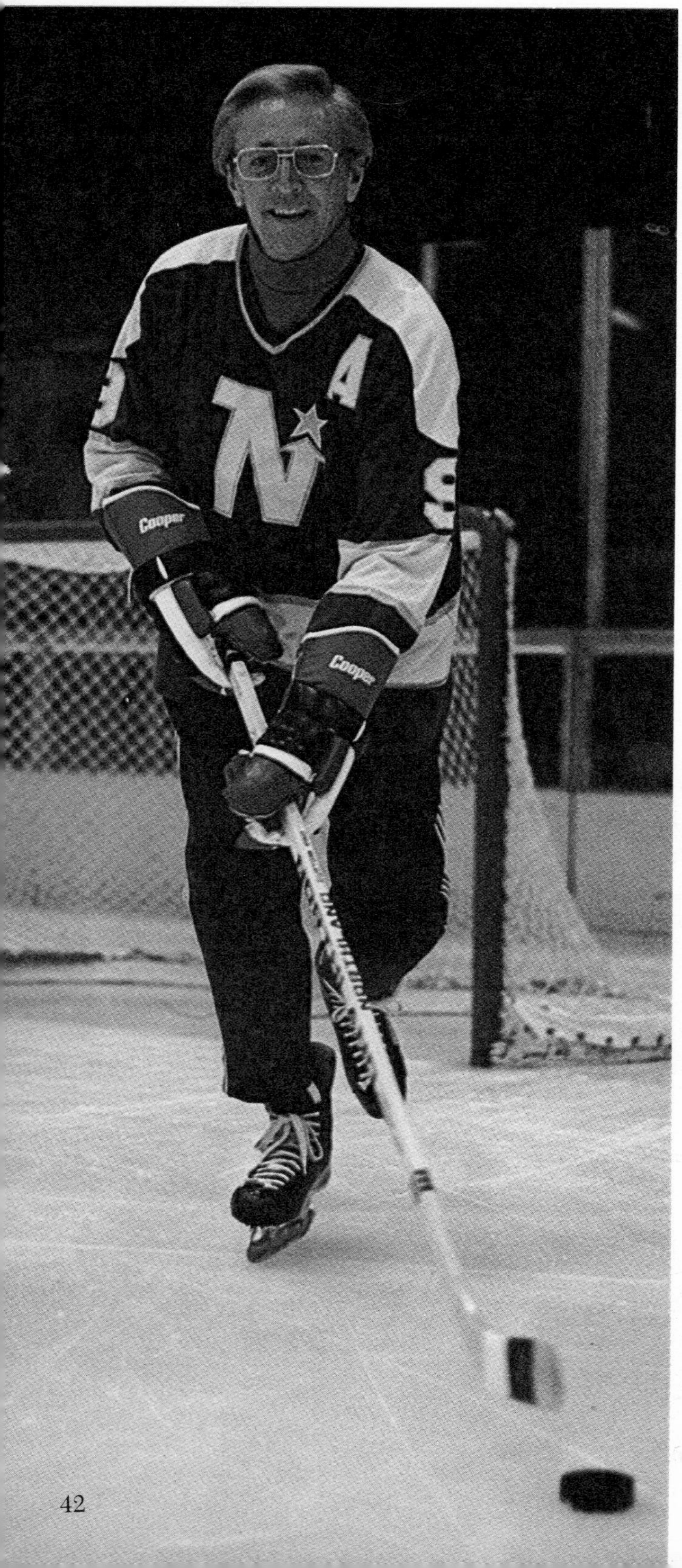

A
Cooper
Cooper

Sparky (*left*) also manages to play ice hockey at least once or twice a week at the magnificent Redwood Empire Ice Arena, which he built just a block from his studio. This, of course, led to some animated sequences of Snoopy playing hockey. It also led to the creation of four network ice-skating specials involving Snoopy, stars from Shipstads and Johnson Ice Follies, and other top skaters. Thus Snoopy skated with the great Peggy Fleming (*below*) . . .

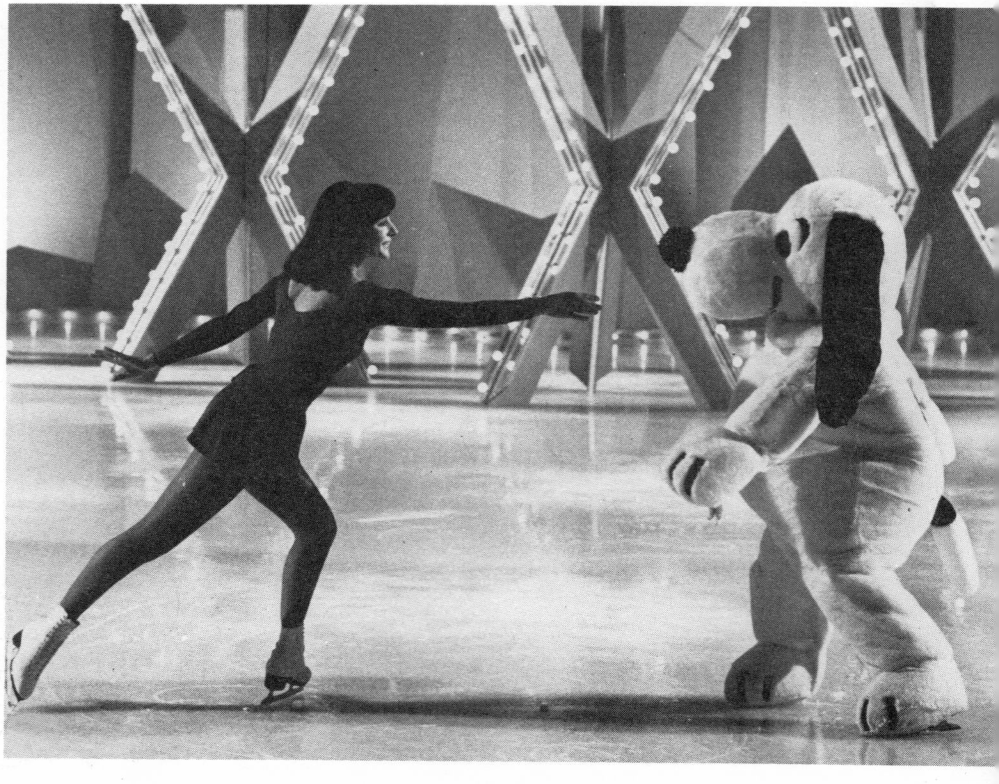

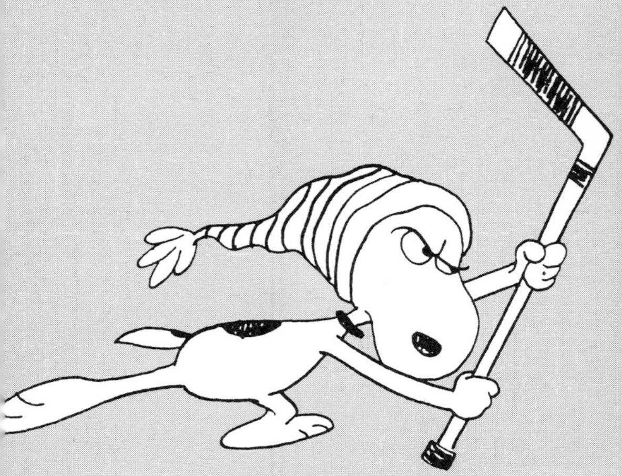

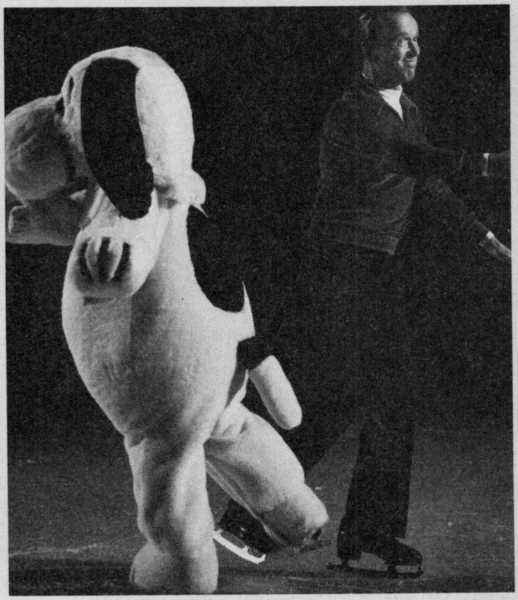

. . . with the incomparable Mr. Frick, who was celebrating forty years as an international star . . .

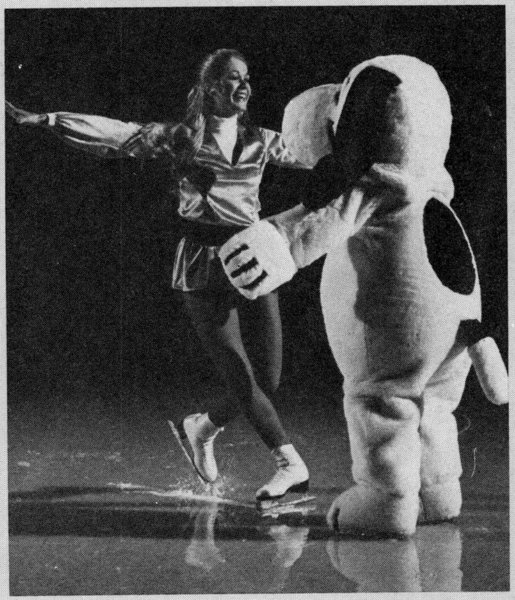

. . . with the beautiful Ice Follies star Karen Kresge . . .

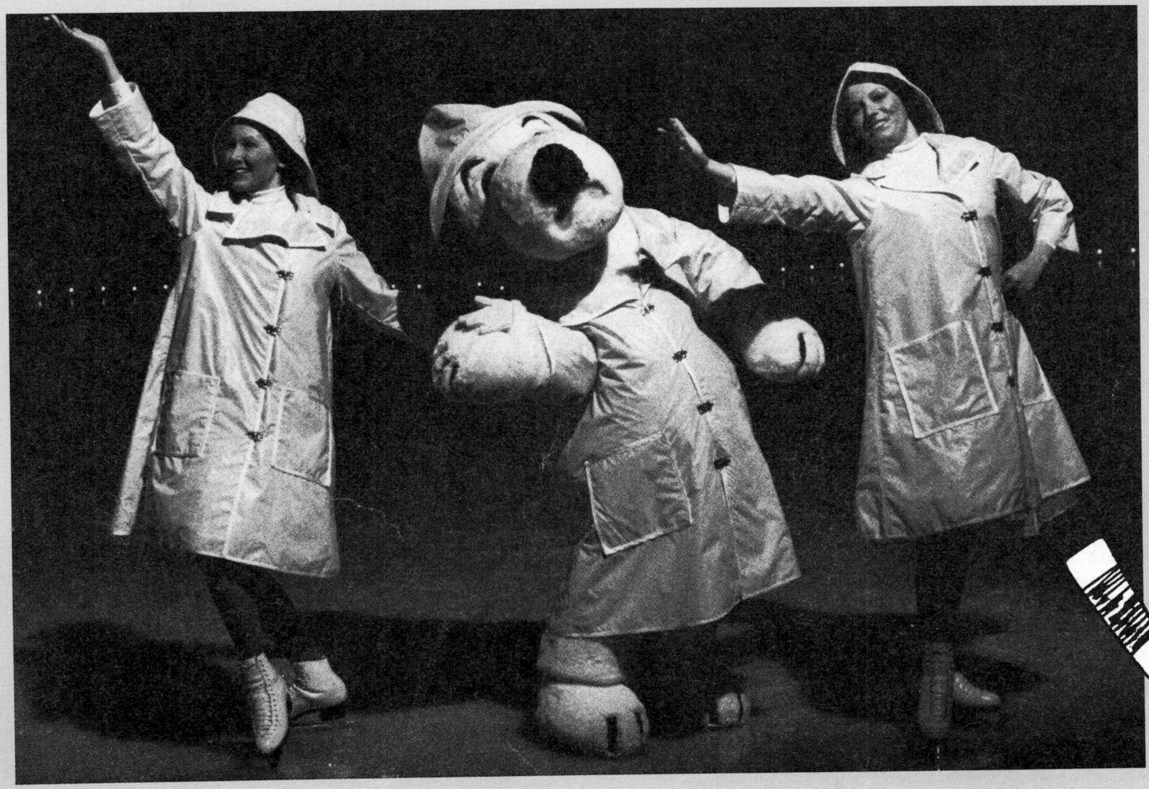

. . . and with Sparky's daughter Amy (*left*) and Mary Ellen Kinsey.

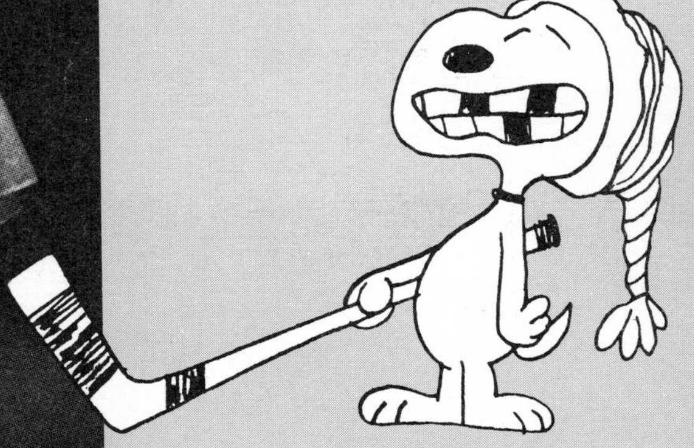

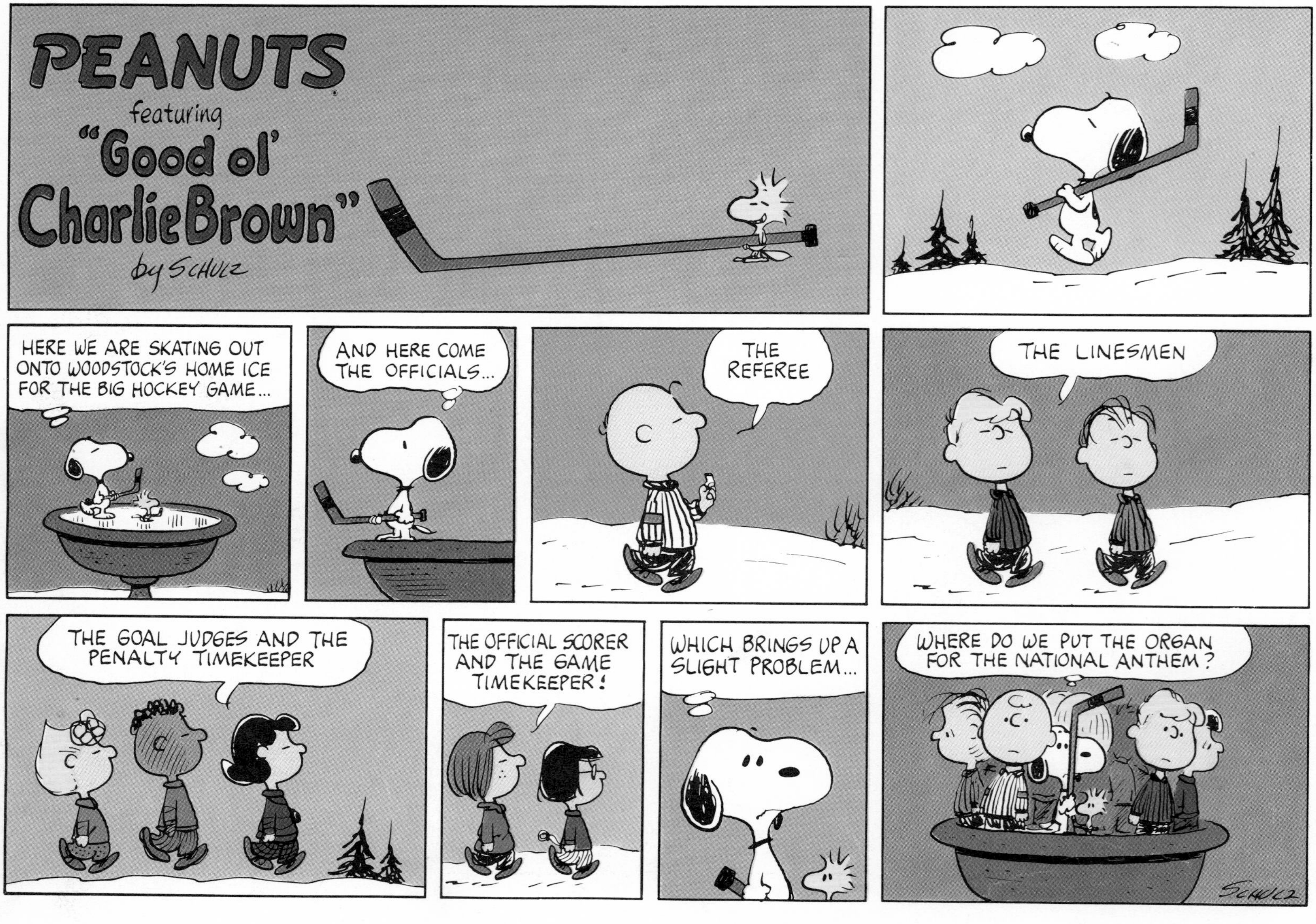
PEANUTS
featuring
"Good ol' Charlie Brown"
by SCHULZ
HERE WE ARE SKATING OUT ONTO WOODSTOCK'S HOME ICE FOR THE BIG HOCKEY GAME...
AND HERE COME THE OFFICIALS...
THE REFEREE
THE LINESMEN
THE GOAL JUDGES AND THE PENALTY TIMEKEEPER
THE OFFICIAL SCORER AND THE GAME TIMEKEEPER!
WHICH BRINGS UP A SLIGHT PROBLEM...
WHERE DO WE PUT THE ORGAN FOR THE NATIONAL ANTHEM?
SCHULZ

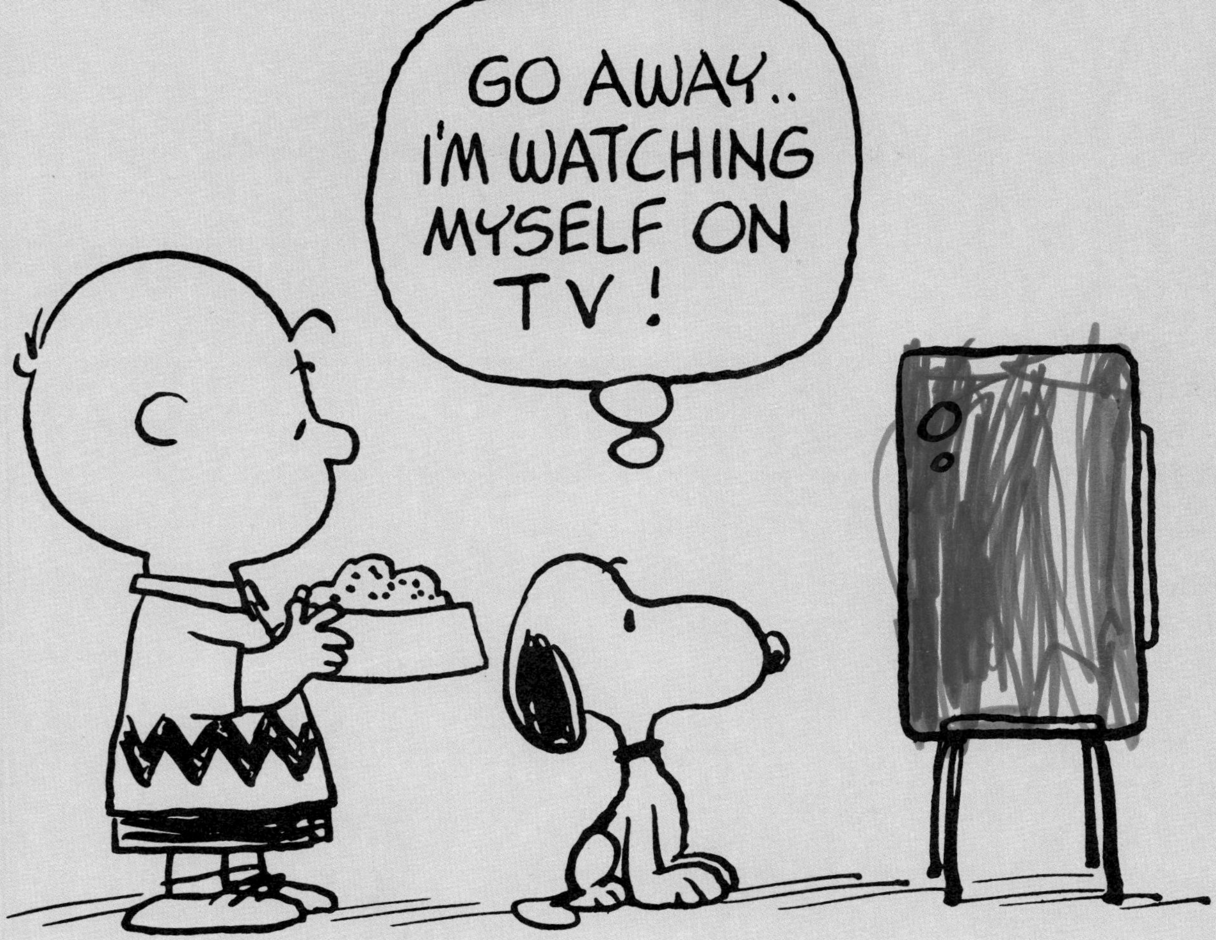
GO AWAY..
I'M WATCHING
MYSELF ON
TV!

When we started the animated specials back in 1965, Snoopy presented us with a major problem. By that time in the comic strip, Snoopy's thoughts had become one of the major outlets of humor for the strip. We considered printing those thoughts on the animated shows, but we then realized that young children wouldn't be able to read them. Then we discussed the idea of using a funny voice to actually verbalize Snoopy's thoughts, because we didn't want to lose all those great gags. But this idea was discarded also. We finally decided that Snoopy would have to emulate the great Harpo Marx — all in pantomime.

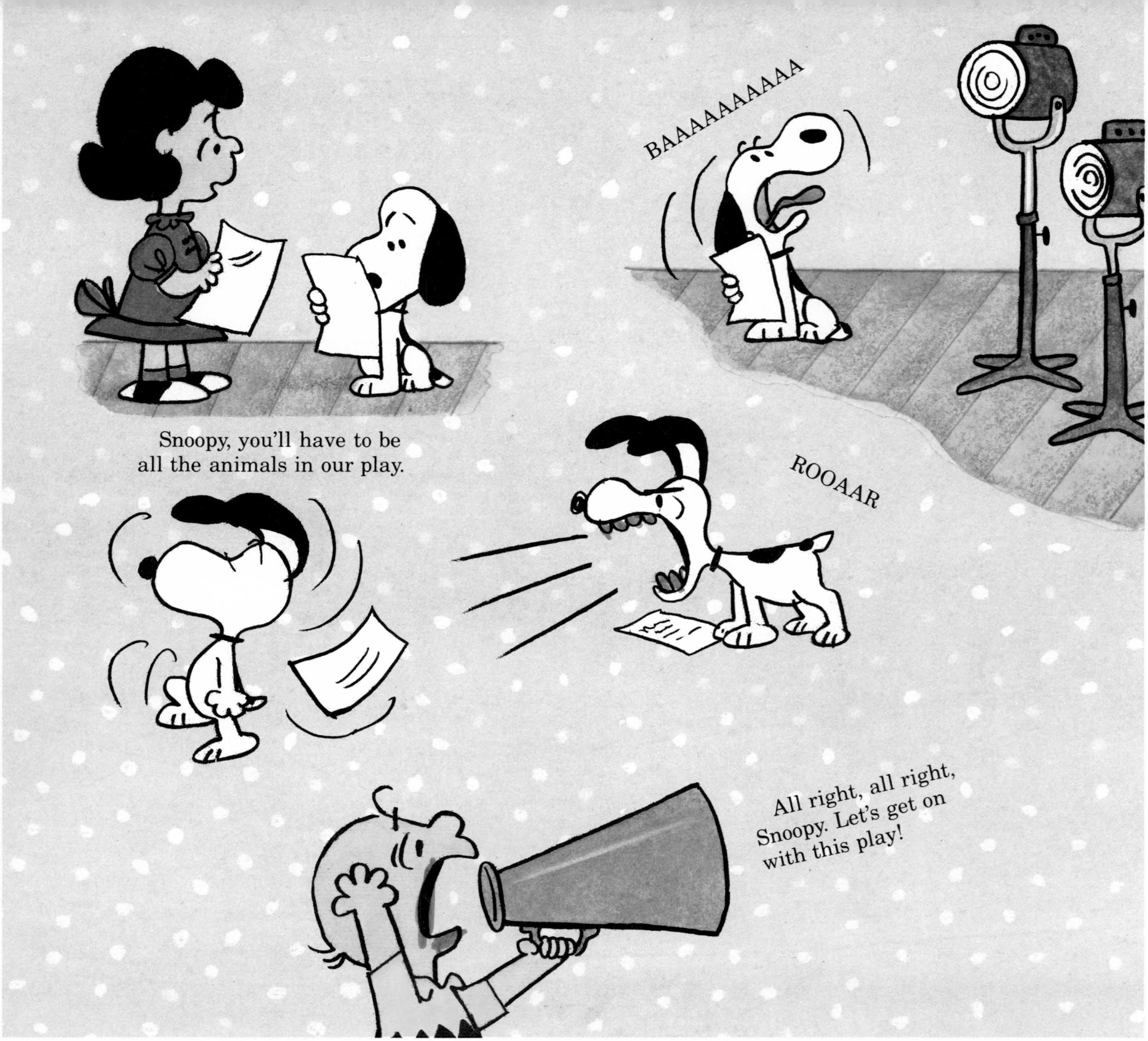
Snoopy, you'll have to be
all the animals in our play.
BAAAAAAAAAAA
ROOAAR
All right, all right,
Snoopy. Let's get on
with this play!

We started Snoopy out slowly, with just a few scenes in *A Charlie Brown Christmas*. We had to see just how far we could go with him in pantomime.

Then, in *It's the Great Pumpkin, Charlie Brown*, we gave Snoopy a five-minute animated scene as he chased the infamous Red Baron. This proved that Snoopy could be a "star" without ever talking.

By the 1970's Snoopy had become the leading animated character as he performed in two Emmy-winning shows — the Moto-Cross performer in *Good Sport* and . . .

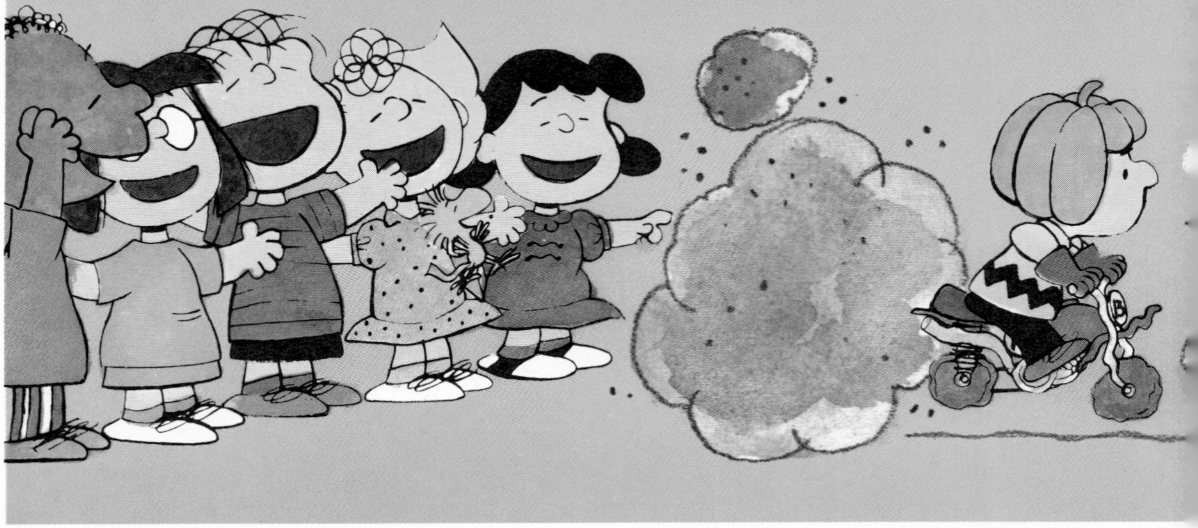

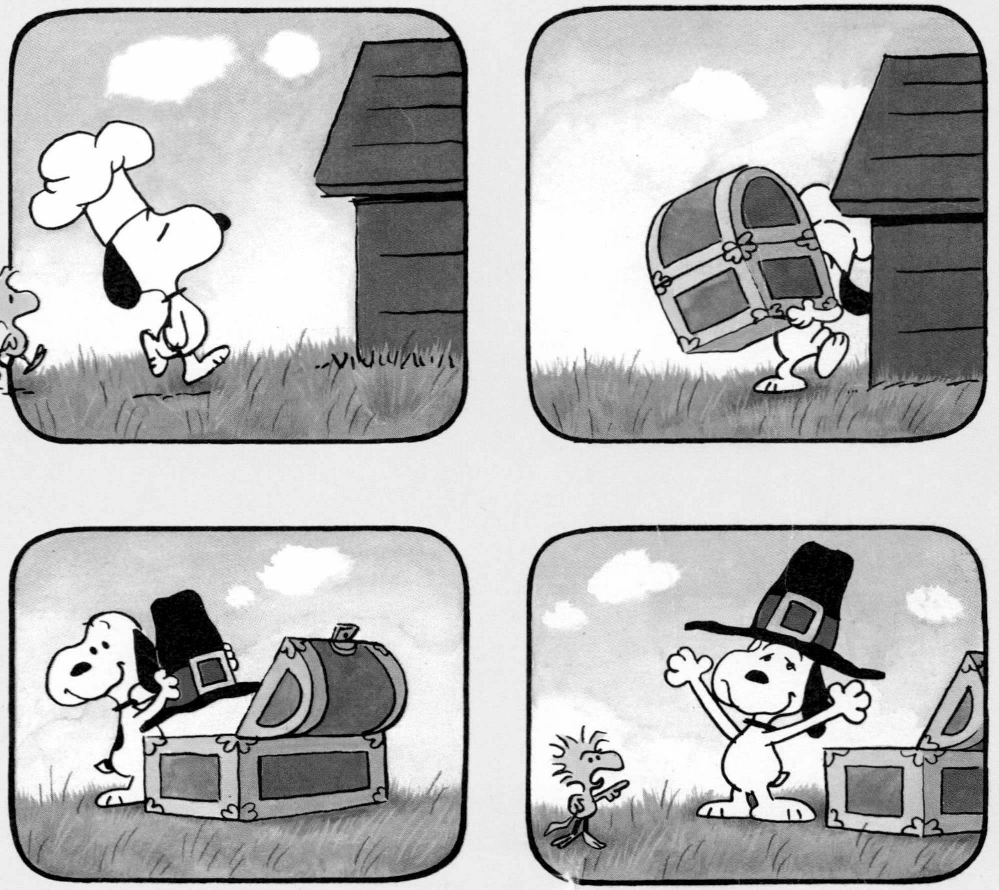

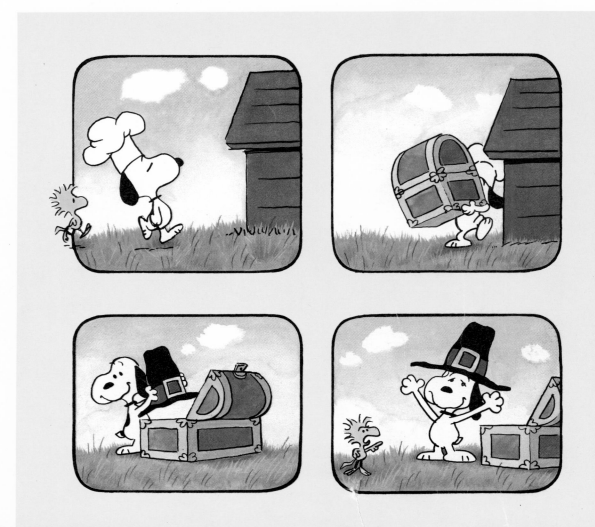

. . . the pilgrim in *A Charlie Brown Thanksgiving*.

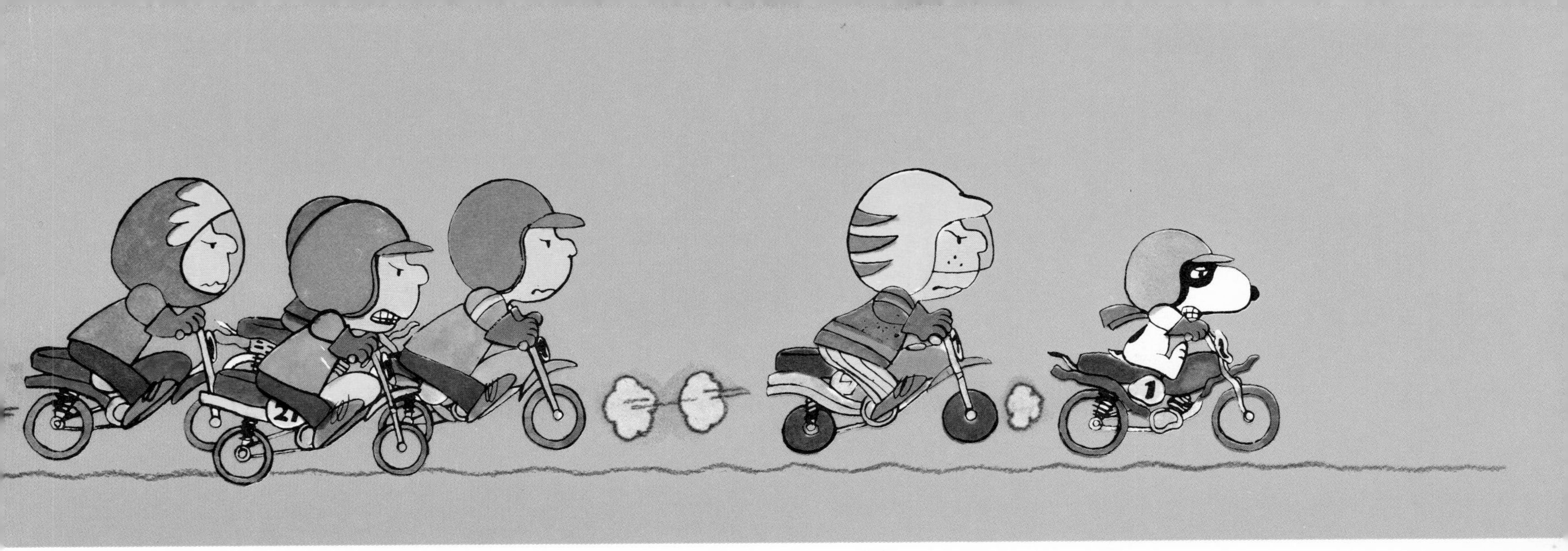

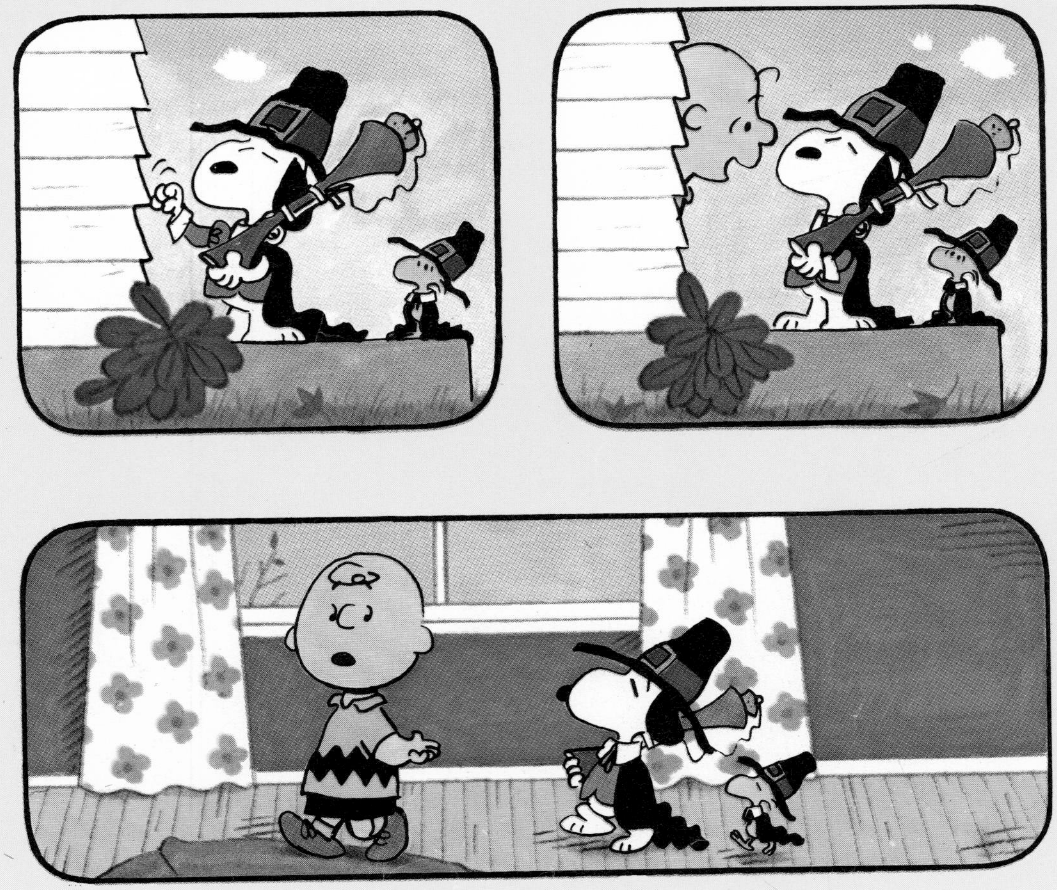

Snoopy! How can you serve food in that ridiculous costume? Why aren't you wearing your chef's hat?

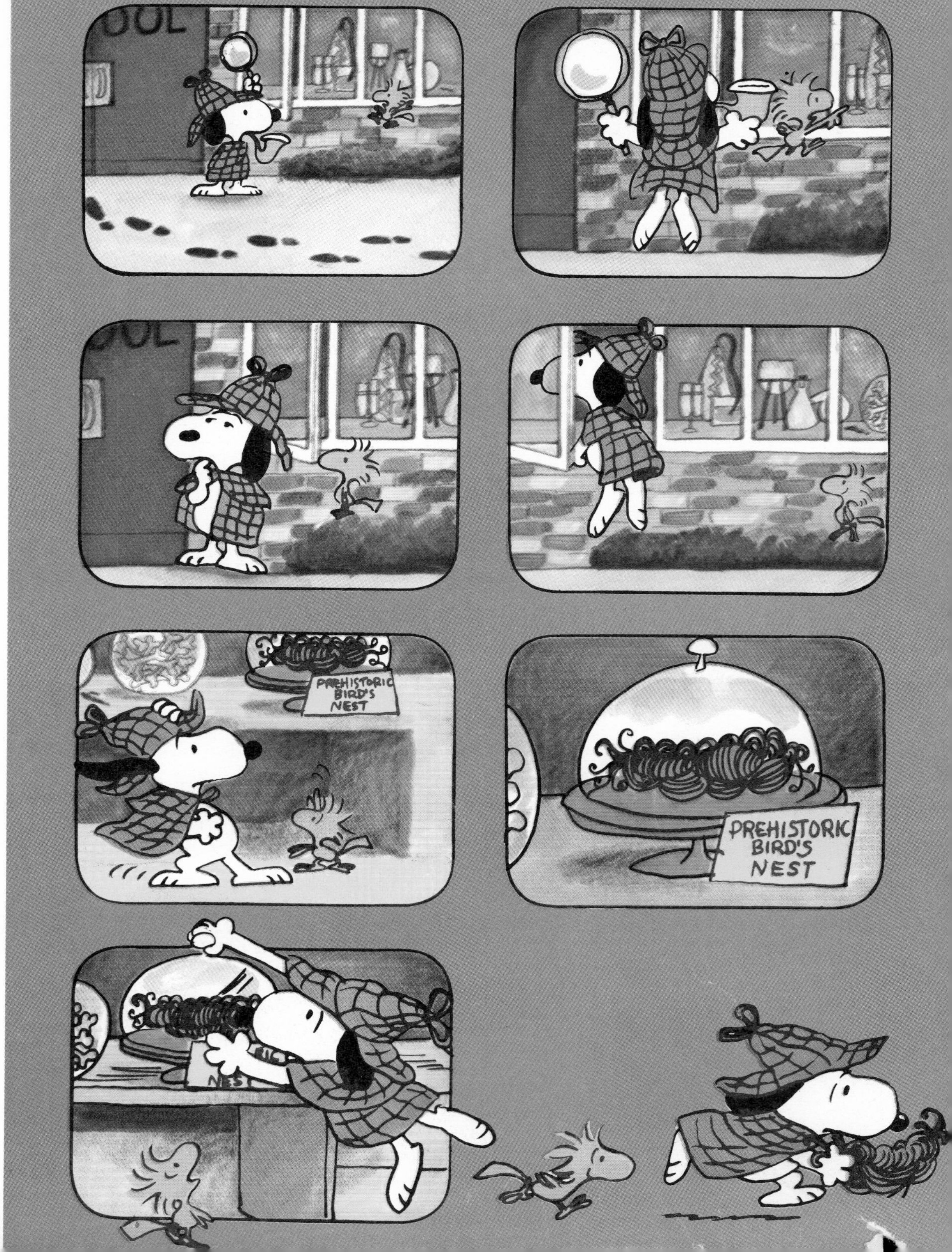
PREHISTORIC
BIRD'S
NEST
PREHISTORIC
BIRD'S
NEST

He even performed as Sherlock Holmes in *It's a Mystery, Charlie Brown* when he had to find who had "stolen" Woodstock's bird nest. Snoopy wouldn't rest until the case was solved.

Sally was the culprit: she needed an exhibit for school. Snoopy recovered the nest and returned it to his friend.

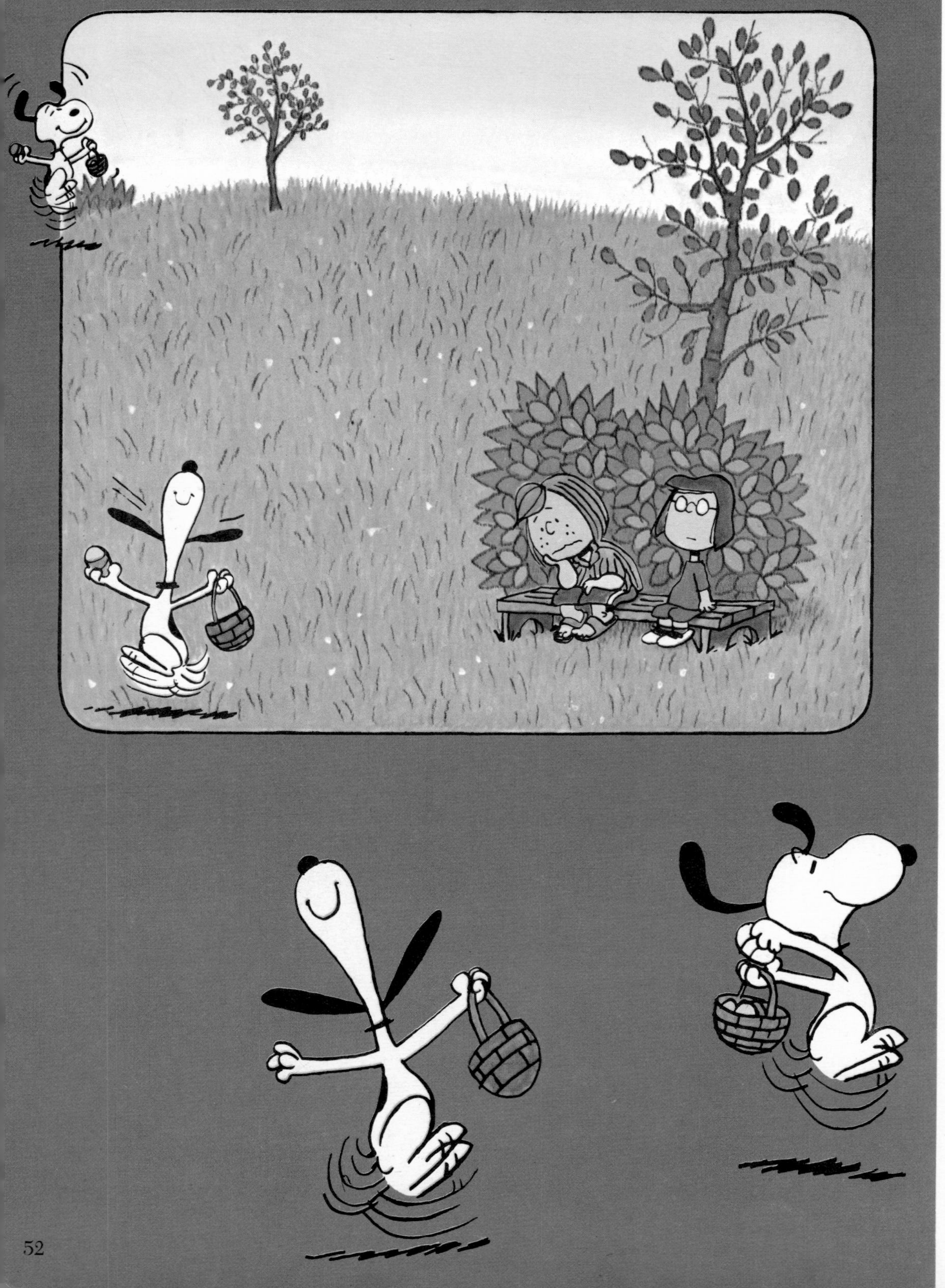

In *It's the Easter Beagle, Charlie Brown*, Snoopy spied on Lucy as she hid the eggs, then quickly gathered them up, and distributed them as the Easter Beagle, infuriating Lucy.

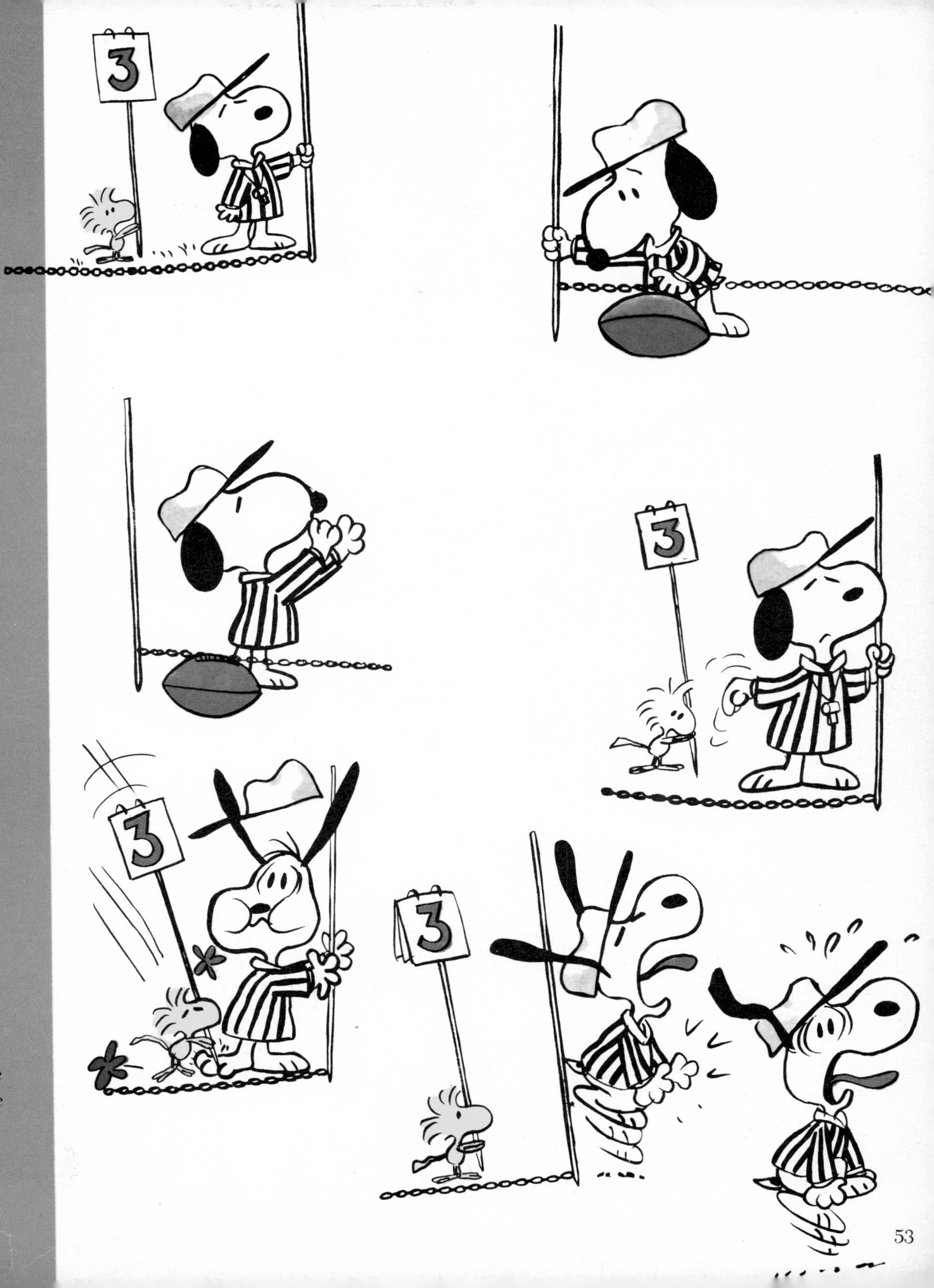
3
3
3
3

In *First Kiss*, Snoopy became a referee, but he had a little trouble with his assistant . . .

Finally, by the eighteenth TV special, Sparky and Bill Melendez decided that Snoopy had earned his own show, and they planned a half-hour special almost completely in pantomime, something that I doubt has ever been done in animation before.

Sparky had been reading an article about husky dogs at the North Pole. He wondered what might happen if an overly civilized dog like Snoopy were suddenly forced to survive in the Arctic with sled dogs.

Consequently (*see right*) one night Snoopy cooks and eats too many pizzas, which leads to some stomach aches as he goes to sleep, which leads to *What a Nightmare, Charlie Brown . . .*

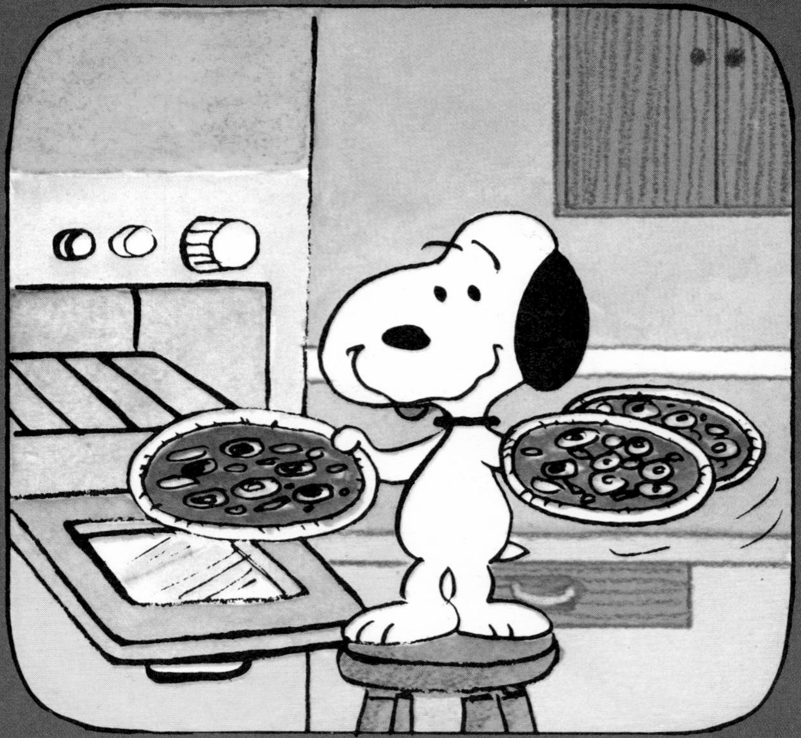

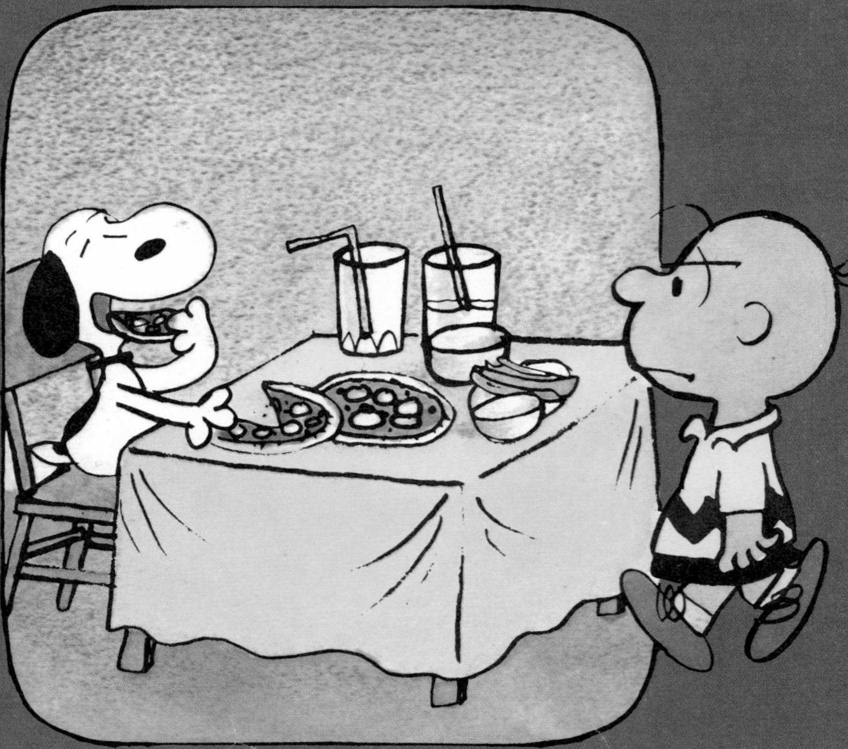

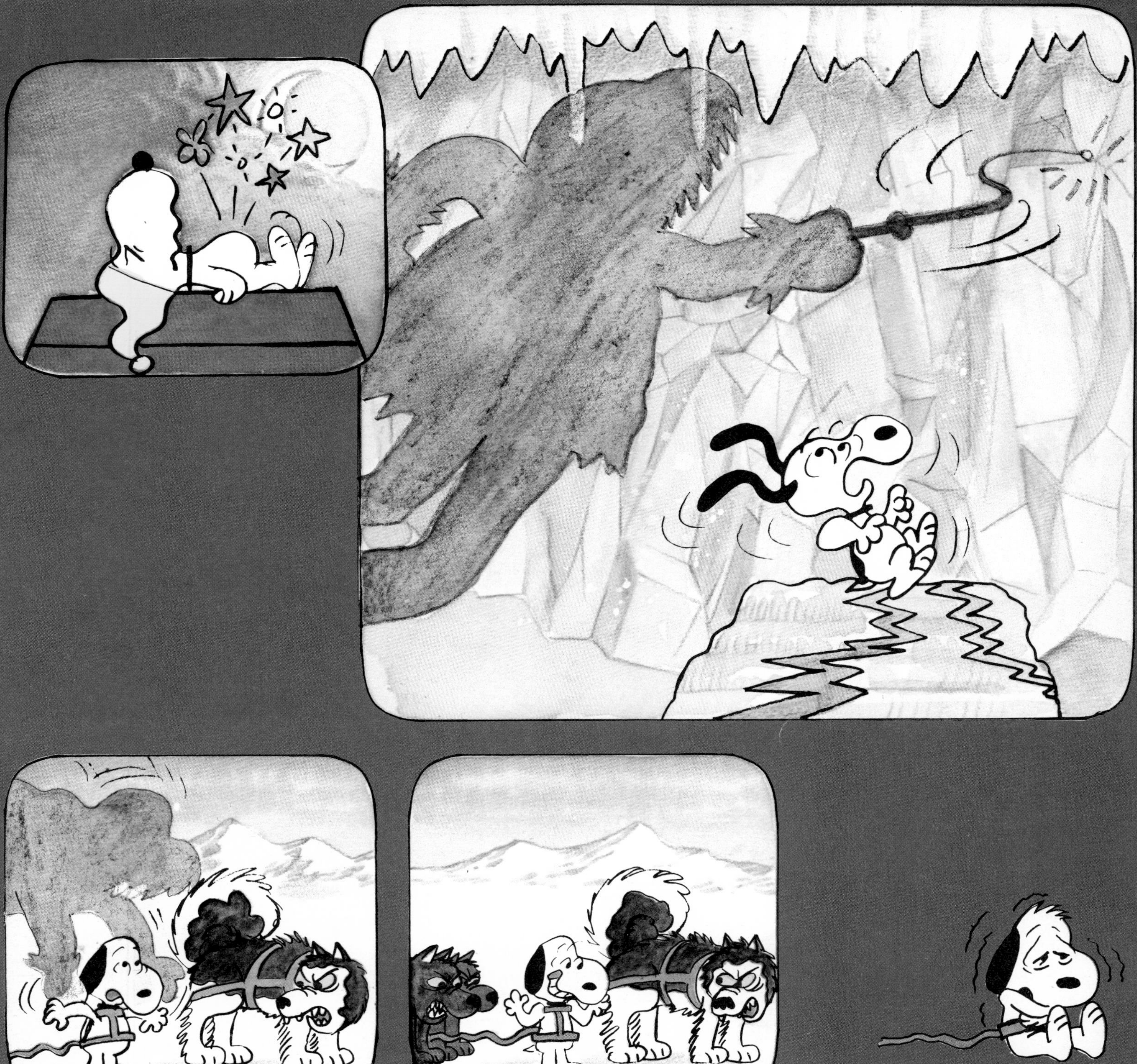

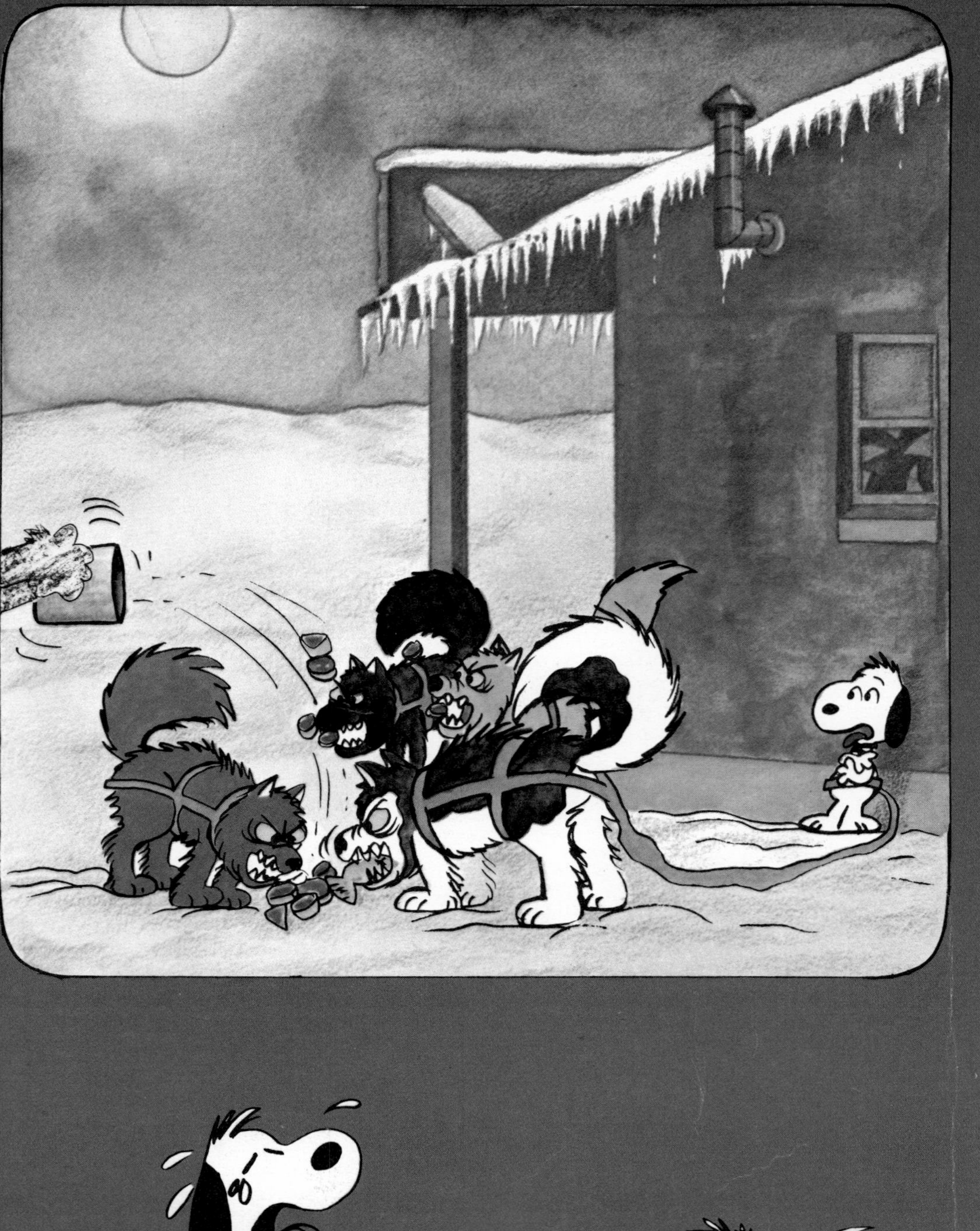

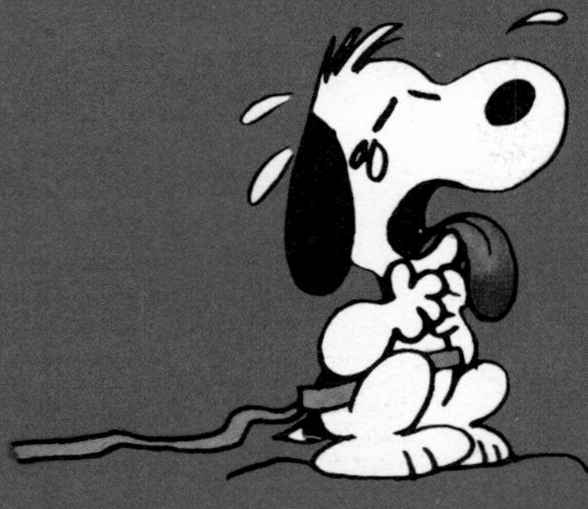

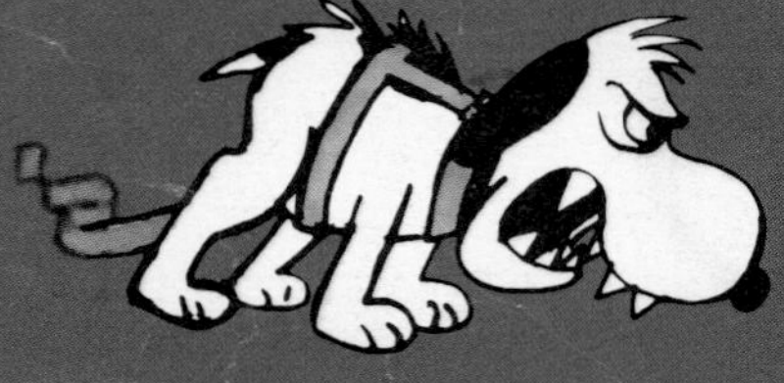

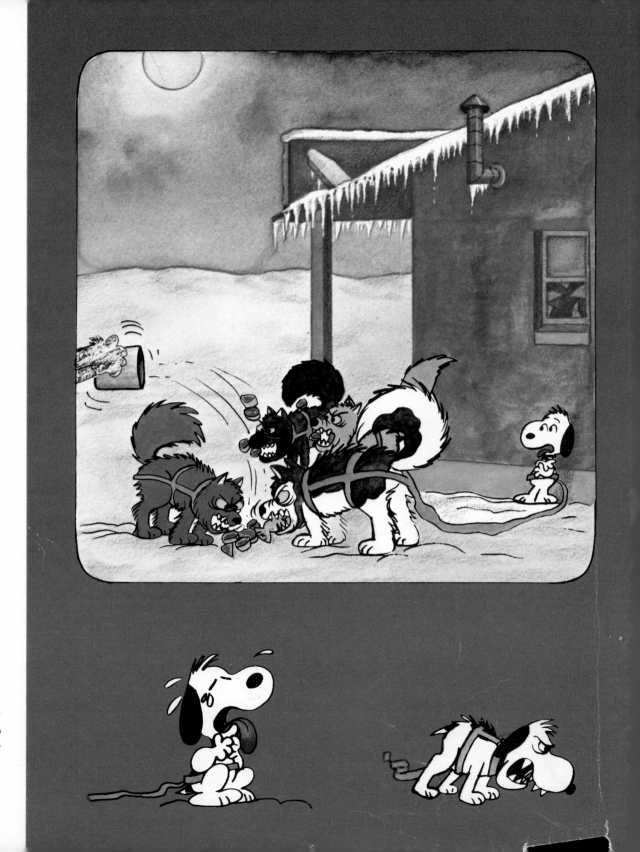

At first Snoopy is terribly mistreated by the sled dogs, who run him ragged and then deny him any food.

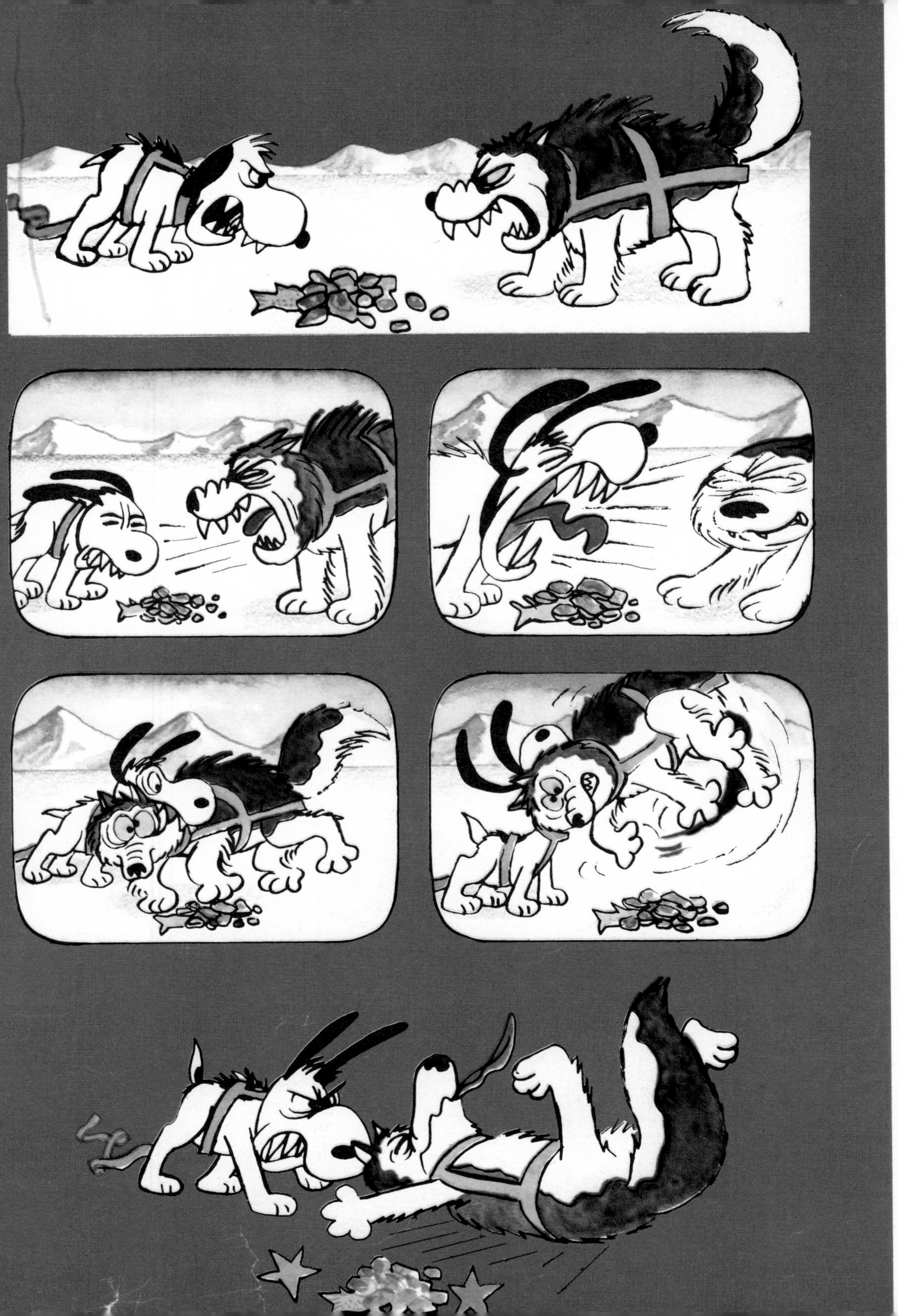

Snoopy finally decides to turn into a "real" dog and he challenges the lead dog to a fight.

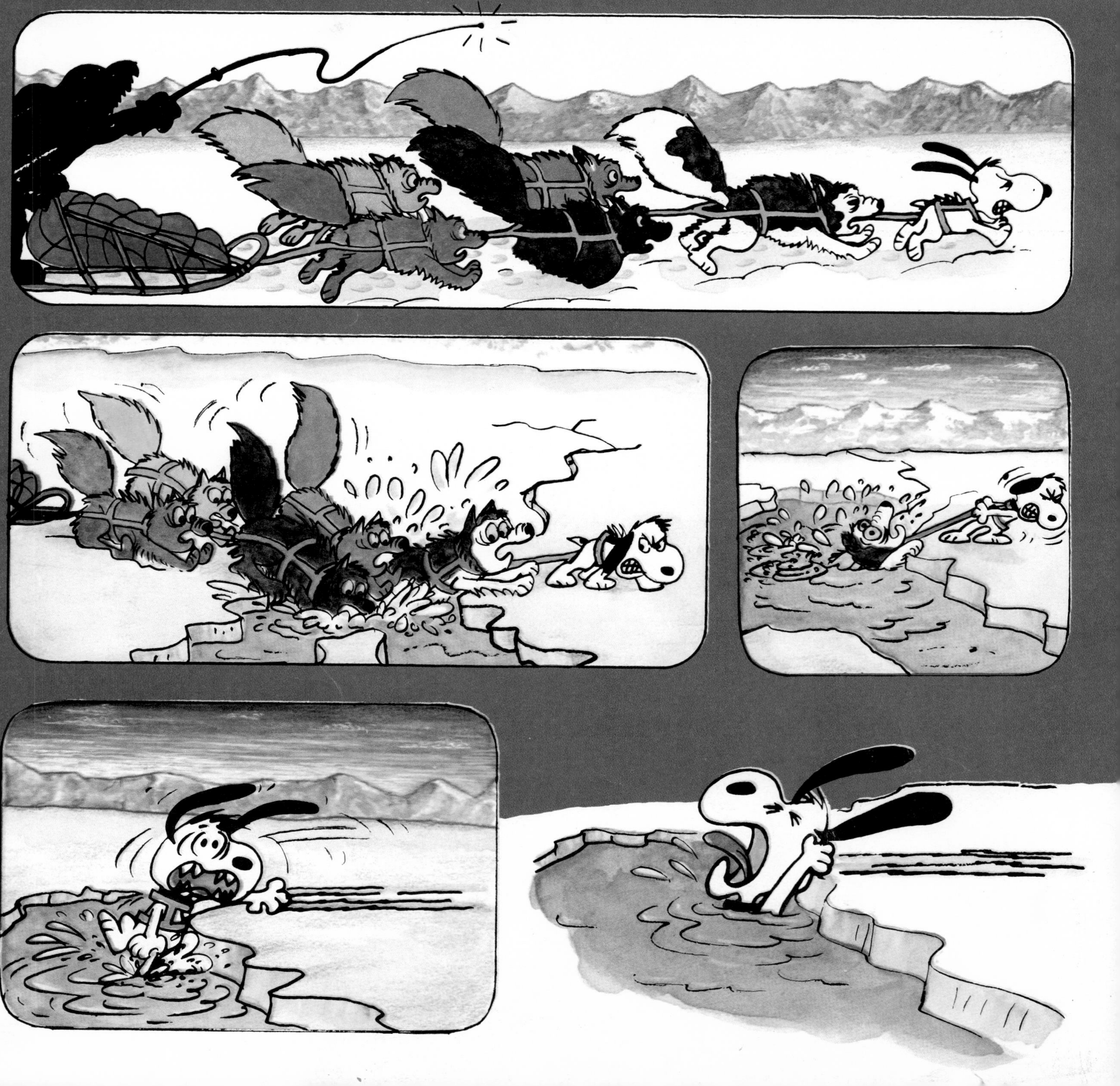

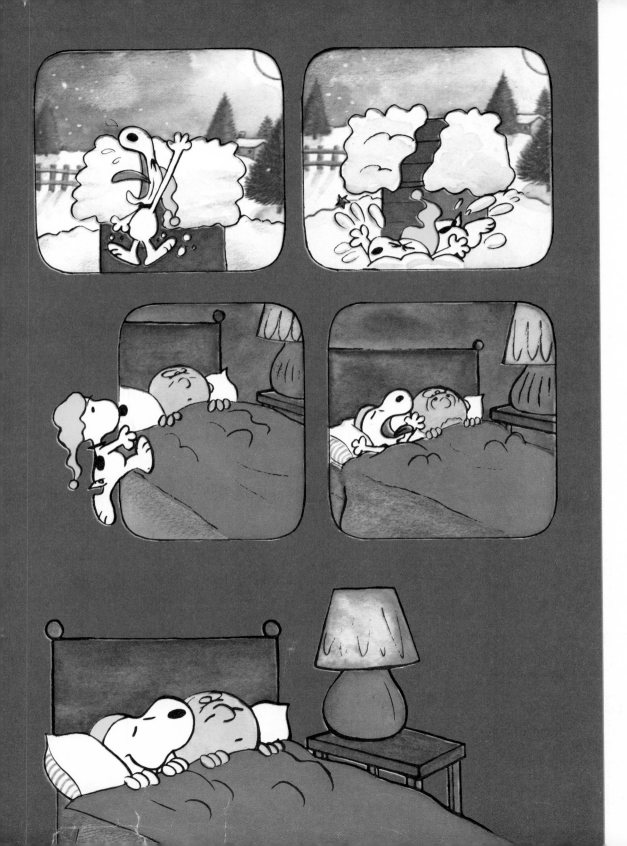

Snoopy then becomes the lead dog and gets himself into even worse difficulty.

When he finally awakes from his nightmare, Snoopy rushes to the bed of his master for a much more comfortable sleep.

59

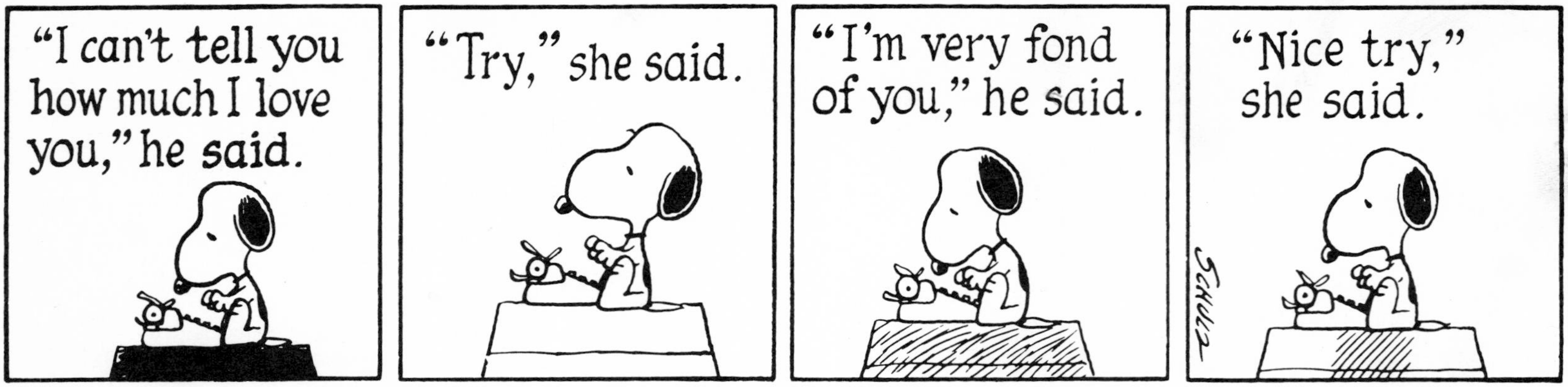
"I can't tell you how much I love you," he said.
"Try," she said.
"I'm very fond of you," he said.
"Nice try," she said.
SCHULZ

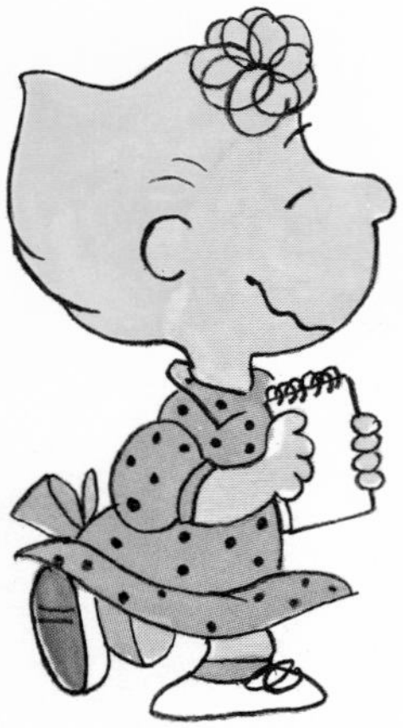

We asked Sparky to select some of his favorite Snoopy comic strips from the past two years, and these appear on the next nine pages. I once asked him if Charlie Brown was the way he (and we) often acted and felt much of the time and if Snoopy was the way he (and we) would like to *be* much of the time. He replied, "I guess I'm kind of a humble egotist, so I must be a little of both of them."

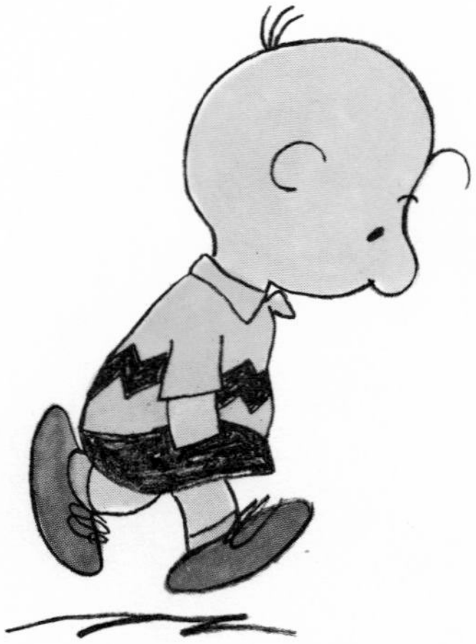

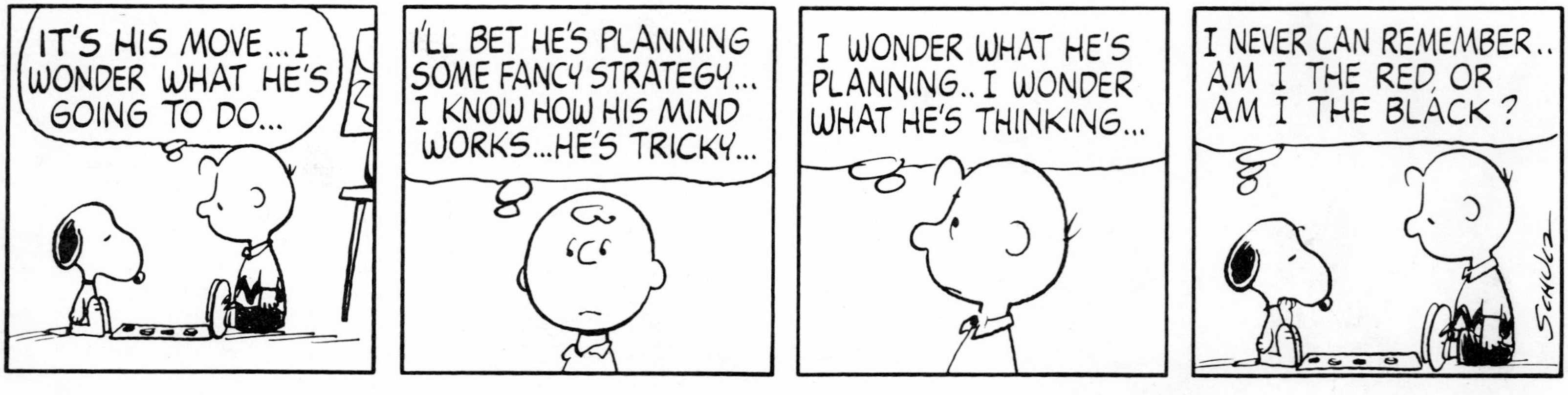
IT'S HIS MOVE...I WONDER WHAT HE'S GOING TO DO...
I'LL BET HE'S PLANNING SOME FANCY STRATEGY... I KNOW HOW HIS MIND WORKS...HE'S TRICKY...
I WONDER WHAT HE'S PLANNING.. I WONDER WHAT HE'S THINKING...
I NEVER CAN REMEMBER.. AM I THE RED, OR AM I THE BLACK?
SCHULZ

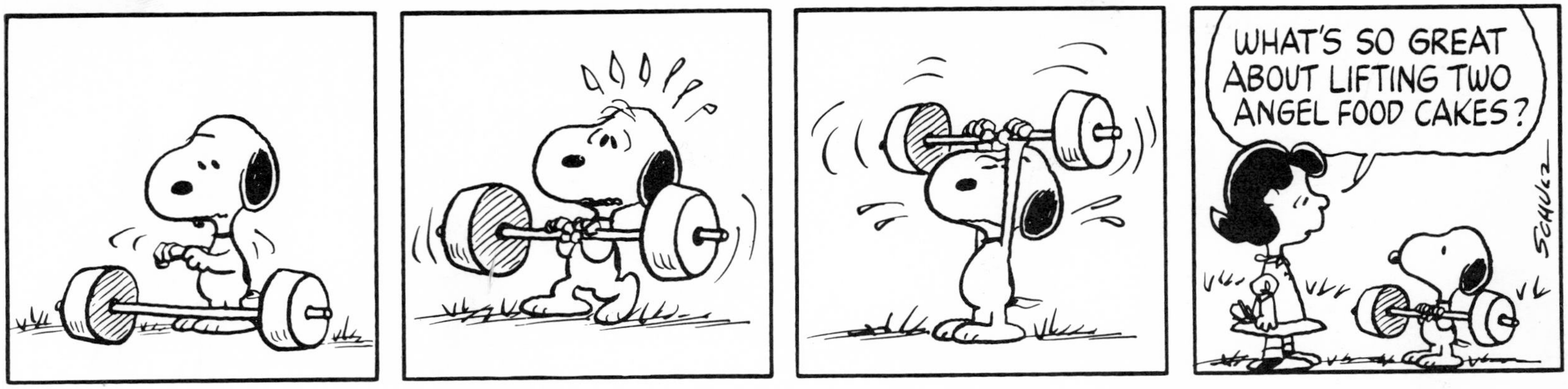
WHAT'S SO GREAT ABOUT LIFTING TWO ANGEL FOOD CAKES?
SCHULZ

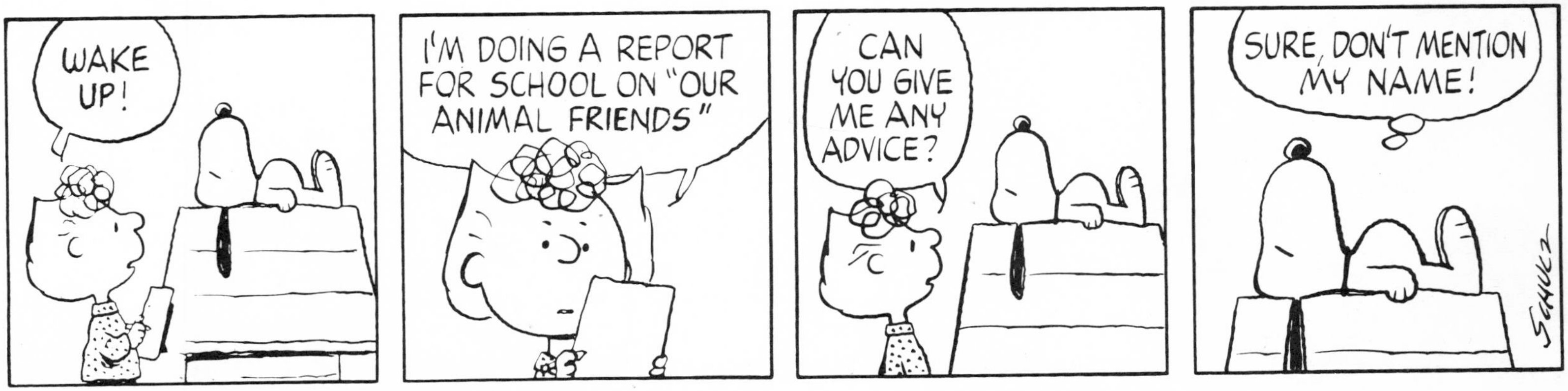
WAKE UP!
I'M DOING A REPORT FOR SCHOOL ON "OUR ANIMAL FRIENDS"
CAN YOU GIVE ME ANY ADVICE?
SURE, DON'T MENTION MY NAME!
SCHULZ

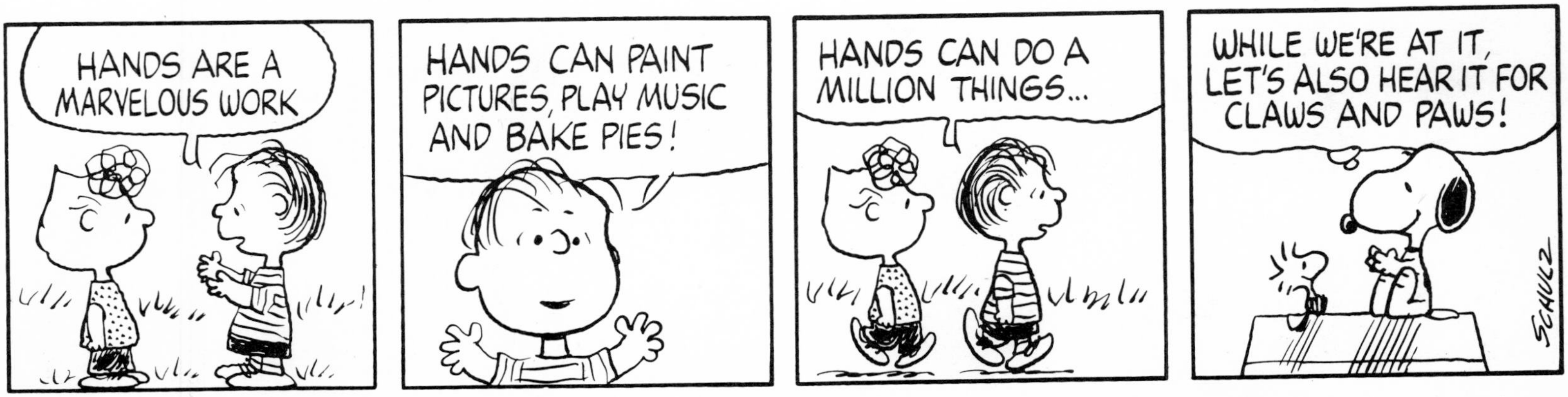
HANDS ARE A MARVELOUS WORK
HANDS CAN PAINT PICTURES, PLAY MUSIC AND BAKE PIES!
HANDS CAN DO A MILLION THINGS...
WHILE WE'RE AT IT, LET'S ALSO HEAR IT FOR CLAWS AND PAWS!
SCHULZ

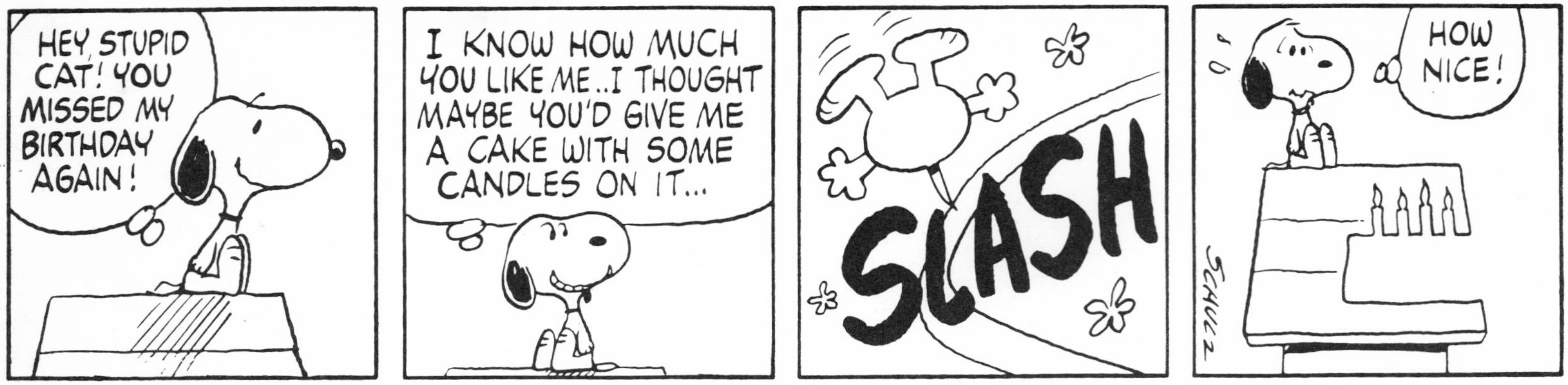
HEY, STUPID CAT! YOU MISSED MY BIRTHDAY AGAIN!
I KNOW HOW MUCH YOU LIKE ME..I THOUGHT MAYBE YOU'D GIVE ME A CAKE WITH SOME CANDLES ON IT...
SLASH
HOW NICE!
SCHULZ

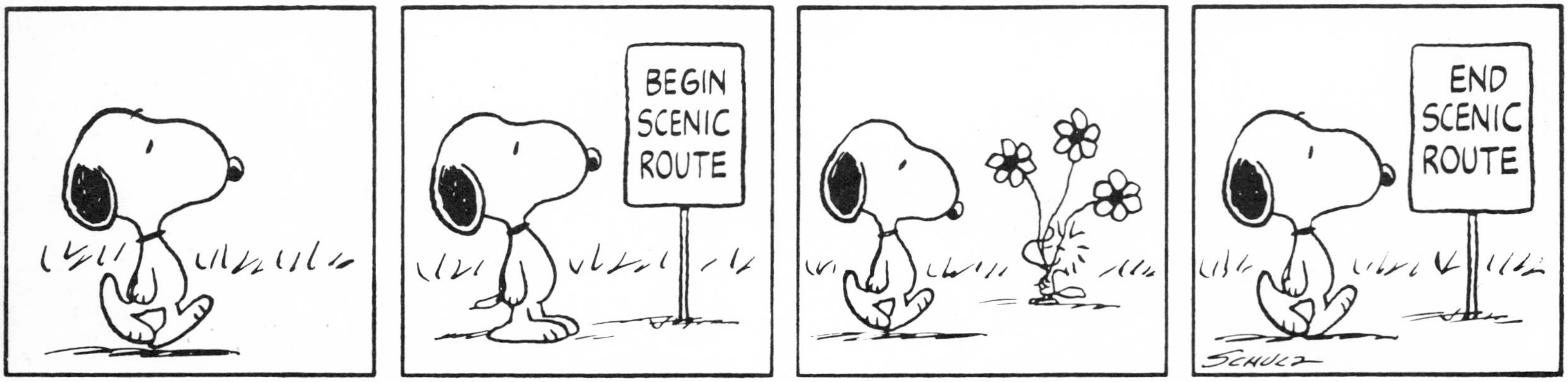
BEGIN SCENIC ROUTE
END SCENIC ROUTE
SCHULZ

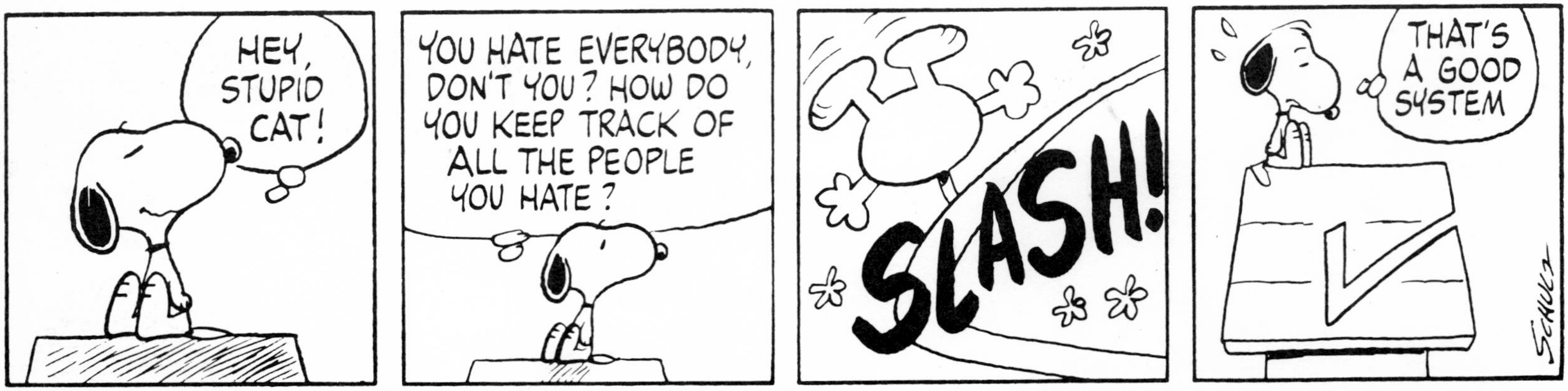
HEY, STUPID CAT!
YOU HATE EVERYBODY, DON'T YOU? HOW DO YOU KEEP TRACK OF ALL THE PEOPLE YOU HATE?
SLASH!
THAT'S A GOOD SYSTEM
SCHULZ

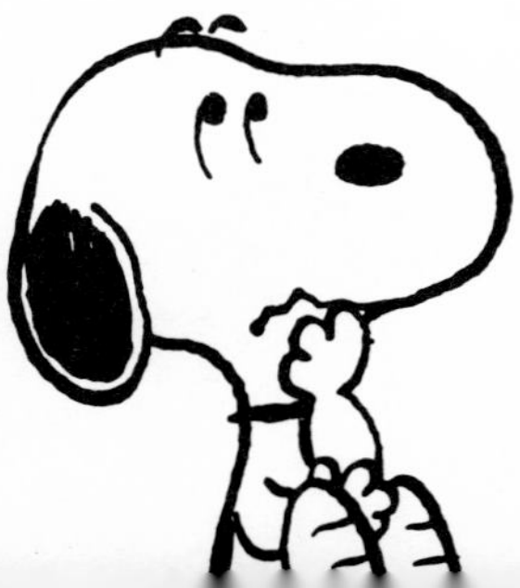

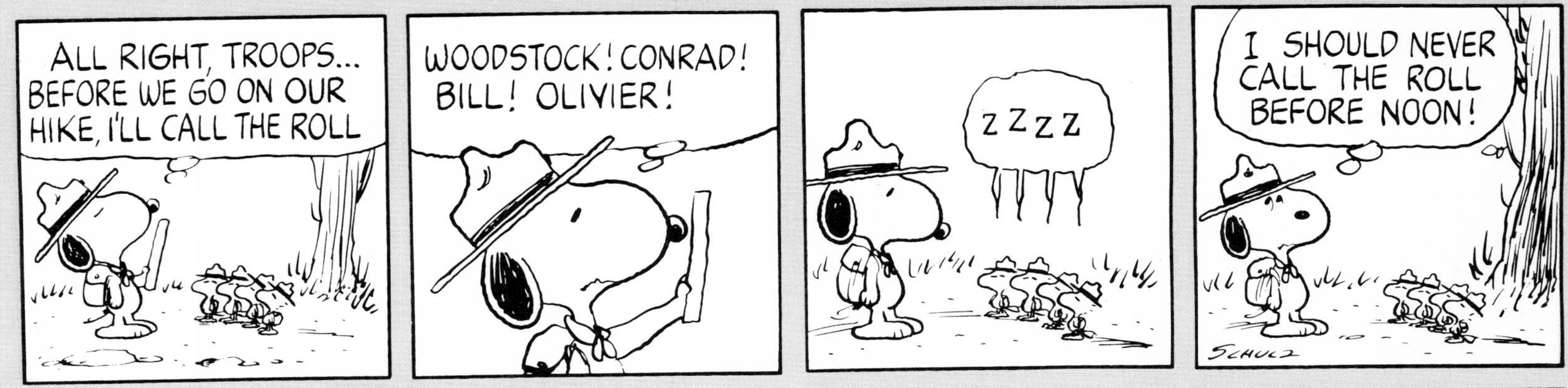
ALL RIGHT, TROOPS... BEFORE WE GO ON OUR HIKE, I'LL CALL THE ROLL
WOODSTOCK! CONRAD! BILL! OLIVIER!
Z Z Z Z
I SHOULD NEVER CALL THE ROLL BEFORE NOON!

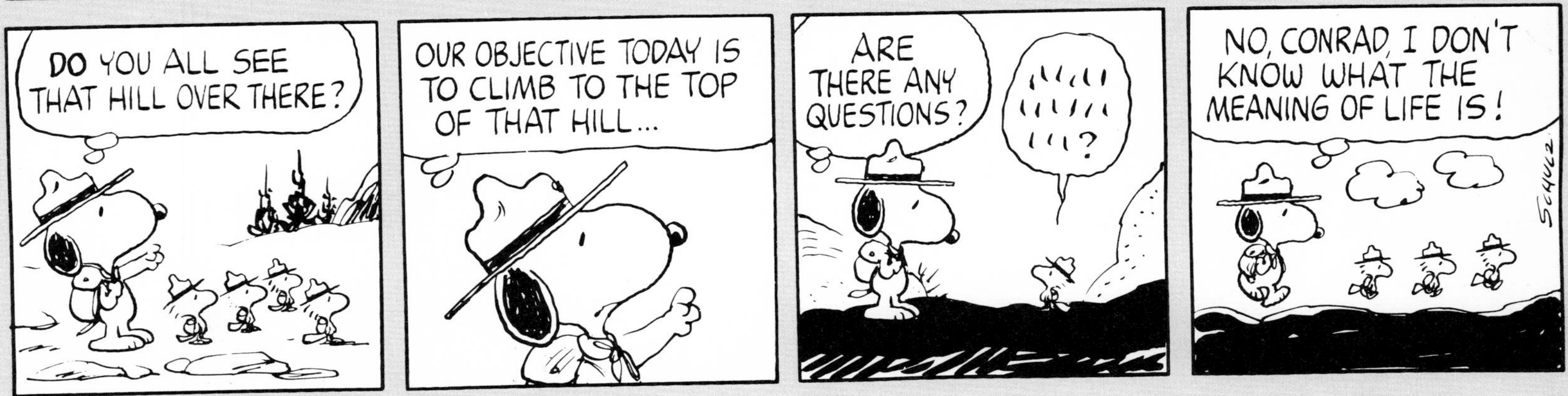
DO YOU ALL SEE THAT HILL OVER THERE?
OUR OBJECTIVE TODAY IS TO CLIMB TO THE TOP OF THAT HILL...
ARE THERE ANY QUESTIONS?
NO, CONRAD, I DON'T KNOW WHAT THE MEANING OF LIFE IS!

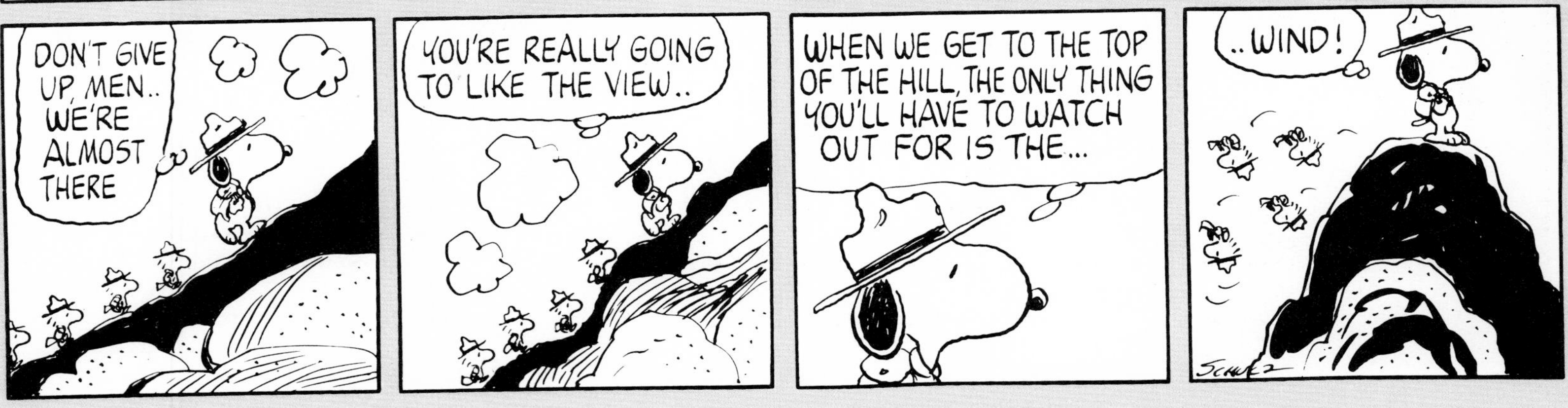
DON'T GIVE UP, MEN.. WE'RE ALMOST THERE
YOU'RE REALLY GOING TO LIKE THE VIEW..
WHEN WE GET TO THE TOP OF THE HILL, THE ONLY THING YOU'LL HAVE TO WATCH OUT FOR IS THE...
..WIND!

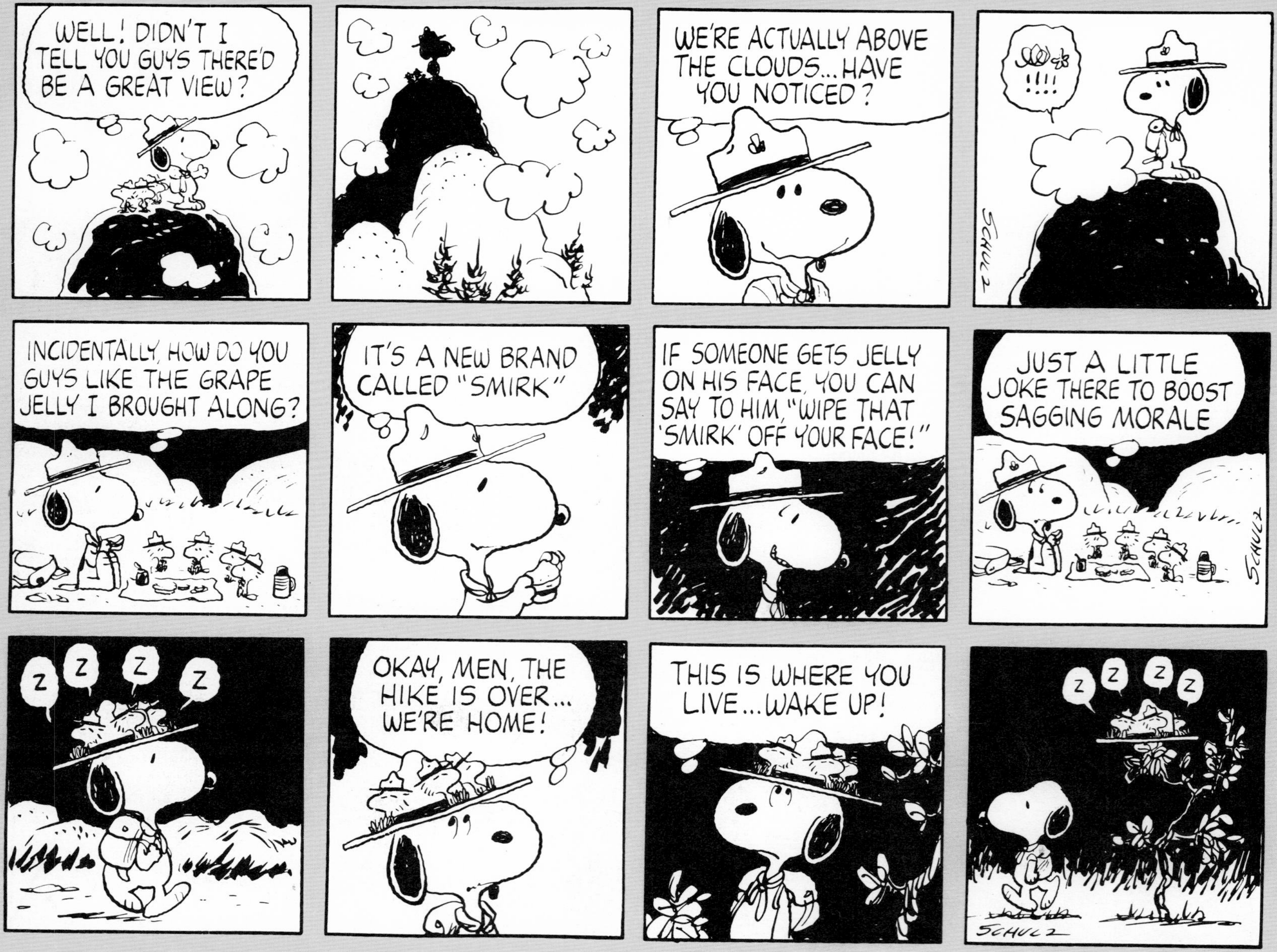
WELL! DIDN'T I TELL YOU GUYS THERE'D BE A GREAT VIEW?
WE'RE ACTUALLY ABOVE THE CLOUDS...HAVE YOU NOTICED?
!!!!
SCHULZ
INCIDENTALLY, HOW DO YOU GUYS LIKE THE GRAPE JELLY I BROUGHT ALONG?
IT'S A NEW BRAND CALLED "SMIRK"
IF SOMEONE GETS JELLY ON HIS FACE, YOU CAN SAY TO HIM, "WIPE THAT 'SMIRK' OFF YOUR FACE!"
JUST A LITTLE JOKE THERE TO BOOST SAGGING MORALE
SCHULZ
Z Z Z Z
OKAY, MEN, THE HIKE IS OVER... WE'RE HOME!
THIS IS WHERE YOU LIVE...WAKE UP!
Z Z Z Z
SCHULZ

We asked Sparky about Snoopy's next-door cat that we never see. "Years ago I drew a cat in the strip, but there were two things wrong with that. First, this cat started to make Snoopy act like a real dog, and of course, he shouldn't act like a real dog. And the second thing I discovered was that I couldn't draw cats very well. So we got rid of the cat for about fifteen years. And then I got this idea to have an offstage cat, and it's really worked out well."

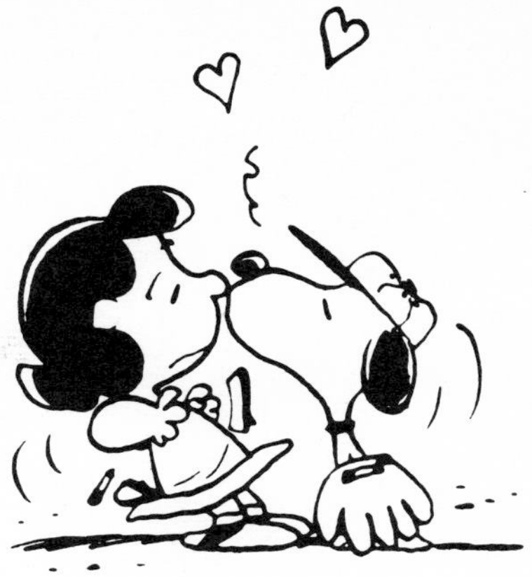

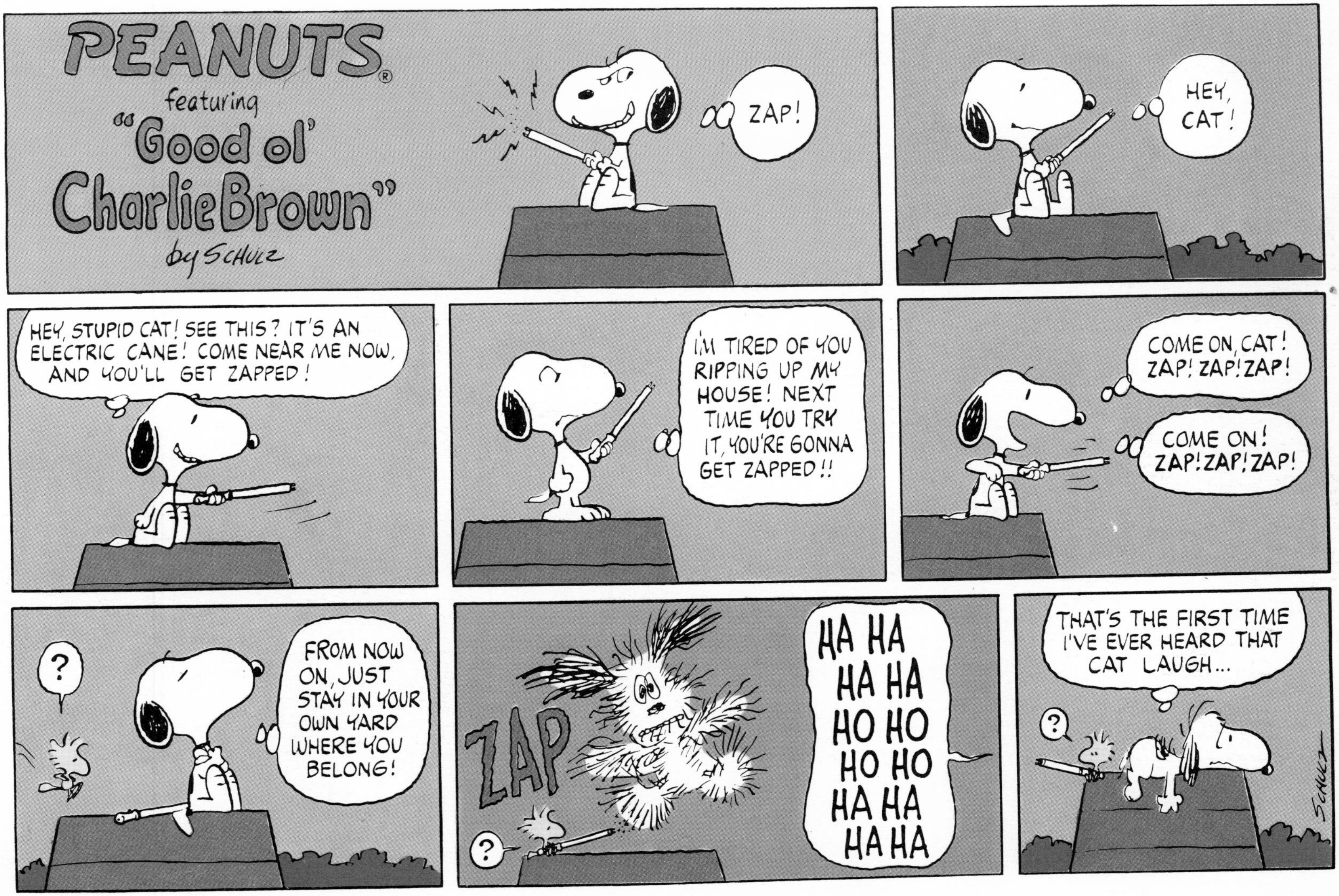
PEANUTS®
featuring
"Good ol' Charlie Brown"
by SCHULZ
ZAP!
HEY, CAT!
HEY, STUPID CAT! SEE THIS? IT'S AN ELECTRIC CANE! COME NEAR ME NOW, AND YOU'LL GET ZAPPED!
I'M TIRED OF YOU RIPPING UP MY HOUSE! NEXT TIME YOU TRY IT, YOU'RE GONNA GET ZAPPED!!
COME ON, CAT! ZAP! ZAP! ZAP!
COME ON! ZAP! ZAP! ZAP!
?
FROM NOW ON, JUST STAY IN YOUR OWN YARD WHERE YOU BELONG!
ZAP
?
HA HA HA HA HO HO HO HO HA HA HA HA
THAT'S THE FIRST TIME I'VE EVER HEARD THAT CAT LAUGH...
?
SCHULZ

MEMORIES... ⅟♪ SIGH ♪⅟

MEMORIES WILL DRIVE YOU CRAZY

I WONDER WHATEVER HAPPENED TO MY DAD

"HEY, PUPS, YOU WANNA GO FOR A LITTLE RUN?" HE USED TO ASK...

WE'D GO SCAMPERING OFF LIKE A BUNCH OF BOOBIES FALLING ALL OVER OURSELVES

IN THE EVENING DAD WOULD INVITE A FEW RABBITS OVER...DAD NEVER CHASED RABBITS...

INSTEAD, HE'D INVITE THEM OVER TO PLAY CARDS

THOSE WERE GOOD DAYS...

I REMEMBER THE TIME A PREACHER CAME AROUND TELLING ABOUT HOW THE WOLF AND THE LAMB WILL LIE DOWN TOGETHER...

"AND THE LEOPARD AND GOATS WILL BE AT PEACE...COWS WILL GRAZE AMONG BEARS..."

MY DAD STOOD UP AND SHOUTED,"HOW ABOUT THE BEAGLES AND THE BUNNIES?"

IT BROKE UP THE MEETING

YES, THOSE WERE GOOD DAYS...

ANYWAY, HAPPY FATHER'S DAY, DAD, WHEREVER YOU ARE... AND SAY HELLO TO ALL THE RABBITS!

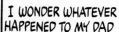

PEANUTS featuring "Good ol' Charlie Brown" by SCHULZ

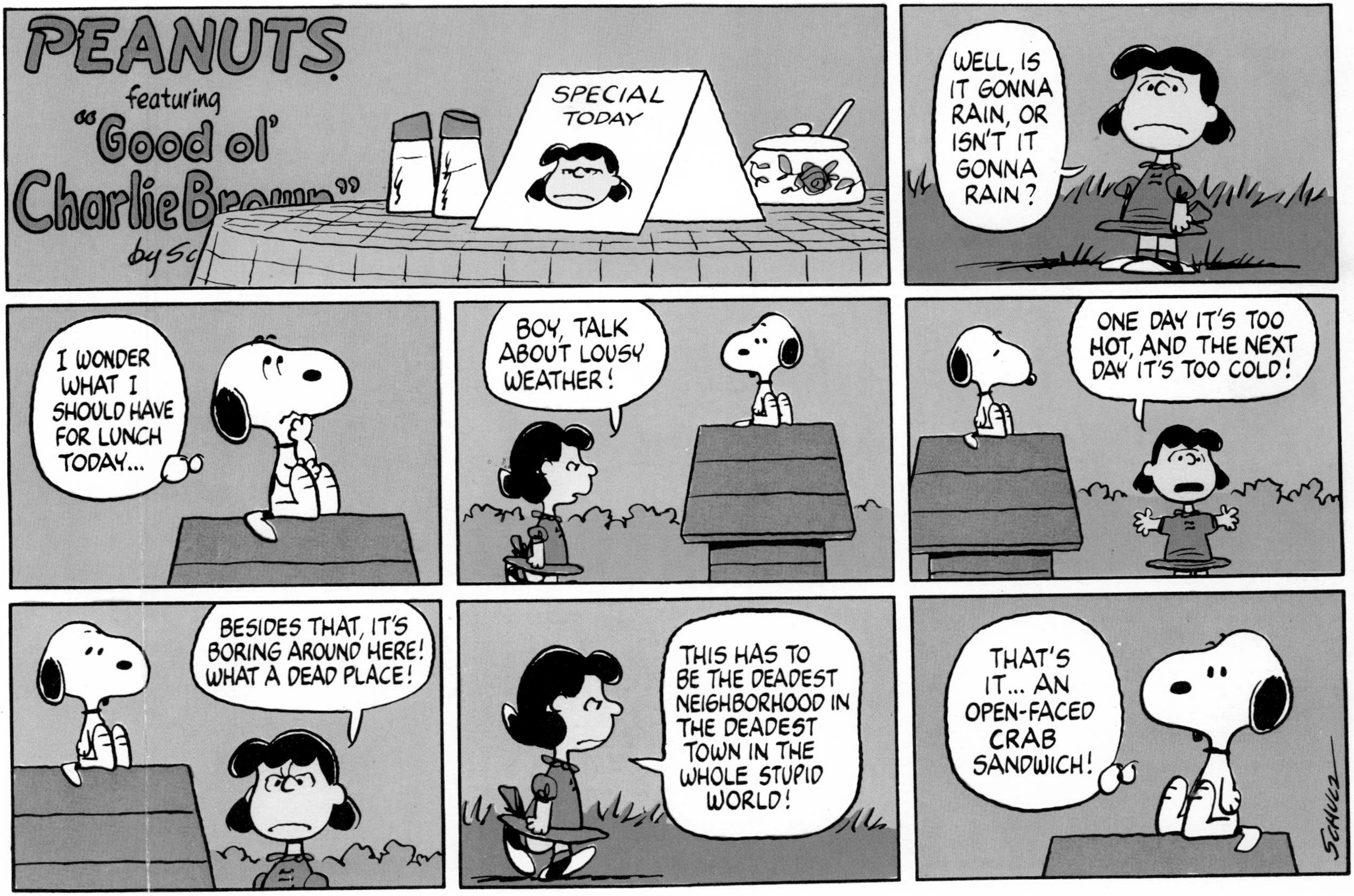
PEANUTS
featuring
“Good ol’
CharlieB
by Sc
SPECIAL TODAY
WELL, IS IT GONNA RAIN, OR ISN'T IT GONNA RAIN?
I WONDER WHAT I SHOULD HAVE FOR LUNCH TODAY...
BOY, TALK ABOUT LOUSY WEATHER!
ONE DAY IT'S TOO HOT, AND THE NEXT DAY IT'S TOO COLD!
BESIDES THAT, IT'S BORING AROUND HERE! WHAT A DEAD PLACE!
THIS HAS TO BE THE DEADEST NEIGHBORHOOD IN THE DEADEST TOWN IN THE WHOLE STUPID WORLD!
THAT'S IT... AN OPEN-FACED CRAB SANDWICH!
SCHULZ

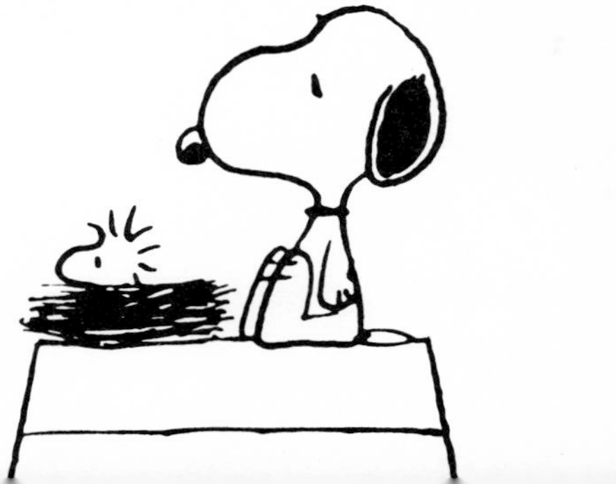

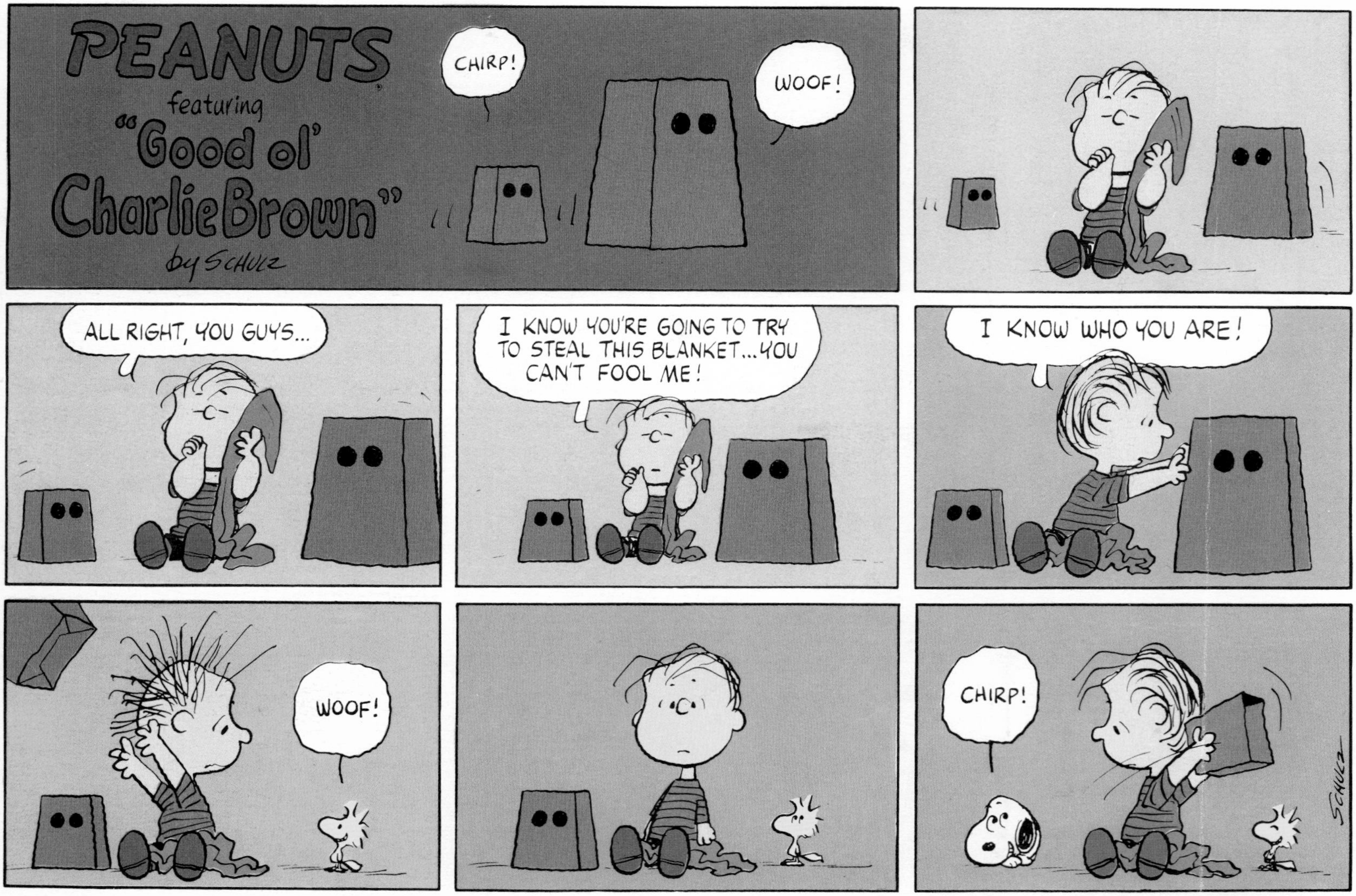
PEANUTS
featuring
"Good ol' Charlie Brown"
by SCHULZ
CHIRP!
WOOF!
ALL RIGHT, YOU GUYS...
I KNOW YOU'RE GOING TO TRY TO STEAL THIS BLANKET...YOU CAN'T FOOL ME!
I KNOW WHO YOU ARE!
WOOF!
CHIRP!
SCHULZ

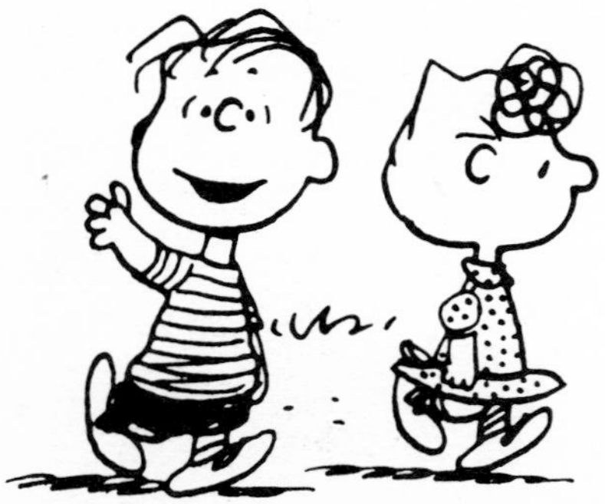

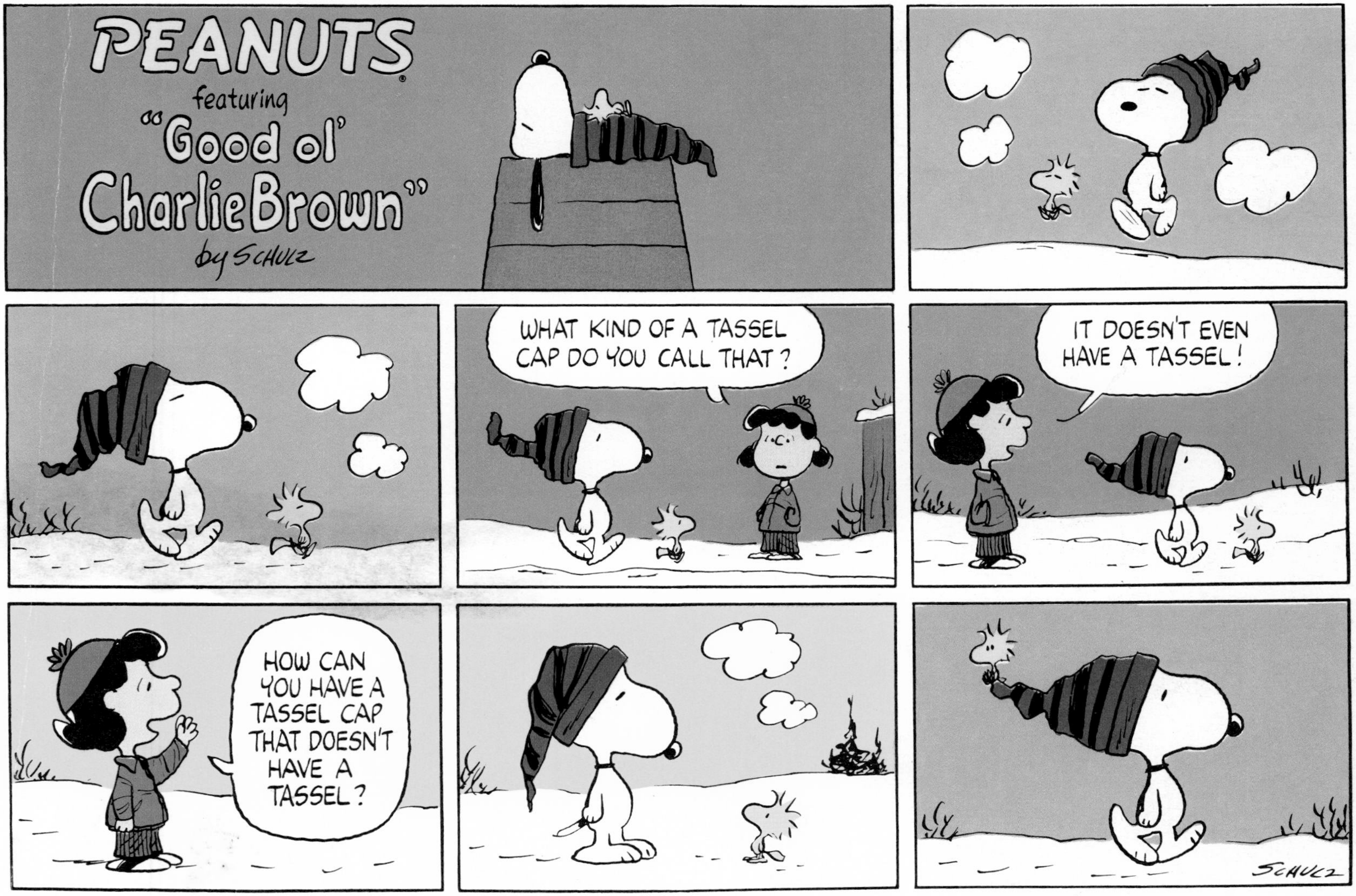
PEANUTS
featuring
"Good ol' CharlieBrown"
by SCHULZ
WHAT KIND OF A TASSEL CAP DO YOU CALL THAT ?
IT DOESN'T EVEN HAVE A TASSEL !
HOW CAN YOU HAVE A TASSEL CAP THAT DOESN'T HAVE A TASSEL ?
SCHULZ

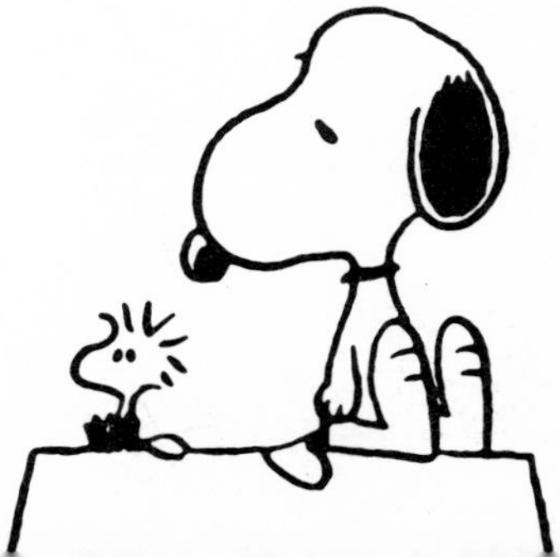

I think the best series of comic strips that Sparky ever drew were those inspired by the great Hank Aaron. When Aaron was approaching Babe Ruth's home-run record, 99.99 percent of Americans cheered him on. But there were many bigots who were writing hate mail to Aaron because they were angry that a black man was challenging the Babe's fantastic record. Sparky read about this, and the following strips soon started to appear in 1,700 newspapers across the country:

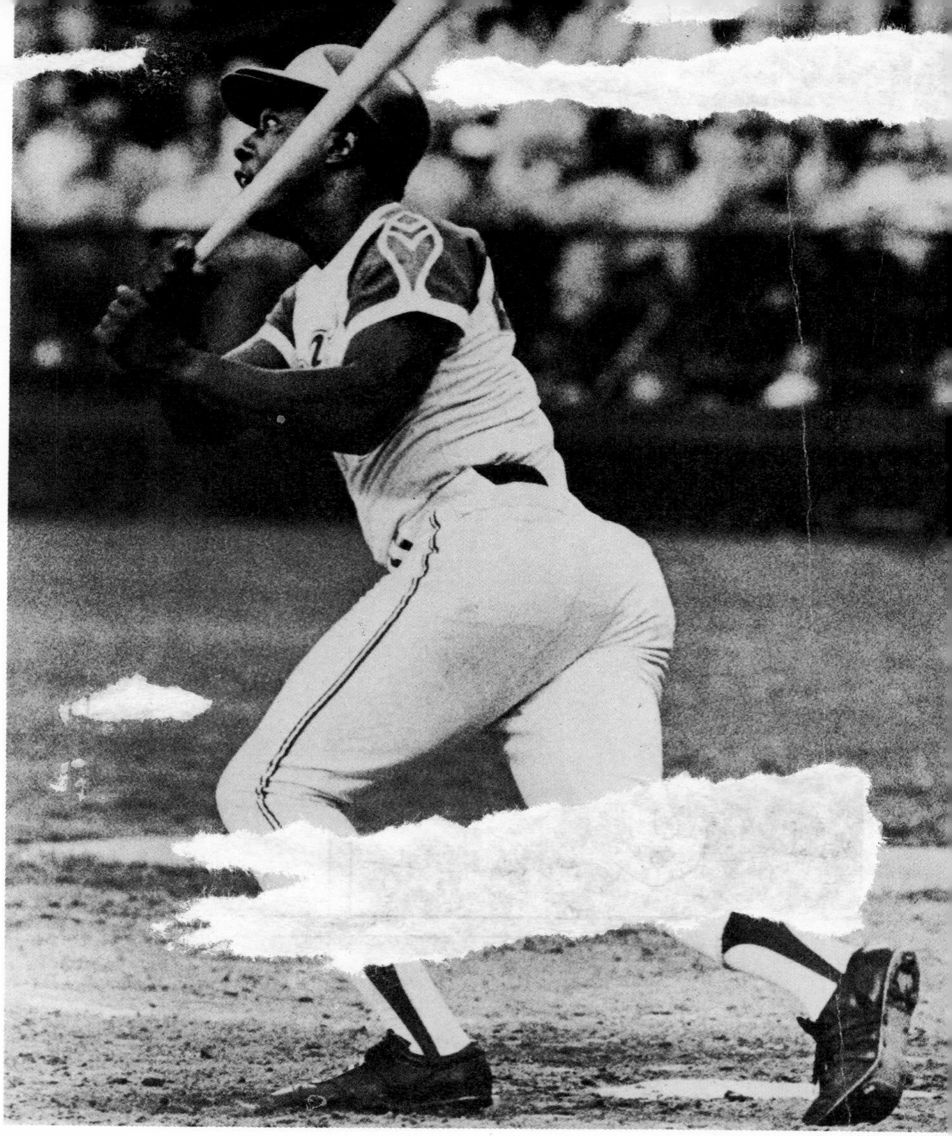

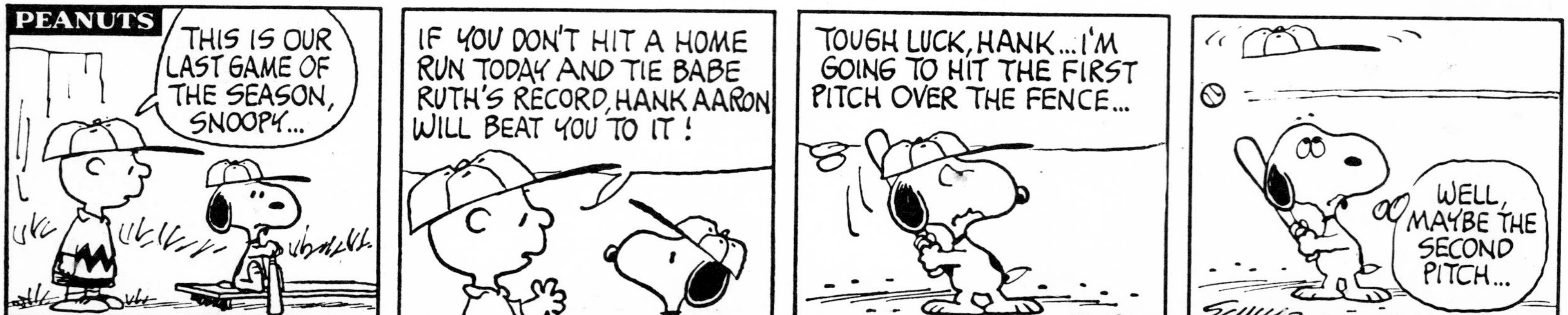

PEANUTS
THIS IS OUR LAST GAME OF THE SEASON, SNOOPY...
IF YOU DON'T HIT A HOME RUN TODAY AND TIE BABE RUTH'S RECORD, HANK AARON WILL BEAT YOU TO IT!
TOUGH LUCK, HANK...I'M GOING TO HIT THE FIRST PITCH OVER THE FENCE...
WELL, MAYBE THE SECOND PITCH...
SCHULZ

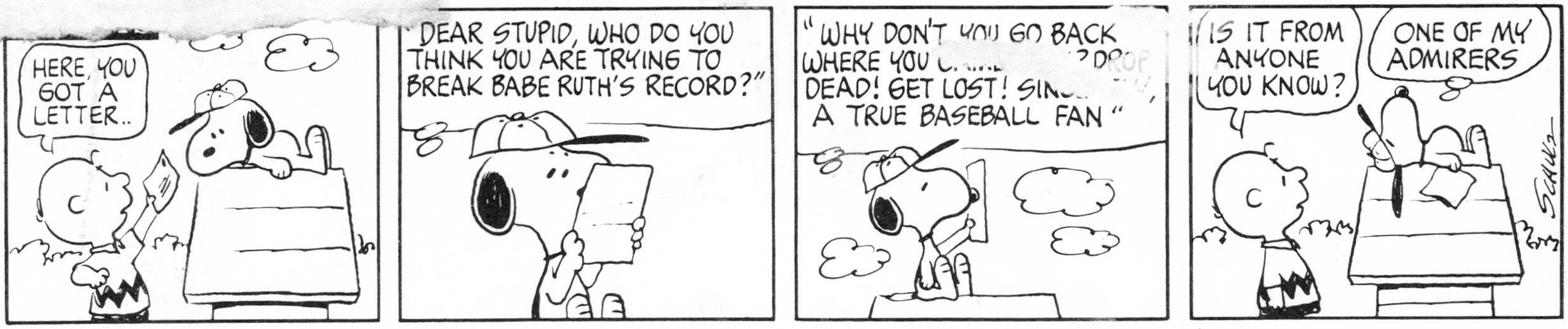
PEANUTS
HERE, YOU GOT A LETTER..
"DEAR STUPID, WHO DO YOU THINK YOU ARE TRYING TO BREAK BABE RUTH'S RECORD?"
"WHY DON'T YOU GO BACK WHERE YOU ... DROP DEAD! GET LOST! SIN... A TRUE BASEBALL FAN"
IS IT FROM ANYONE YOU KNOW?
ONE OF MY ADMIRERS
SCHULZ

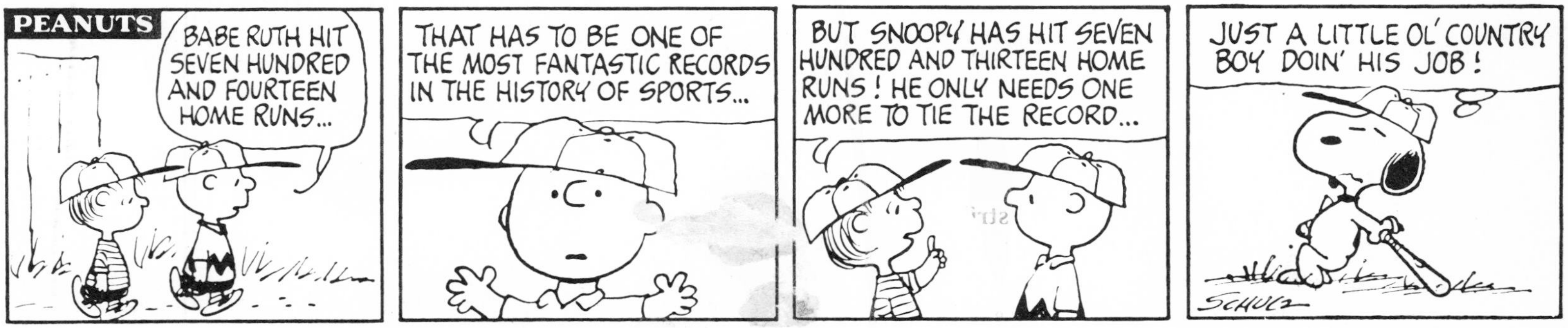
PEANUTS
BABE RUTH HIT SEVEN HUNDRED AND FOURTEEN HOME RUNS...
THAT HAS TO BE ONE OF THE MOST FANTASTIC RECORDS IN THE HISTORY OF SPORTS...
BUT SNOOPY HAS HIT SEVEN HUNDRED AND THIRTEEN HOME RUNS! HE ONLY NEEDS ONE MORE TO TIE THE RECORD...
JUST A LITTLE OL' COUNTRY BOY DOIN' HIS JOB!
SCHULZ

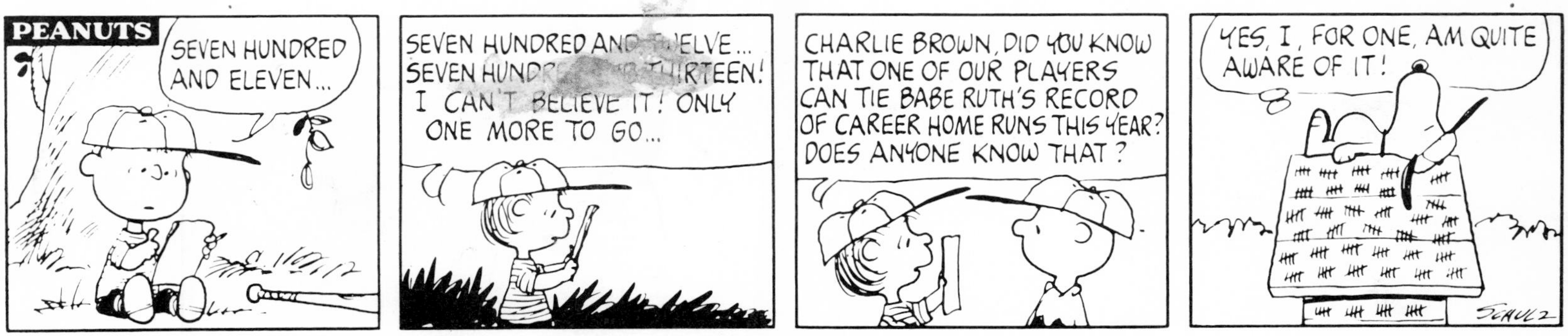
PEANUTS
SEVEN HUNDRED AND ELEVEN...
SEVEN HUNDRED AND ...ELVE... SEVEN HUNDR... THIRTEEN! I CAN'T BELIEVE IT! ONLY ONE MORE TO GO...
CHARLIE BROWN, DID YOU KNOW THAT ONE OF OUR PLAYERS CAN TIE BABE RUTH'S RECORD OF CAREER HOME RUNS THIS YEAR? DOES ANYONE KNOW THAT?
YES, I, FOR ONE, AM QUITE AWARE OF IT!
SCHULZ

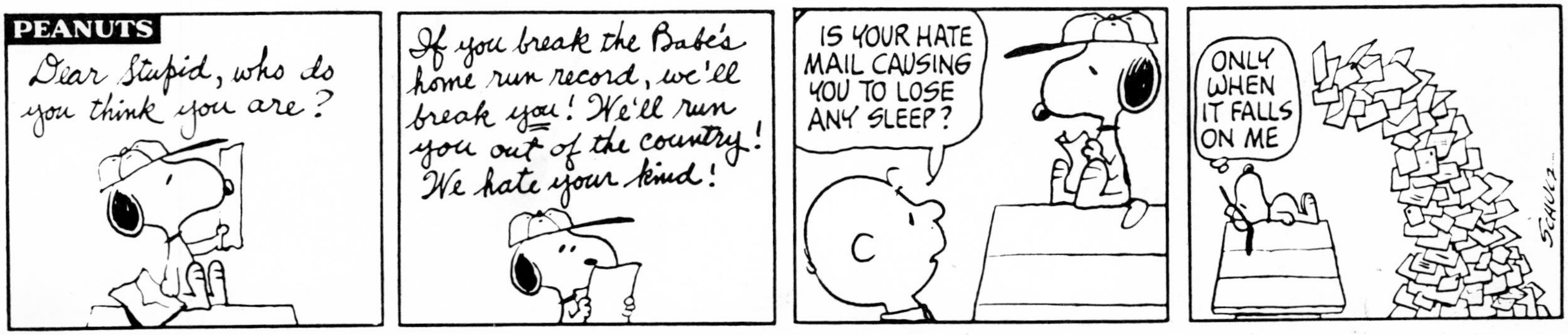
PEANUTS
Dear Stupid, who do you think you are?
If you break the Babe's home run record, we'll break you! We'll run you out of the country! We hate your kind!
IS YOUR HATE MAIL CAUSING YOU TO LOSE ANY SLEEP?
ONLY WHEN IT FALLS ON ME
SCHULZ

In the late 1960's (*right*) Snoopy was adopted as the official emblem of NASA for outstanding achievement within the organization. Of course, Snoopy had already logged many hours on the moon.

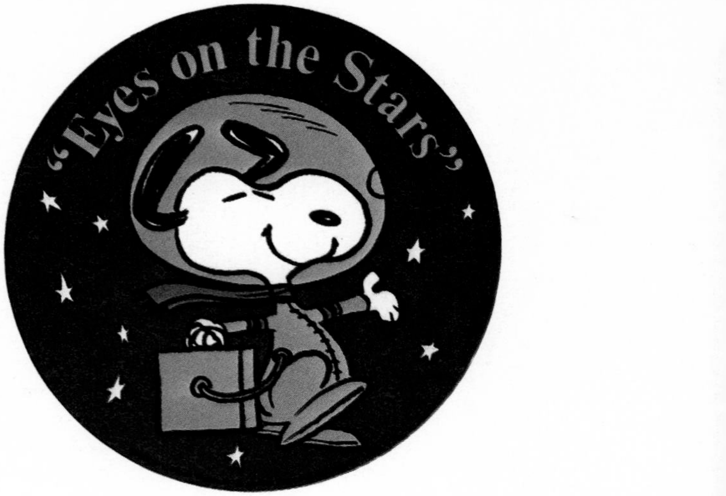
"Eyes on the Stars"

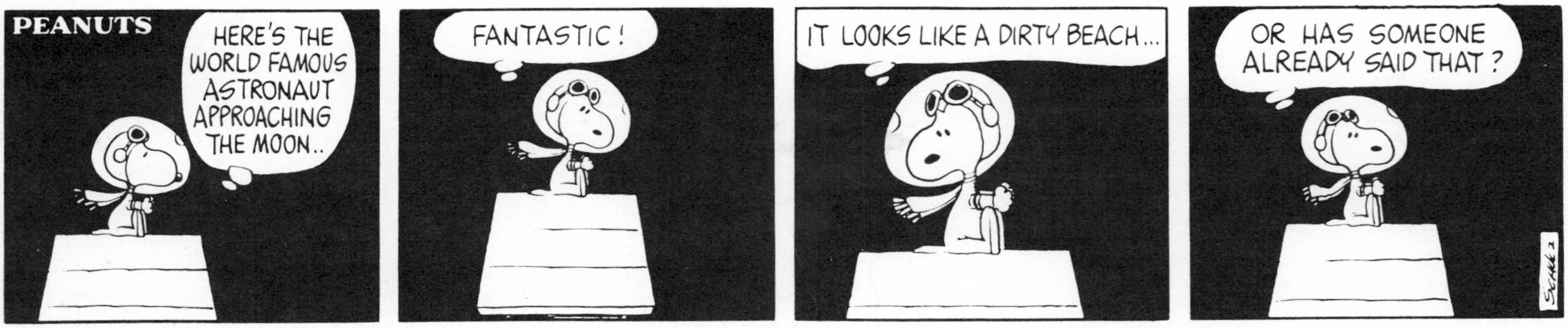
PEANUTS
HERE'S THE WORLD FAMOUS ASTRONAUT APPROACHING THE MOON..
FANTASTIC!
IT LOOKS LIKE A DIRTY BEACH...
OR HAS SOMEONE ALREADY SAID THAT?

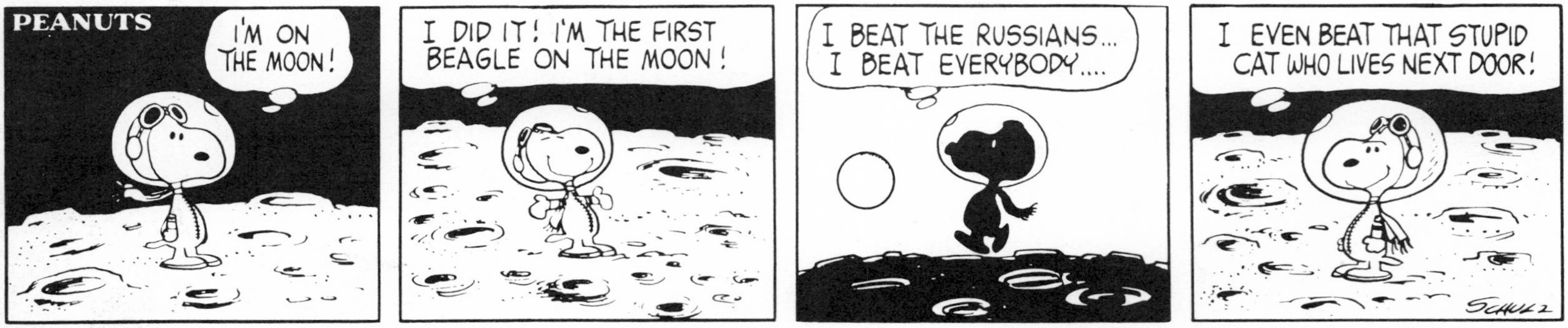
PEANUTS
I'M ON THE MOON!
I DID IT! I'M THE FIRST BEAGLE ON THE MOON!
I BEAT THE RUSSIANS... I BEAT EVERYBODY....
I EVEN BEAT THAT STUPID CAT WHO LIVES NEXT DOOR!

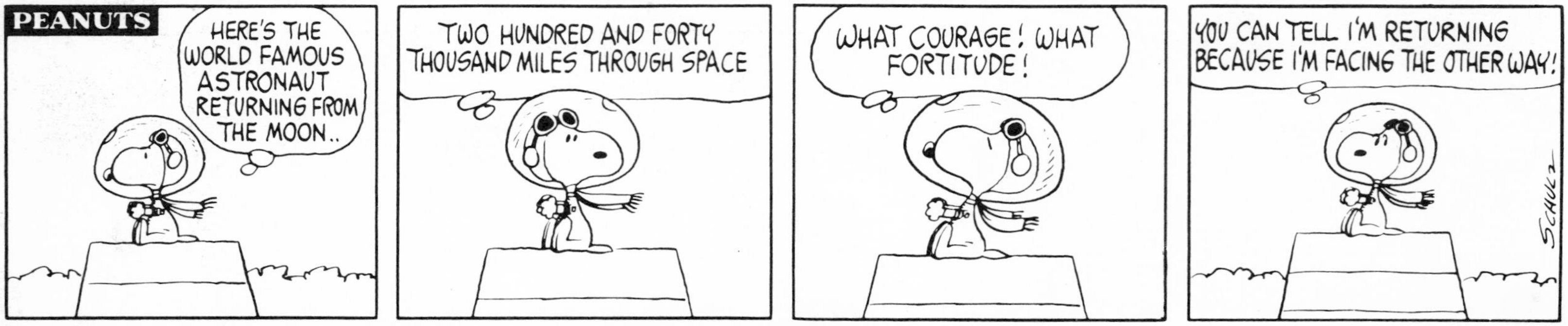
PEANUTS
HERE'S THE WORLD FAMOUS ASTRONAUT RETURNING FROM THE MOON..
TWO HUNDRED AND FORTY THOUSAND MILES THROUGH SPACE
WHAT COURAGE! WHAT FORTITUDE!
YOU CAN TELL I'M RETURNING BECAUSE I'M FACING THE OTHER WAY!

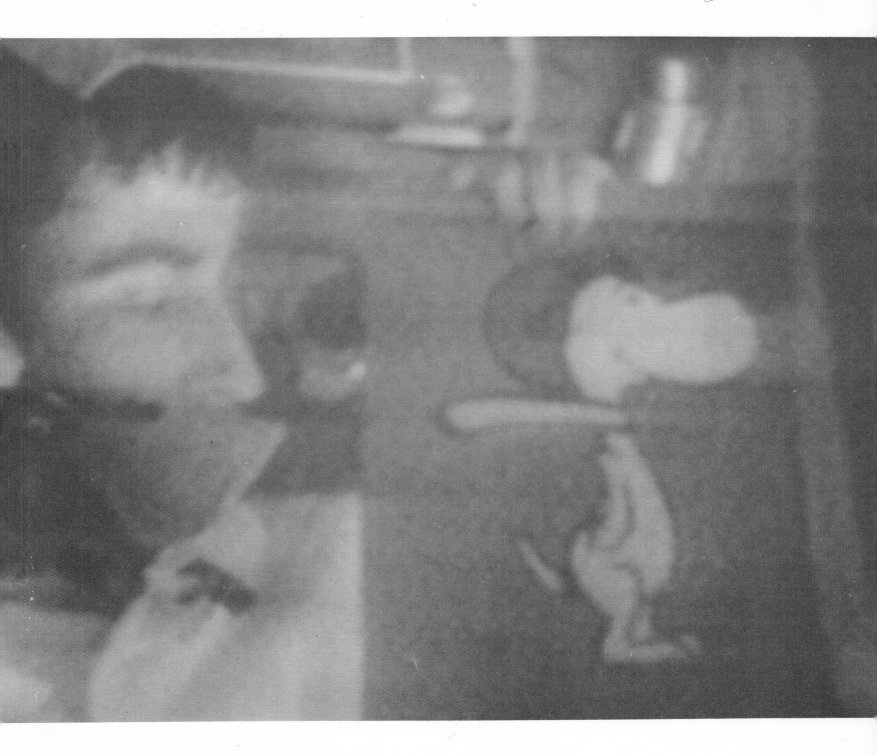

Snoopy also was honored from outer space when Apollo 10's astronaut John Young transmitted this picture back to earth from 110,000 miles away.

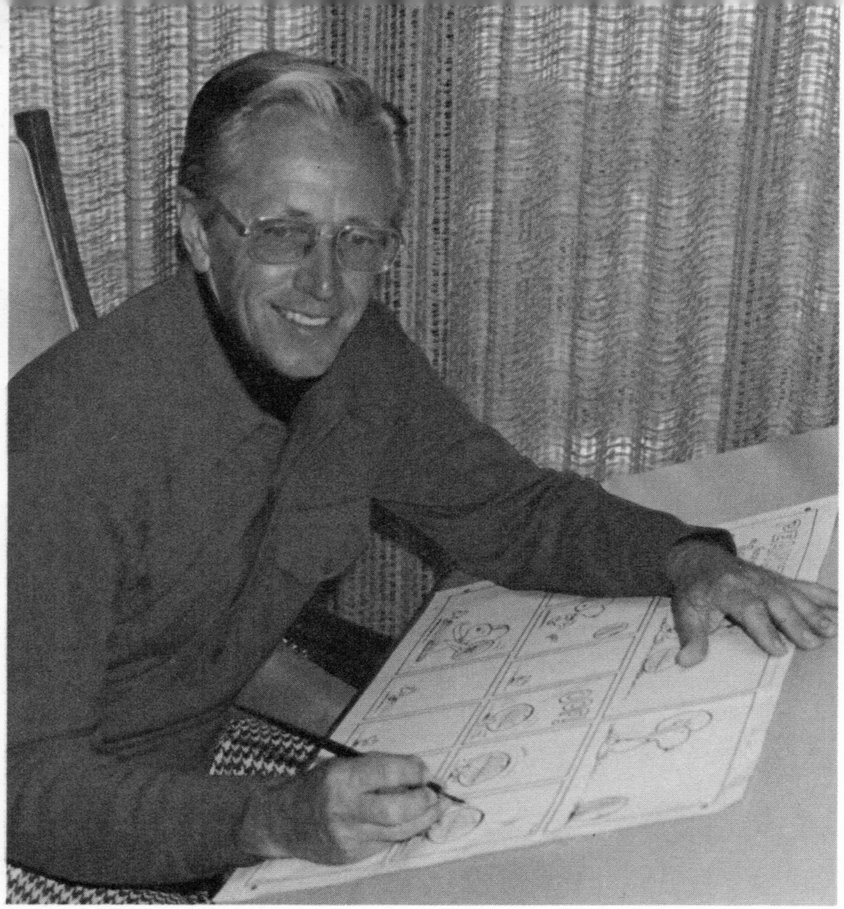

And then came the Van Pelts... Linus and Lucy

On January 6, 1952, fifteen months after Charlie Brown and Snoopy had launched *Peanuts*, Lucy made her boisterous appearance. She didn't look like the Lucy of today, but she surely did act like her.

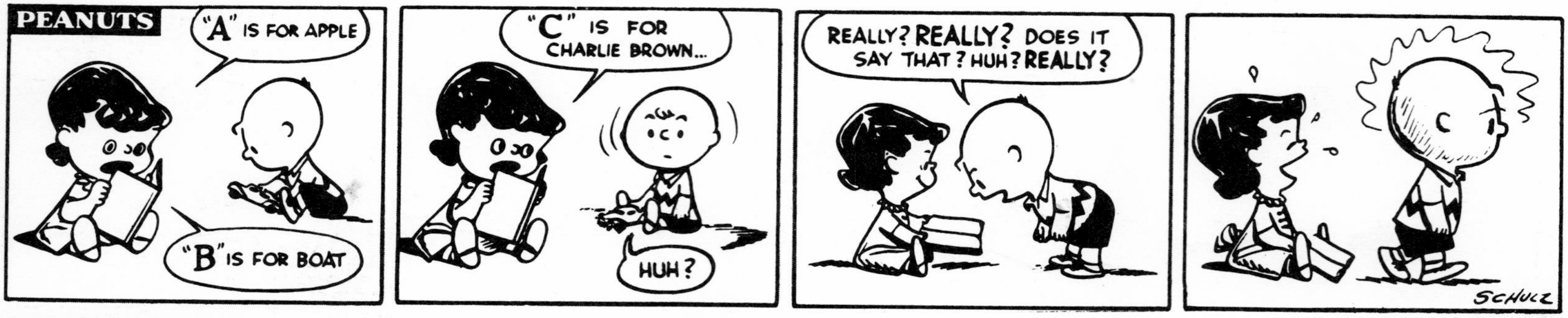
PEANUTS
"A" IS FOR APPLE
"B" IS FOR BOAT
"C" IS FOR CHARLIE BROWN...
HUH?
REALLY? REALLY? DOES IT SAY THAT? HUH? REALLY?
SCHULZ

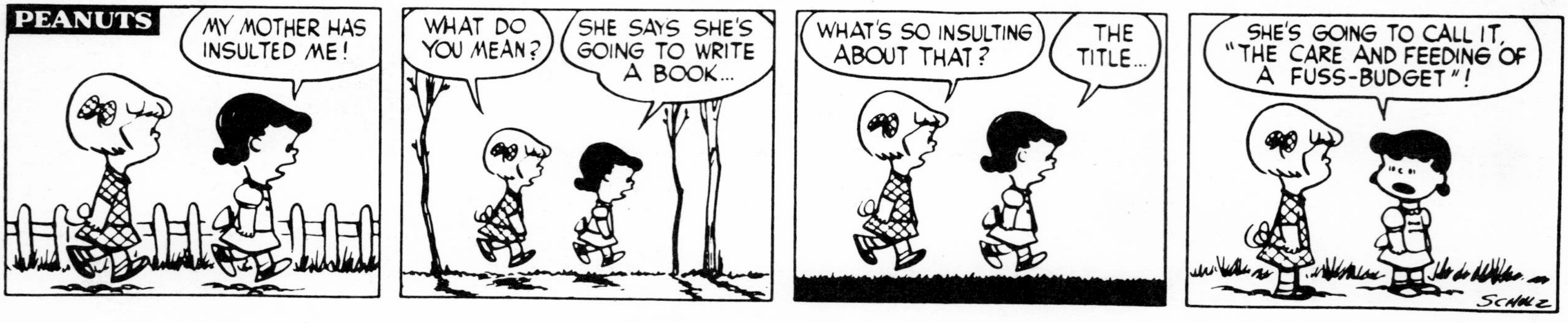
PEANUTS
MY MOTHER HAS INSULTED ME!
WHAT DO YOU MEAN?
SHE SAYS SHE'S GOING TO WRITE A BOOK...
WHAT'S SO INSULTING ABOUT THAT?
THE TITLE...
SHE'S GOING TO CALL IT, "THE CARE AND FEEDING OF A FUSS-BUDGET"!
SCHULZ

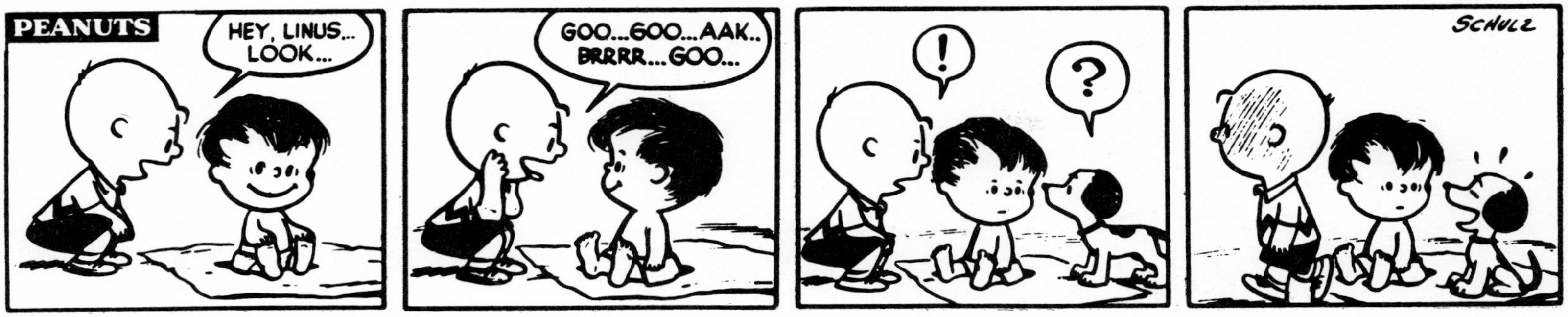
PEANUTS
HEY, LINUS... LOOK...
GOO...GOO...AAK.. BRRRR...GOO...
!
?
SCHULZ

Later that year Lucy was joined by a baby brother; and his name was Linus . . .

By the late 1950's, Lucy's appearance had changed and Linus had grown up.

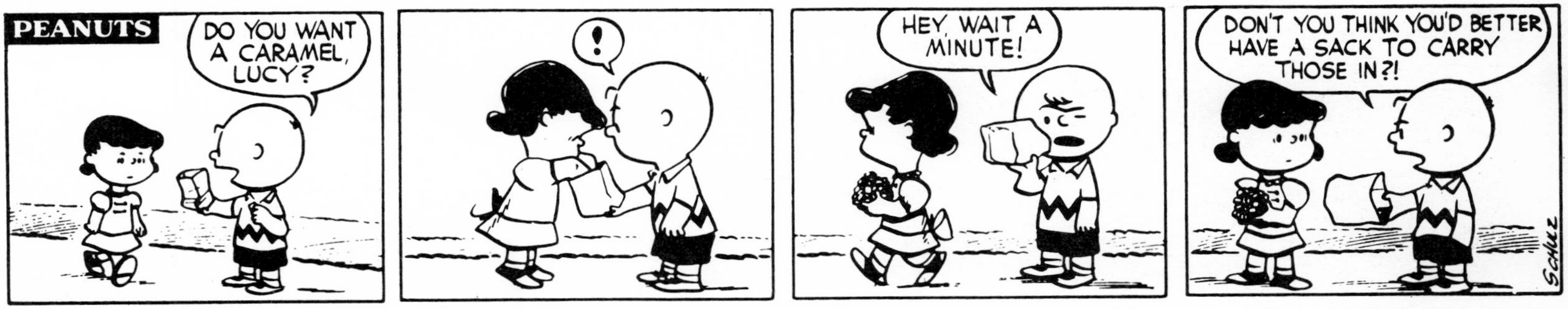
PEANUTS
DO YOU WANT A CARAMEL, LUCY?
!
HEY, WAIT A MINUTE!
DON'T YOU THINK YOU'D BETTER HAVE A SACK TO CARRY THOSE IN?!
SCHULZ

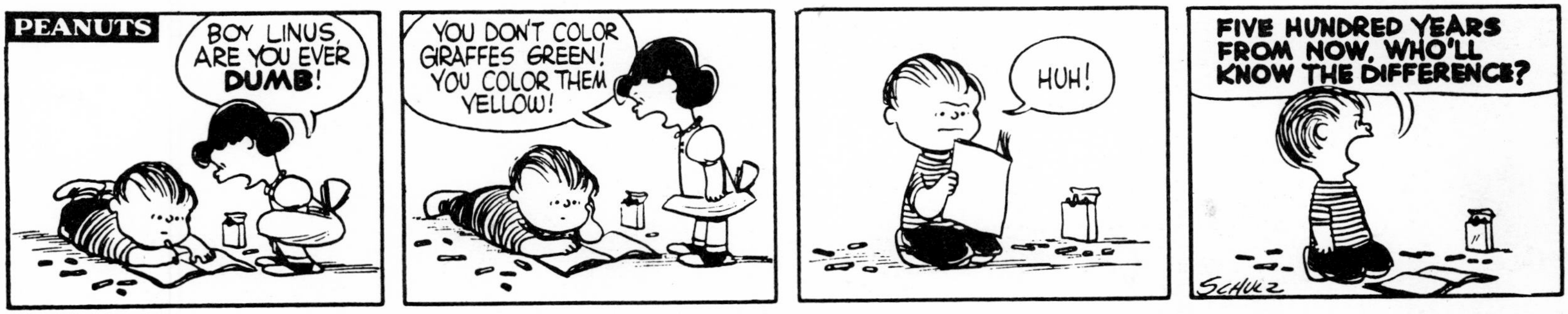
PEANUTS
BOY LINUS, ARE YOU EVER DUMB!
YOU DON'T COLOR GIRAFFES GREEN! YOU COLOR THEM YELLOW!
HUH!
FIVE HUNDRED YEARS FROM NOW, WHO'LL KNOW THE DIFFERENCE?
SCHULZ

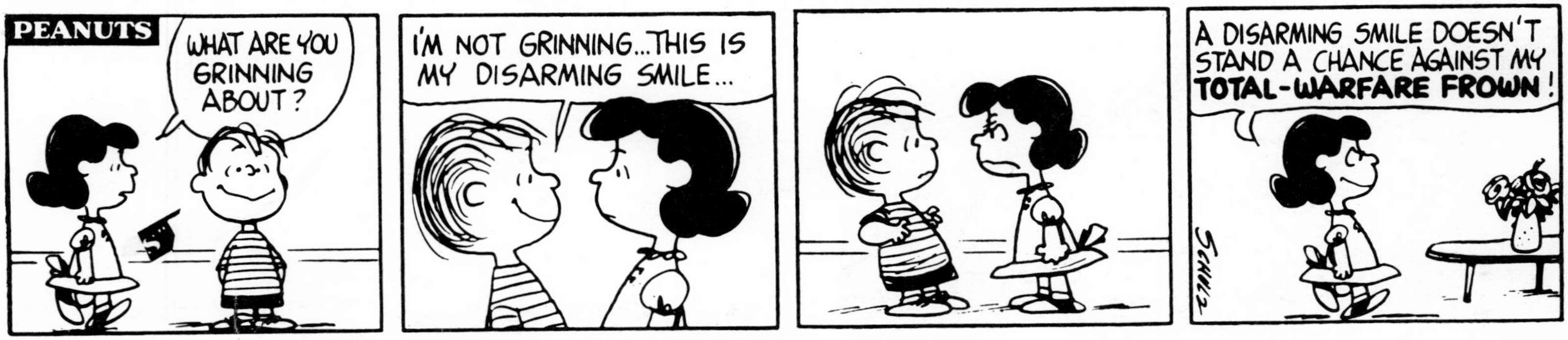
PEANUTS
WHAT ARE YOU GRINNING ABOUT?
I'M NOT GRINNING...THIS IS MY DISARMING SMILE...
A DISARMING SMILE DOESN'T STAND A CHANCE AGAINST MY TOTAL-WARFARE FROWN!
SCHULZ

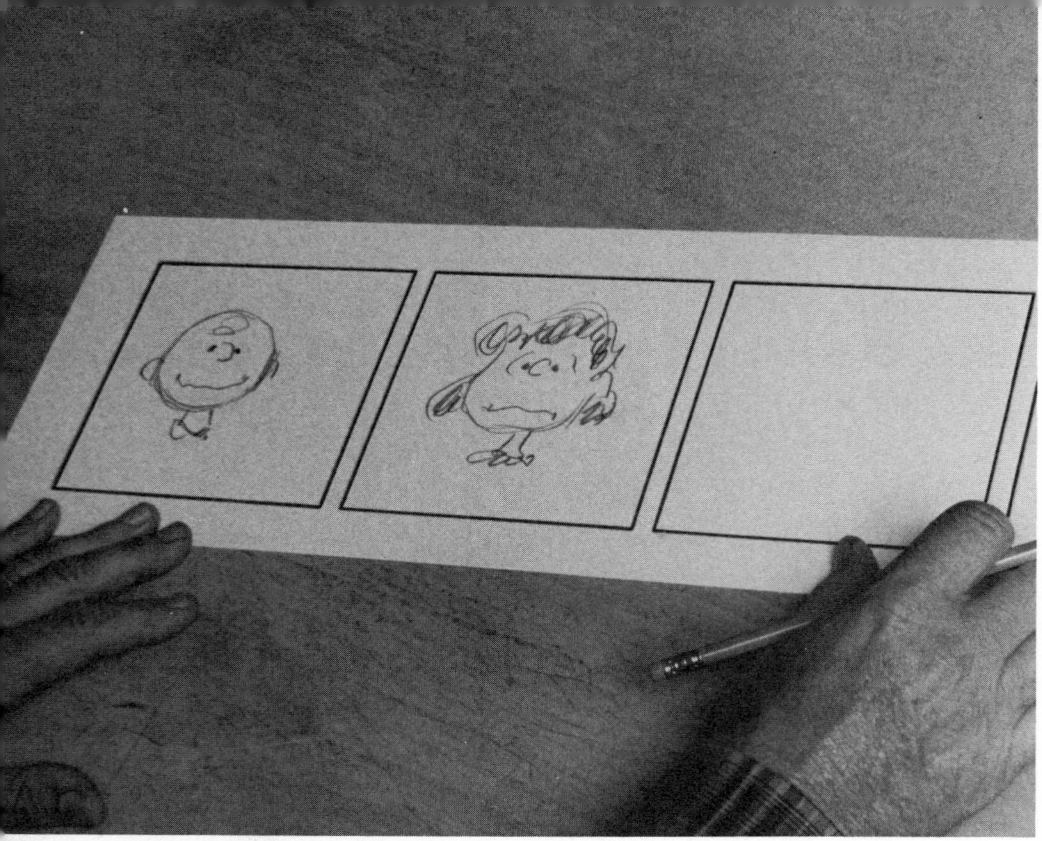

We asked Sparky about Linus and Lucy. "I sometimes wonder when Lucy is staring back at me from the comic strip what she might be thinking. But Lucy's a lot of fun to draw. I like giving her those wild expressions of anger and terror and anxiety that she often expresses. She's fun to work with because she has this violence within her. Lucy's kind of a composite of all the fussbudgets I've known in the world . . . both men and women.

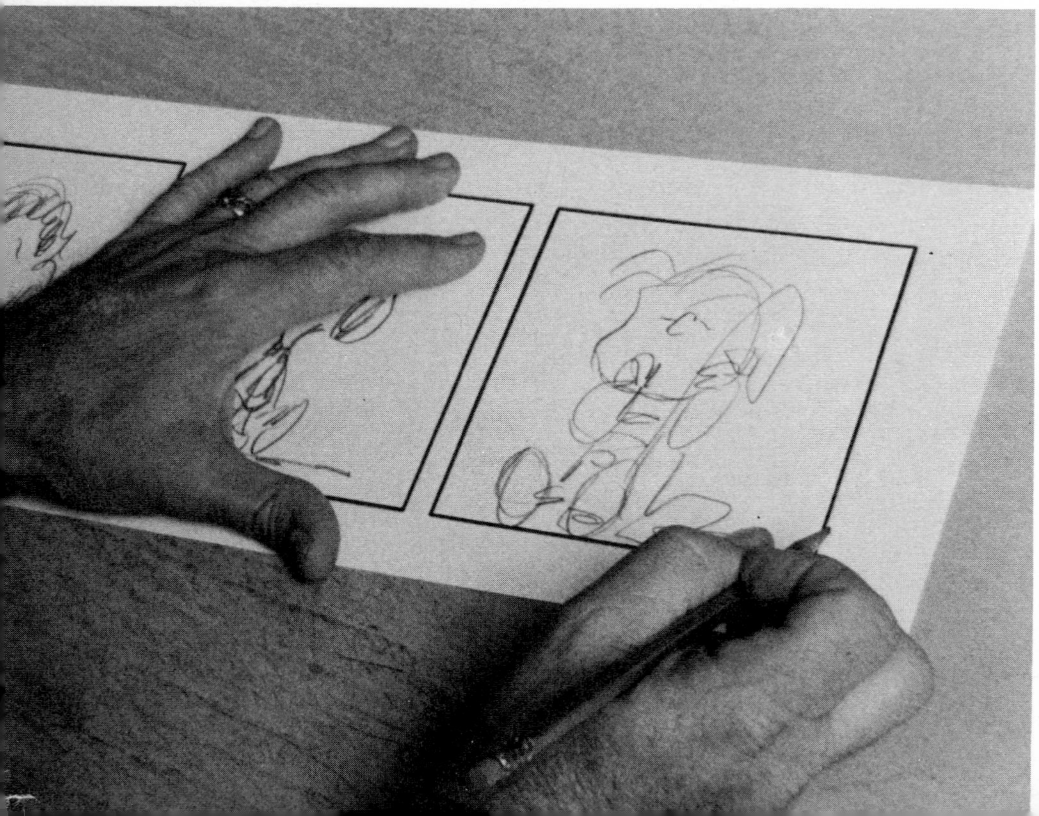

"As for Linus . . . one day I drew this funny little character with funny hair, and I thought he might be a good little brother for Lucy. So that's how Linus got started. Linus is a lot of fun to draw. He is very flexible, especially his hair, and it's fun to draw wild expressions on Linus . . . like when Lucy is yelling at him. I'm very proud of the overall character of Linus. I think he's the most well-rounded individual in the group."

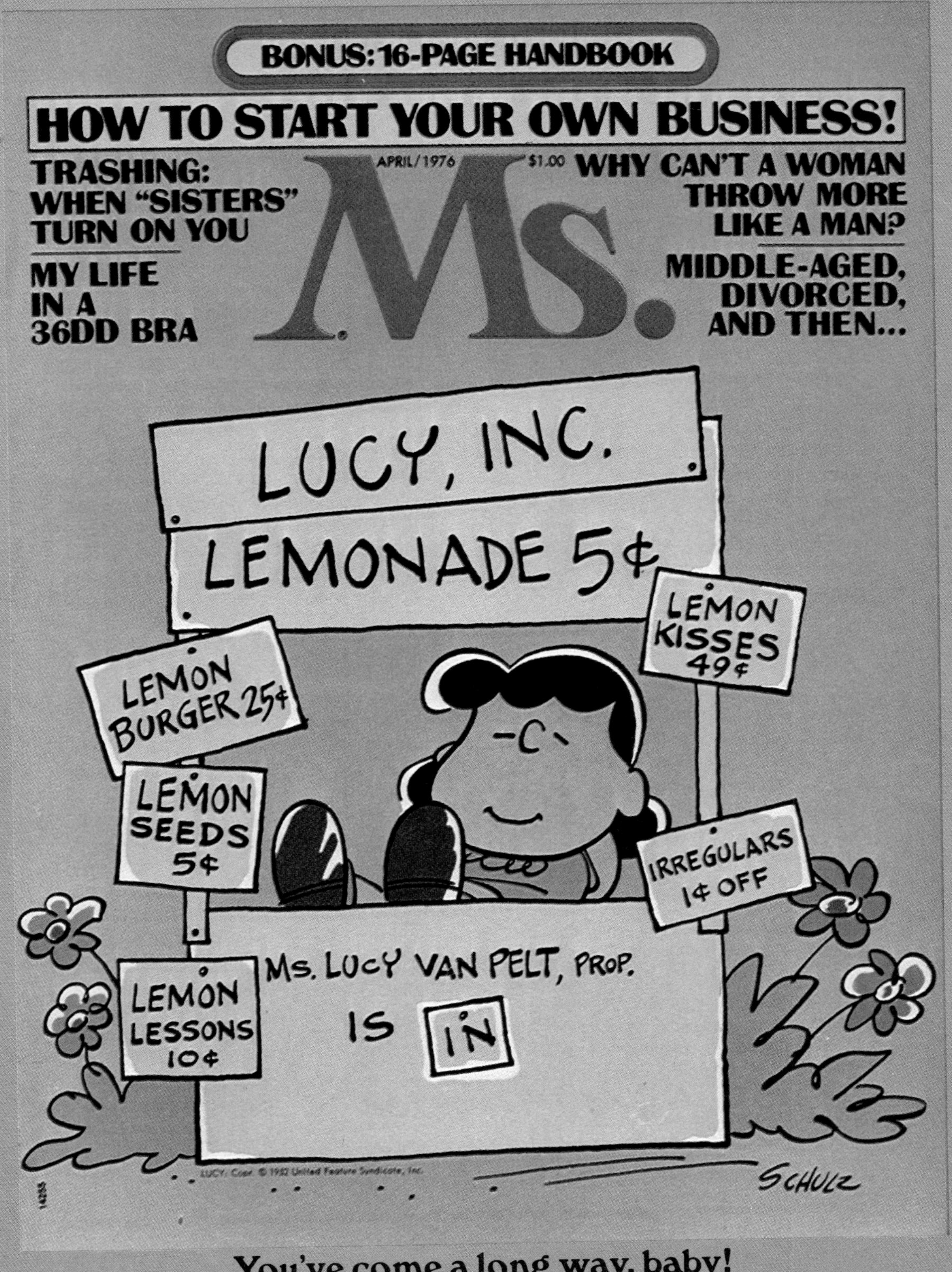
BONUS: 16-PAGE HANDBOOK
HOW TO START YOUR OWN BUSINESS!
APRIL/1976
$1.00
Ms.
TRASHING: WHEN "SISTERS" TURN ON YOU
MY LIFE IN A 36DD BRA
WHY CAN'T A WOMAN THROW MORE LIKE A MAN?
MIDDLE-AGED, DIVORCED, AND THEN...
LUCY, INC.
LEMONADE 5¢
LEMON KISSES 49¢
LEMON BURGER 25¢
LEMON SEEDS 5¢
IRREGULARS 1¢ OFF
LEMON LESSONS 10¢
Ms. LUCY VAN PELT, PROP.
IS IN
SCHULZ

You've come a long way, baby!

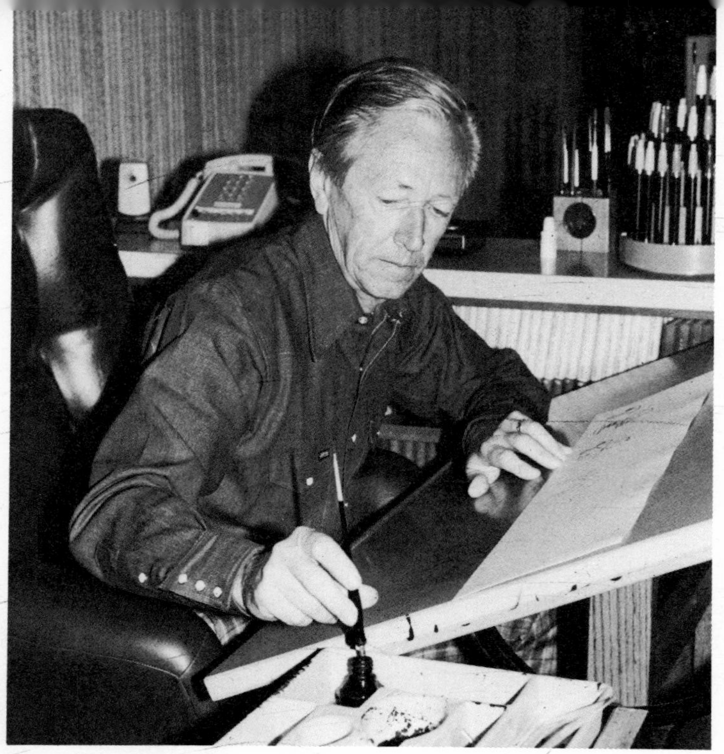

We asked Sparky to select some of his favorite strips featuring Linus and Lucy, and they are found on these next six pages . . .

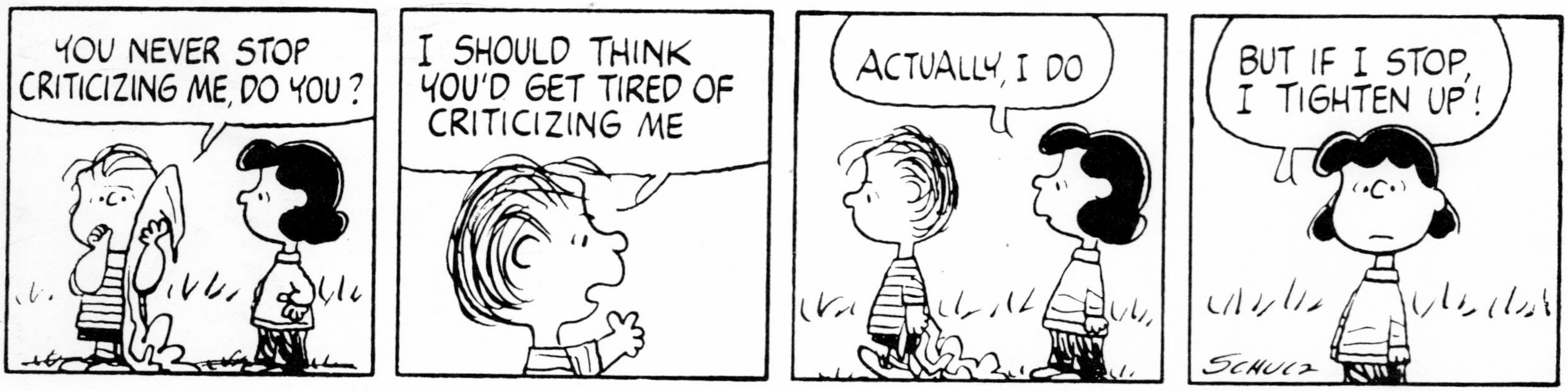
YOU NEVER STOP CRITICIZING ME, DO YOU?
I SHOULD THINK YOU'D GET TIRED OF CRITICIZING ME
ACTUALLY, I DO
BUT IF I STOP, I TIGHTEN UP!
SCHULZ

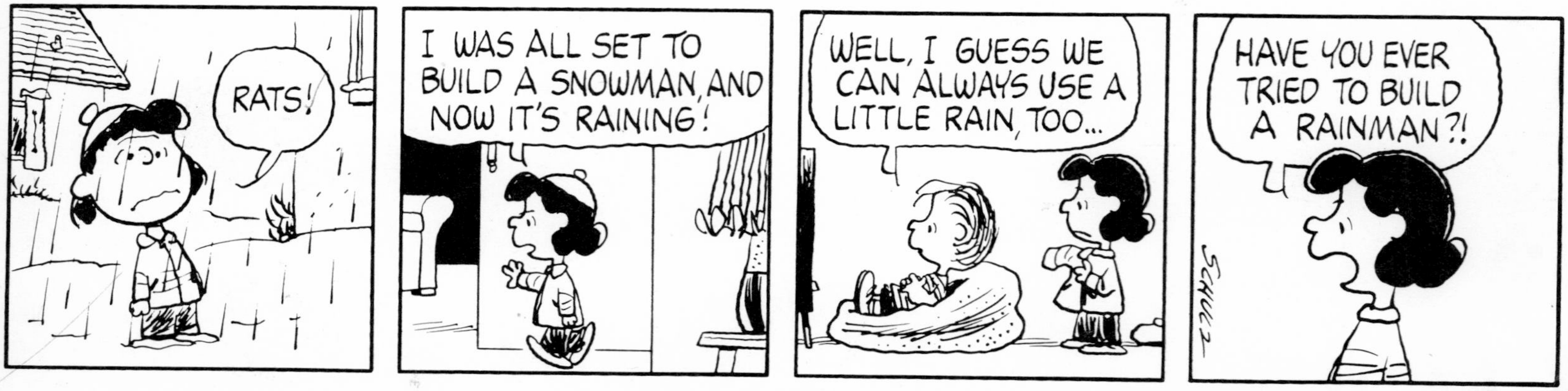
RATS!
I WAS ALL SET TO BUILD A SNOWMAN, AND NOW IT'S RAINING!
WELL, I GUESS WE CAN ALWAYS USE A LITTLE RAIN, TOO...
HAVE YOU EVER TRIED TO BUILD A RAINMAN?!
SCHULZ

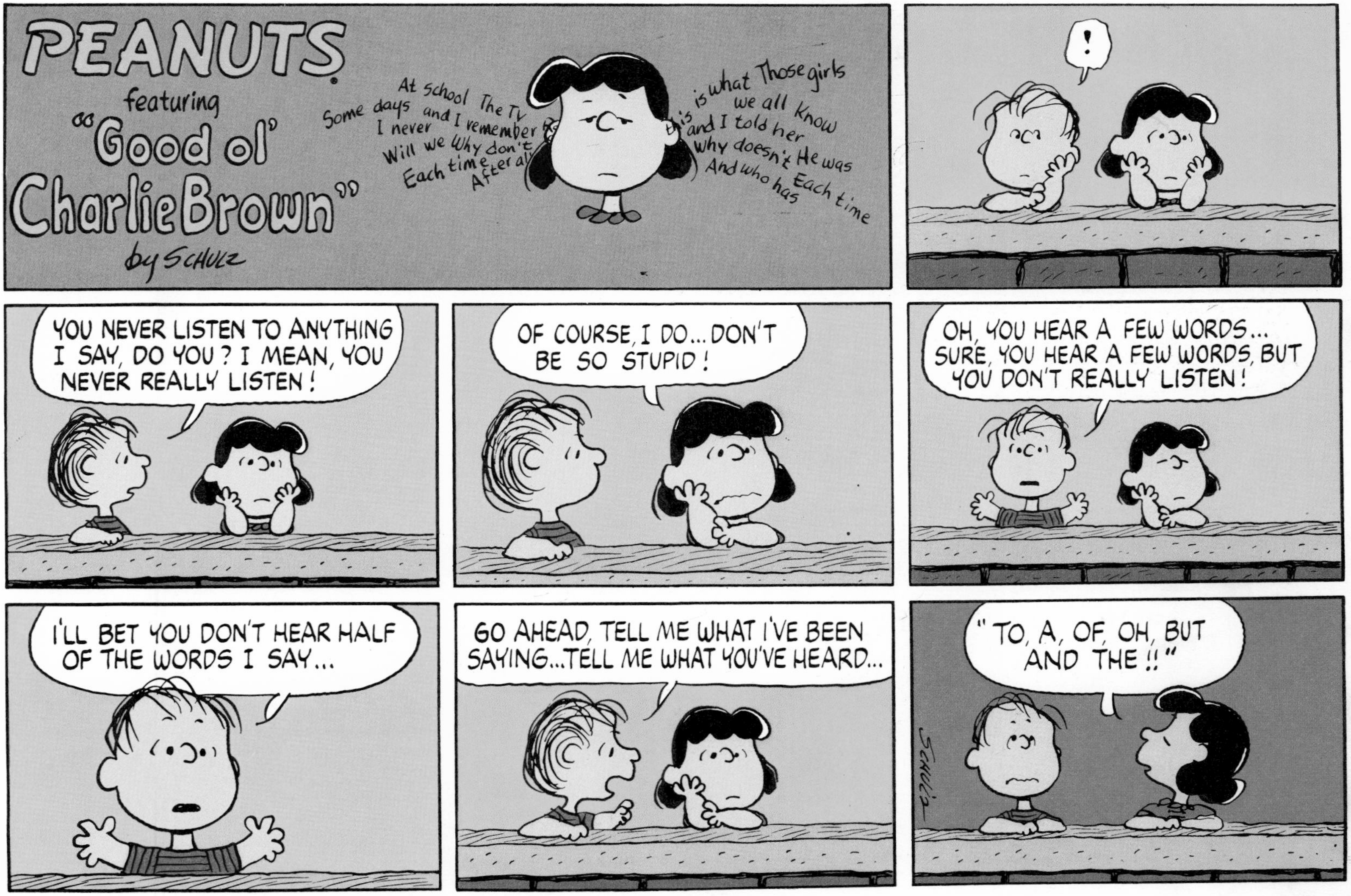
PEANUTS
featuring
"Good ol' Charlie Brown"
by SCHULZ
At school The TV
Some days and I remember
I never
Will we Why don't
Each time After all
this is what Those girls
we all know
and I told her
Why doesn't He was
And who has Each time
!
YOU NEVER LISTEN TO ANYTHING I SAY, DO YOU? I MEAN, YOU NEVER REALLY LISTEN!
OF COURSE, I DO...DON'T BE SO STUPID!
OH, YOU HEAR A FEW WORDS... SURE, YOU HEAR A FEW WORDS, BUT YOU DON'T REALLY LISTEN!
I'LL BET YOU DON'T HEAR HALF OF THE WORDS I SAY...
GO AHEAD, TELL ME WHAT I'VE BEEN SAYING...TELL ME WHAT YOU'VE HEARD...
"TO, A, OF, OH, BUT AND THE!!"
SCHULZ

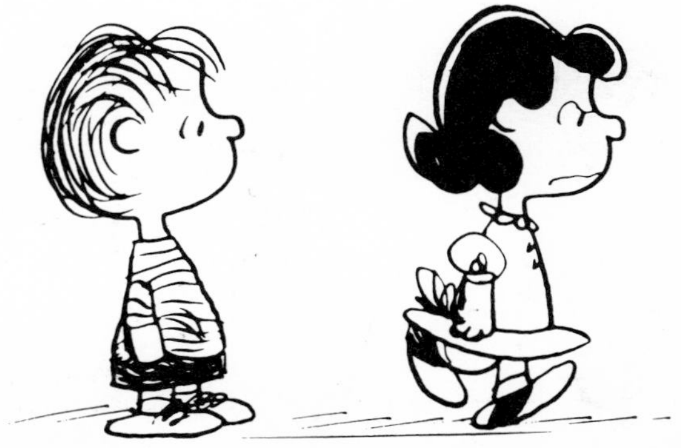

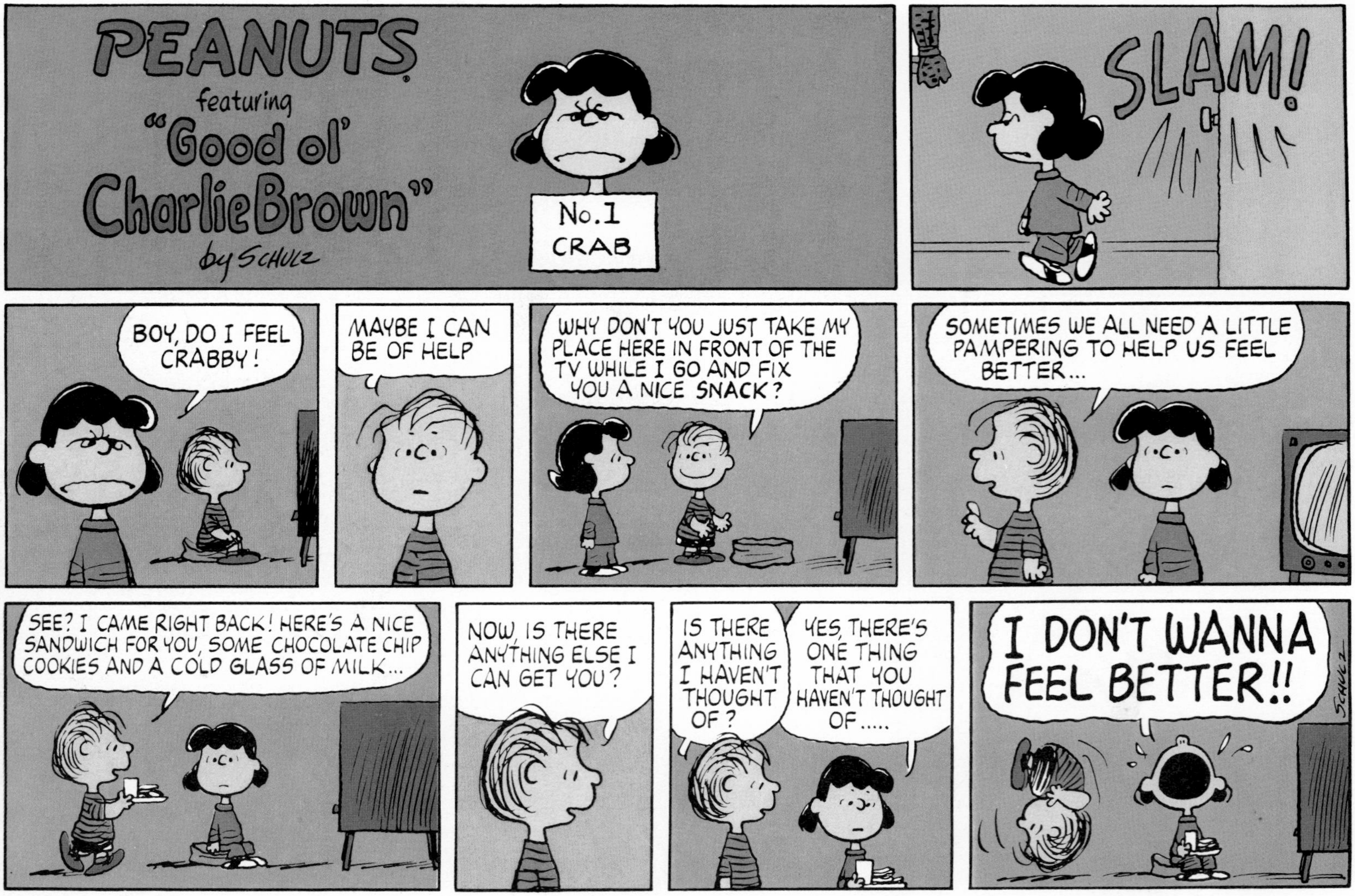
PEANUTS
featuring
"Good ol' Charlie Brown"
by SCHULZ
No.1
CRAB
SLAM!
BOY, DO I FEEL CRABBY!
MAYBE I CAN BE OF HELP
WHY DON'T YOU JUST TAKE MY PLACE HERE IN FRONT OF THE TV WHILE I GO AND FIX YOU A NICE SNACK?
SOMETIMES WE ALL NEED A LITTLE PAMPERING TO HELP US FEEL BETTER...
SEE? I CAME RIGHT BACK! HERE'S A NICE SANDWICH FOR YOU, SOME CHOCOLATE CHIP COOKIES AND A COLD GLASS OF MILK...
NOW, IS THERE ANYTHING ELSE I CAN GET YOU?
IS THERE ANYTHING I HAVEN'T THOUGHT OF?
YES, THERE'S ONE THING THAT YOU HAVEN'T THOUGHT OF.....
I DON'T WANNA FEEL BETTER!!
SCHULZ

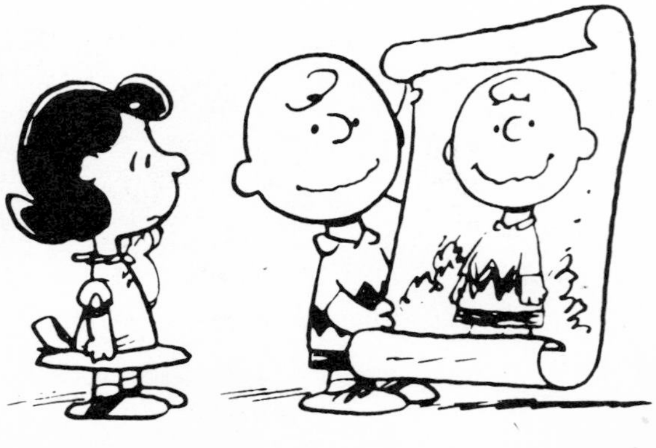

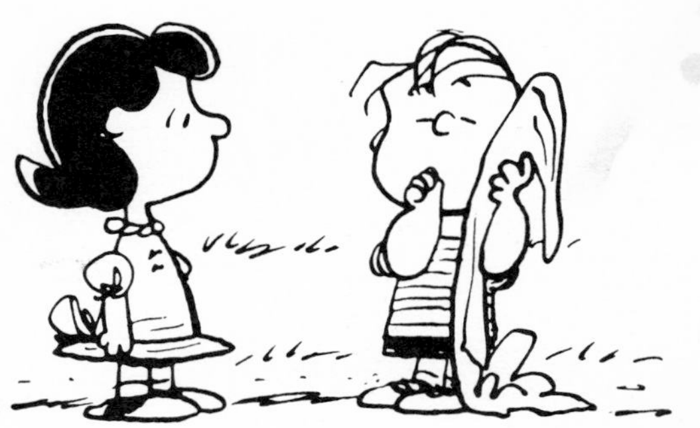

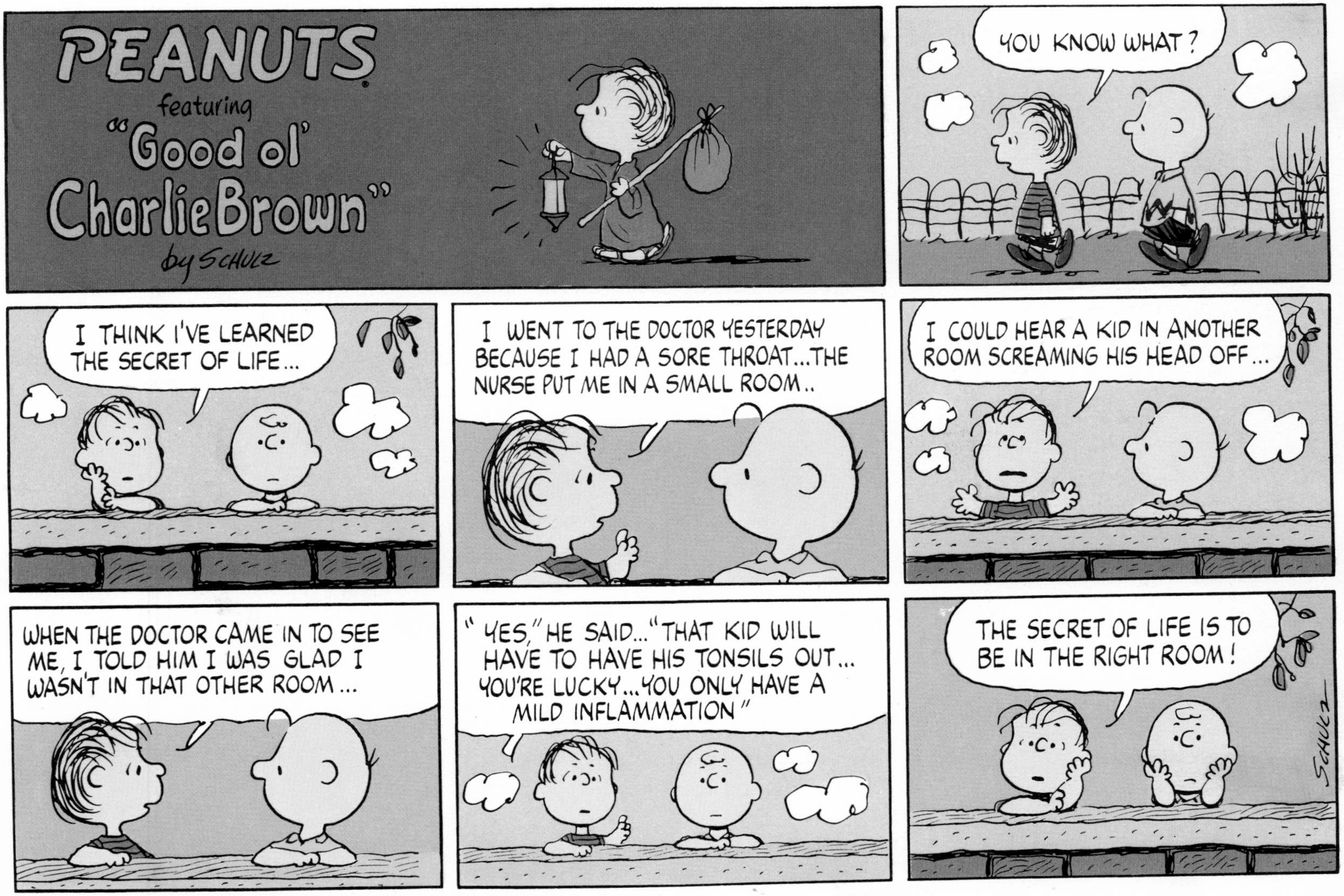
PEANUTS
featuring
"Good ol' Charlie Brown"
by SCHULZ
YOU KNOW WHAT?
I THINK I'VE LEARNED THE SECRET OF LIFE...
I WENT TO THE DOCTOR YESTERDAY BECAUSE I HAD A SORE THROAT...THE NURSE PUT ME IN A SMALL ROOM..
I COULD HEAR A KID IN ANOTHER ROOM SCREAMING HIS HEAD OFF...
WHEN THE DOCTOR CAME IN TO SEE ME, I TOLD HIM I WAS GLAD I WASN'T IN THAT OTHER ROOM...
"YES," HE SAID..."THAT KID WILL HAVE TO HAVE HIS TONSILS OUT... YOU'RE LUCKY...YOU ONLY HAVE A MILD INFLAMMATION"
THE SECRET OF LIFE IS TO BE IN THE RIGHT ROOM!
SCHULZ

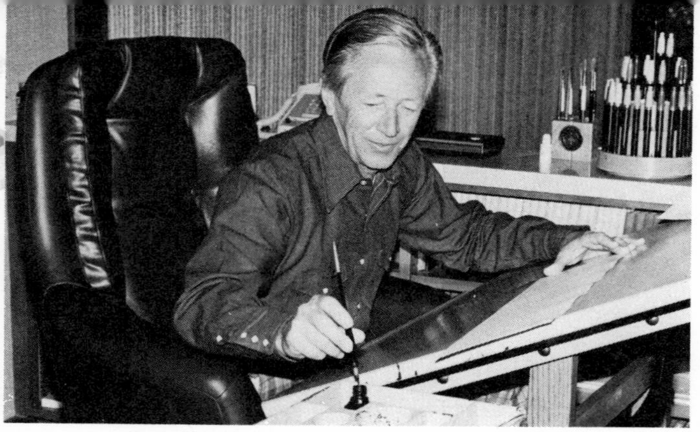

Of all the ideas that Sparky has developed over the past thirty years, I think he is most proud of the idea of Linus' security blanket. Not only was this a funny concept but it also struck an early blow for "kids' rights." One of my favorite *Peanuts* series of strips concerned Linus and his blanket-hating grandma . . .

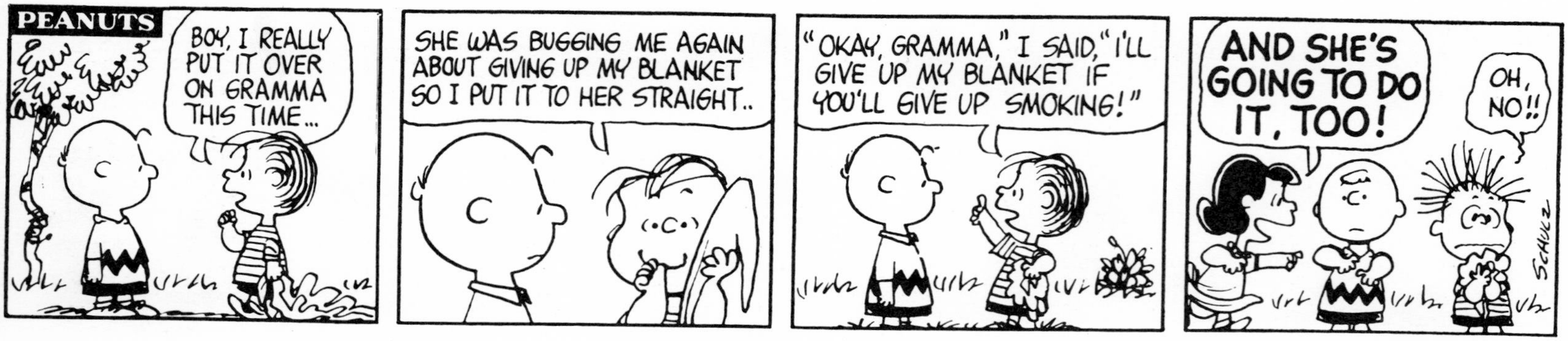

PEANUTS
BOY, I REALLY PUT IT OVER ON GRAMMA THIS TIME...
SHE WAS BUGGING ME AGAIN ABOUT GIVING UP MY BLANKET SO I PUT IT TO HER STRAIGHT..
"OKAY, GRAMMA," I SAID, "I'LL GIVE UP MY BLANKET IF YOU'LL GIVE UP SMOKING!"
AND SHE'S GOING TO DO IT, TOO!
OH, NO!!
SCHULZ

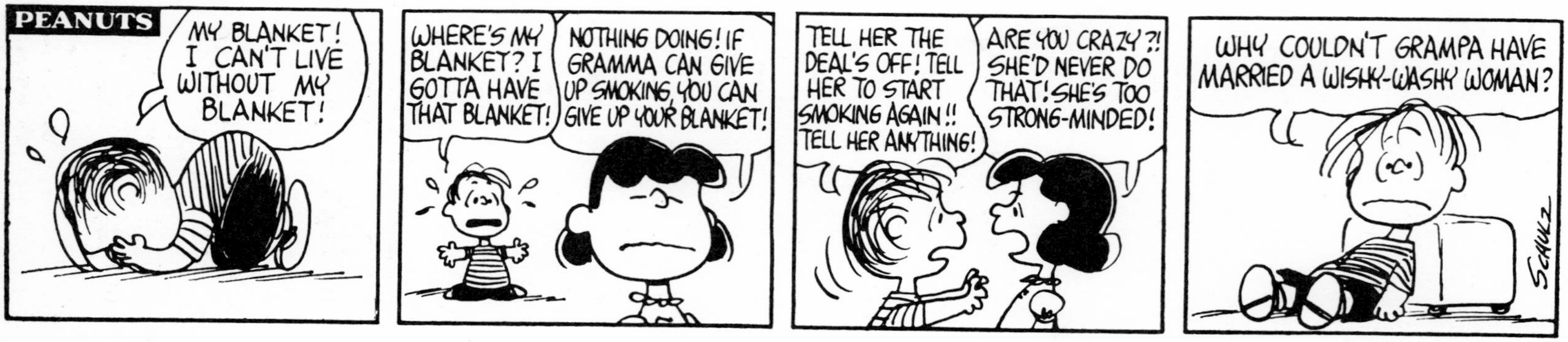

PEANUTS
MY BLANKET! I CAN'T LIVE WITHOUT MY BLANKET!
WHERE'S MY BLANKET? I GOTTA HAVE THAT BLANKET!
NOTHING DOING! IF GRAMMA CAN GIVE UP SMOKING, YOU CAN GIVE UP YOUR BLANKET!
TELL HER THE DEAL'S OFF! TELL HER TO START SMOKING AGAIN!! TELL HER ANYTHING!
ARE YOU CRAZY?! SHE'D NEVER DO THAT! SHE'S TOO STRONG-MINDED!
WHY COULDN'T GRAMPA HAVE MARRIED A WISHY-WASHY WOMAN?
SCHULZ

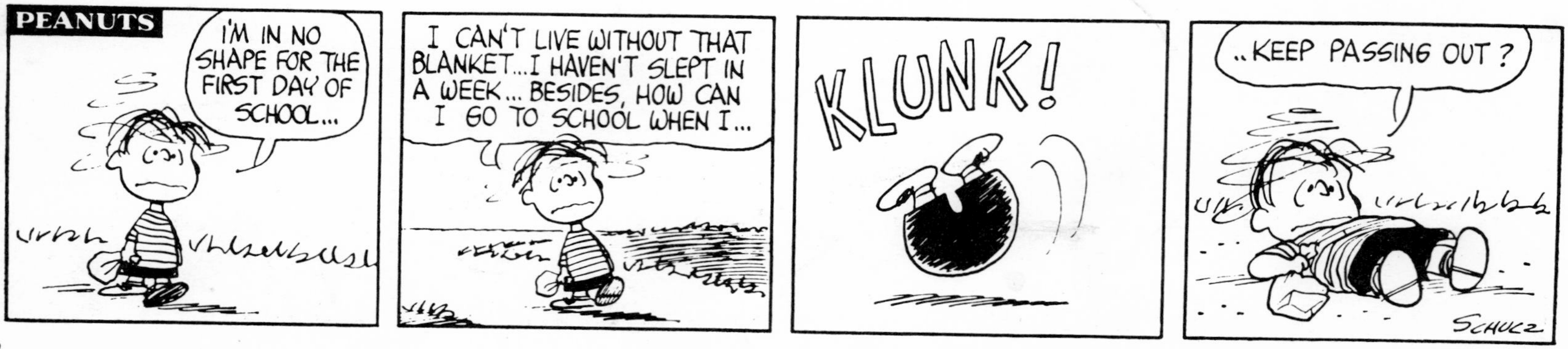

PEANUTS
I'M IN NO SHAPE FOR THE FIRST DAY OF SCHOOL...
I CAN'T LIVE WITHOUT THAT BLANKET...I HAVEN'T SLEPT IN A WEEK... BESIDES, HOW CAN I GO TO SCHOOL WHEN I...
KLUNK!
..KEEP PASSING OUT?
SCHULZ

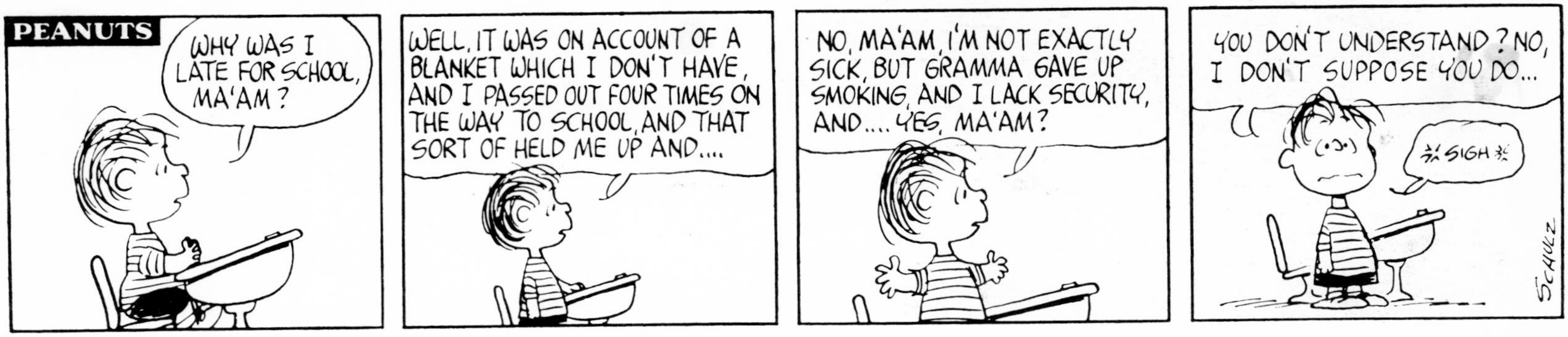
PEANUTS
WHY WAS I LATE FOR SCHOOL, MA'AM?
WELL, IT WAS ON ACCOUNT OF A BLANKET WHICH I DON'T HAVE, AND I PASSED OUT FOUR TIMES ON THE WAY TO SCHOOL, AND THAT SORT OF HELD ME UP AND....
NO, MA'AM, I'M NOT EXACTLY SICK, BUT GRAMMA GAVE UP SMOKING, AND I LACK SECURITY, AND.... YES, MA'AM?
YOU DON'T UNDERSTAND? NO, I DON'T SUPPOSE YOU DO...
SIGH
SCHULZ

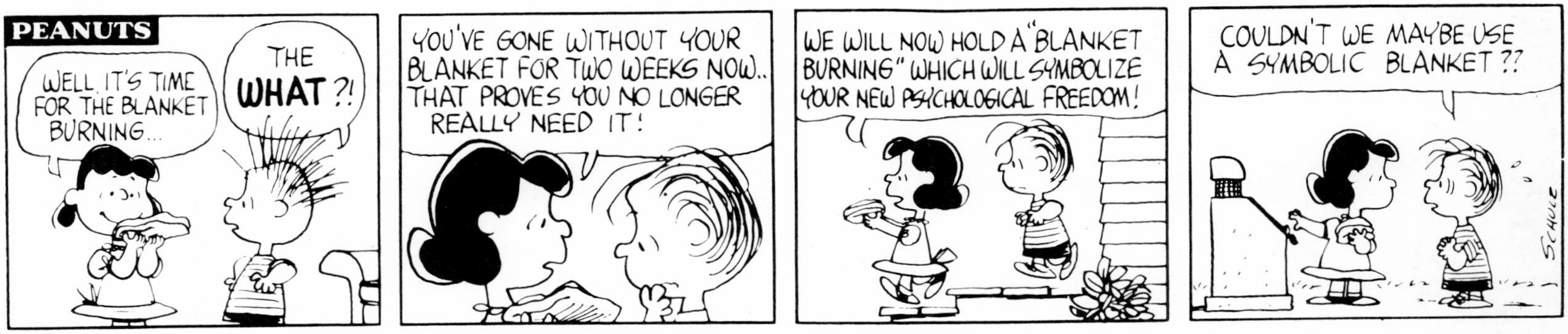
PEANUTS
WELL, IT'S TIME FOR THE BLANKET BURNING...
THE WHAT?!
YOU'VE GONE WITHOUT YOUR BLANKET FOR TWO WEEKS NOW.. THAT PROVES YOU NO LONGER REALLY NEED IT!
WE WILL NOW HOLD A "BLANKET BURNING" WHICH WILL SYMBOLIZE YOUR NEW PSYCHOLOGICAL FREEDOM!
COULDN'T WE MAYBE USE A SYMBOLIC BLANKET??
SCHULZ

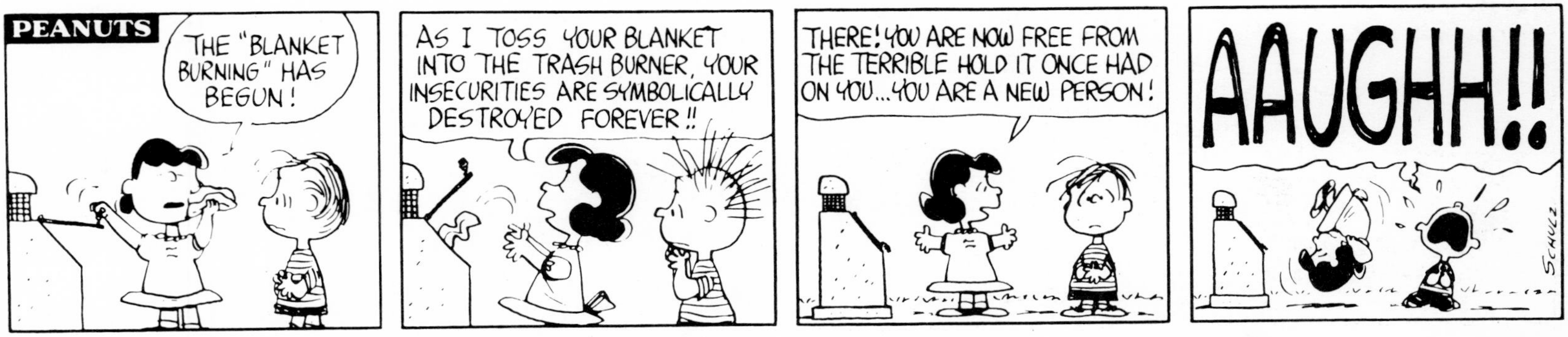
PEANUTS
THE "BLANKET BURNING" HAS BEGUN!
AS I TOSS YOUR BLANKET INTO THE TRASH BURNER, YOUR INSECURITIES ARE SYMBOLICALLY DESTROYED FOREVER!!
THERE! YOU ARE NOW FREE FROM THE TERRIBLE HOLD IT ONCE HAD ON YOU...YOU ARE A NEW PERSON!
AAUGHH!!
SCHULZ

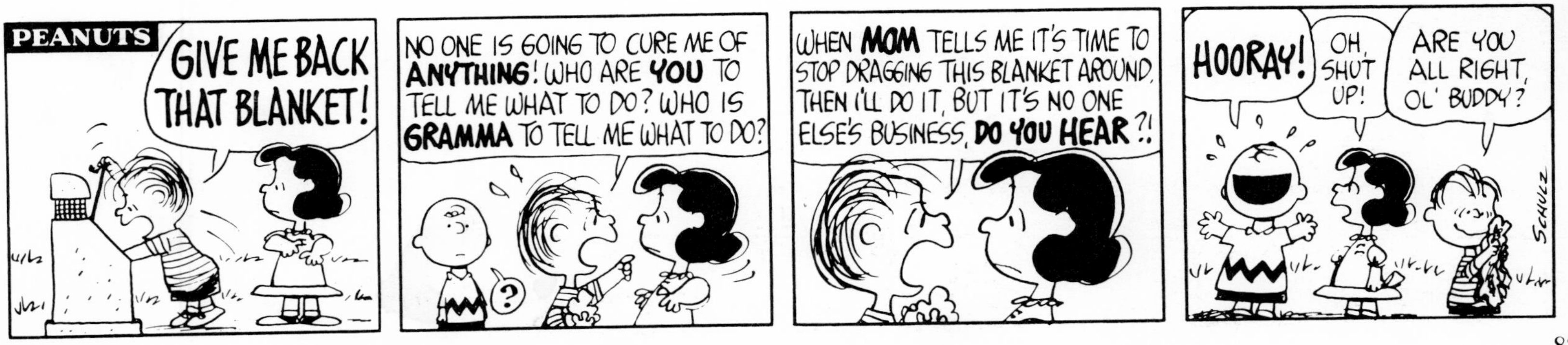
PEANUTS
GIVE ME BACK THAT BLANKET!
NO ONE IS GOING TO CURE ME OF ANYTHING! WHO ARE YOU TO TELL ME WHAT TO DO? WHO IS GRAMMA TO TELL ME WHAT TO DO?
?
WHEN MOM TELLS ME IT'S TIME TO STOP DRAGGING THIS BLANKET AROUND, THEN I'LL DO IT, BUT IT'S NO ONE ELSE'S BUSINESS, DO YOU HEAR?!
HOORAY!
OH, SHUT UP!
ARE YOU ALL RIGHT, OL' BUDDY?
SCHULZ

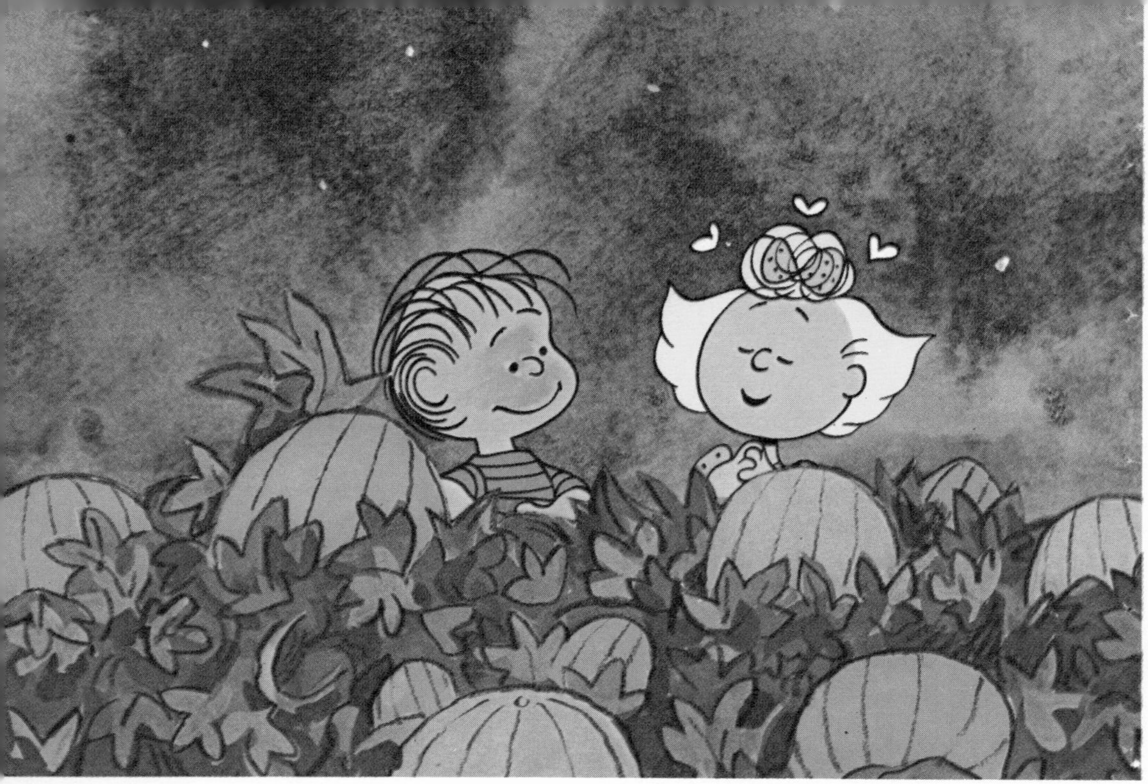

Another idea of Sparky's that has brought him great satisfaction was his creation of the Great Pumpkin, again involving Linus. Says Sparky: "Linus and the pumpkin patch came to me as an idea one year when I was trying to imagine what would happen if a child suddenly got one holiday ahead of himself and began to wait for presents on Halloween rather than Christmas. Then, of course, he had to wait for someone to bring him these presents. And who would it be on Halloween night other than — obviously — someone named the Great Pumpkin. I really am very proud of this whole idea, and it may be the most original — or unique — of all my ideas during these past thirty years."

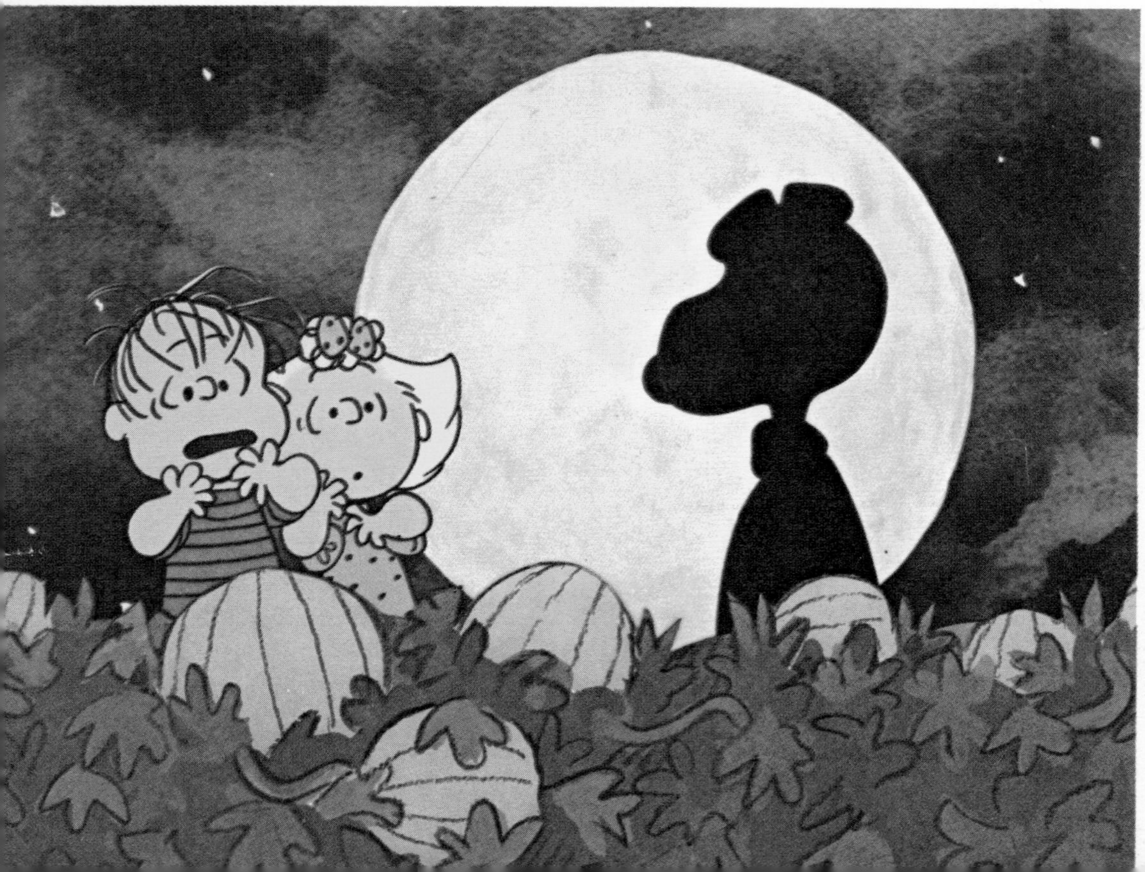

In *It's the Great Pumpkin, Charlie Brown*, Linus talked Sally into joining him at the pumpkin patch to wait for the arrival of the Great Pumpkin.

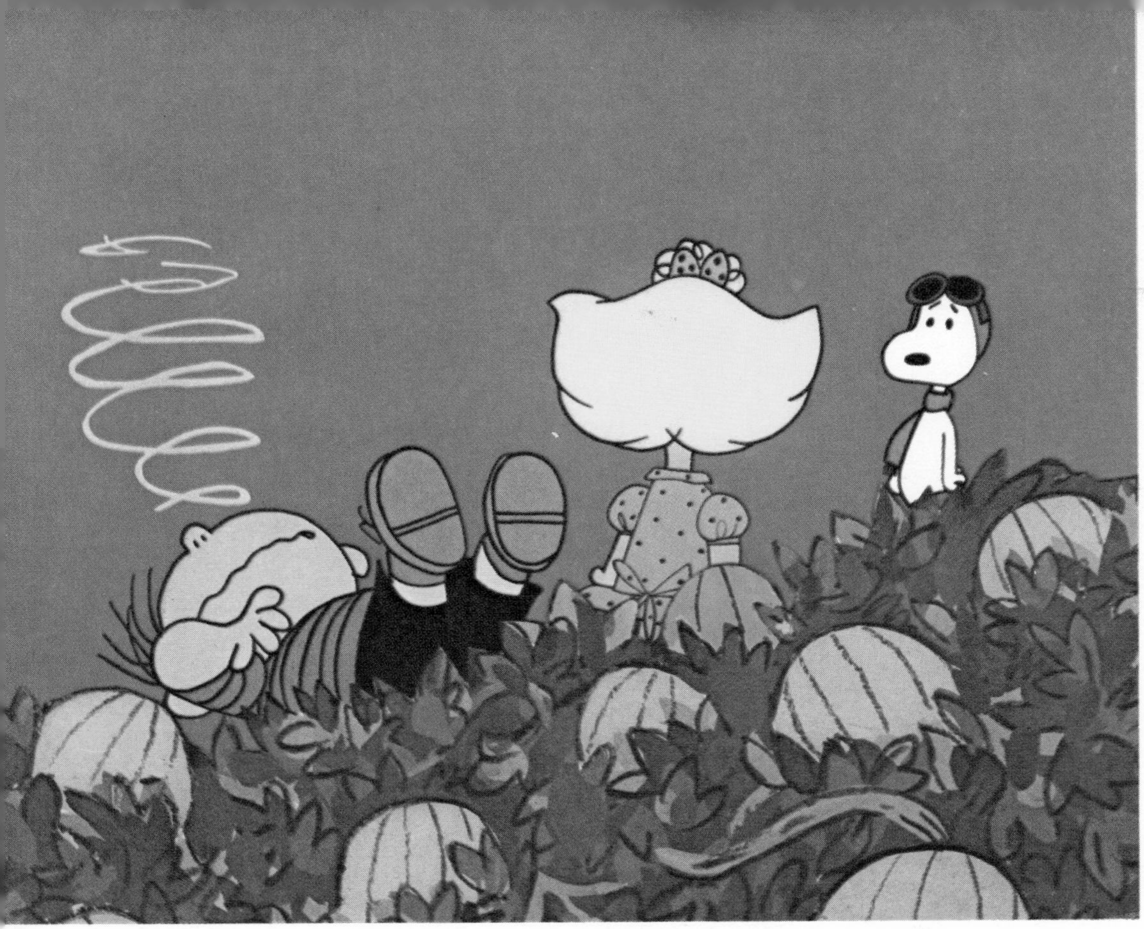

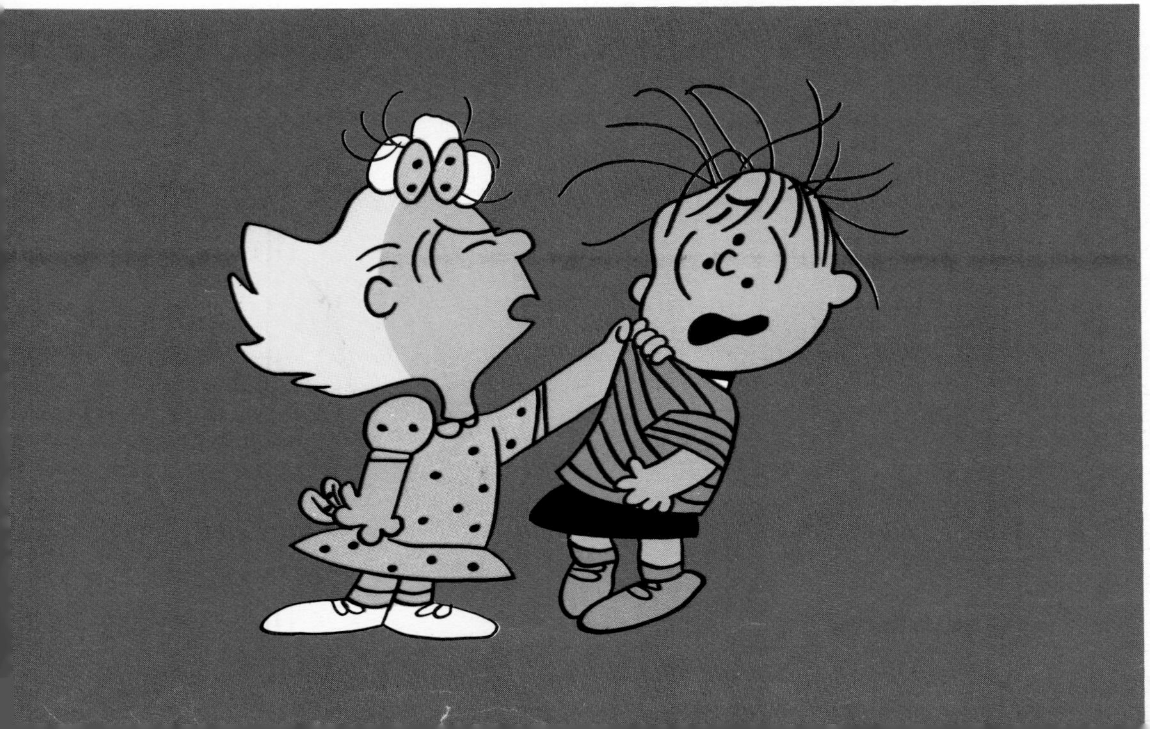

But after a long wait, only Snoopy arrived. Furious, Sally abandoned the whole idea and went home. But Linus and many of his fans still believe in the Great Pumpkin.

You're hopeless, Charlie Brown, completely hopeless.

HA! HA! HA! HA! HA!

It was in the first TV show, *A Charlie Brown Christmas*, that Linus had perhaps his "finest" moment. He and Charlie Brown had returned to the scene of the Christmas play with the sad little tree that Charlie Brown had selected. Everyone made fun of the scraggly tree, and Charlie Brown felt totally defeated. When Charlie Brown asks, "Doesn't anyone know what Christmas is all about?" Linus steps forward and quotes from the Bible . . .

I guess you were right, Linus. I shouldn't have picked this little tree. I guess I really don't know what Christmas is all about. Isn't there anyone who knows what Christmas is all about????

Sure, Charlie Brown, I can tell you what Christmas is all about.

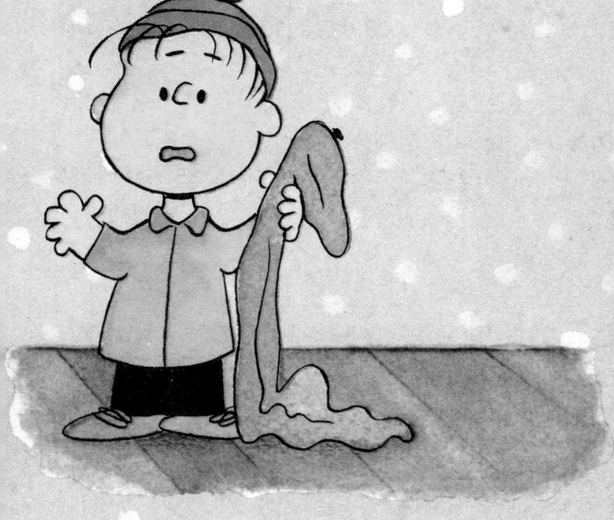

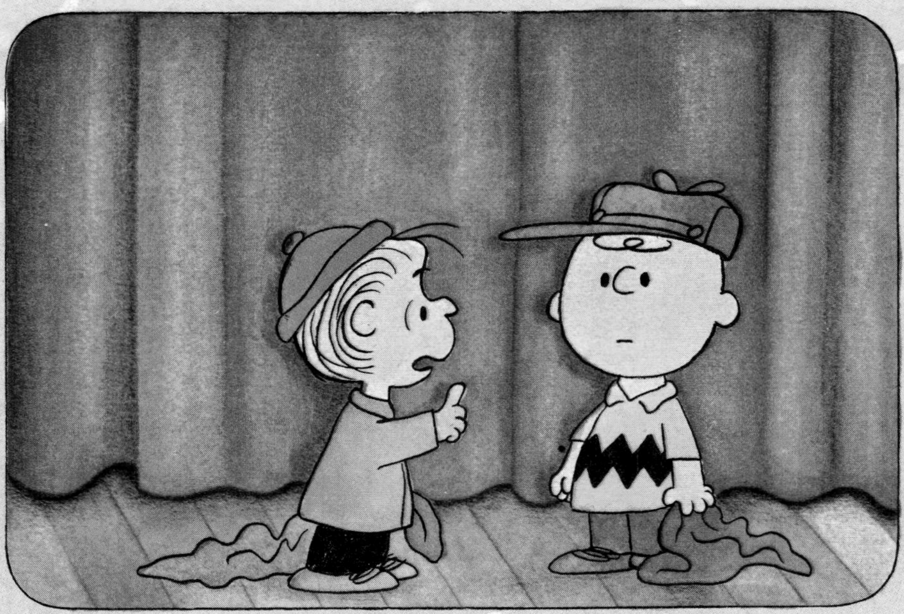

And there were in the same country shepherds abiding in the field, keeping watch over their flock by night.

And, lo, the angel of the Lord came upon them, and the glory of the Lord shone round about them: and they were sore afraid.

And the angel said unto them, Fear not: for, behold, I bring you tidings of great joy, which shall be to all people.

For unto you is born this day in the city of David a Saviour, which is Christ the Lord.

And this shall be a sign unto you; Ye shall find the babe wrapped in swaddling clothes, lying in a manger.

And suddenly there was with the angel a multitude of the heavenly host praising God, and saying,

Glory to God in the highest, and on earth peace, good will toward men.

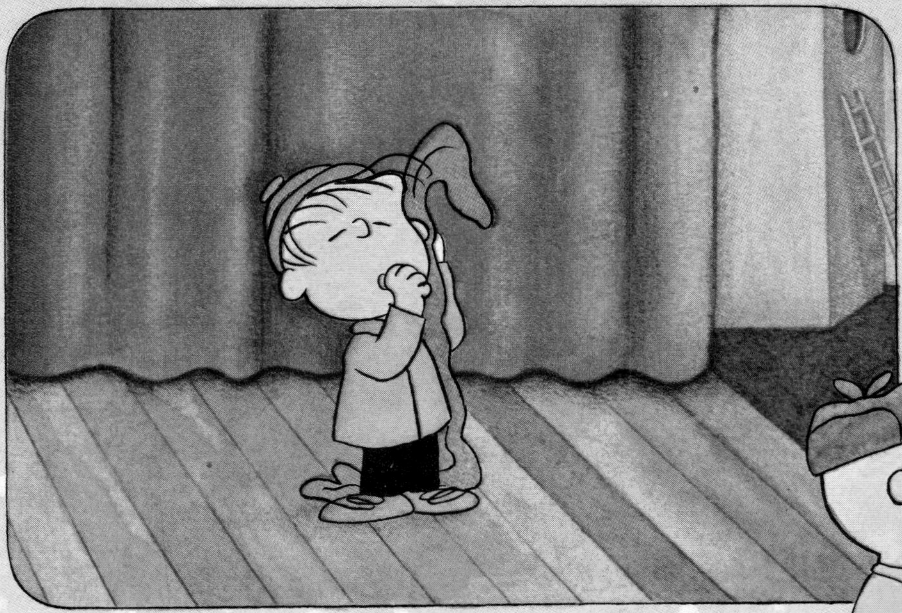

And that's what Christmas is all about, Charlie Brown.

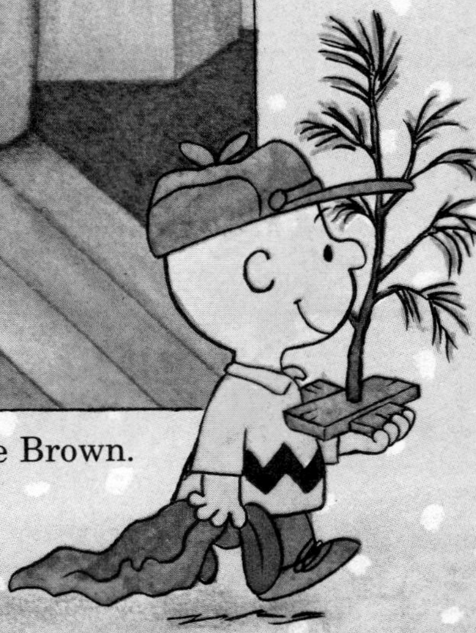

It says here that it is probable the valentine was the first of all greeting cards. Get it, Schroeder? The valentine was *first*. Love comes *first*.

"Originally, Valentine's Day was set aside as a lovers' festival." Oh, Schroeder, isn't that romantic? A lovers' festival.

Sometimes I think you don't realize that you could lose me. Are you sure you want to suffer the tortures of the memory of a lost love? Do you know the tortures of the memory of a lost love?

Originally we had thought that Lucy would be one of the major "stars" of the TV shows. But we found that her often abrasive nature and raucous behavior were frequently too intrusive on the TV shows.

From time to time, however, as in our Valentine special, she found her way into animation.

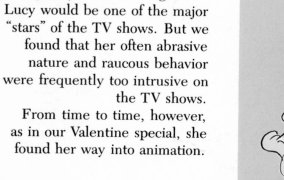

IT'S AWFUL!

IT WILL HAUNT YOU NIGHT AND DAY! YOU'LL
WAKE UP AT NIGHT SCREAMING! YOU CAN'T EAT!
YOU CAN'T SLEEP! YOU'LL WANT TO SMASH THINGS!

YOU'LL HATE YOURSELF AND THE WORLD AND
EVERYBODY IN IT! OOOOH . . . OOO!!!

Are you sure you want to risk losing me?

In *Be My Valentine, Charlie Brown,* Lucy discussed love with Schroeder.

89

As a matter of fact, Sparky thinks the best animated scene of all the shows we have done was Bill Melendez' creation of the arm-wrestling scene in *It Was a Short Summer, Charlie Brown*.

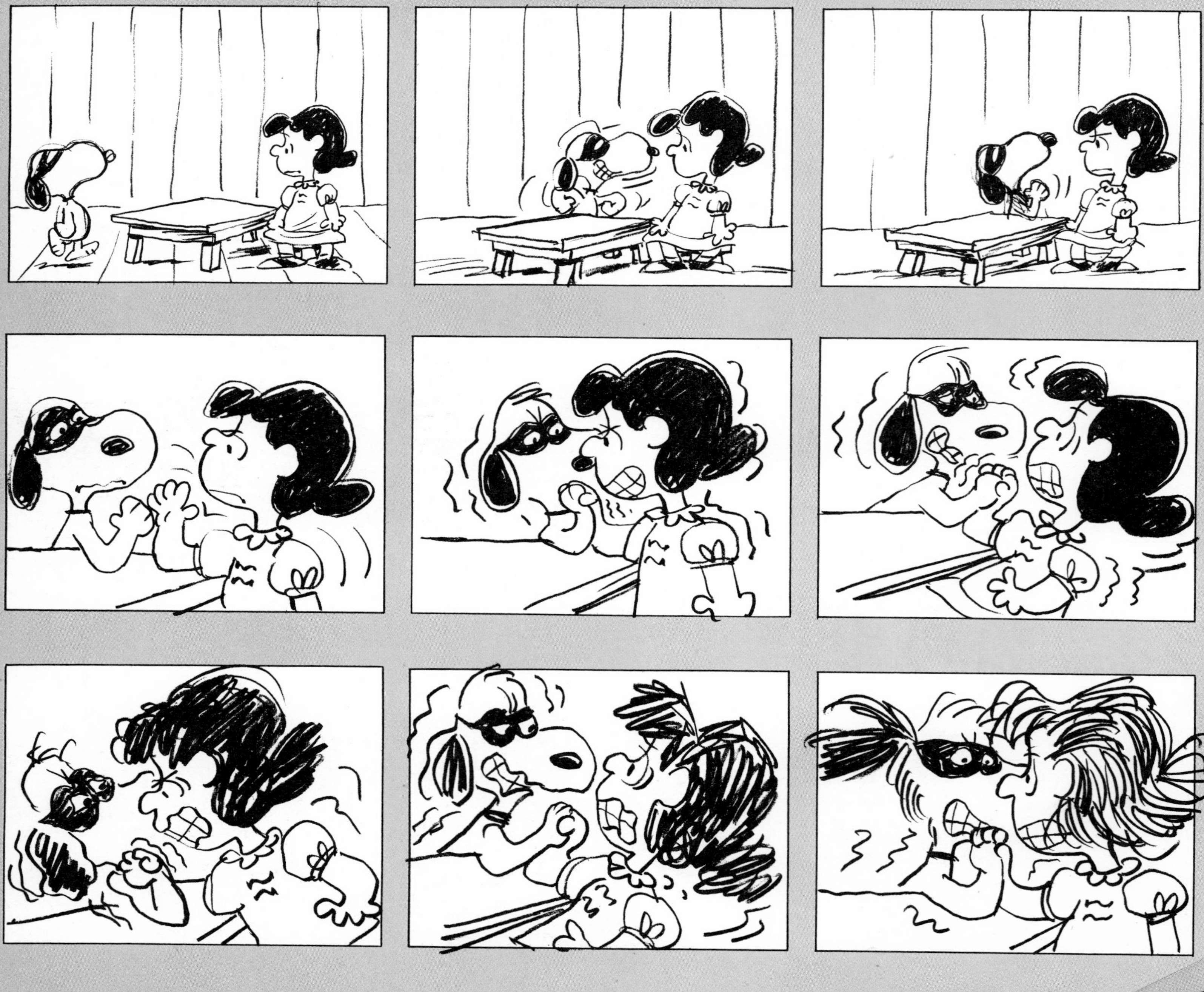

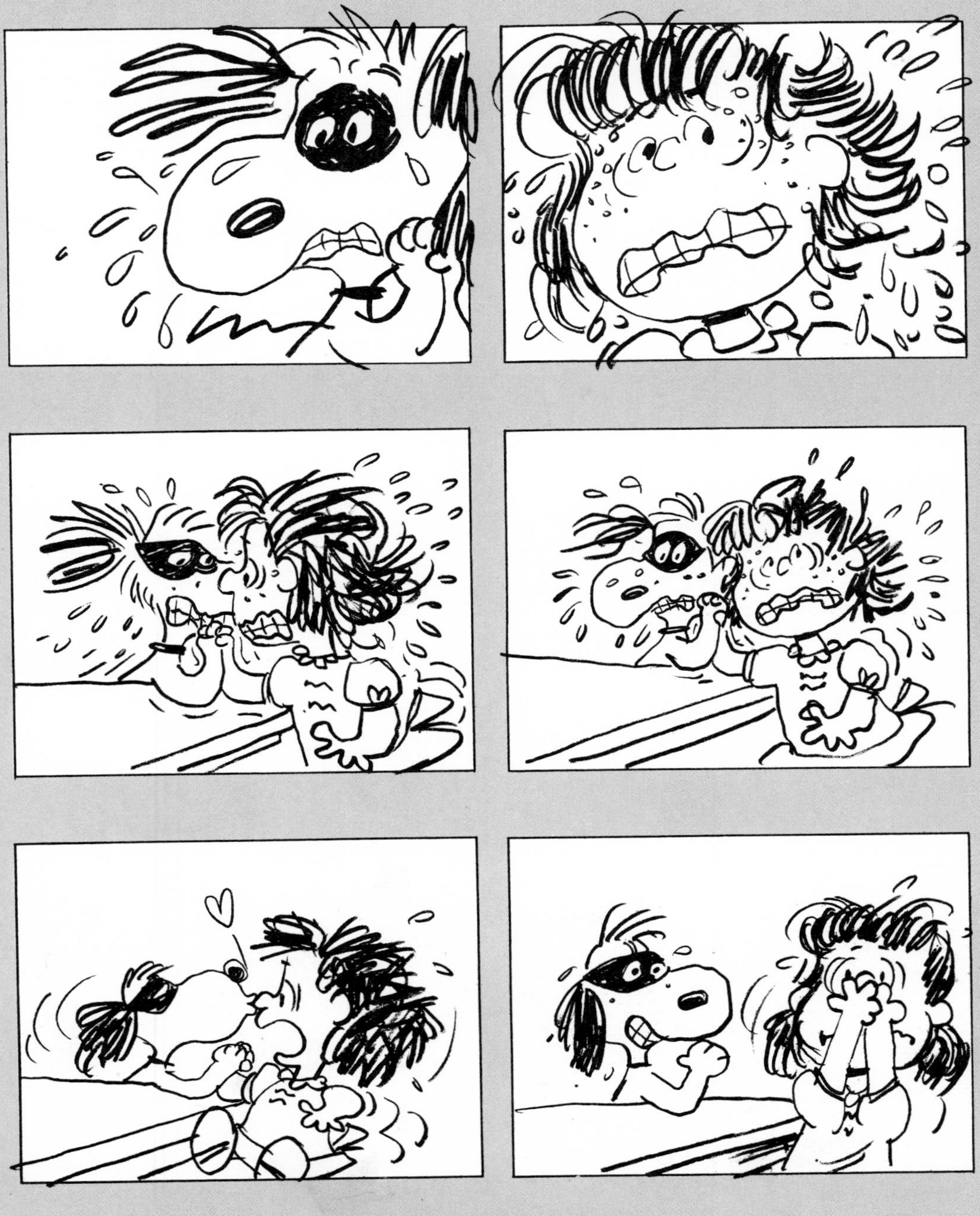

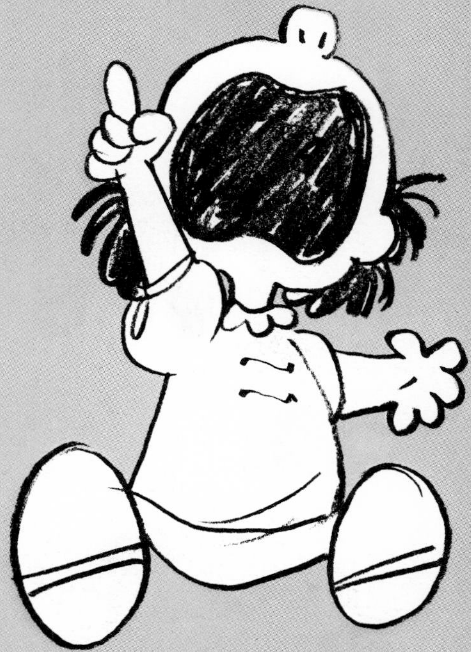

I WAS ROBBED. I'VE BEEN
KISSED BY DOG LIPS! ARGHH!

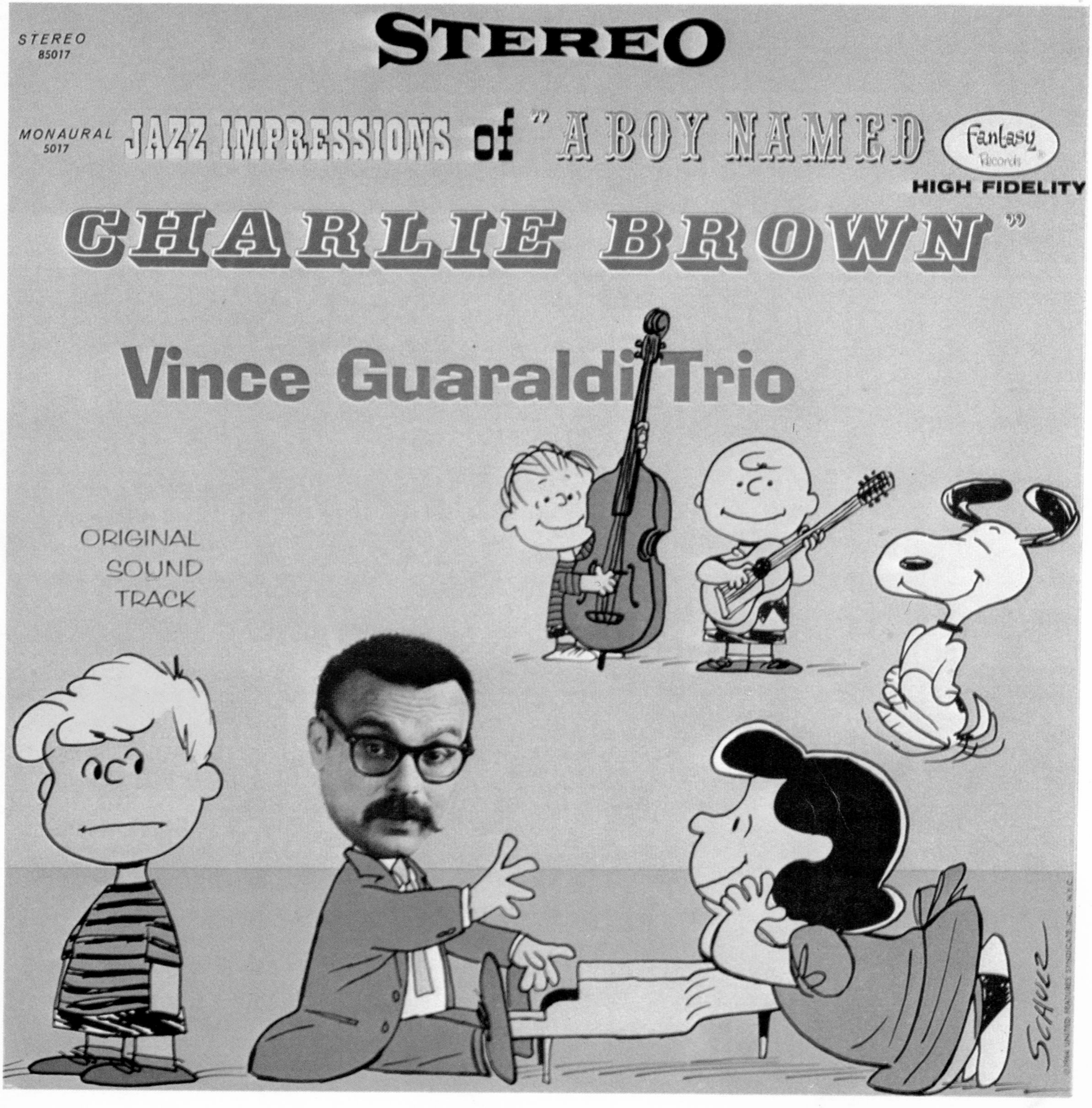
STEREO
85017
STEREO
MONAURAL
5017
JAZZ IMPRESSIONS of "A BOY NAMED
Fantasy
Records
HIGH FIDELITY
CHARLIE BROWN"
Vince Guaraldi Trio
ORIGINAL
SOUND
TRACK
SCHULZ

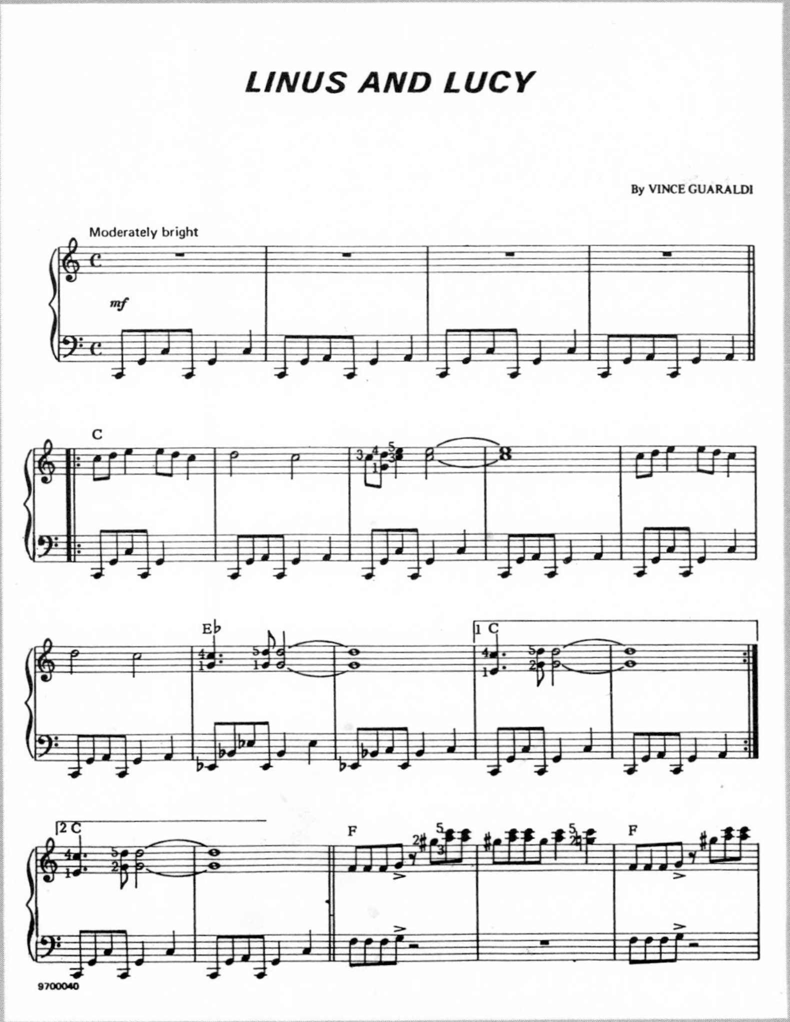
LINUS AND LUCY
By VINCE GUARALDI
Moderately bright
mf
C
E♭
1 C
2 C
F
F
9700040

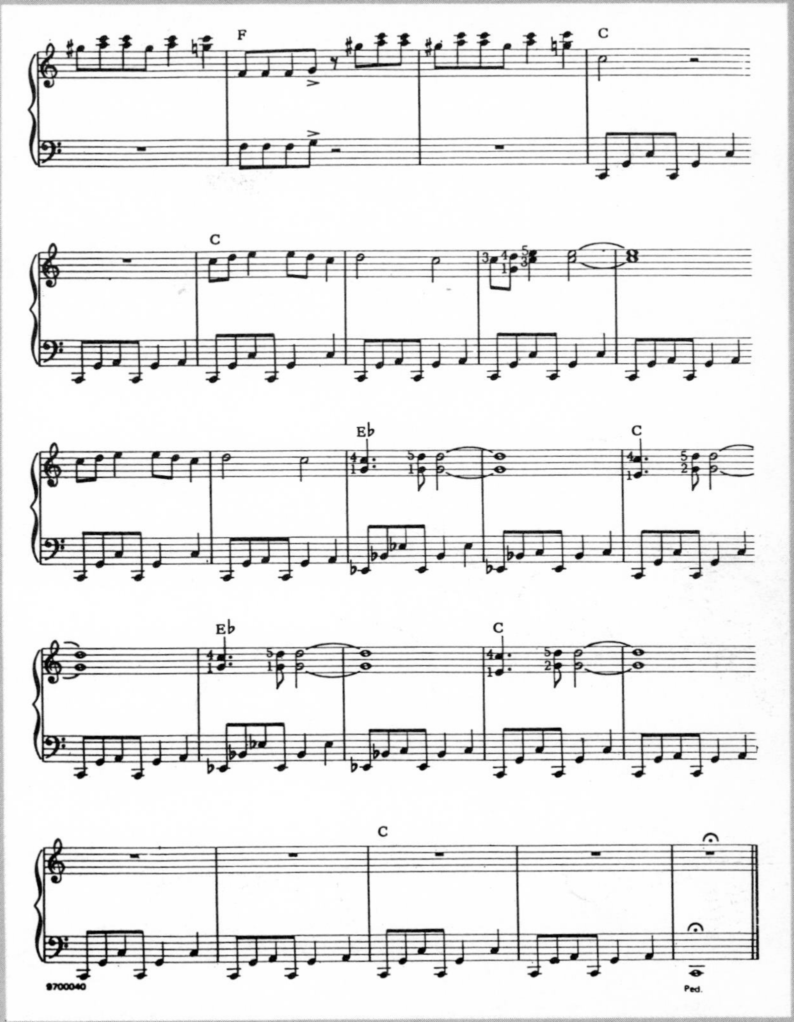
F
C
C
E♭
C
E♭
C
C
9700040
Ped.

While Linus and Lucy have not really been major "stars" in most of the TV shows, their influence on the music for all the shows was crucial. We wanted to get away from the usual "cartoon music," so we asked a San Francisco composer-musician to develop a jazz-oriented score for *A Charlie Brown Christmas*. A few weeks later the composer called me and said he wanted to play a song over the phone for me. He was very excited. As soon as I heard it, I realized why. The song was just what we were looking for. It was called "Linus and Lucy" and the composer was the late Vince Guaraldi, who had already won a Grammy for his "Cast Your Fate to the Wind." Vince went on to compose and perform all of the music for our first sixteen TV specials before his untimely death. His musical genius deserves a great deal of the credit for the success of the television specials. I think we have received as much mail requesting his music as anything else.

And then came Peppermint Patty and Marcie

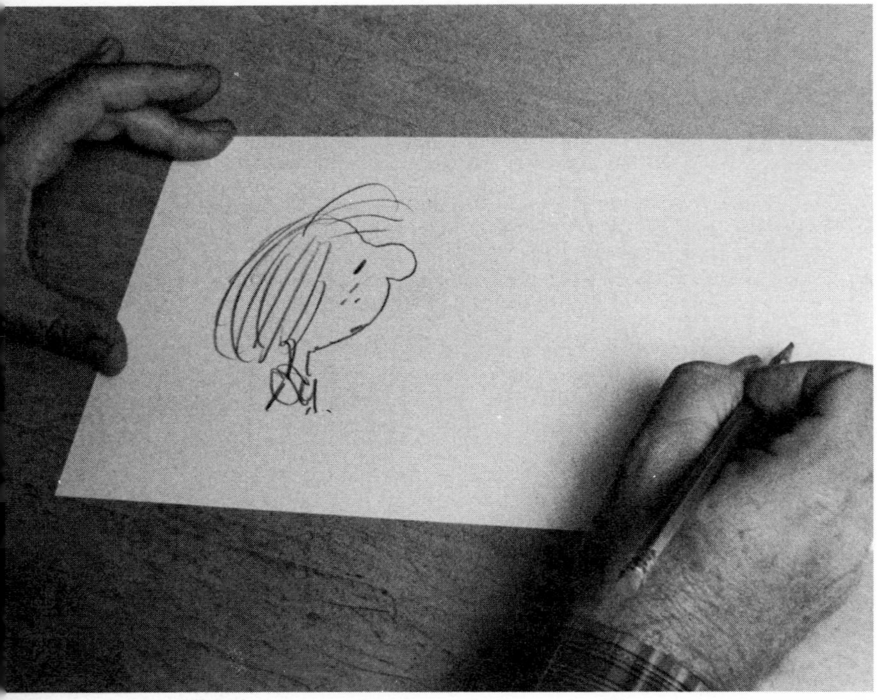

Peppermint Patty joined the *Peanuts* gang in the late 1960's, and she looked then just as she looks today. I always thought that Sparky brought her into the strip as sort of a reflection of the new independent woman. Sparky, though he agrees there might have been some of this involved, believes that she simply was brought into *Peanuts* for entertainment factors. He says, "One day I looked at some candy in a dish, and I thought of how funny the name Peppermint Patty would be. Also, I wanted to develop someone who was from another neighborhood who could challenge Charlie Brown's team, and perhaps challenge Lucy too. I also believe that a comic artist and a comic strip have to *grow*. If you just stand still and play off past successes, you're liable to fail in the long run. Since fifteen years had passed since I had brought Linus and Lucy into the strip — and eight years since Sally had started — I thought I needed a new major character. I'm very glad that I created Peppermint Patty, because she has been an important factor in the growth of the strip, and especially in the various TV shows.

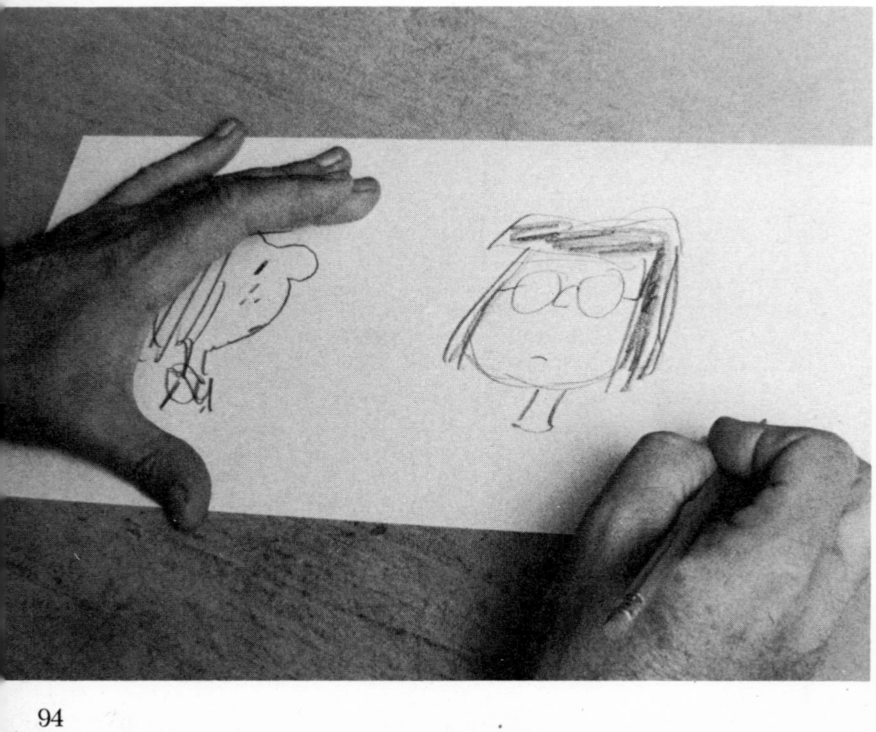

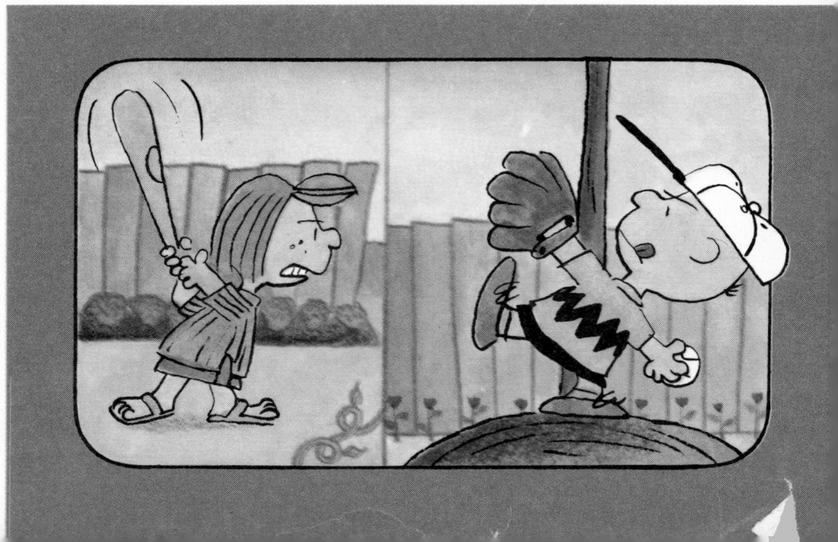

"Then a few years after Peppermint Patty caught on, I decided that she needed a friend, to further develop this 'second neighborhood.' So I created the character of Marcie. At first Marcie didn't do much more than repeat what Peppermint Patty said. But then Marcie started calling Peppermint Patty 'sir,' and this drove her crazy. As the years rolled by, Marcie developed her own personality. She's now become one of my favorite characters, and I especially like the cute voice we have for her on the TV shows."

Kid, I want to ask you something. How come you're always calling me "sir" when I keep asking you not to, huh?
Don't you know how annoying that can be?

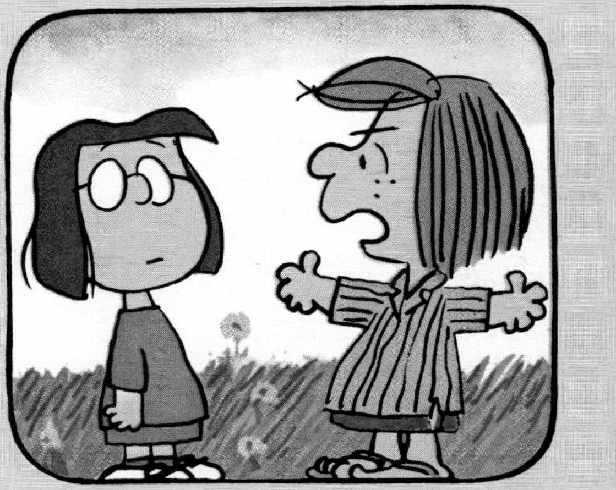

No, ma'am.

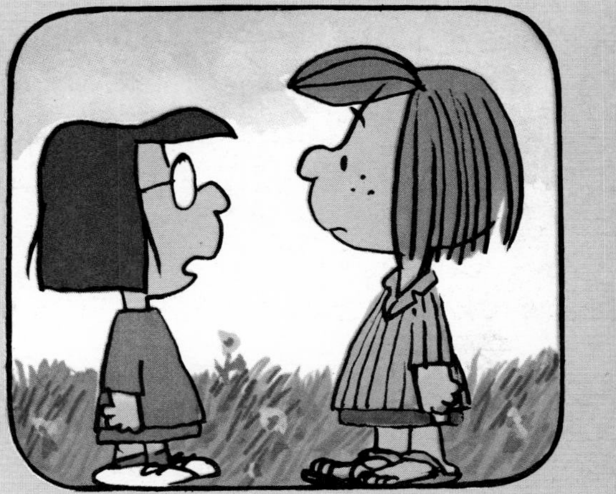

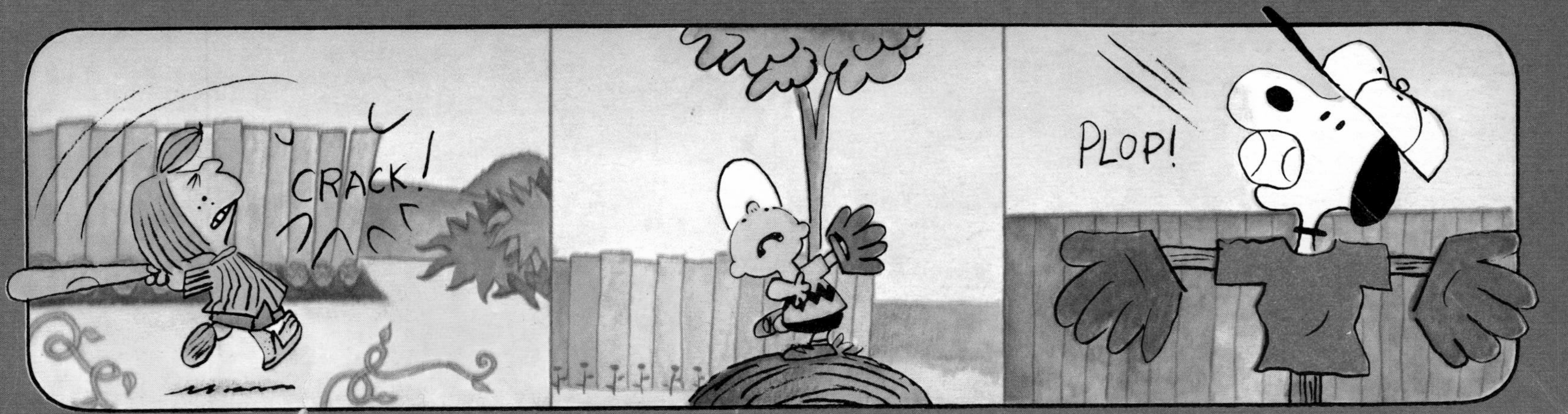
CRACK!
PLOP!

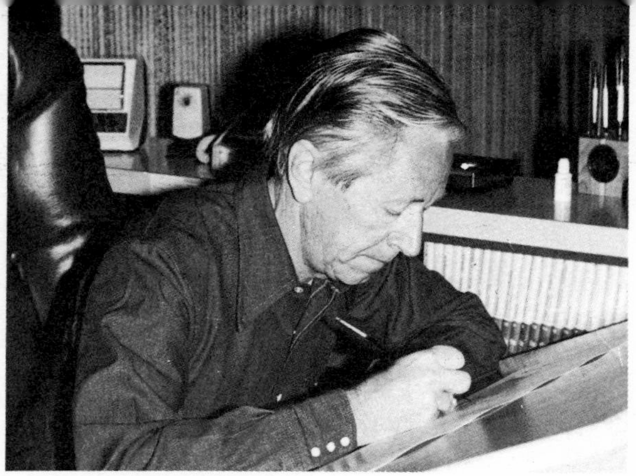

"In fact, probably the longest series of a single idea I ever drew concerned Peppermint Patty and Marcie and skating. It ran five weeks. Upon looking back at these strips, I was so pleased with the humor involved that I decided to make this story the basis of our newest TV show, *She's a Winner, Charlie Brown*, which will debut in 1980."

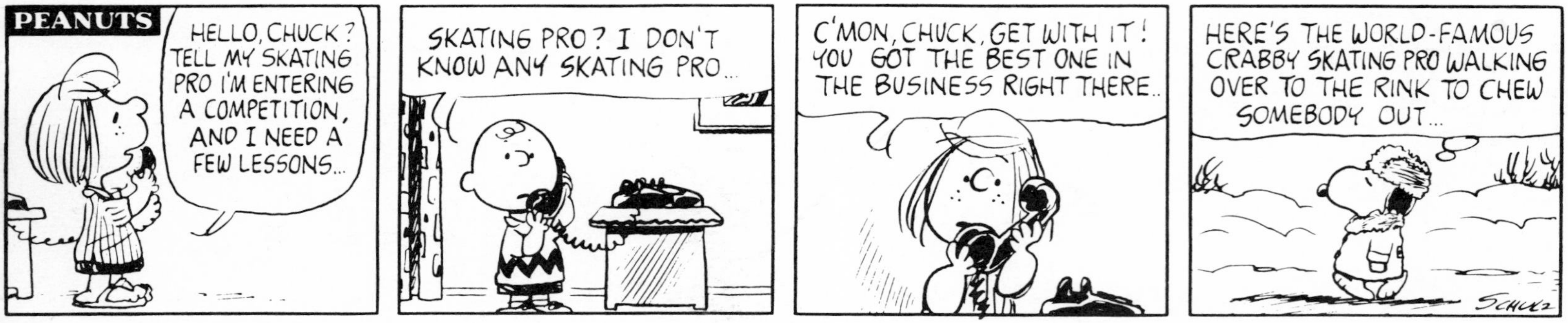
PEANUTS
HELLO, CHUCK? TELL MY SKATING PRO I'M ENTERING A COMPETITION, AND I NEED A FEW LESSONS...
SKATING PRO? I DON'T KNOW ANY SKATING PRO...
C'MON, CHUCK, GET WITH IT! YOU GOT THE BEST ONE IN THE BUSINESS RIGHT THERE..
HERE'S THE WORLD-FAMOUS CRABBY SKATING PRO WALKING OVER TO THE RINK TO CHEW SOMEBODY OUT...
SCHULZ

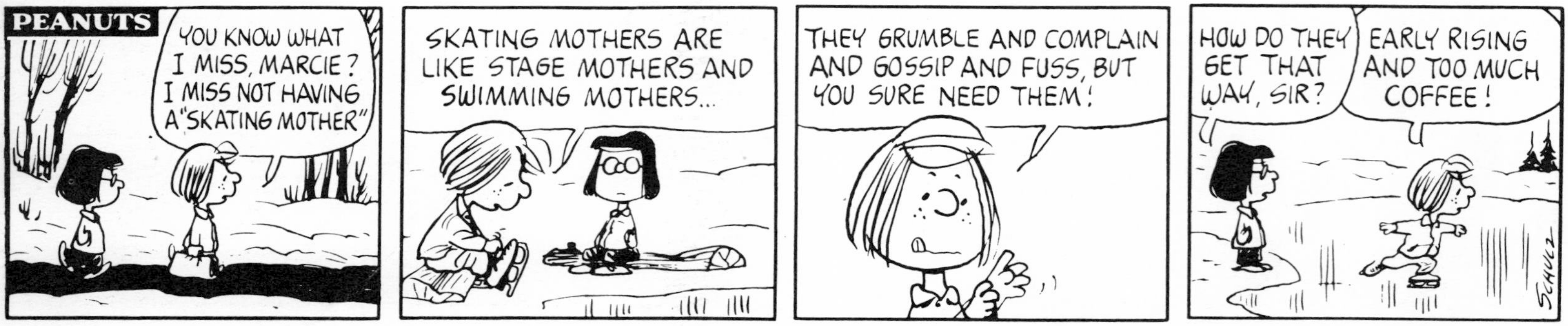
PEANUTS
YOU KNOW WHAT I MISS, MARCIE? I MISS NOT HAVING A "SKATING MOTHER"
SKATING MOTHERS ARE LIKE STAGE MOTHERS AND SWIMMING MOTHERS...
THEY GRUMBLE AND COMPLAIN AND GOSSIP AND FUSS, BUT YOU SURE NEED THEM!
HOW DO THEY GET THAT WAY, SIR?
EARLY RISING AND TOO MUCH COFFEE!
SCHULZ

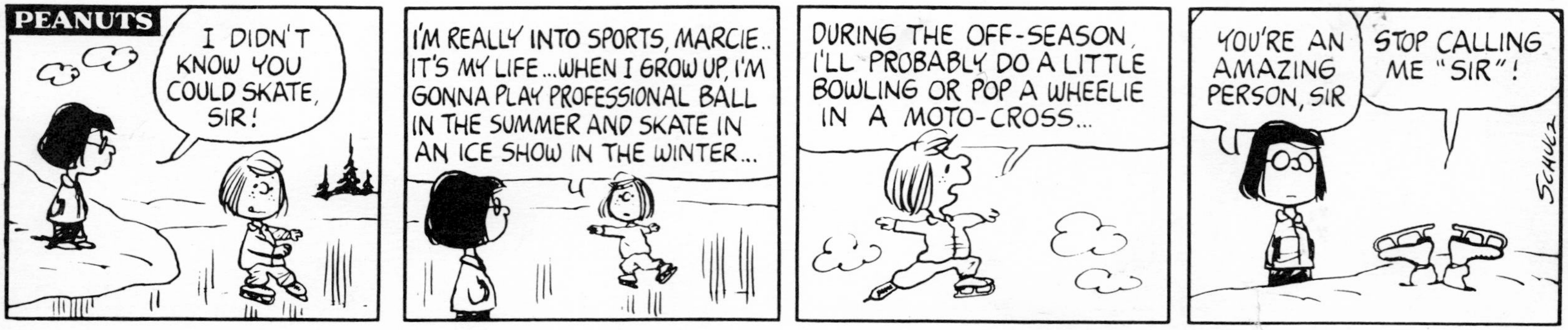
PEANUTS
I DIDN'T KNOW YOU COULD SKATE, SIR!
I'M REALLY INTO SPORTS, MARCIE.. IT'S MY LIFE...WHEN I GROW UP, I'M GONNA PLAY PROFESSIONAL BALL IN THE SUMMER AND SKATE IN AN ICE SHOW IN THE WINTER...
DURING THE OFF-SEASON, I'LL PROBABLY DO A LITTLE BOWLING OR POP A WHEELIE IN A MOTO-CROSS...
YOU'RE AN AMAZING PERSON, SIR
STOP CALLING ME "SIR"!
SCHULZ

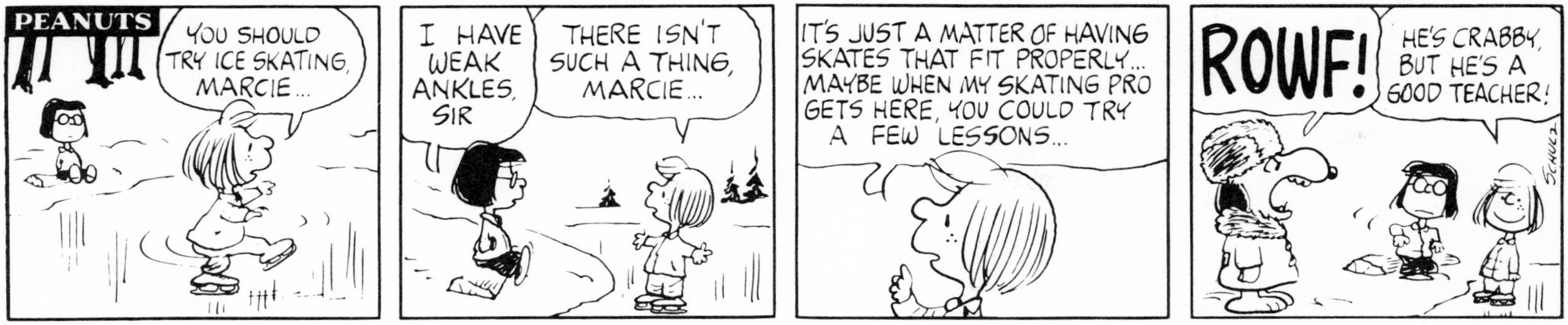
PEANUTS
YOU SHOULD TRY ICE SKATING, MARCIE...
I HAVE WEAK ANKLES, SIR
THERE ISN'T SUCH A THING, MARCIE...
IT'S JUST A MATTER OF HAVING SKATES THAT FIT PROPERLY... MAYBE WHEN MY SKATING PRO GETS HERE, YOU COULD TRY A FEW LESSONS...
ROWF!
HE'S CRABBY, BUT HE'S A GOOD TEACHER!
SCHULZ

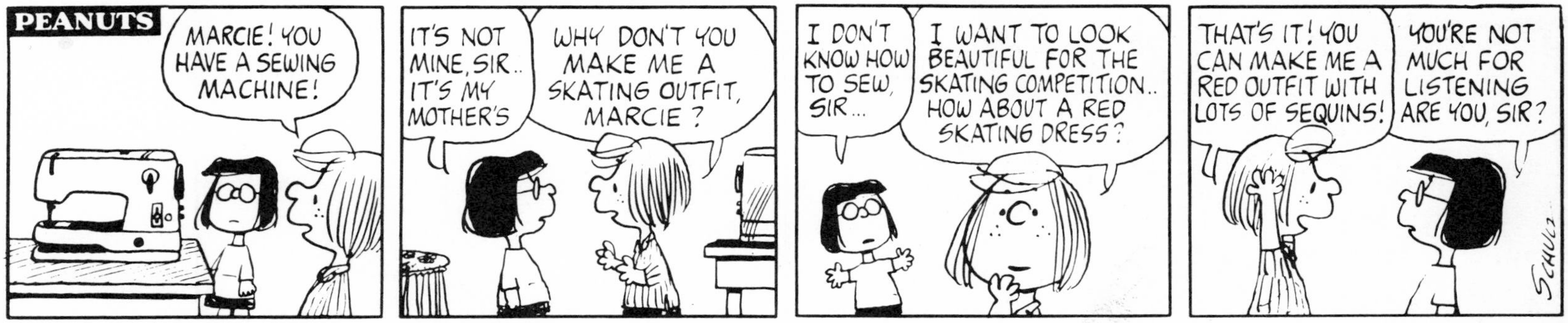
PEANUTS
MARCIE! YOU HAVE A SEWING MACHINE!
IT'S NOT MINE, SIR.. IT'S MY MOTHER'S
WHY DON'T YOU MAKE ME A SKATING OUTFIT, MARCIE ?
I DON'T KNOW HOW TO SEW, SIR...
I WANT TO LOOK BEAUTIFUL FOR THE SKATING COMPETITION.. HOW ABOUT A RED SKATING DRESS?
THAT'S IT! YOU CAN MAKE ME A RED OUTFIT WITH LOTS OF SEQUINS!
YOU'RE NOT MUCH FOR LISTENING ARE YOU, SIR?
SCHULZ

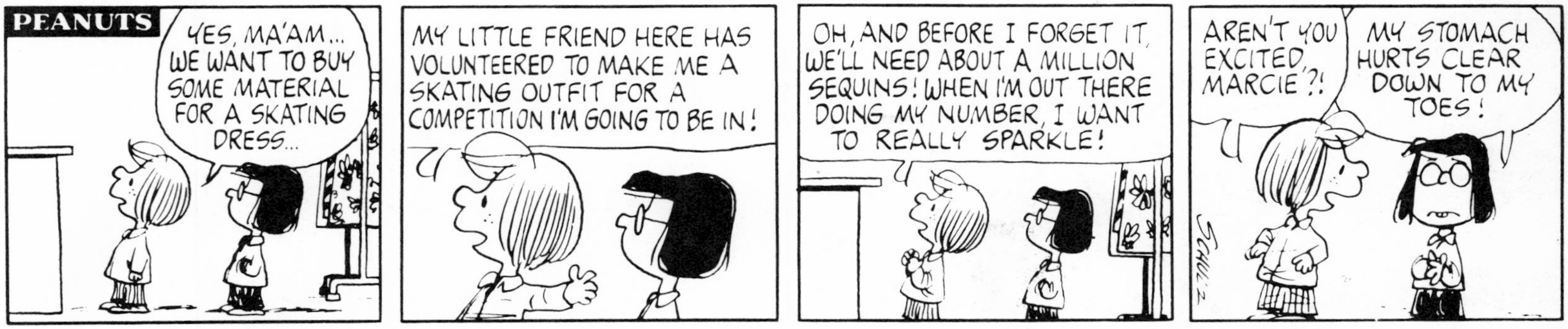
PEANUTS
YES, MA'AM... WE WANT TO BUY SOME MATERIAL FOR A SKATING DRESS...
MY LITTLE FRIEND HERE HAS VOLUNTEERED TO MAKE ME A SKATING OUTFIT FOR A COMPETITION I'M GOING TO BE IN!
OH, AND BEFORE I FORGET IT, WE'LL NEED ABOUT A MILLION SEQUINS! WHEN I'M OUT THERE DOING MY NUMBER, I WANT TO REALLY SPARKLE!
AREN'T YOU EXCITED, MARCIE?!
MY STOMACH HURTS CLEAR DOWN TO MY TOES!
SCHULZ

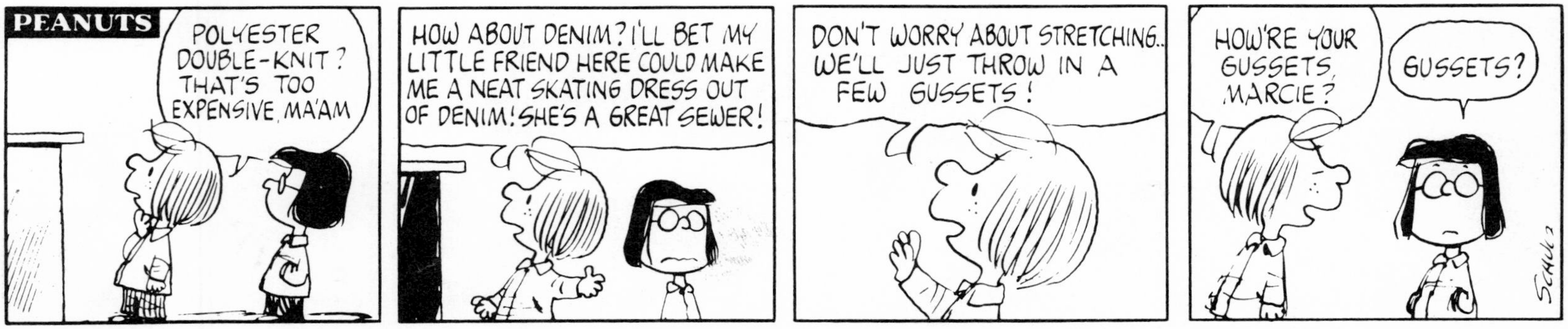
PEANUTS
POLYESTER DOUBLE-KNIT? THAT'S TOO EXPENSIVE, MA'AM
HOW ABOUT DENIM? I'LL BET MY LITTLE FRIEND HERE COULD MAKE ME A NEAT SKATING DRESS OUT OF DENIM! SHE'S A GREAT SEWER!
DON'T WORRY ABOUT STRETCHING.. WE'LL JUST THROW IN A FEW GUSSETS!
HOW'RE YOUR GUSSETS, MARCIE?
GUSSETS?
SCHULZ

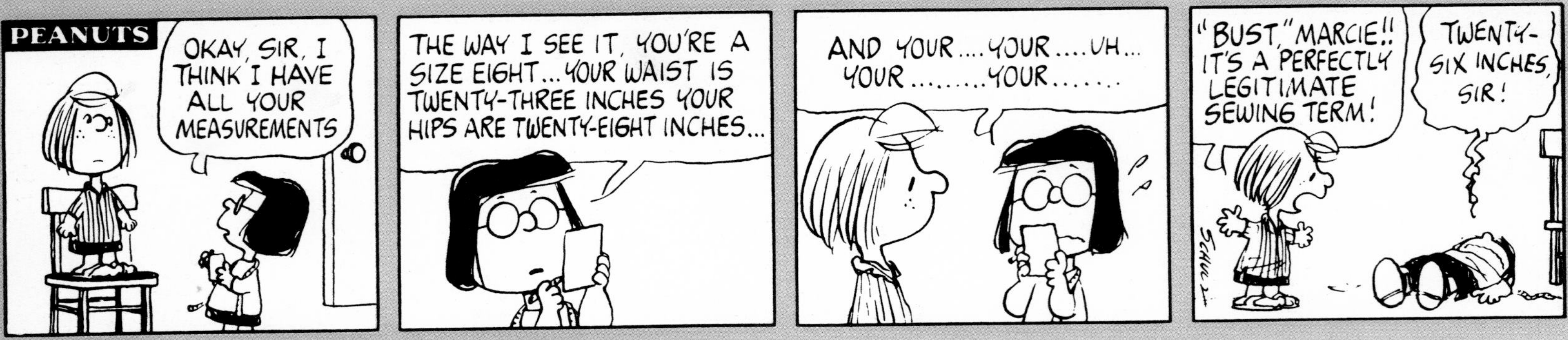
PEANUTS
OKAY, SIR, I THINK I HAVE ALL YOUR MEASUREMENTS
THE WAY I SEE IT, YOU'RE A SIZE EIGHT... YOUR WAIST IS TWENTY-THREE INCHES YOUR HIPS ARE TWENTY-EIGHT INCHES...
AND YOUR.... YOUR.... UH... YOUR........ YOUR......
"BUST," MARCIE!! IT'S A PERFECTLY LEGITIMATE SEWING TERM!
TWENTY-SIX INCHES, SIR!
SCHULZ

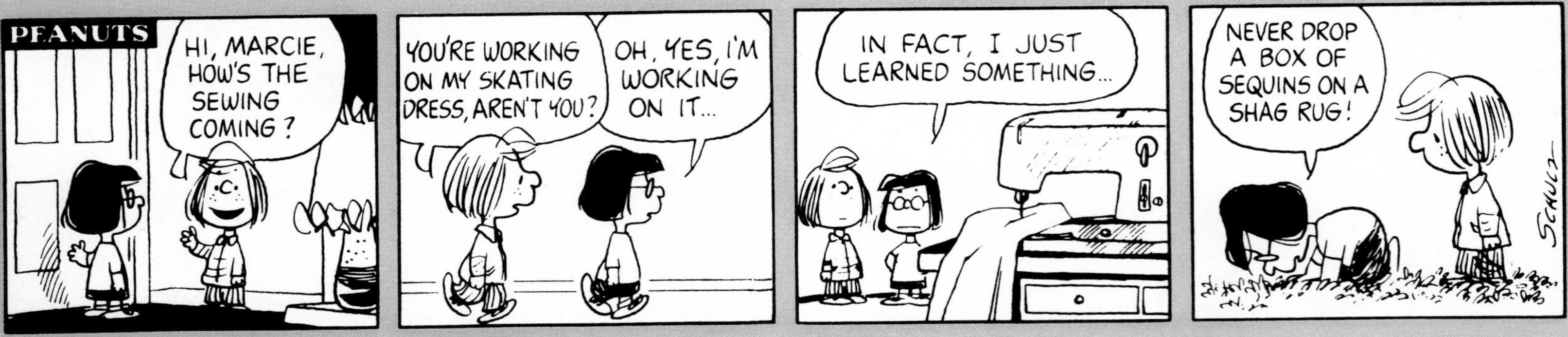
PEANUTS
HI, MARCIE, HOW'S THE SEWING COMING?
YOU'RE WORKING ON MY SKATING DRESS, AREN'T YOU?
OH, YES, I'M WORKING ON IT...
IN FACT, I JUST LEARNED SOMETHING...
NEVER DROP A BOX OF SEQUINS ON A SHAG RUG!
SCHULZ

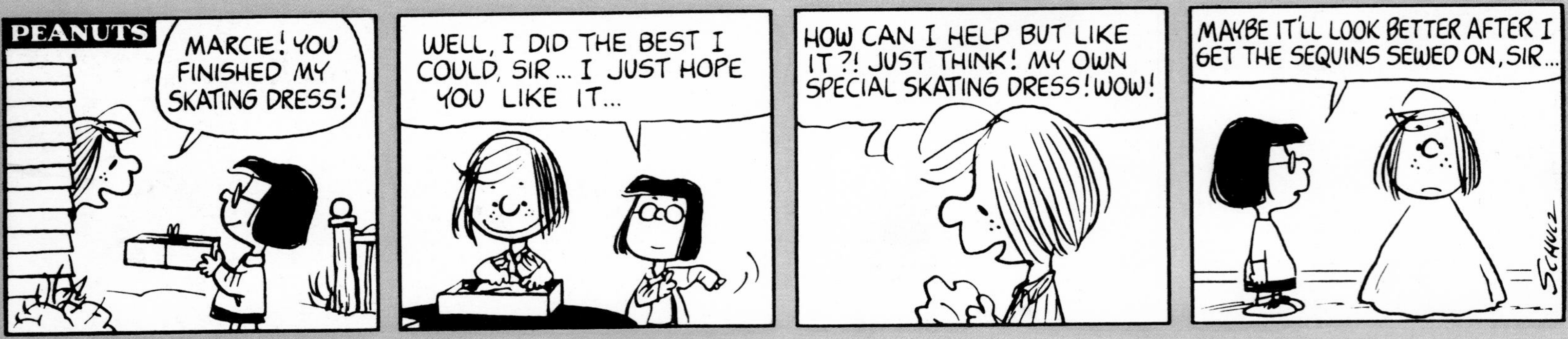
PEANUTS
MARCIE! YOU FINISHED MY SKATING DRESS!
WELL, I DID THE BEST I COULD, SIR... I JUST HOPE YOU LIKE IT...
HOW CAN I HELP BUT LIKE IT?! JUST THINK! MY OWN SPECIAL SKATING DRESS! WOW!
MAYBE IT'LL LOOK BETTER AFTER I GET THE SEQUINS SEWED ON, SIR...
SCHULZ

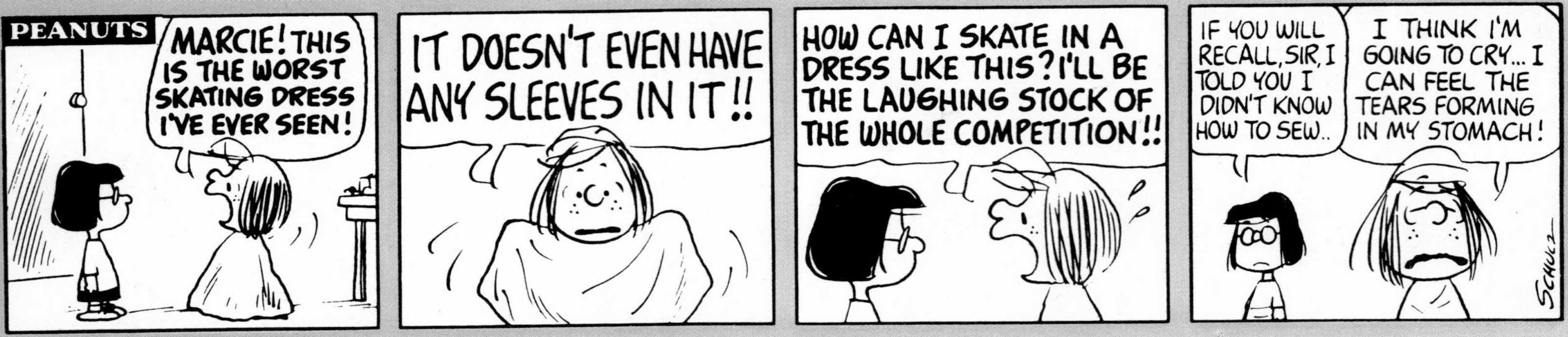
PEANUTS
MARCIE! THIS IS THE WORST SKATING DRESS I'VE EVER SEEN!
IT DOESN'T EVEN HAVE ANY SLEEVES IN IT!!
HOW CAN I SKATE IN A DRESS LIKE THIS? I'LL BE THE LAUGHING STOCK OF THE WHOLE COMPETITION!!
IF YOU WILL RECALL, SIR, I TOLD YOU I DIDN'T KNOW HOW TO SEW..
I THINK I'M GOING TO CRY... I CAN FEEL THE TEARS FORMING IN MY STOMACH!
SCHULZ

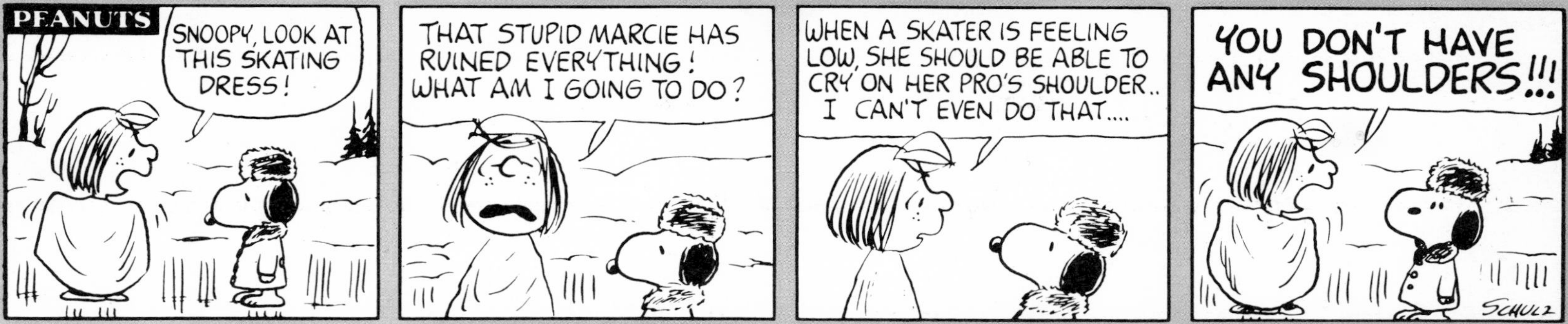
PEANUTS
SNOOPY, LOOK AT THIS SKATING DRESS!
THAT STUPID MARCIE HAS RUINED EVERYTHING! WHAT AM I GOING TO DO?
WHEN A SKATER IS FEELING LOW, SHE SHOULD BE ABLE TO CRY ON HER PRO'S SHOULDER.. I CAN'T EVEN DO THAT....
YOU DON'T HAVE ANY SHOULDERS!!!
SCHULZ

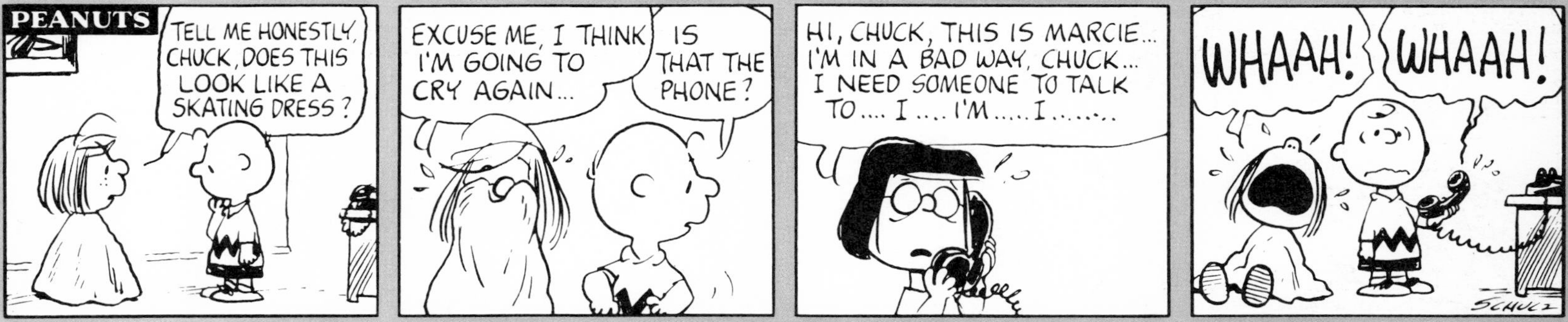
PEANUTS
TELL ME HONESTLY, CHUCK, DOES THIS LOOK LIKE A SKATING DRESS?
EXCUSE ME, I THINK I'M GOING TO CRY AGAIN...
IS THAT THE PHONE?
HI, CHUCK, THIS IS MARCIE... I'M IN A BAD WAY, CHUCK... I NEED SOMEONE TO TALK TO.... I.... I'M..... I.......
WHAAAH!
WHAAAH!
SCHULZ

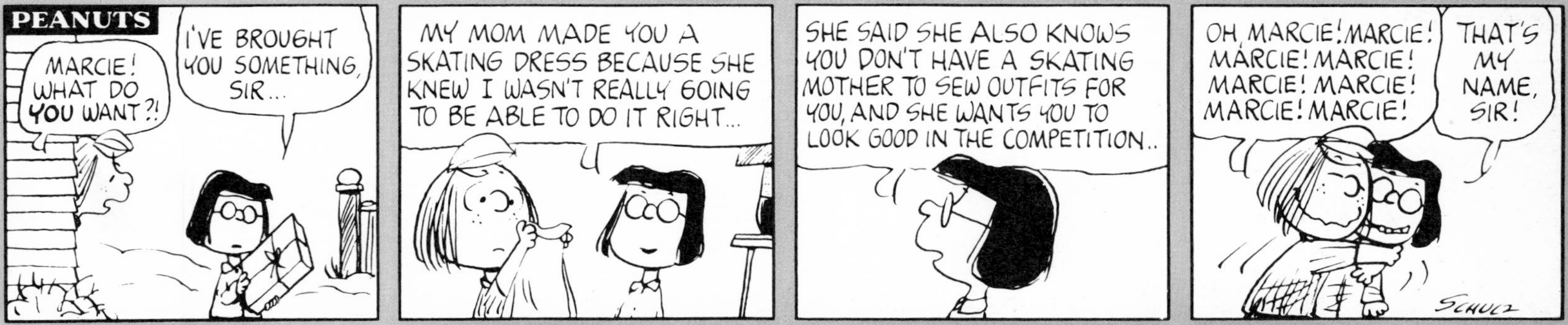
PEANUTS
MARCIE! WHAT DO YOU WANT?!
I'VE BROUGHT YOU SOMETHING, SIR...
MY MOM MADE YOU A SKATING DRESS BECAUSE SHE KNEW I WASN'T REALLY GOING TO BE ABLE TO DO IT RIGHT...
SHE SAID SHE ALSO KNOWS YOU DON'T HAVE A SKATING MOTHER TO SEW OUTFITS FOR YOU, AND SHE WANTS YOU TO LOOK GOOD IN THE COMPETITION..
OH, MARCIE! MARCIE! MARCIE! MARCIE! MARCIE! MARCIE! MARCIE! MARCIE!
THAT'S MY NAME, SIR!
SCHULZ

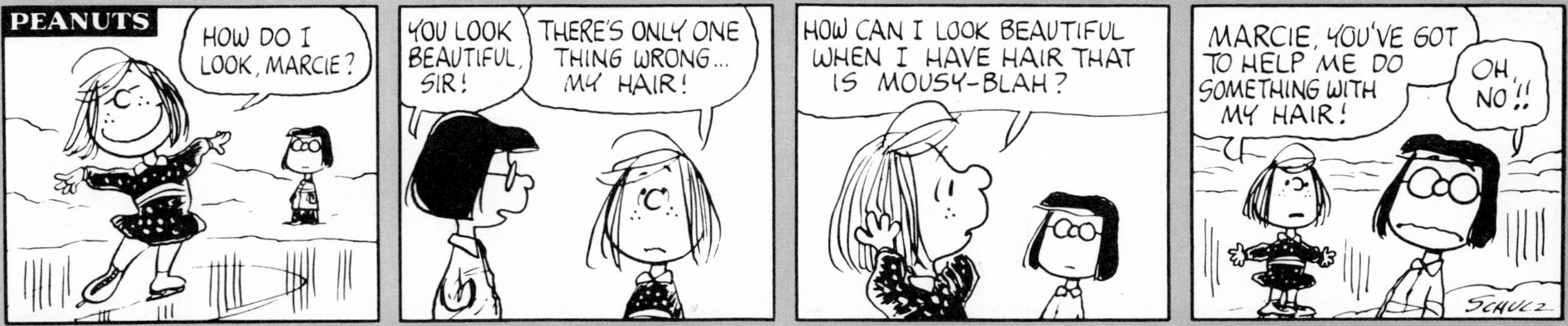
PEANUTS
HOW DO I LOOK, MARCIE?
YOU LOOK BEAUTIFUL, SIR!
THERE'S ONLY ONE THING WRONG... MY HAIR!
HOW CAN I LOOK BEAUTIFUL WHEN I HAVE HAIR THAT IS MOUSY-BLAH?
MARCIE, YOU'VE GOT TO HELP ME DO SOMETHING WITH MY HAIR!
OH, NO!!
SCHULZ

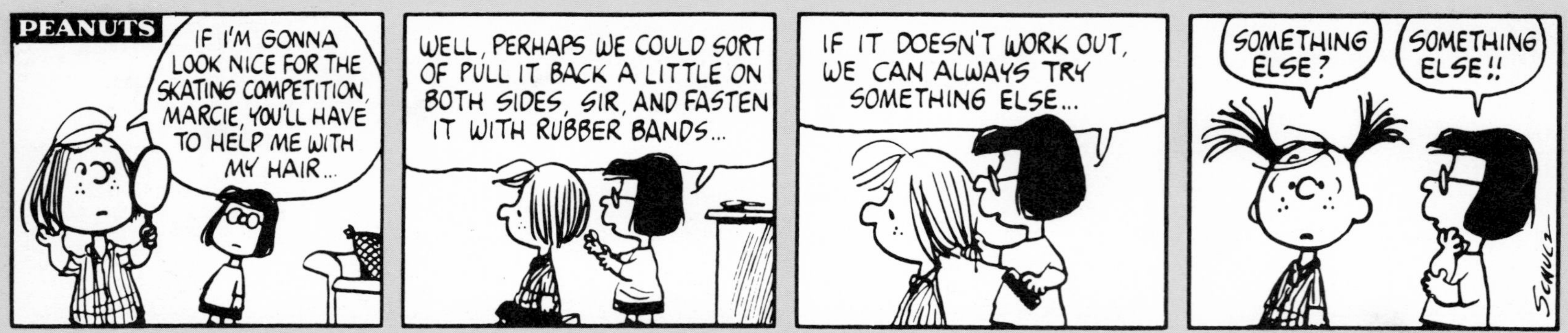
PEANUTS
IF I'M GONNA LOOK NICE FOR THE SKATING COMPETITION, MARCIE, YOU'LL HAVE TO HELP ME WITH MY HAIR...
WELL, PERHAPS WE COULD SORT OF PULL IT BACK A LITTLE ON BOTH SIDES, SIR, AND FASTEN IT WITH RUBBER BANDS...
IF IT DOESN'T WORK OUT, WE CAN ALWAYS TRY SOMETHING ELSE...
SOMETHING ELSE?
SOMETHING ELSE!!

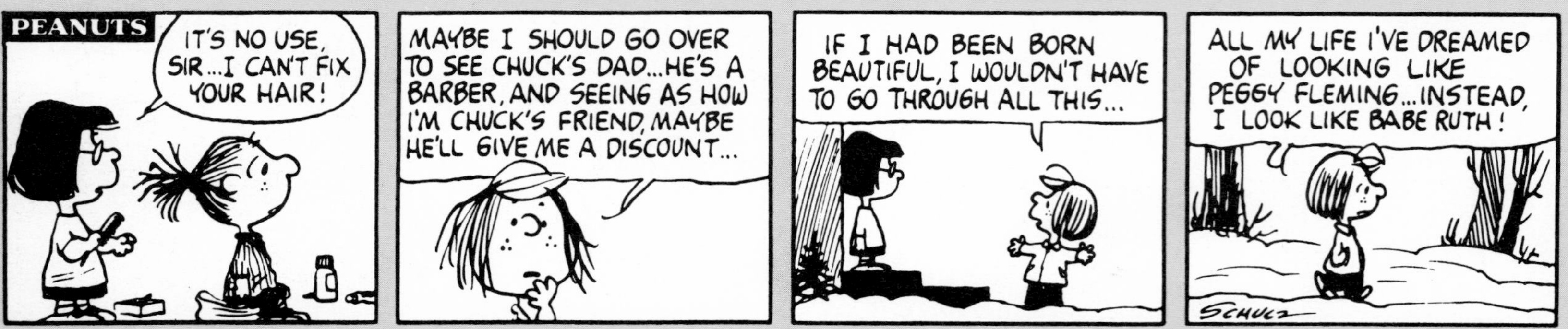
PEANUTS
IT'S NO USE, SIR...I CAN'T FIX YOUR HAIR!
MAYBE I SHOULD GO OVER TO SEE CHUCK'S DAD...HE'S A BARBER, AND SEEING AS HOW I'M CHUCK'S FRIEND, MAYBE HE'LL GIVE ME A DISCOUNT...
IF I HAD BEEN BORN BEAUTIFUL, I WOULDN'T HAVE TO GO THROUGH ALL THIS...
ALL MY LIFE I'VE DREAMED OF LOOKING LIKE PEGGY FLEMING...INSTEAD, I LOOK LIKE BABE RUTH!

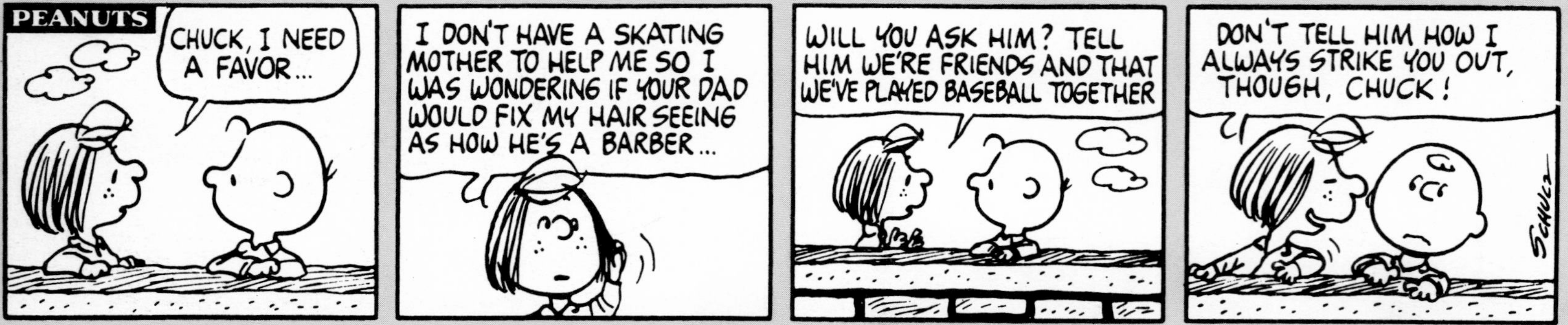
PEANUTS
CHUCK, I NEED A FAVOR...
I DON'T HAVE A SKATING MOTHER TO HELP ME SO I WAS WONDERING IF YOUR DAD WOULD FIX MY HAIR SEEING AS HOW HE'S A BARBER...
WILL YOU ASK HIM? TELL HIM WE'RE FRIENDS AND THAT WE'VE PLAYED BASEBALL TOGETHER
DON'T TELL HIM HOW I ALWAYS STRIKE YOU OUT, THOUGH, CHUCK!

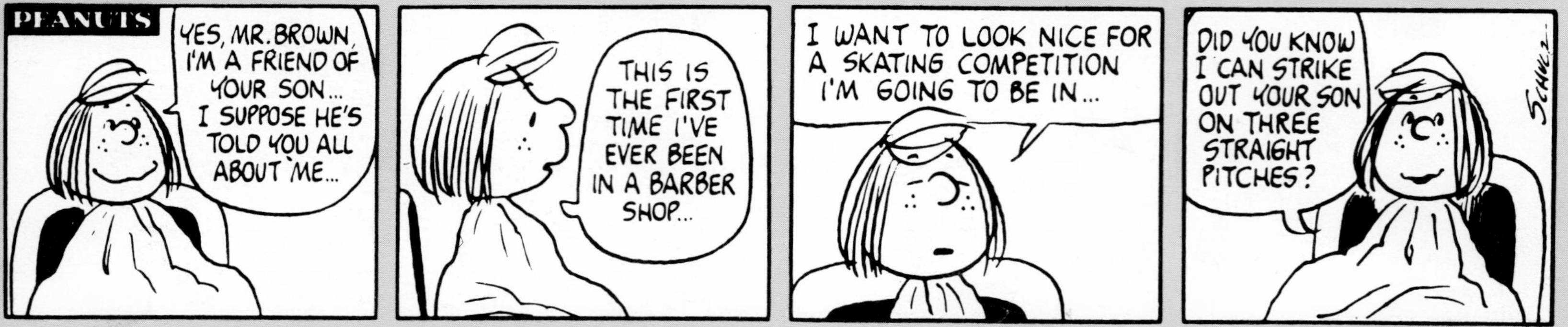
PEANUTS
YES, MR. BROWN, I'M A FRIEND OF YOUR SON... I SUPPOSE HE'S TOLD YOU ALL ABOUT ME...
THIS IS THE FIRST TIME I'VE EVER BEEN IN A BARBER SHOP...
I WANT TO LOOK NICE FOR A SKATING COMPETITION I'M GOING TO BE IN...
DID YOU KNOW I CAN STRIKE OUT YOUR SON ON THREE STRAIGHT PITCHES?

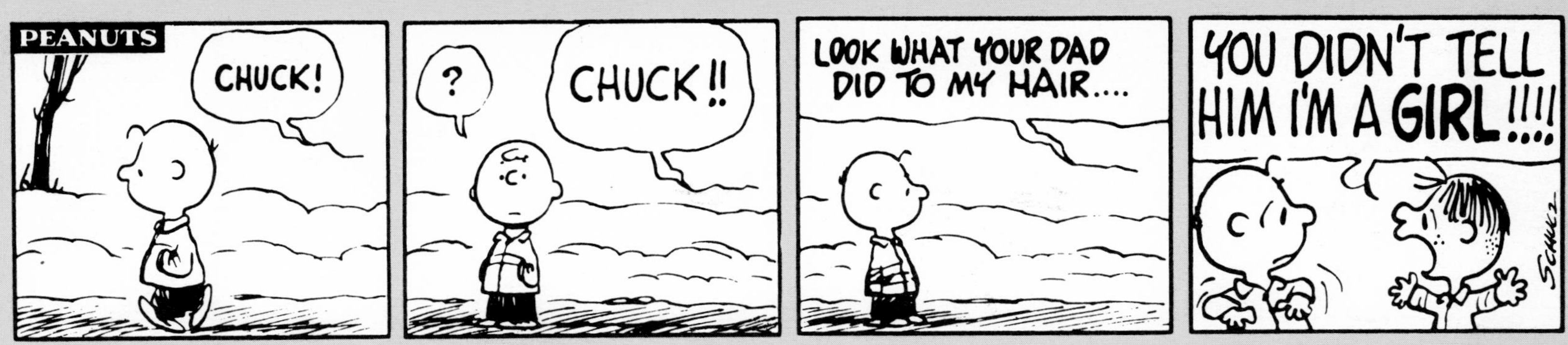
PEANUTS
CHUCK!
?
CHUCK!!
LOOK WHAT YOUR DAD DID TO MY HAIR....
YOU DIDN'T TELL HIM I'M A GIRL!!!!

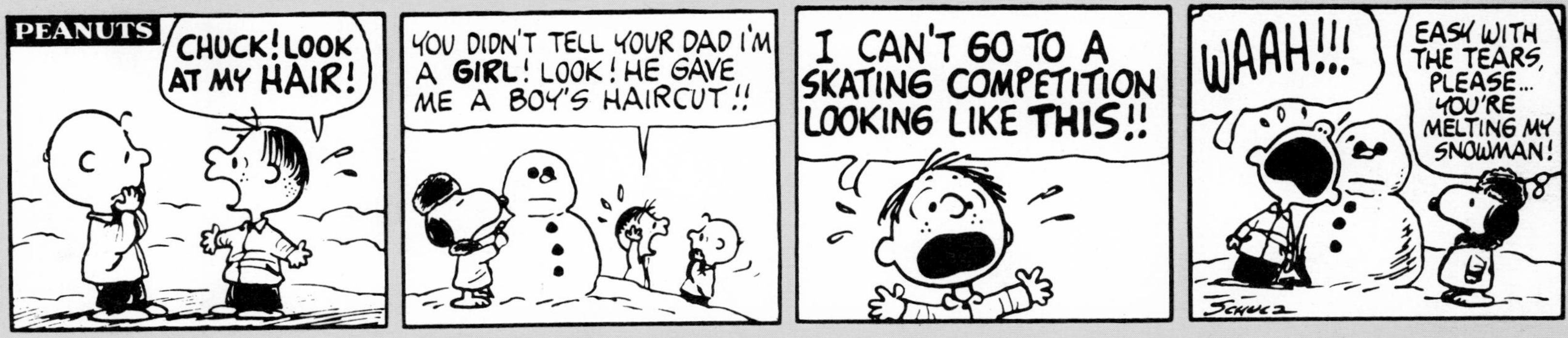
PEANUTS
CHUCK! LOOK AT MY HAIR!
YOU DIDN'T TELL YOUR DAD I'M A GIRL! LOOK! HE GAVE ME A BOY'S HAIRCUT!!
I CAN'T GO TO A SKATING COMPETITION LOOKING LIKE THIS!!
WAAH!!!
EASY WITH THE TEARS, PLEASE... YOU'RE MELTING MY SNOWMAN!

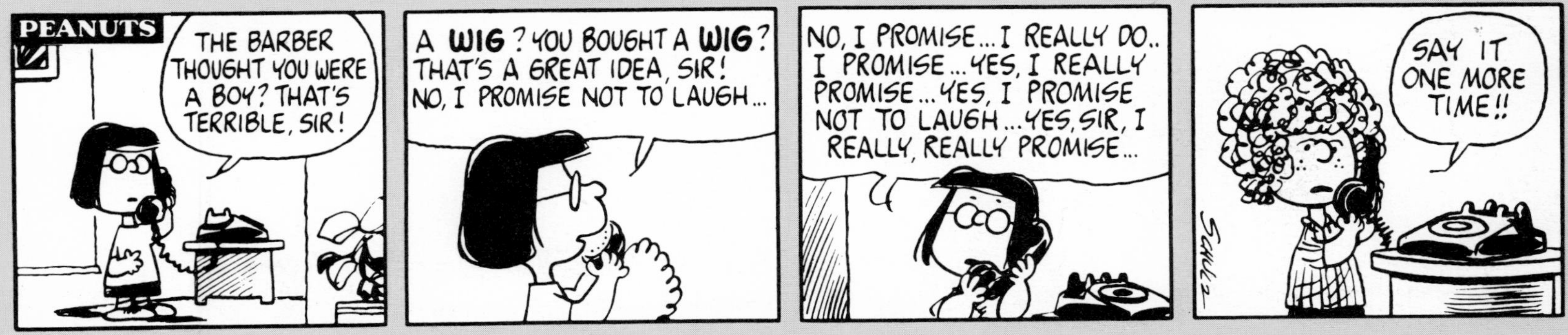
PEANUTS
THE BARBER THOUGHT YOU WERE A BOY? THAT'S TERRIBLE, SIR!
A WIG? YOU BOUGHT A WIG? THAT'S A GREAT IDEA, SIR! NO, I PROMISE NOT TO LAUGH...
NO, I PROMISE...I REALLY DO.. I PROMISE...YES, I REALLY PROMISE...YES, I PROMISE NOT TO LAUGH...YES, SIR, I REALLY, REALLY PROMISE...
SAY IT ONE MORE TIME!!

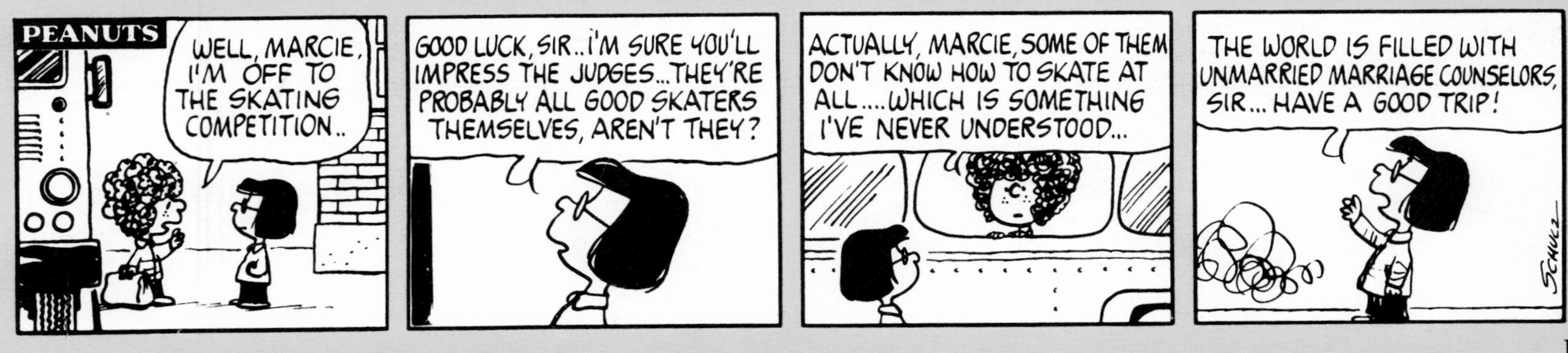
PEANUTS
WELL, MARCIE, I'M OFF TO THE SKATING COMPETITION..
GOOD LUCK, SIR..I'M SURE YOU'LL IMPRESS THE JUDGES...THEY'RE PROBABLY ALL GOOD SKATERS THEMSELVES, AREN'T THEY?
ACTUALLY, MARCIE, SOME OF THEM DON'T KNOW HOW TO SKATE AT ALL....WHICH IS SOMETHING I'VE NEVER UNDERSTOOD...
THE WORLD IS FILLED WITH UNMARRIED MARRIAGE COUNSELORS, SIR... HAVE A GOOD TRIP!

PEANUTS
YES, MA'AM.. I'M HERE FOR THE SKATING COMPETITION...
SKATERS Register HERE!
HOW ABOUT PRACTICE TIME, MA'AM? NOW? GOOD! I'LL PUT MY SKATES ON...
WHAT ARE YOU LOOKING AT, KID?!
YOUR SKATES...I THINK YOU'VE MADE A LITTLE MISTAKE
THIS IS A ROLLER SKATING COMPETITION!
SCHULZ

PEANUTS
I JUST REMEMBERED SOMETHING, SNOOPY...
I STILL OWE YOU FOR MY SKATING LESSONS, DON'T I?
WELL, I DON'T HAVE ANY MONEY, BUT I HAVE SOMETHING ELSE THAT I CAN GIVE YOU...

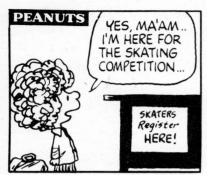

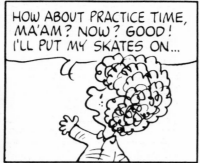

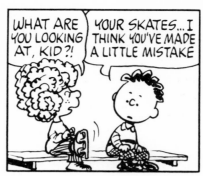

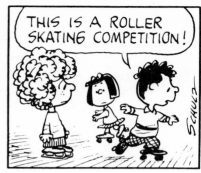

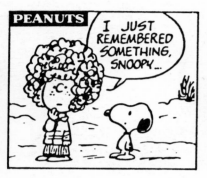

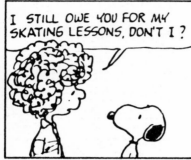

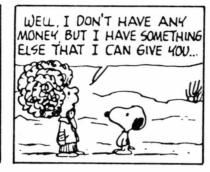

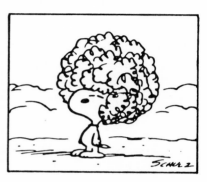

"Where do you get the voices?"

I guess we're asked that question more than any other in relation to the TV specials. For one example, when we started to look for the "voice" of Peppermint Patty, we really didn't know how she should sound. Weeks passed, and we hadn't found the right sound. Then one evening I was having a hamburger with my associate, Walt DeFaria, and with his three children. His oldest daughter, Gai, yelled "PASS THE MUSTARD, PLEASE." I jumped from my chair and yelled "THAT'S IT! THAT'S PEPPERMINT PATTY." And so the husky, gravelly voice became our model. Subsequently, Gai's younger sister Lisa and younger brother Kip also played Peppermint Patty, because they all had the same "sound."

For the past few years, Laura Planting played that role, but she was discovered in a more conventional way: every two years we re-cast the voices by auditioning hundreds of children — usually ages nine to eleven — from various schools located near our northern California office.

I'm always looking and listening for new voices. Recently I was waiting to board a plane at San Francisco Airport. I heard this fantastic voice from a young boy who looked about six or seven years old. I secretly started to follow him around the airport so that I could hear more of his voice. Suddenly his mother looked at me very suspiciously, and then angrily. I hastily presented my business card. "Why are you following my son?" she demanded, ignoring the card. "Look," I started to reply, "I produce the Charlie Brown TV shows and—" She interrupted, "We don't have a TV and I never heard of Charlie Brown. Now, just what's going on here?" "Well, if you'll just call the number on my card there, I'd like to audition your son and see . . ." She really started fuming. "If you don't leave us alone, I'm calling the airport police," she said, and she stormed off with her son. I suppose I picked one of the few mothers in America who had never heard of Charlie Brown.

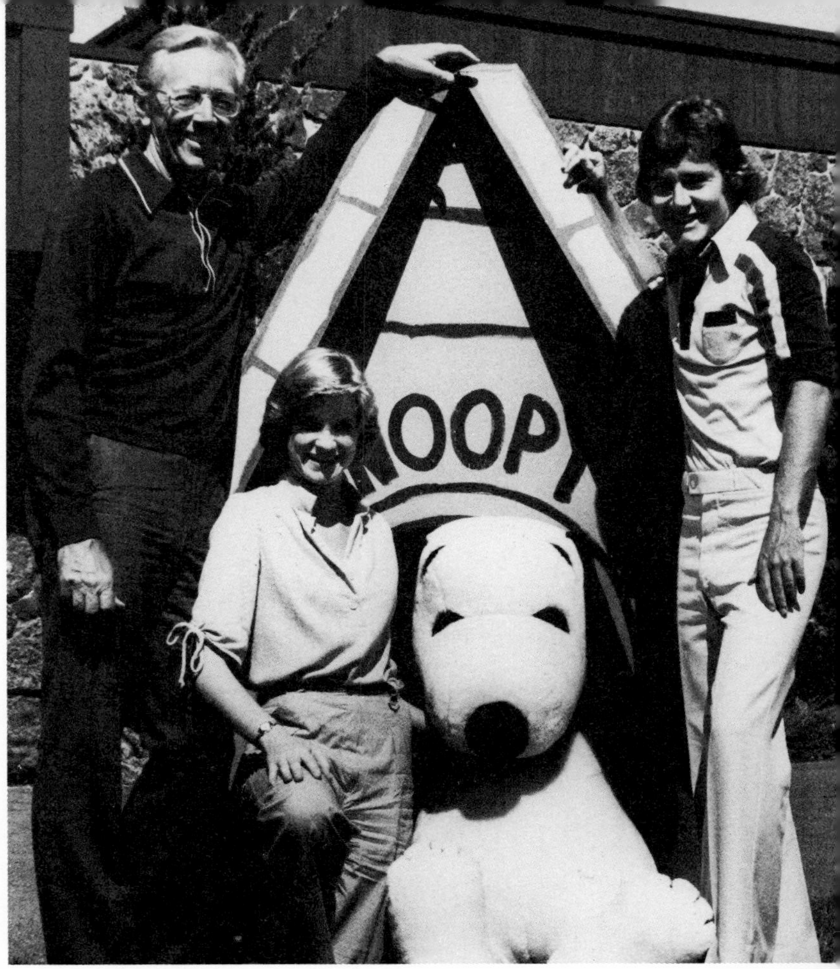
OOP

Fourteen years after we produced the first three Charlie Brown specials we had a reunion of the original Charlie Brown (Peter Robbins, *right*), the Lucy from the *Great Pumpkin* show (Sally Dryer, *center*) and Sparky (*left*).

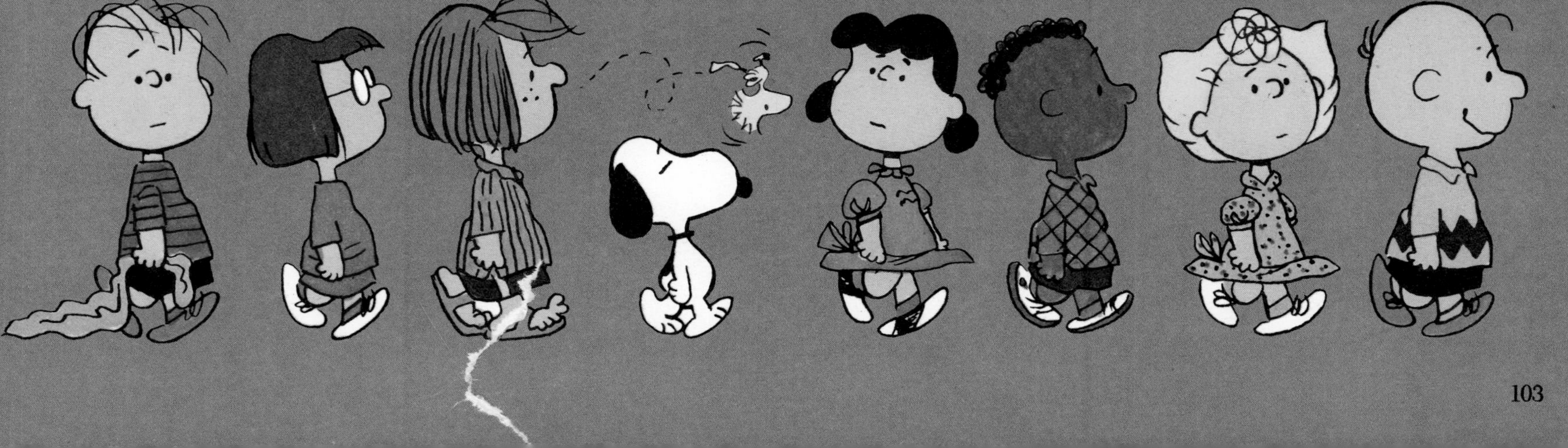

On the previous page we saw Sally "Lucy" Dryer as she looks today. Here she is (*far left*) fourteen years ago during a recording session. Next is Gai DeFaria (Peppermint Patty); Peter Robbins (Charlie Brown); Chris Shea (Linus); and producer-director Bill Melendez, who also plays the voice of "Snoopy" when Snoopy grunts, laughs, or groans.

Our decision in 1965 to use the voices of children was unique and crucial. Up to that time, most animators had used adults pretending to be children. The use of real kids gave us a sound of spontaneity that was essential to the success of the shows. Each actor for Charlie Brown has the difficult task of sounding "blah" but also having good expression — that's a tough combination. Lucy has to be tough but not raucous. Linus needs to combine intelligence with a poetic lilt. In the final selecting process, however, each new cast must emulate the original voices of *A Charlie Brown Christmas*, because that's what the public now expects.

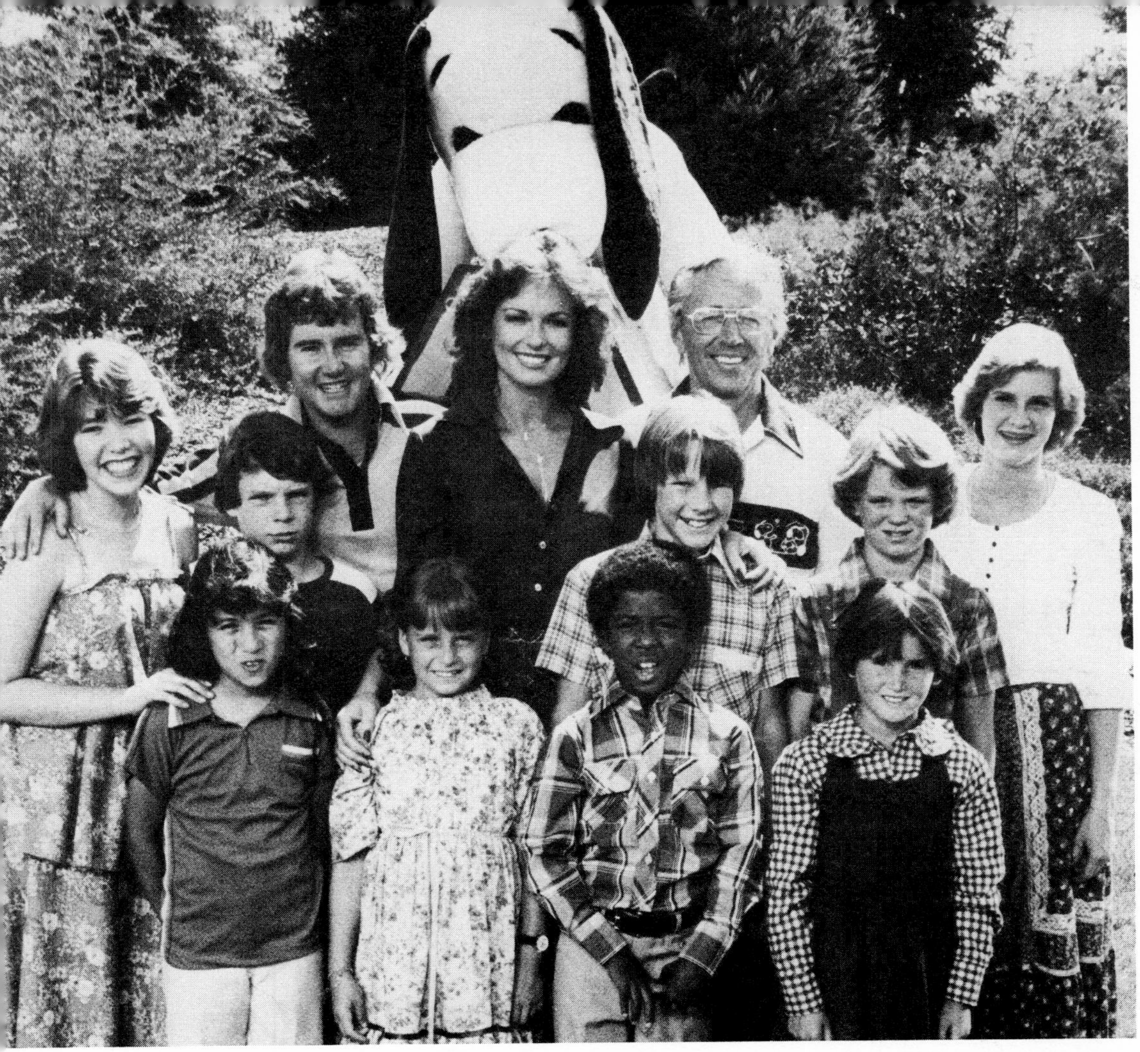

For our special *Happy Birthday, Charlie Brown* we brought our most current cast together with some of the originals. In the back row (*left to right*) are Peter Robbins, host Phyllis George, Sparky, and Sally Dryer. In the front row are Leticia Ortiz (who plays a new character, Dolores); Annalisa Bortolin (Sally); Ronald Hendrix (Franklin); and Casey Carlson (Marcie). In the middle row are Michelle Muller (Lucy); Daniel Anderson (Linus); Arrin Skelley (Charlie Brown); and Laura Planting (Peppermint Patty).

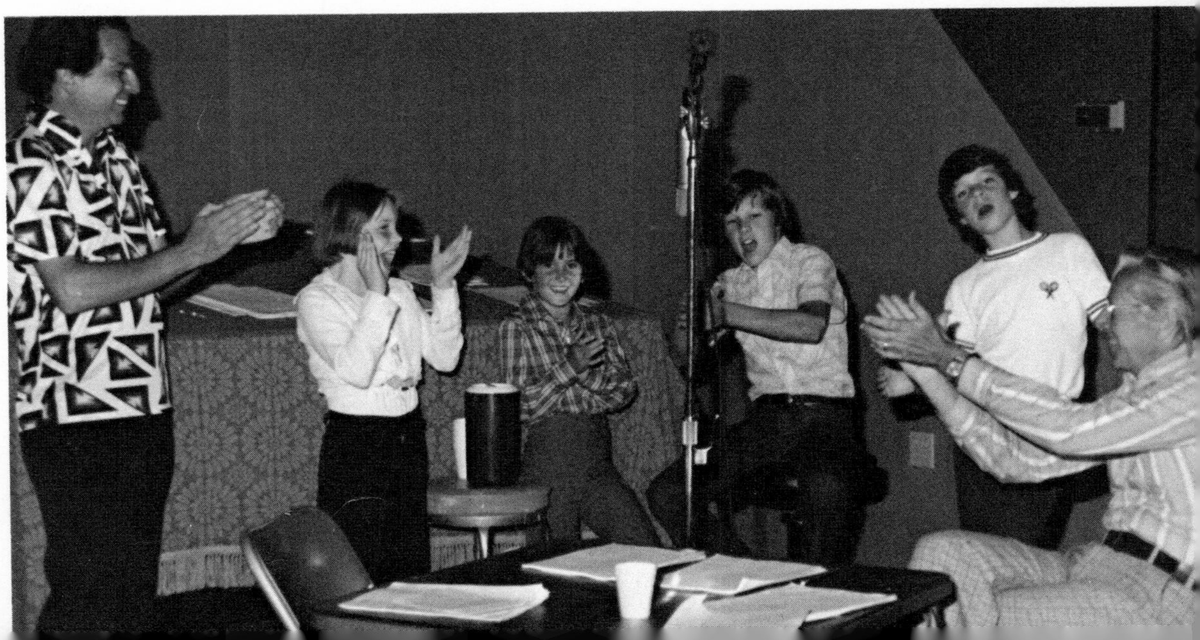

This is a recording session for our new movie, with Sparky and me directing (*left to right*) Patricia Patts (the new Peppermint Patty), Casey Carlson, Arrin Skelley, and Daniel Anderson.

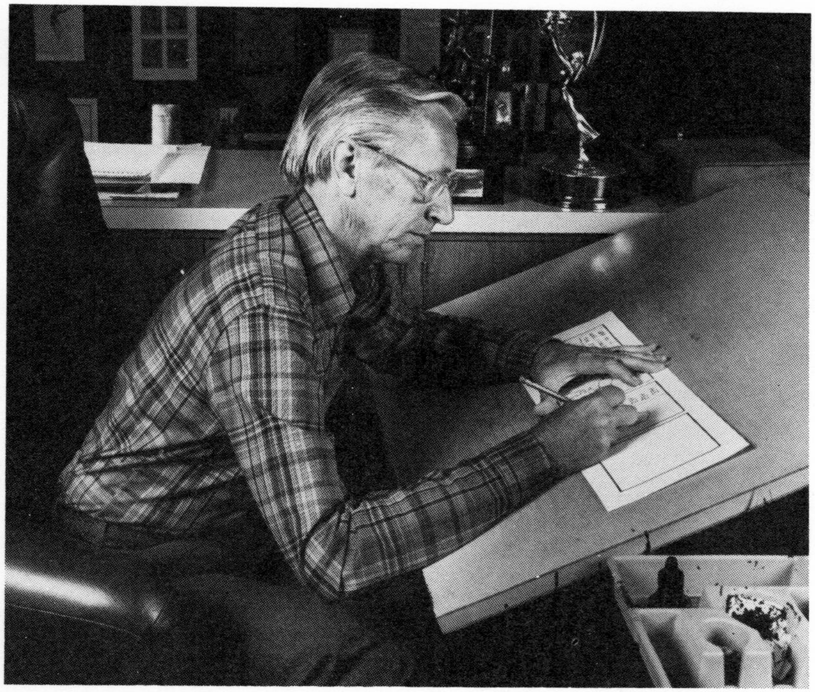

And then came Woodstock...

Woodstock was introduced in the strip in 1970 and was named after the famous rock festival. Sparky told us: "At first a lot of readers didn't seem to like Woodstock, but I decided to stick with him, and I'm glad I did. He's a good change of pace for the strip. Every now and then I can do outrageous things with him that I can't do with the other characters. I think he's finally caught on with the readers, too."

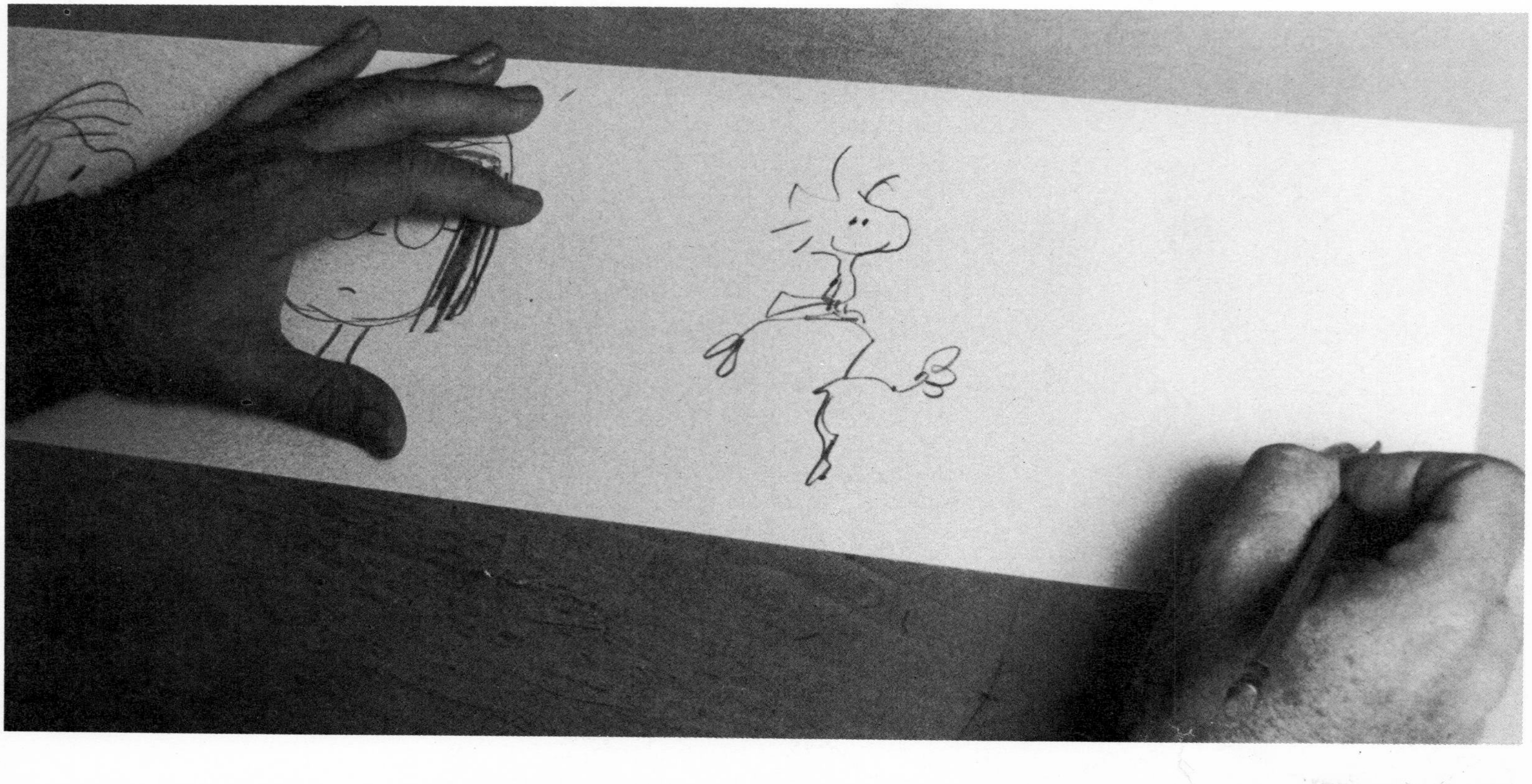

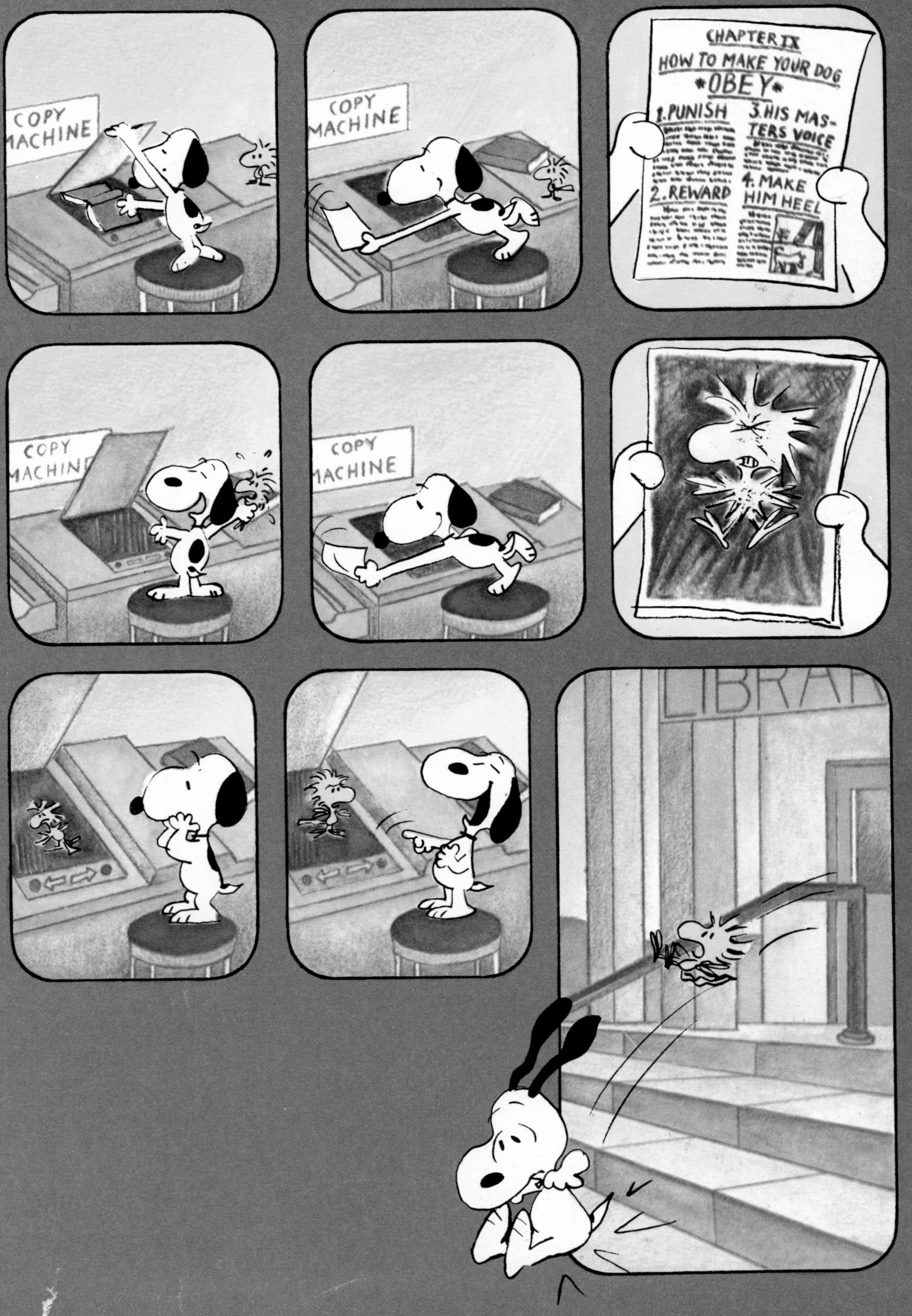
COPY MACHINE
COPY MACHINE
CHAPTER IX
HOW TO MAKE YOUR DOG
OBEY
1. PUNISH
3. HIS MAS-
TERS VOICE
2. REWARD
4. MAKE
HIM HEEL
COPY MACHINE
COPY MACHINE
LIBRAR

Until now, Woodstock's television career has been somewhat limited, usually as a foil for Snoopy. In this scene from *It's Arbor Day, Charlie Brown*, Snoopy wants to make a copy of a book about obedience training. Somehow he picks up Woodstock by mistake and makes a copy of a smashed Woodstock.

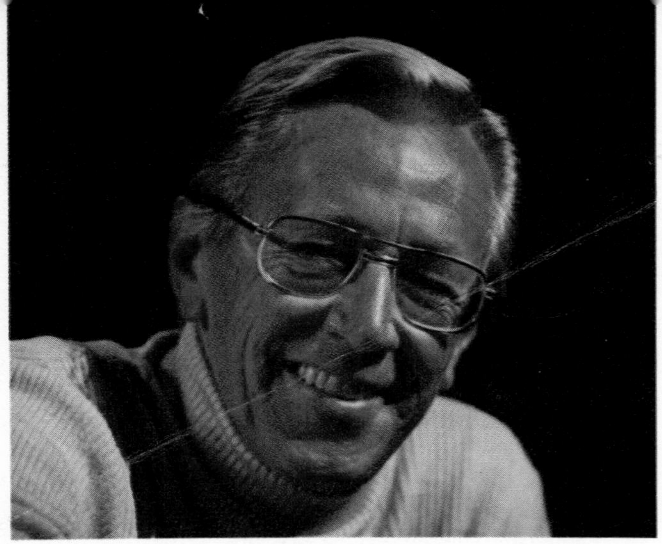

We haven't used Woodstock on the TV shows to any extent because he is much more difficult to animate than, say, Snoopy. But these strips give a clue to his future on television:

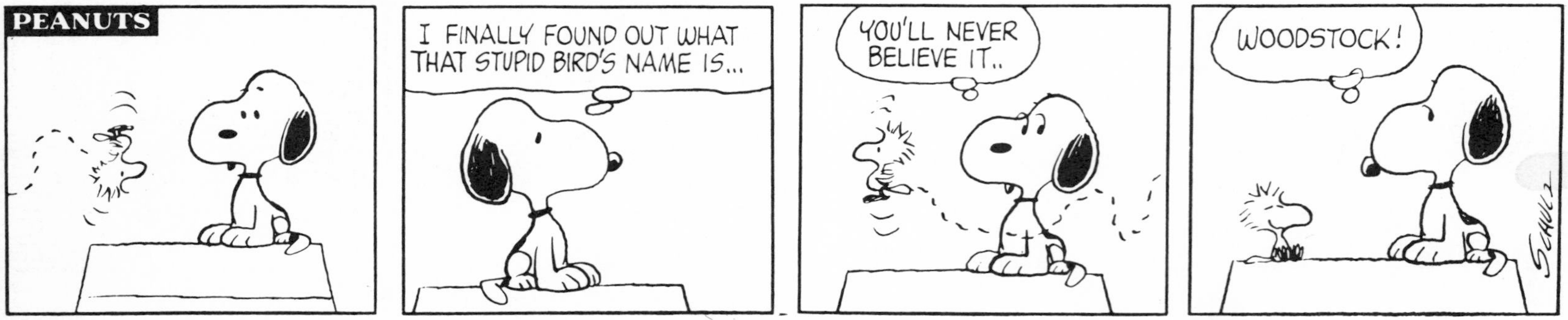
PEANUTS
I FINALLY FOUND OUT WHAT THAT STUPID BIRD'S NAME IS...
YOU'LL NEVER BELIEVE IT..
WOODSTOCK!
SCHULZ

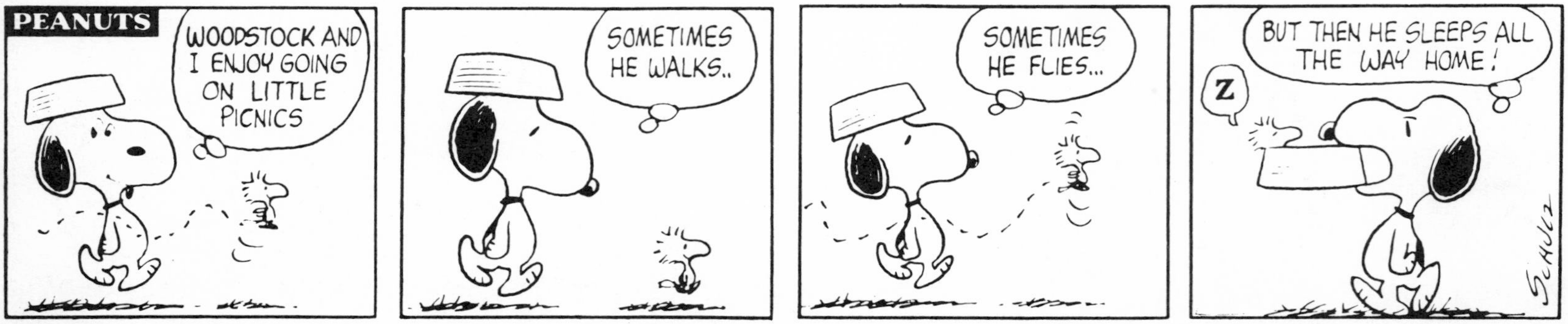
PEANUTS
WOODSTOCK AND I ENJOY GOING ON LITTLE PICNICS
SOMETIMES HE WALKS..
SOMETIMES HE FLIES...
Z
BUT THEN HE SLEEPS ALL THE WAY HOME!
SCHULZ

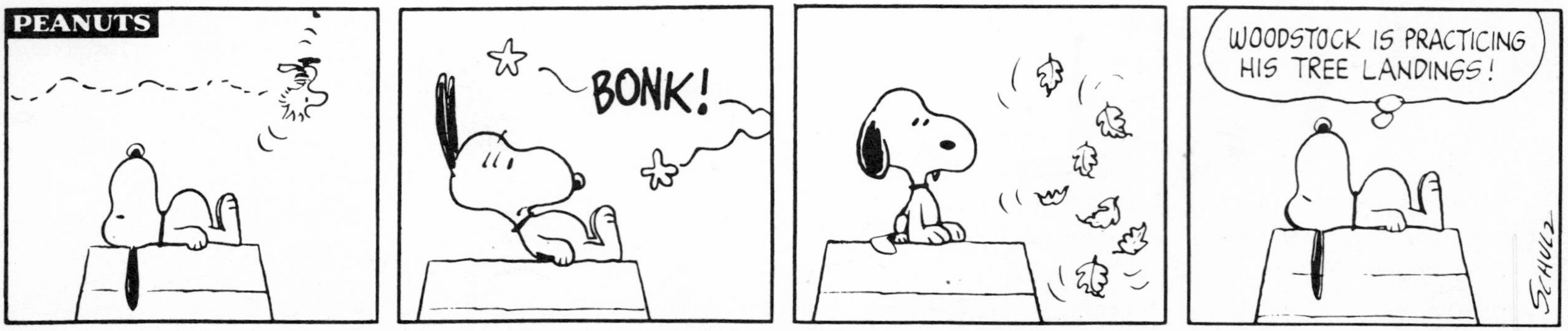
PEANUTS
BONK!
WOODSTOCK IS PRACTICING HIS TREE LANDINGS!
SCHULZ

About one year ago I received a phone call from a man named Jason Serinus. He told me that he did bird whistles. I thanked him for calling and abruptly hung up. He called me right back and said that he whistled with symphony orchestras. I thought he was kidding, but I asked him to send me a tape. The tape was sensational, but I called him back and told him I just

didn't have any use for his talent. Then a few months ago Sparky, Bill Melendez and I were planning our newest TV special for 1980. A climactic scene with Woodstock was suggested, but we couldn't, as usual, figure out how to do it. Suddenly the idea of the bird whistler hit me, and consequently Jason Serinus will make his network debut whistling Puccini's "O mio babbino caro." Moral: never hang up on a bird whistler!

She's your sister, Charlie Brown!

Sally joined *Peanuts* in 1959, nearly ten years after the introduction of the strip. As Sally grew up, she embodied all the confusion and frustration that many little kids suffer in school.

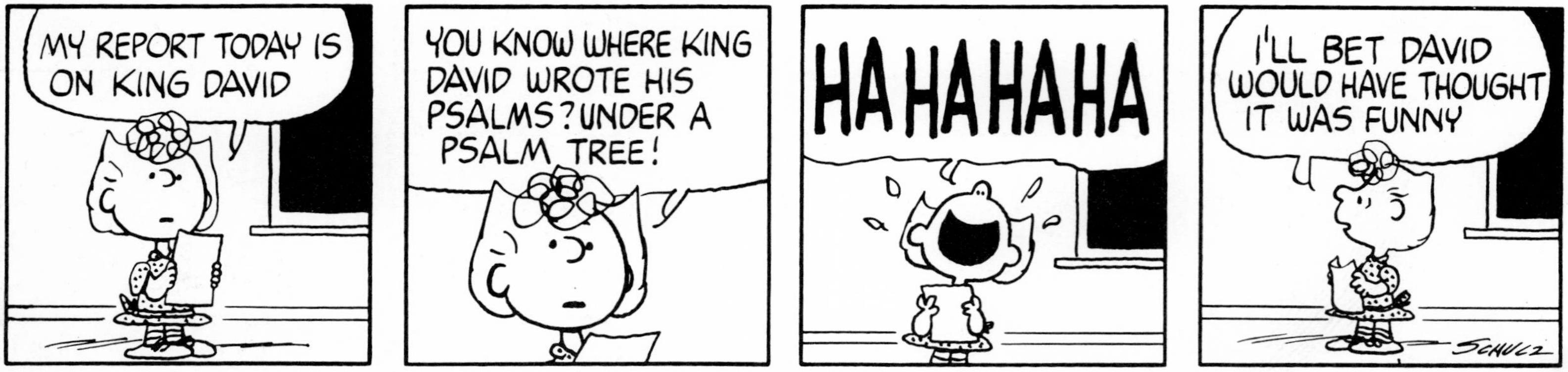
MY REPORT TODAY IS ON KING DAVID
YOU KNOW WHERE KING DAVID WROTE HIS PSALMS? UNDER A PSALM TREE!
HAHAHAHA
I'LL BET DAVID WOULD HAVE THOUGHT IT WAS FUNNY
SCHULZ

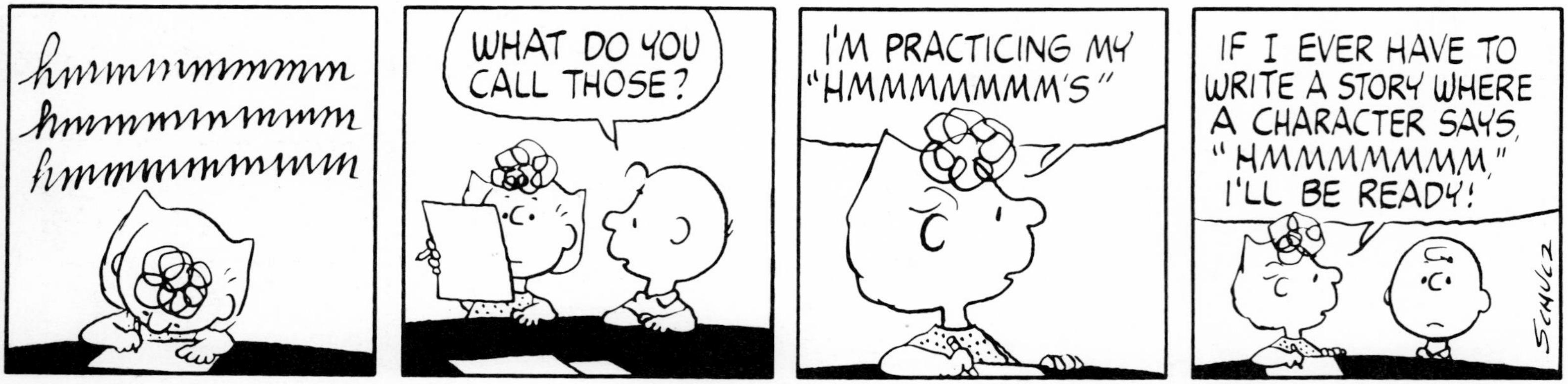
hmmmmmmmm
hmmmmmmmm
hmmmmmmmm
WHAT DO YOU CALL THOSE?
I'M PRACTICING MY "HMMMMMMM'S"
IF I EVER HAVE TO WRITE A STORY WHERE A CHARACTER SAYS, "HMMMMMMM," I'LL BE READY!
SCHULZ

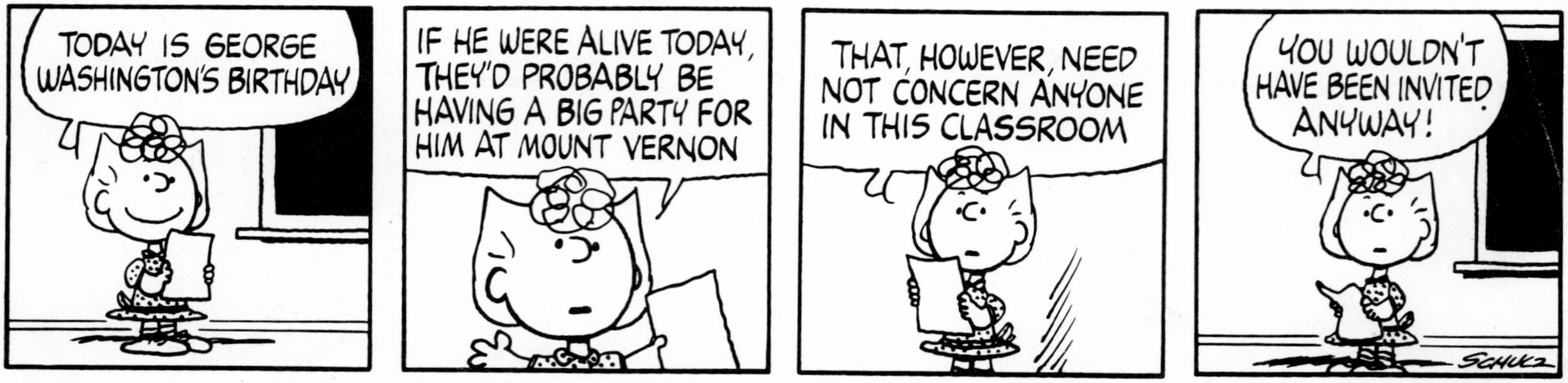
TODAY IS GEORGE WASHINGTON'S BIRTHDAY
IF HE WERE ALIVE TODAY, THEY'D PROBABLY BE HAVING A BIG PARTY FOR HIM AT MOUNT VERNON
THAT, HOWEVER, NEED NOT CONCERN ANYONE IN THIS CLASSROOM
YOU WOULDN'T HAVE BEEN INVITED ANYWAY!
SCHULZ

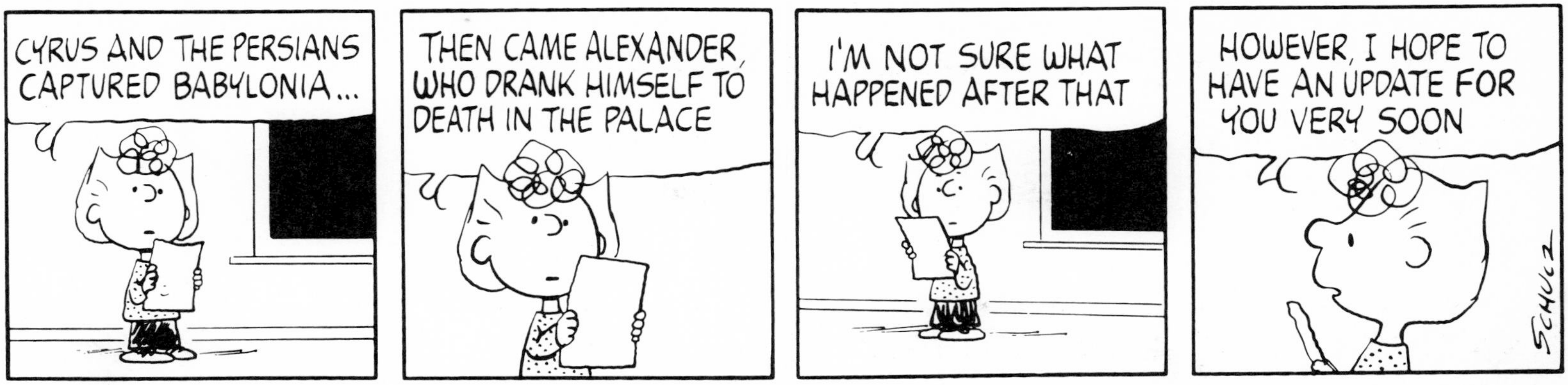
CYRUS AND THE PERSIANS CAPTURED BABYLONIA...
THEN CAME ALEXANDER, WHO DRANK HIMSELF TO DEATH IN THE PALACE
I'M NOT SURE WHAT HAPPENED AFTER THAT
HOWEVER, I HOPE TO HAVE AN UPDATE FOR YOU VERY SOON
SCHULZ

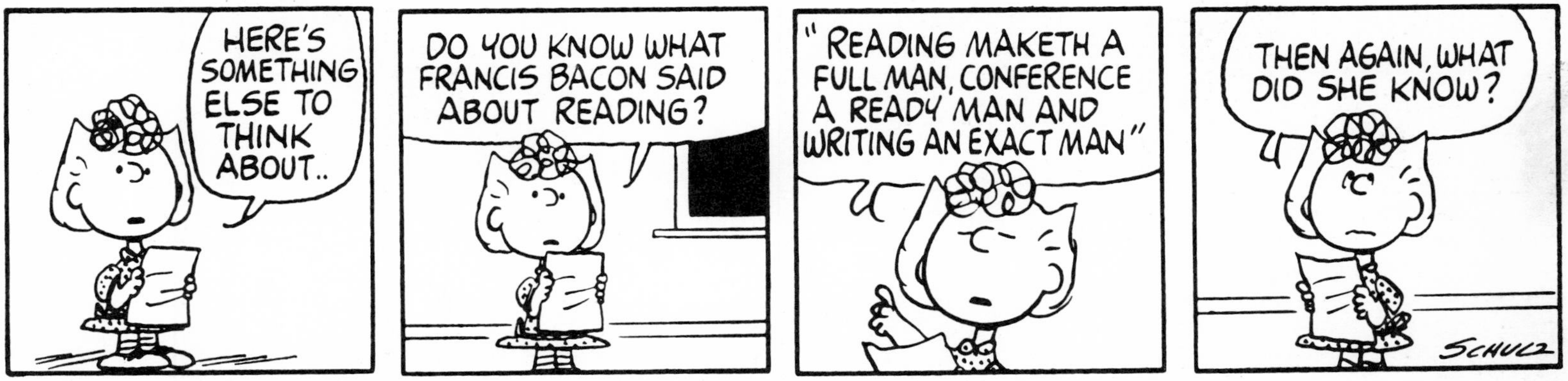
HERE'S SOMETHING ELSE TO THINK ABOUT..
DO YOU KNOW WHAT FRANCIS BACON SAID ABOUT READING?
"READING MAKETH A FULL MAN, CONFERENCE A READY MAN AND WRITING AN EXACT MAN"
THEN AGAIN, WHAT DID SHE KNOW?
SCHULZ

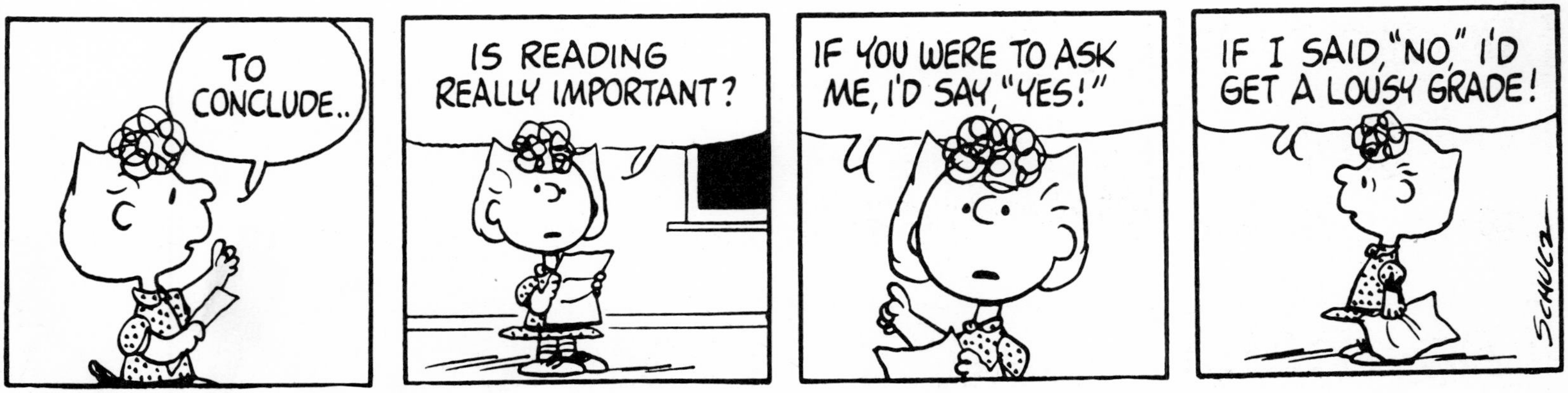
TO CONCLUDE..
IS READING REALLY IMPORTANT?
IF YOU WERE TO ASK ME, I'D SAY, "YES!"
IF I SAID, "NO," I'D GET A LOUSY GRADE!
SCHULZ

I think Sally is my personal favorite of all the characters. Her outrage at the world is so uninhibited that, for me, she's always like a breath of fresh air.

On these two pages and the next two are some of Sparky's favorite strips involving Sally.

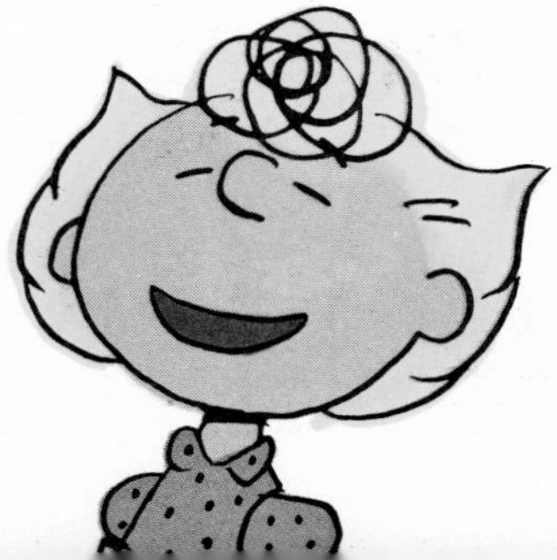

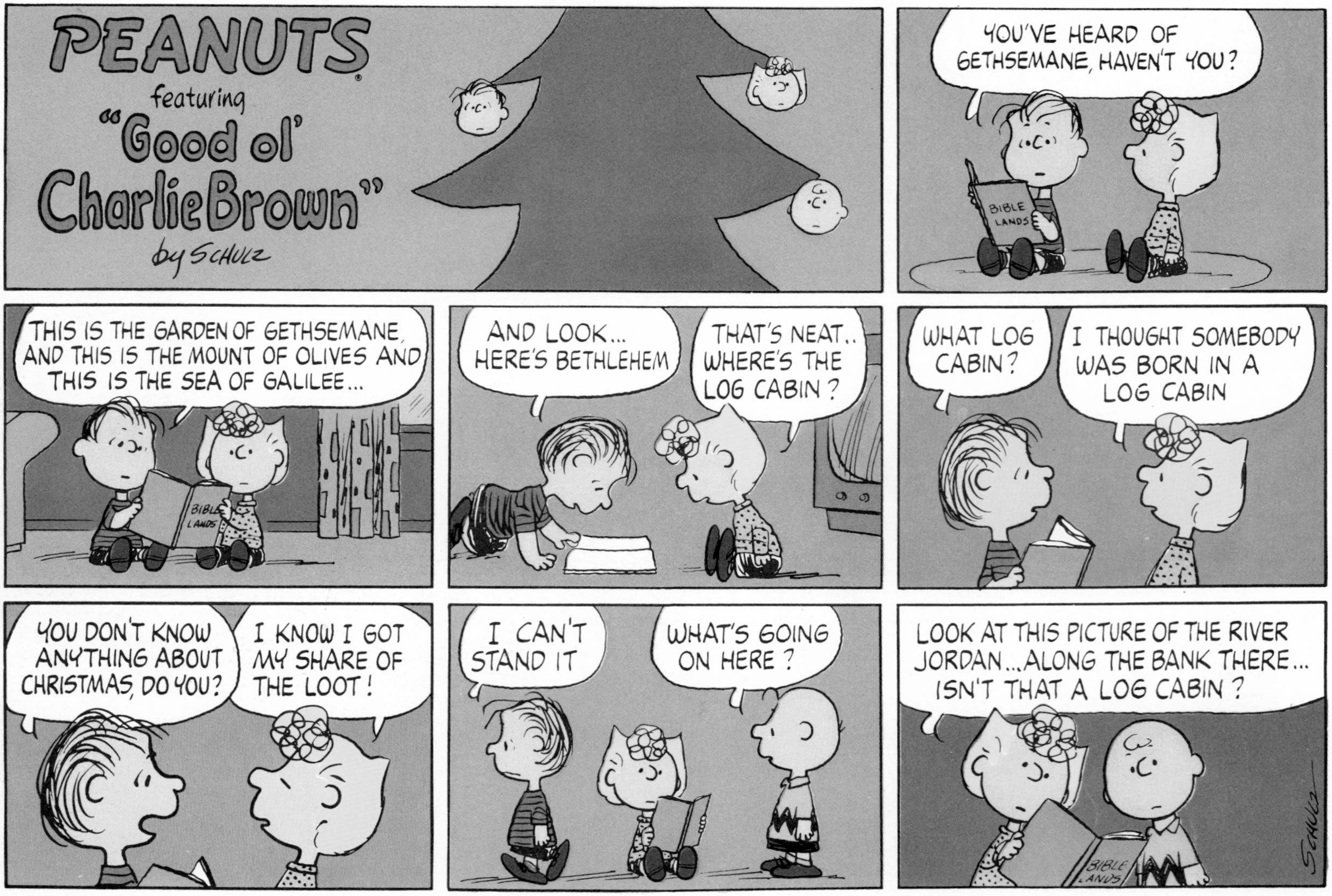
PEANUTS
featuring
"Good ol' CharlieBrown"
by SCHULZ
YOU'VE HEARD OF GETHSEMANE, HAVEN'T YOU?
BIBLE LANDS
THIS IS THE GARDEN OF GETHSEMANE, AND THIS IS THE MOUNT OF OLIVES AND THIS IS THE SEA OF GALILEE...
BIBLE LANDS
AND LOOK... HERE'S BETHLEHEM
THAT'S NEAT.. WHERE'S THE LOG CABIN?
WHAT LOG CABIN?
I THOUGHT SOMEBODY WAS BORN IN A LOG CABIN
YOU DON'T KNOW ANYTHING ABOUT CHRISTMAS, DO YOU?
I KNOW I GOT MY SHARE OF THE LOOT!
I CAN'T STAND IT
WHAT'S GOING ON HERE?
LOOK AT THIS PICTURE OF THE RIVER JORDAN...ALONG THE BANK THERE... ISN'T THAT A LOG CABIN?
BIBLE LANDS
SCHULZ

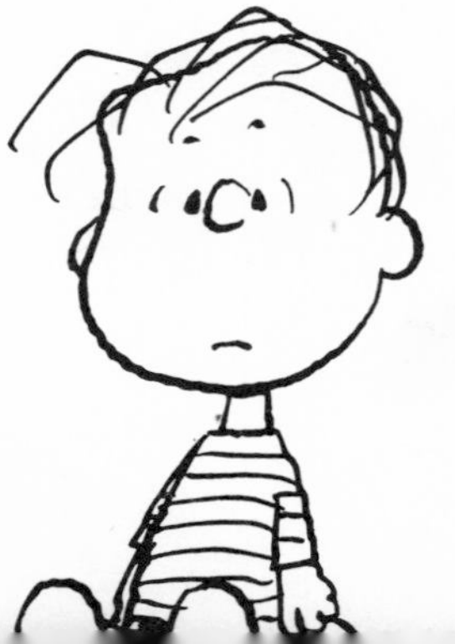

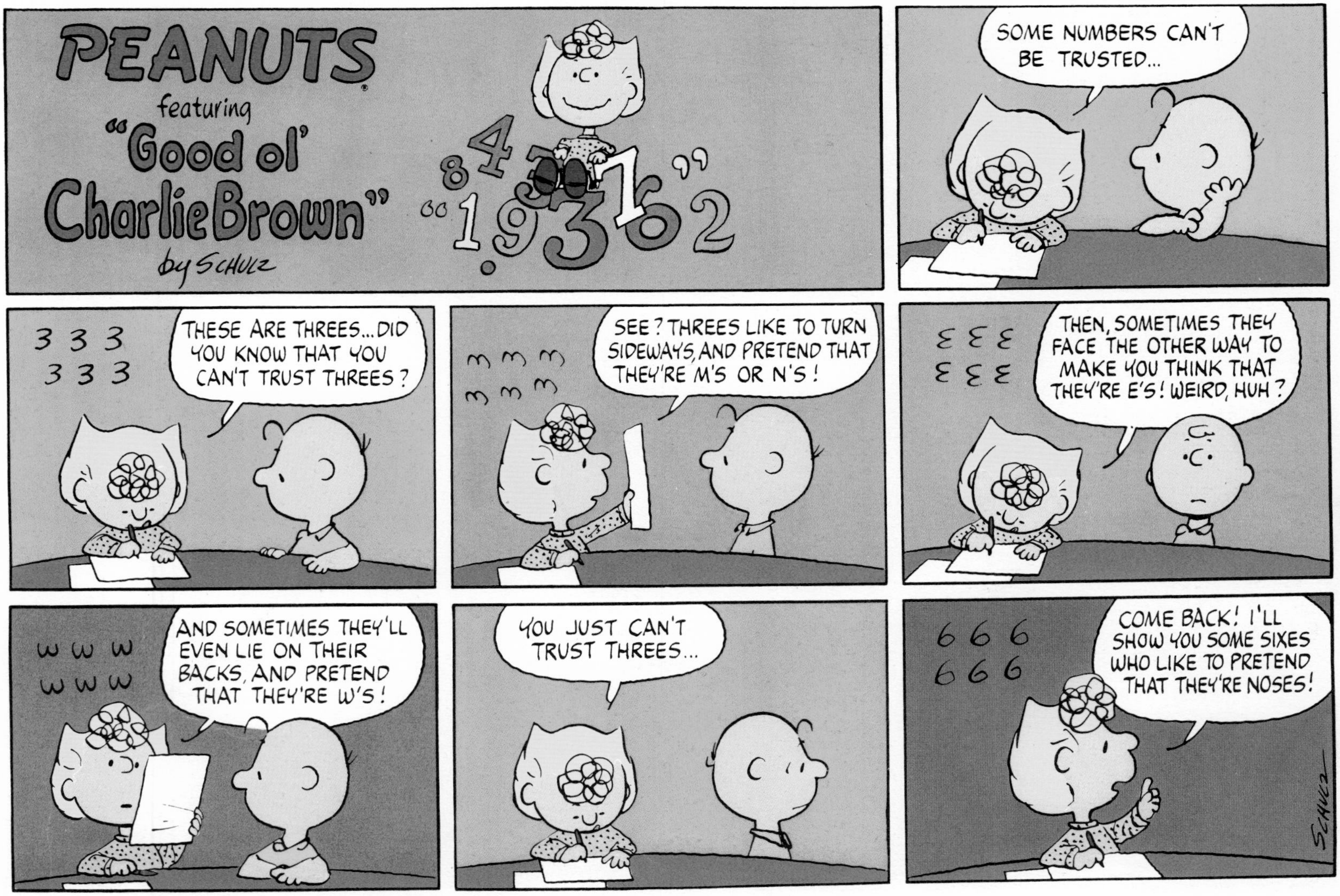
PEANUTS
featuring
"Good ol' CharlieBrown"
by SCHULZ
SOME NUMBERS CAN'T BE TRUSTED...
THESE ARE THREES...DID YOU KNOW THAT YOU CAN'T TRUST THREES?
SEE? THREES LIKE TO TURN SIDEWAYS, AND PRETEND THAT THEY'RE M'S OR N'S!
THEN, SOMETIMES THEY FACE THE OTHER WAY TO MAKE YOU THINK THAT THEY'RE E'S! WEIRD, HUH?
AND SOMETIMES THEY'LL EVEN LIE ON THEIR BACKS, AND PRETEND THAT THEY'RE W'S!
YOU JUST CAN'T TRUST THREES...
COME BACK! I'LL SHOW YOU SOME SIXES WHO LIKE TO PRETEND THAT THEY'RE NOSES!
SCHULZ

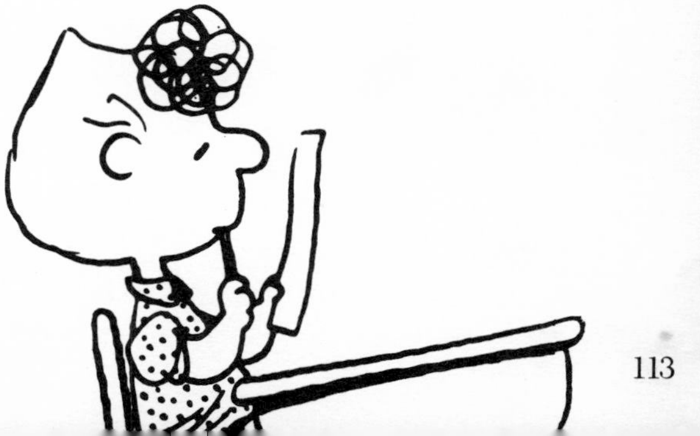

I've been looking for you, big brother. Will you please write a letter to Santa Claus for me? You write it, and I'll tell you what I want you to say.

Dear Santa Claus, how have you been? Did you have a nice summer? How is your wife?

I have been extra good this year. So I have a long list of presents that I want.

Please note the size and color of the items, and send me as many as possible. If it seems too complicated, make it easy on yourself. Send money. How about tens and twenties?

AUGH!!

EVEN MY BABY SISTER!

TENS AND TWENTIES!!!

Sally had a very small part in *A Charlie Brown Christmas*, but it was one that seems to have stuck in the minds of viewers.

You're really something, Sally. Do you know that?

I've never seen anyone who was so uptight about school. Why don't you just relax?

Sally's problems with school in the comic strip carried over to the television shows themselves.

Who can relax?

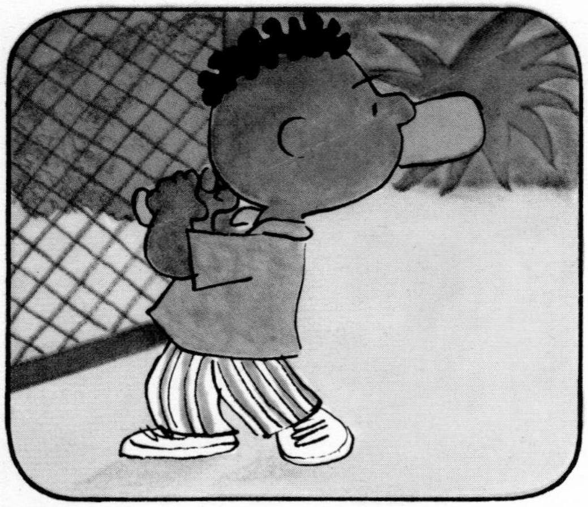

Franklin

Franklin entered the comic strip in 1968. *Newsweek* did an article about his debut, saying that it was great to find out that Charlie Brown wasn't color-blind.

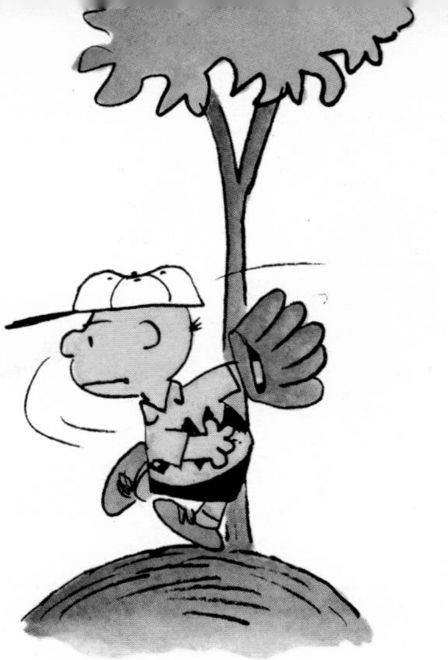

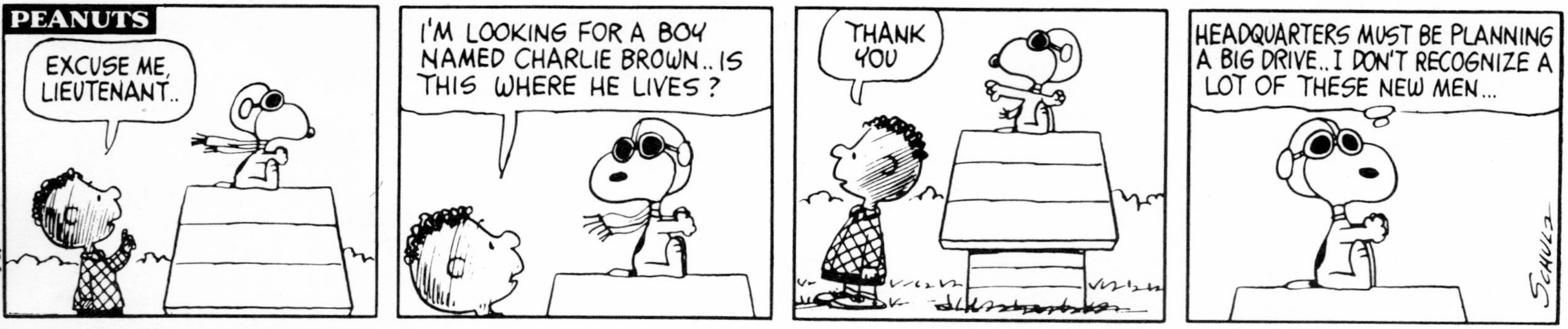
PEANUTS
EXCUSE ME, LIEUTENANT..
I'M LOOKING FOR A BOY NAMED CHARLIE BROWN.. IS THIS WHERE HE LIVES?
THANK YOU
HEADQUARTERS MUST BE PLANNING A BIG DRIVE.. I DON'T RECOGNIZE A LOT OF THESE NEW MEN...
SCHULZ

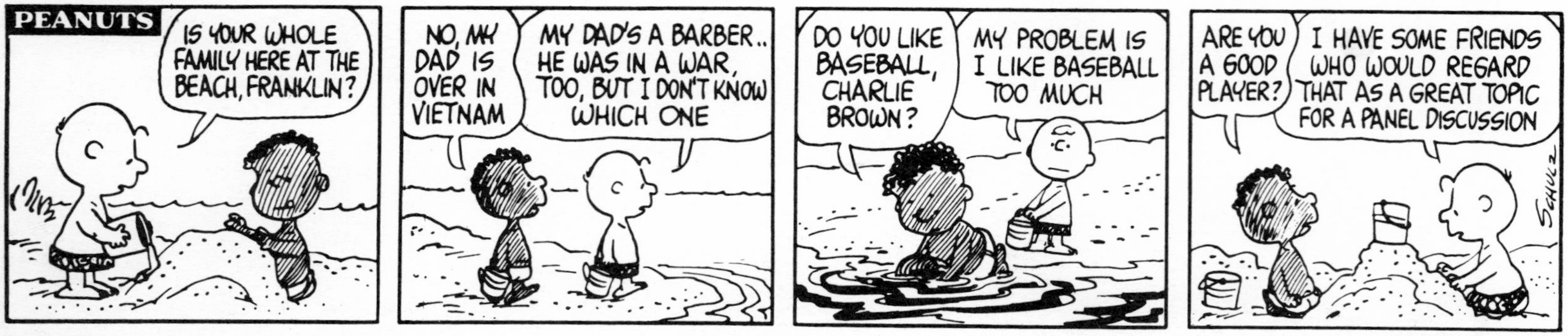
PEANUTS
IS YOUR WHOLE FAMILY HERE AT THE BEACH, FRANKLIN?
NO, MY DAD IS OVER IN VIETNAM
MY DAD'S A BARBER.. HE WAS IN A WAR, TOO, BUT I DON'T KNOW WHICH ONE
DO YOU LIKE BASEBALL, CHARLIE BROWN?
MY PROBLEM IS I LIKE BASEBALL TOO MUCH
ARE YOU A GOOD PLAYER?
I HAVE SOME FRIENDS WHO WOULD REGARD THAT AS A GREAT TOPIC FOR A PANEL DISCUSSION
SCHULZ

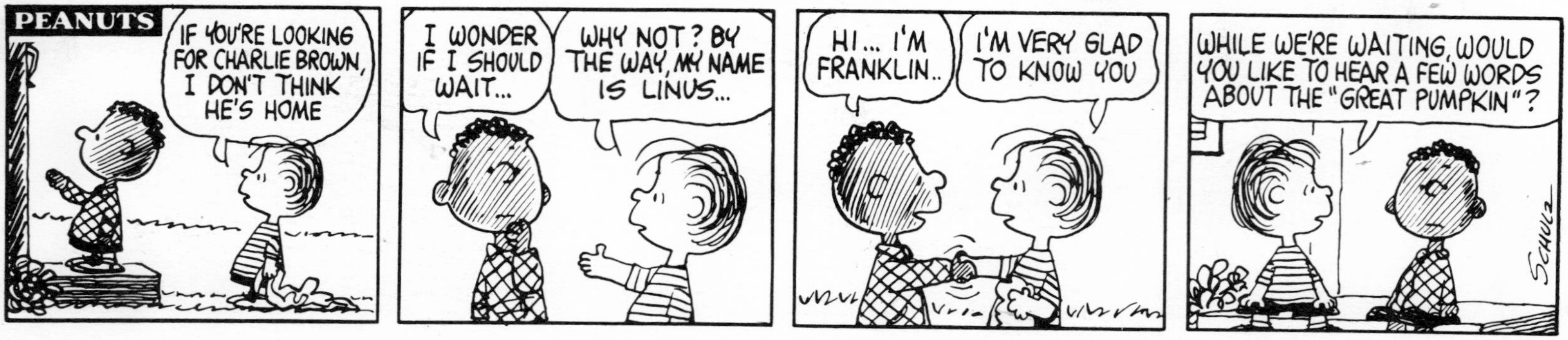
PEANUTS
IF YOU'RE LOOKING FOR CHARLIE BROWN, I DON'T THINK HE'S HOME
I WONDER IF I SHOULD WAIT...
WHY NOT? BY THE WAY, MY NAME IS LINUS...
HI... I'M FRANKLIN..
I'M VERY GLAD TO KNOW YOU
WHILE WE'RE WAITING, WOULD YOU LIKE TO HEAR A FEW WORDS ABOUT THE "GREAT PUMPKIN"?
SCHULZ

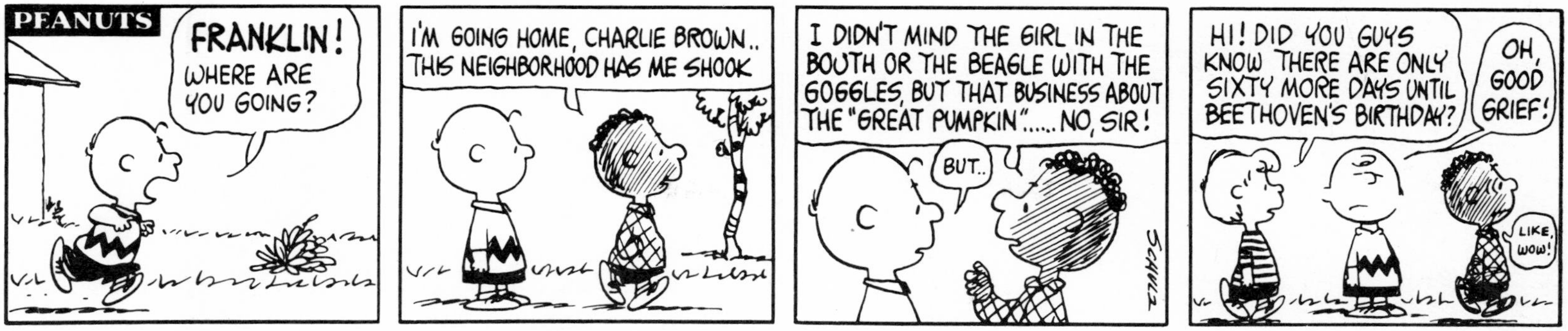
PEANUTS
FRANKLIN! WHERE ARE YOU GOING?
I'M GOING HOME, CHARLIE BROWN.. THIS NEIGHBORHOOD HAS ME SHOOK
I DIDN'T MIND THE GIRL IN THE BOOTH OR THE BEAGLE WITH THE GOGGLES, BUT THAT BUSINESS ABOUT THE "GREAT PUMPKIN"..... NO, SIR!
BUT..
SCHULZ
HI! DID YOU GUYS KNOW THERE ARE ONLY SIXTY MORE DAYS UNTIL BEETHOVEN'S BIRTHDAY?
OH, GOOD GRIEF!
LIKE, WOW!

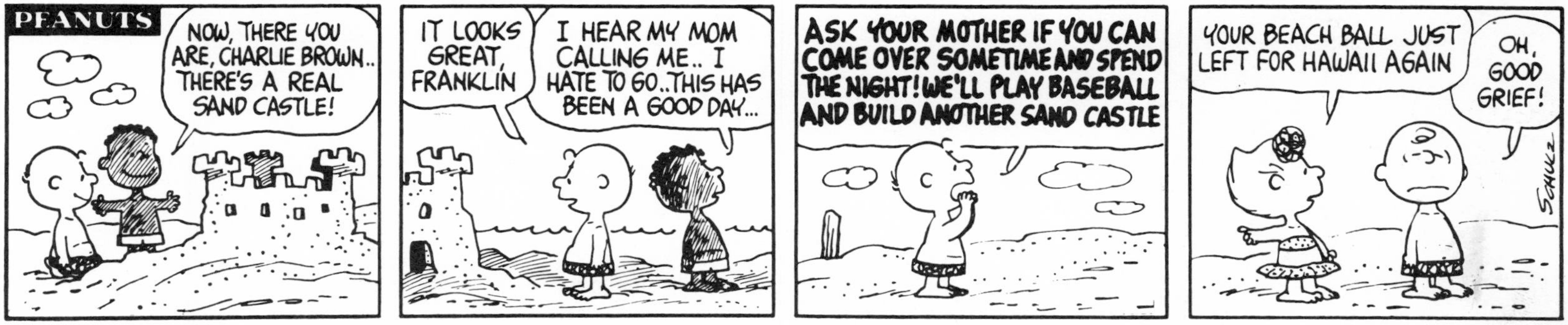
PEANUTS
NOW, THERE YOU ARE, CHARLIE BROWN.. THERE'S A REAL SAND CASTLE!
IT LOOKS GREAT, FRANKLIN
I HEAR MY MOM CALLING ME.. I HATE TO GO..THIS HAS BEEN A GOOD DAY...
ASK YOUR MOTHER IF YOU CAN COME OVER SOMETIME AND SPEND THE NIGHT! WE'LL PLAY BASEBALL AND BUILD ANOTHER SAND CASTLE
YOUR BEACH BALL JUST LEFT FOR HAWAII AGAIN
OH, GOOD GRIEF!
SCHULZ

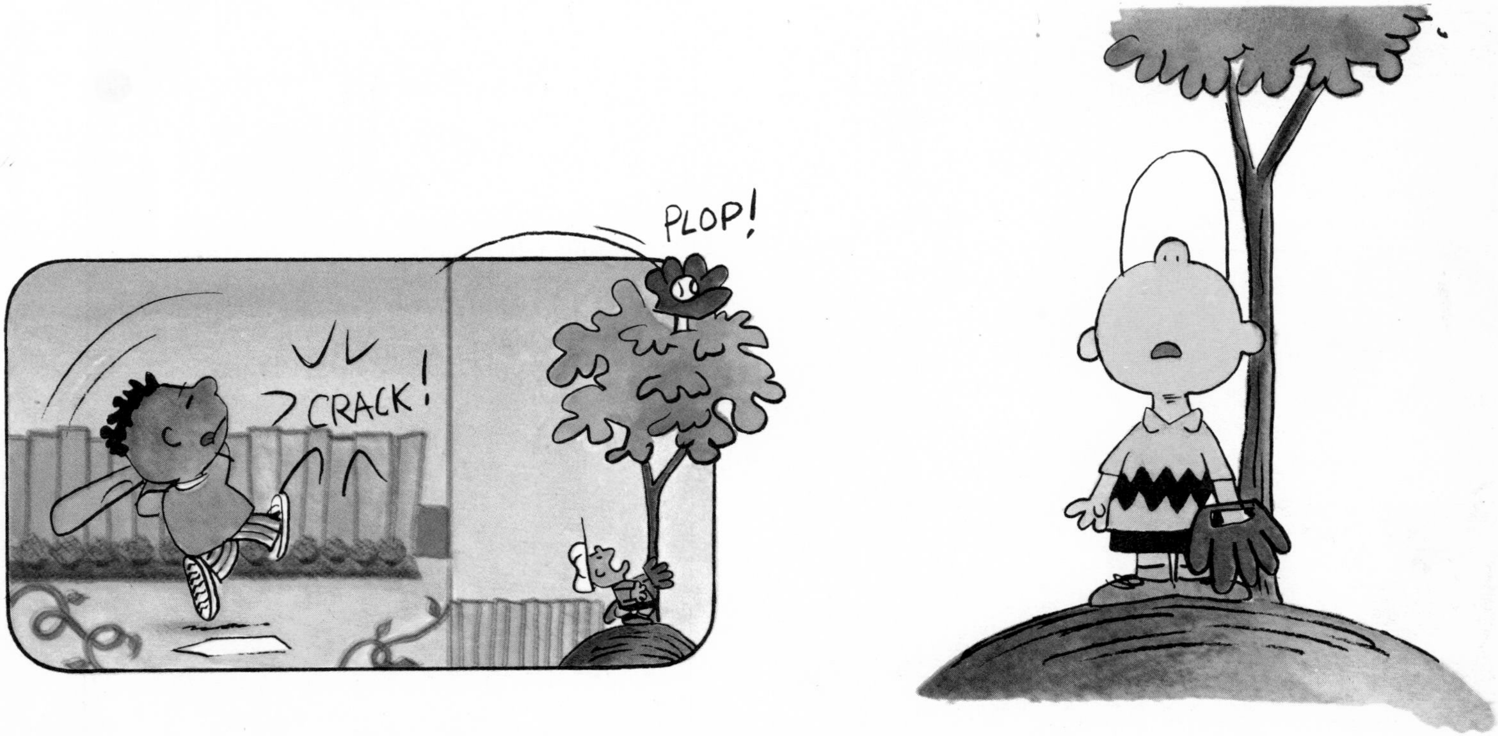
CRACK!
PLOP!

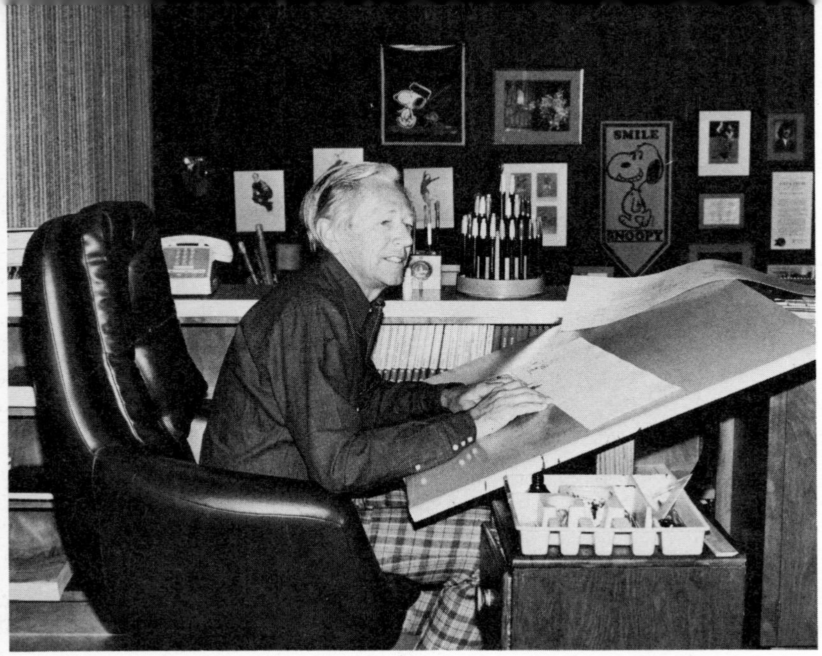

SMILE
SNOOPY

Schroeder

Schroeder entered *Peanuts* way back in 1951. Sparky's lifelong interest in music in general and Beethoven in particular led to Schroeder's playing Beethoven on a toy piano. Schroeder, however, unlike Beethoven, has had to contend with Lucy for nearly thirty years.

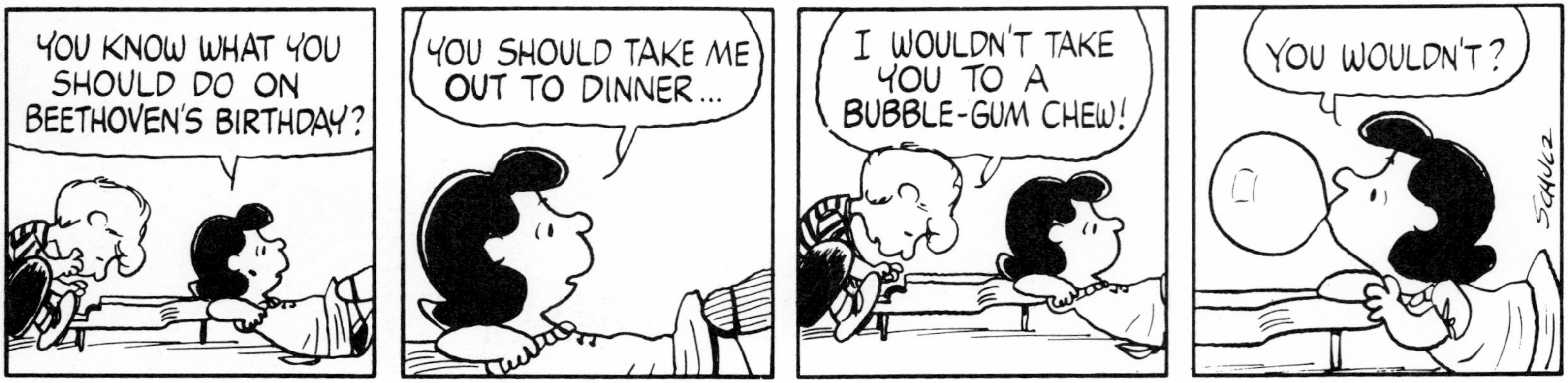

YOU KNOW WHAT YOU SHOULD DO ON BEETHOVEN'S BIRTHDAY?
YOU SHOULD TAKE ME OUT TO DINNER...
I WOULDN'T TAKE YOU TO A BUBBLE-GUM CHEW!
YOU WOULDN'T?
SCHULZ

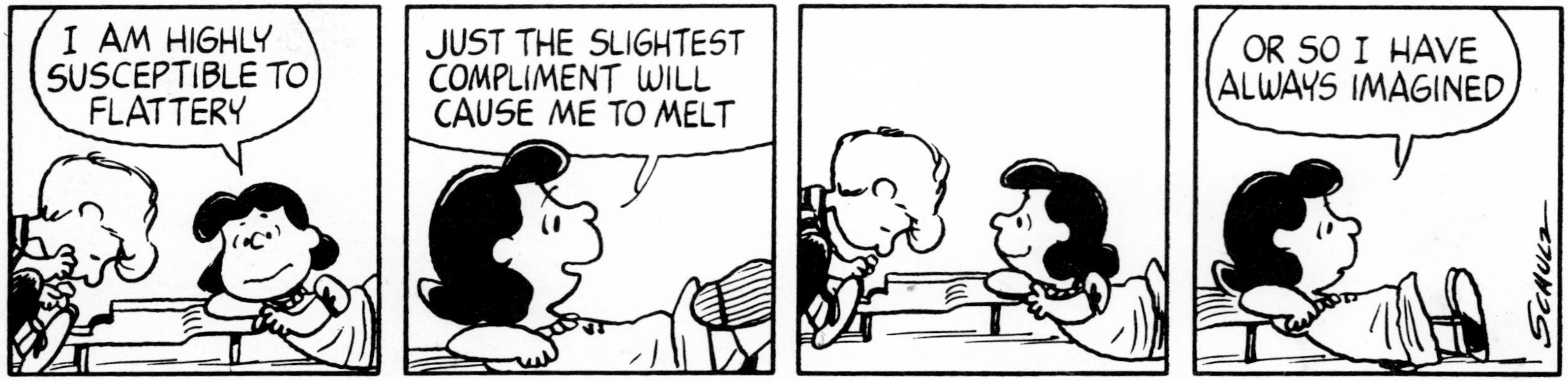

I AM HIGHLY SUSCEPTIBLE TO FLATTERY
JUST THE SLIGHTEST COMPLIMENT WILL CAUSE ME TO MELT
OR SO I HAVE ALWAYS IMAGINED
SCHULZ

Hold on there! What do you think you're doing? Who do you think you are?! Don't you think he has any feelings? You and your friends are the most thoughtless bunch I've ever known! You don't care anything about Charlie Brown. You just hate to feel guilty! And now you have the nerve to come around one day later and offer him a used valentine, just to ease your conscience! Well, let me tell you something. Charlie Brown doesn't need your—

Schroeder hasn't been in many television shows, but when he has appeared he's usually sticking up for his good friend Charlie Brown.

Don't listen to him. I'll take it!

119

Fans of *Peanuts* know of Schroeder's deep affection for Beethoven. A few years ago, when I was on a business trip to Vienna, I went to the cemetery where Beethoven is buried. I usually carry little pins of the various characters to give to people whom I meet along the way.

For some reason, I placed one of the Snoopy pins at Beethoven's grave site. A little Austrian girl was watching me, and she said something that

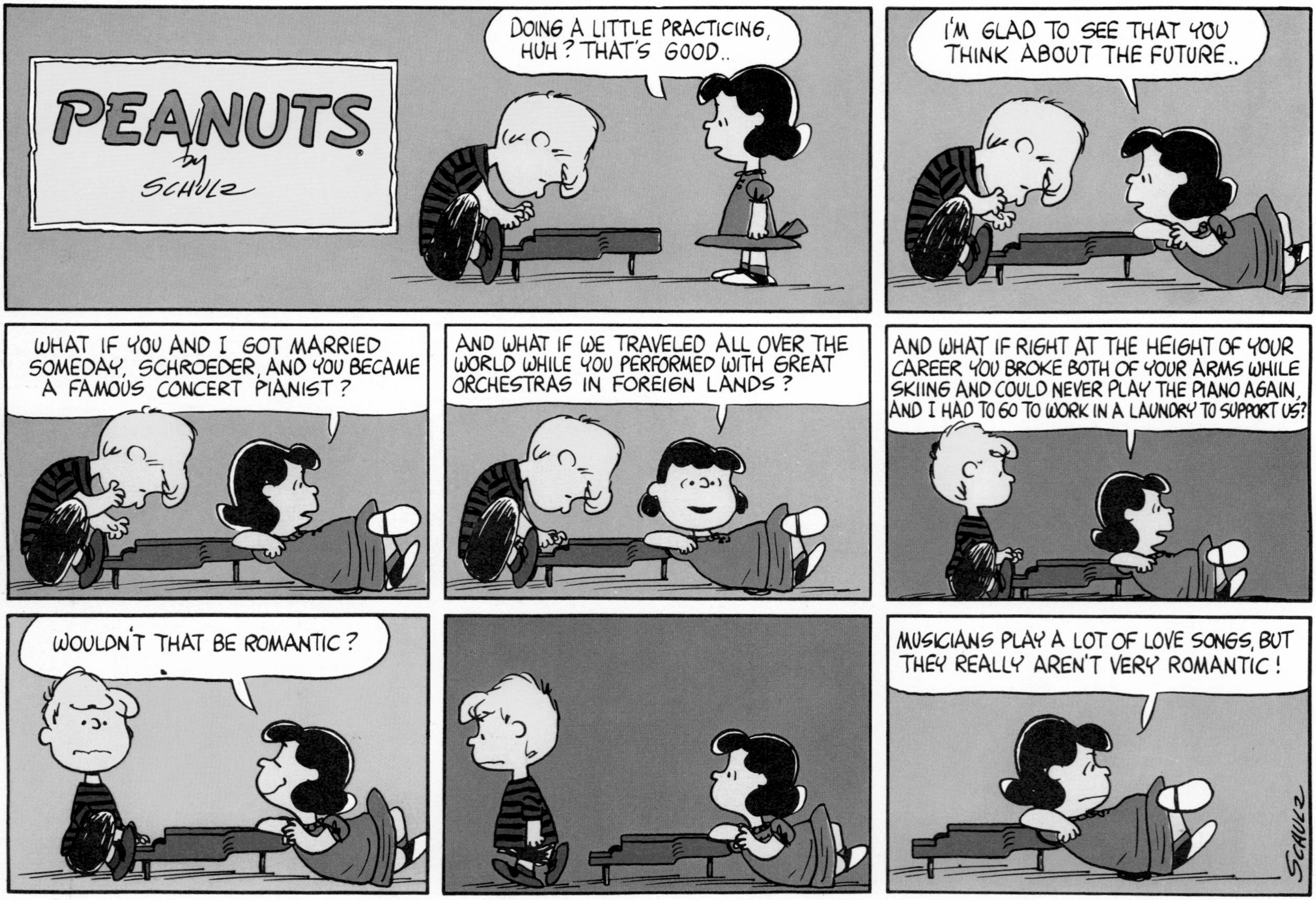
PEANUTS
by SCHULZ
DOING A LITTLE PRACTICING, HUH? THAT'S GOOD..
I'M GLAD TO SEE THAT YOU THINK ABOUT THE FUTURE..
WHAT IF YOU AND I GOT MARRIED SOMEDAY, SCHROEDER, AND YOU BECAME A FAMOUS CONCERT PIANIST?
AND WHAT IF WE TRAVELED ALL OVER THE WORLD WHILE YOU PERFORMED WITH GREAT ORCHESTRAS IN FOREIGN LANDS?
AND WHAT IF RIGHT AT THE HEIGHT OF YOUR CAREER YOU BROKE BOTH OF YOUR ARMS WHILE SKIING AND COULD NEVER PLAY THE PIANO AGAIN, AND I HAD TO GO TO WORK IN A LAUNDRY TO SUPPORT US?
WOULDN'T THAT BE ROMANTIC?
MUSICIANS PLAY A LOT OF LOVE SONGS, BUT THEY REALLY AREN'T VERY ROMANTIC!
SCHULZ

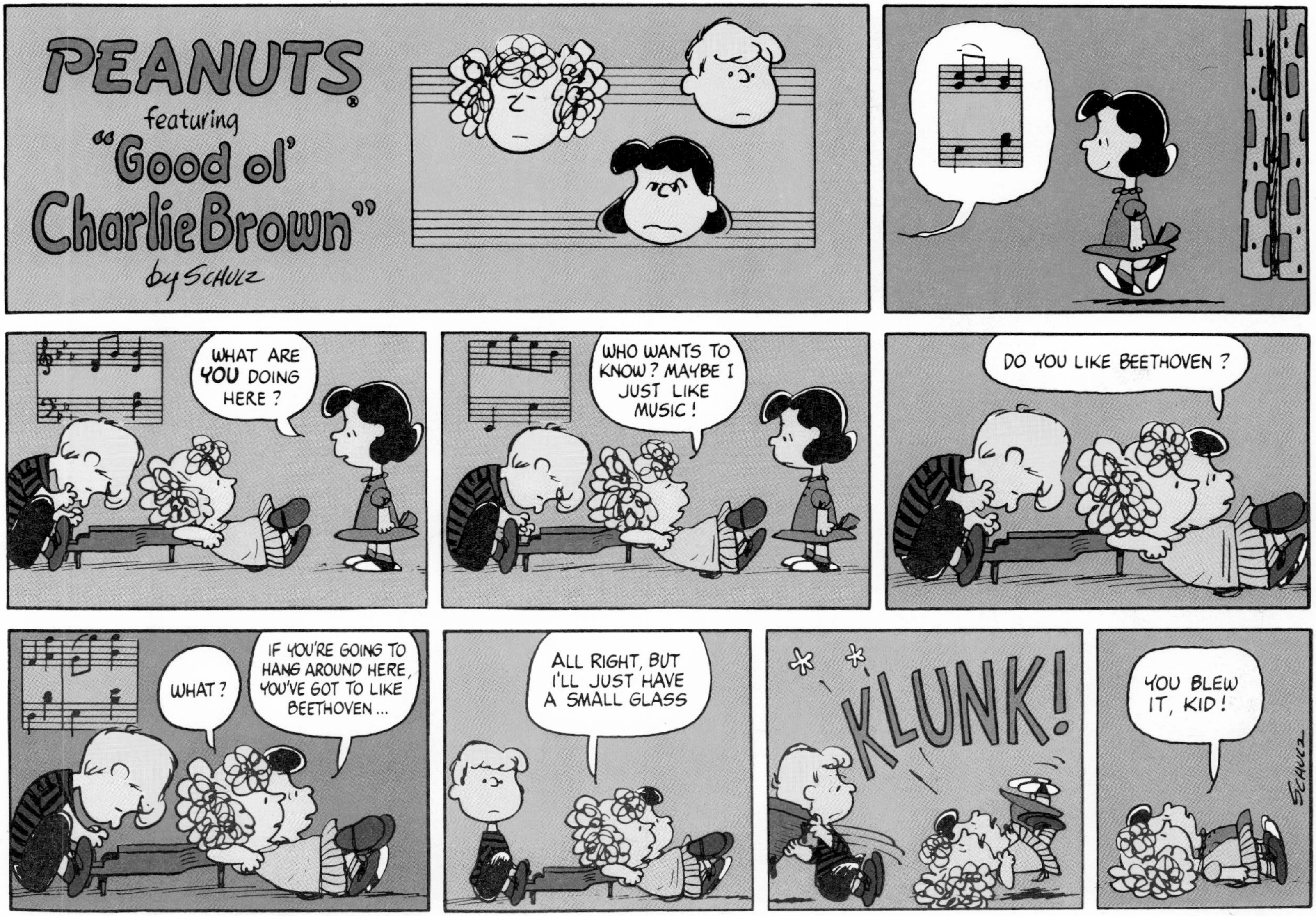
PEANUTS
featuring
"Good ol' Charlie Brown"
by SCHULZ
WHAT ARE YOU DOING HERE ?
WHO WANTS TO KNOW ? MAYBE I JUST LIKE MUSIC !
DO YOU LIKE BEETHOVEN ?
WHAT ?
IF YOU'RE GOING TO HANG AROUND HERE, YOU'VE GOT TO LIKE BEETHOVEN...
ALL RIGHT, BUT I'LL JUST HAVE A SMALL GLASS
KLUNK!
YOU BLEW IT, KID!
SCHULZ

sounded like "Vas der Schroeder?" Her mother, realizing I was an American, said, "She is asking why you place Snoopy there rather than Schroeder?" I excused myself for a moment, went back to my car, found my one Schroeder pin, brought it back, and placed it at the grave site. The mother and little girl both smiled. It was an extremely emotional moment for me — the power and universality of these characters — and the fact that in this strange way Schroeder was finally paying his respects to his hero.

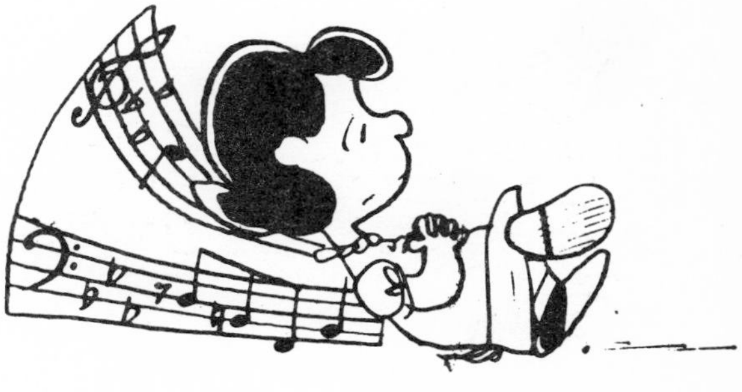

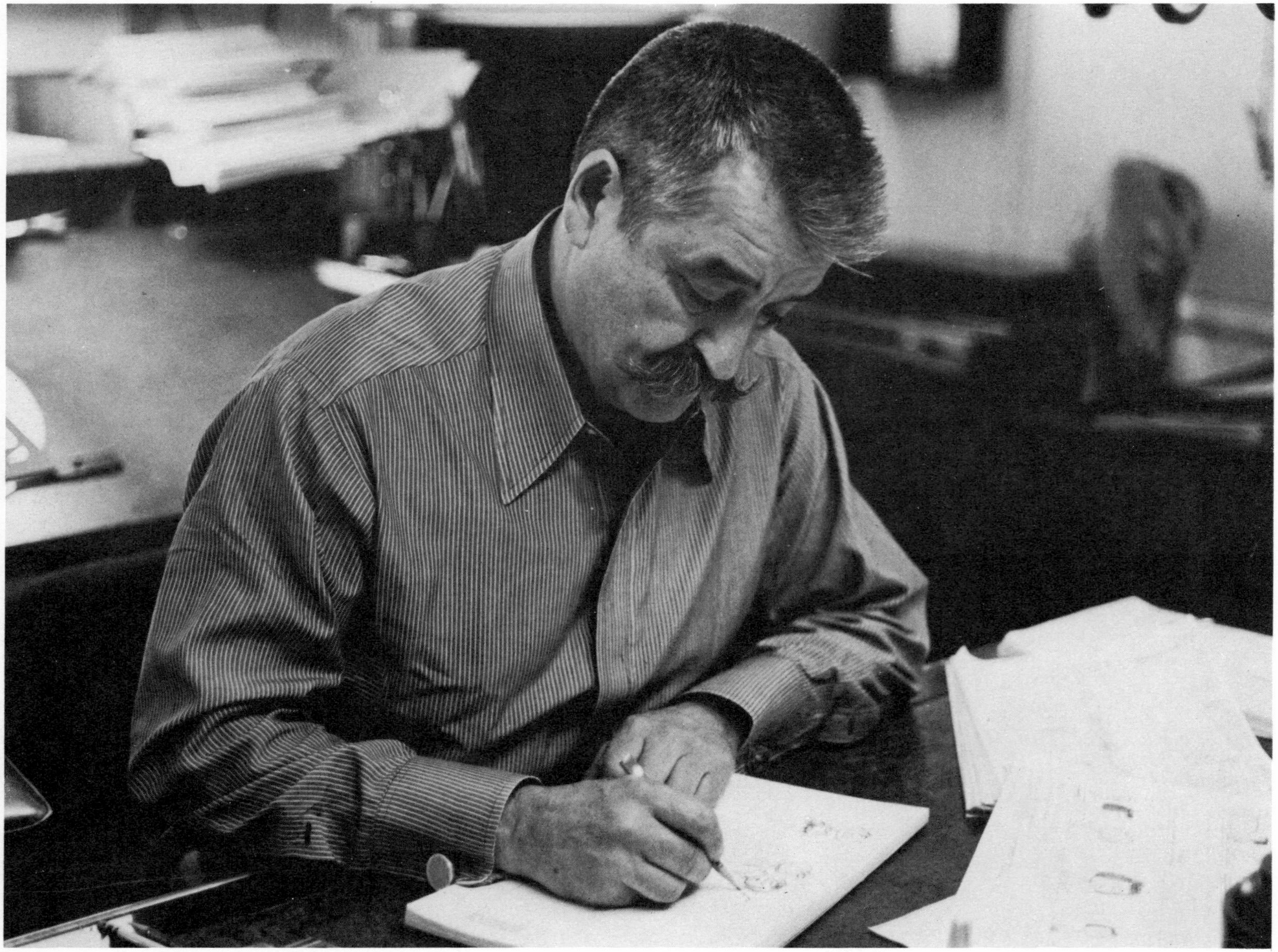

Bill Melendez has been animating *Peanuts* for nearly twenty years, having worked with Sparky on commercials long before we started the TV specials. We asked Bill to describe the different stages of animating Charlie Brown, as he was working on our new feature film, *Bon Voyage, Charlie Brown . . . and Don't Come Back.*

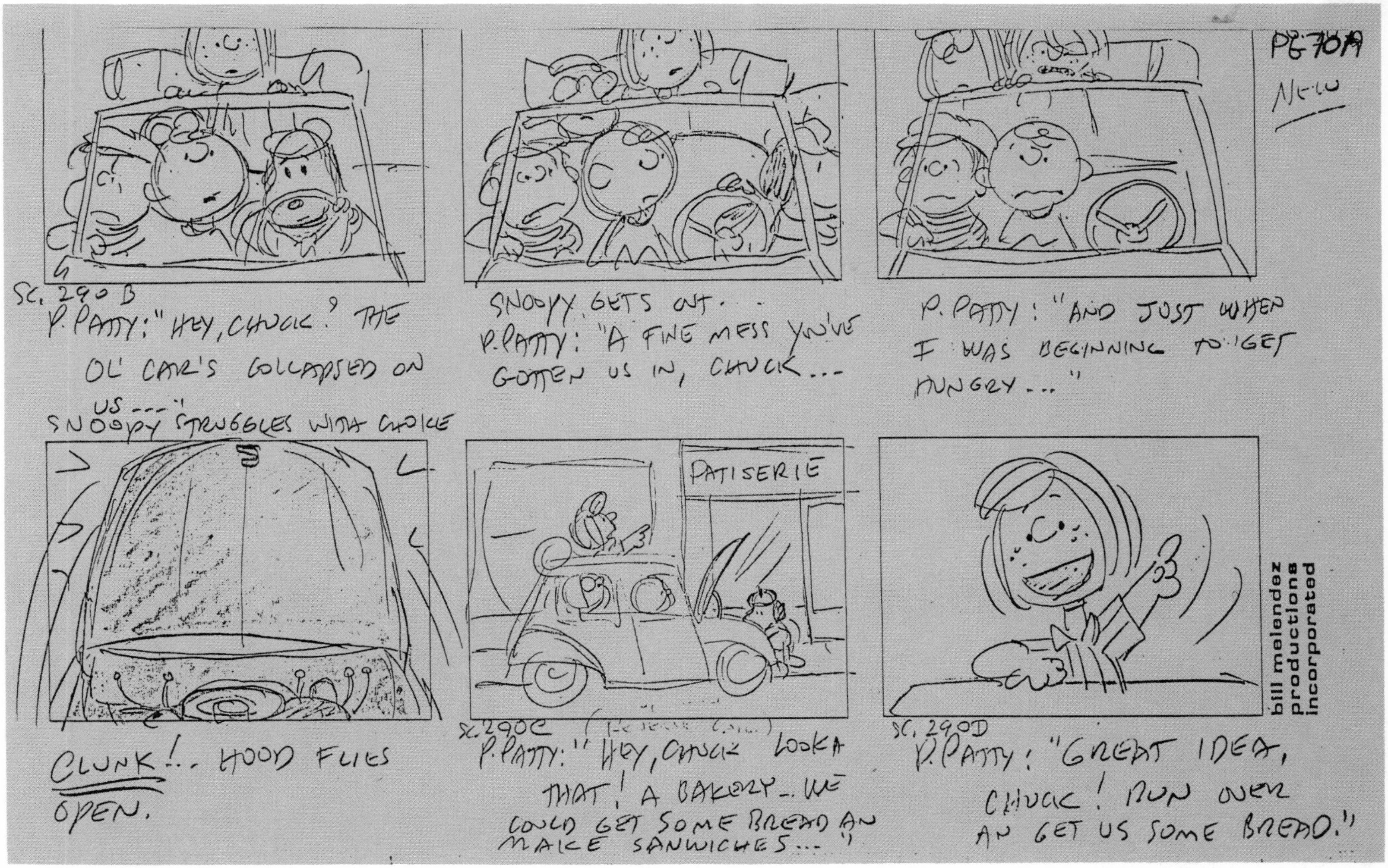
PG 70A
NEW
SC. 290 B
P. PATTY: "HEY, CHUCK? THE OL' CAR'S COLLAPSED ON US ---"
SNOOPY GETS OUT.
P. PATTY: "A FINE MESS YOU'VE GOTTEN US IN, CHUCK..."
P. PATTY: "AND JUST WHEN I WAS BEGINNING TO GET HUNGRY..."
SNOOPY STRUGGLES WITH CHOKE
PATISERIE
bill melendez productions incorporated
CLUNK!.. HOOD FLIES OPEN.
SC. 290C
P. PATTY: "HEY, CHUCK LOOKA THAT! A BAKERY_ WE COULD GET SOME BREAD AN MAKE SANWICHES..."
SC. 290D
P. PATTY: "GREAT IDEA, CHUCK! RUN OVER AN GET US SOME BREAD."

"First, of course, we must create the story — both action and dialogue with Sparky — and then I take his ideas and create a storyboard. A storyboard for a 75-minute feature will consist of about two thousand sketches that outline the entire film.

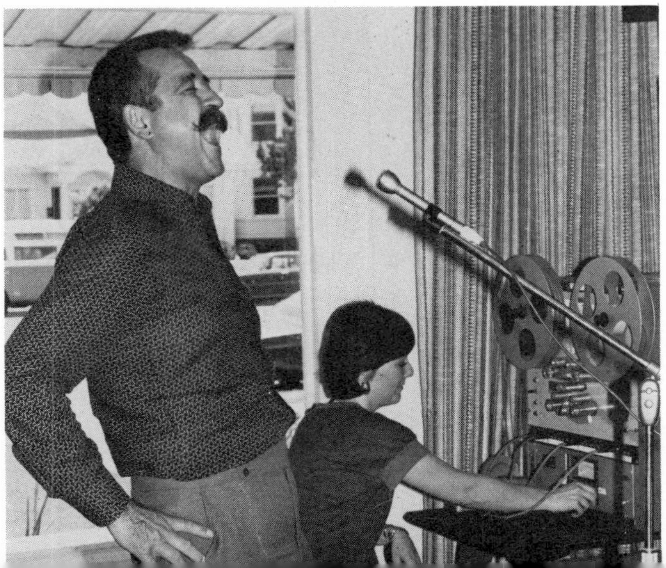

"Then we will record the entire sound track for the characters, with Sparky and Lee directing the voices up in northern California while I direct any in southern California. That's me recording some sounds for Snoopy.

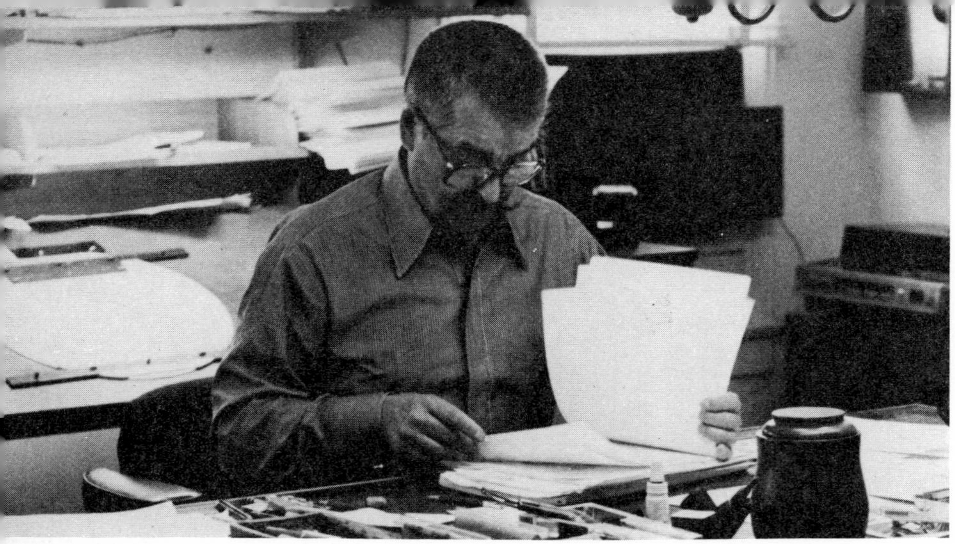

“Then I will make up what we call ‘bar sheets’ or exposure sheets. I take the dialogue from the sound track and direct the animators — by means of these exposure sheets — as to mouth movements and action that I want for each character.

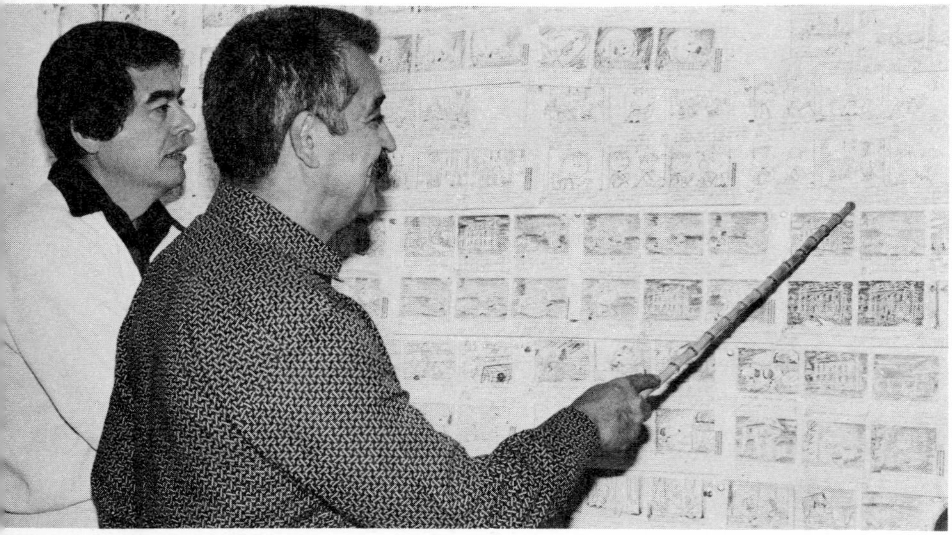

“This is my co-director, Phil Roman, and I going over the storyboard and discussing how we want to plot a particular scene.

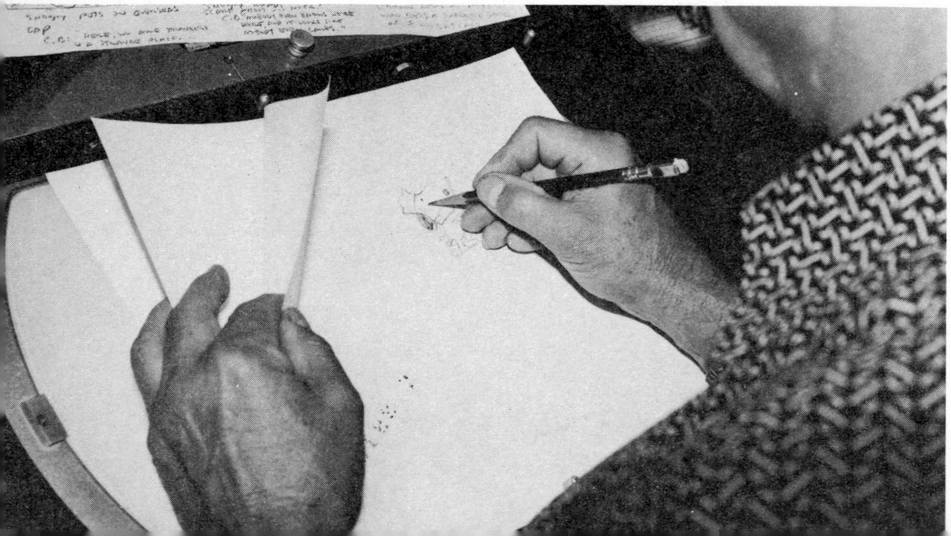

“Next, animators — following the storyboard and my directions — will start to create pencil sketches of the characters. We must use between twelve and twenty-four such sketches of *each* character in a scene for *just one second* of action on the screen. This rapid change of pictures causes the illusion of animation.

"Consequently there will be thousands of pencil sketches for each scene. We do them first in pencil so that we can then do what we call 'pencil test animation.'

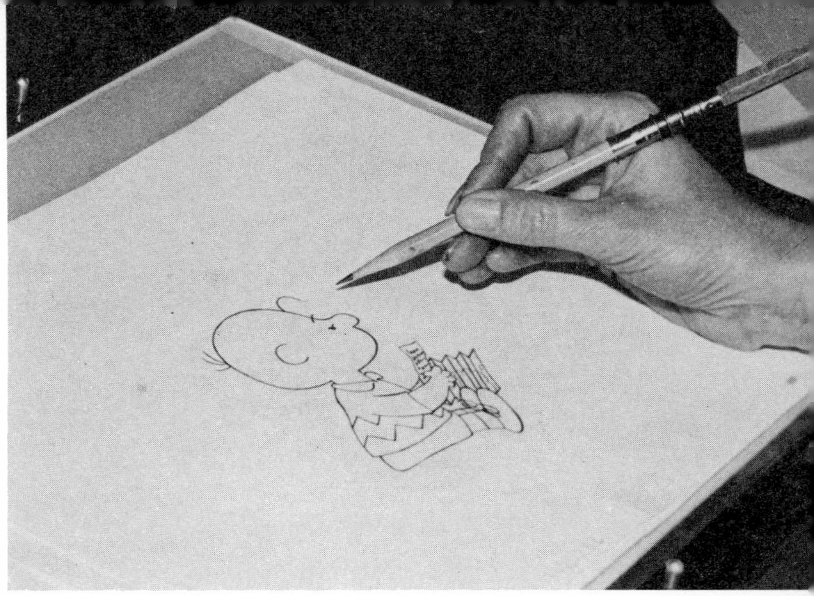

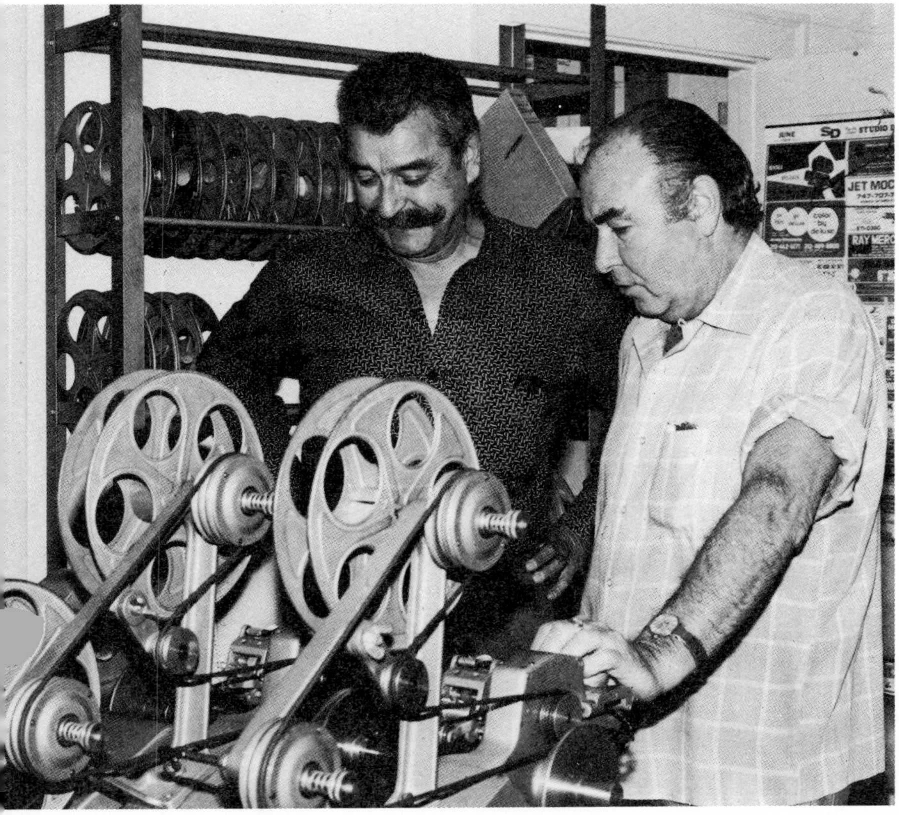

"Next, we will photograph one sketch at a time, and then we (that's editor Roger Donley with me) watch the animated action on our Movieola. This gives us the opportunity to check mouth movements and action before we commit to ink and paint.

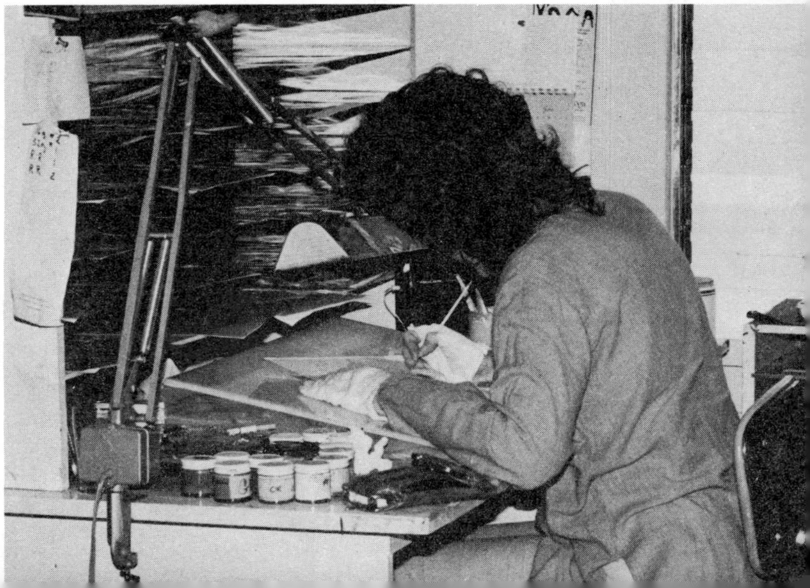

"Once I've approved the pencil tests, then the inking of every pencil sketch begins. This inking is obviously a long, painstaking, meticulous process. The ink lines have to be perfectly consistent.

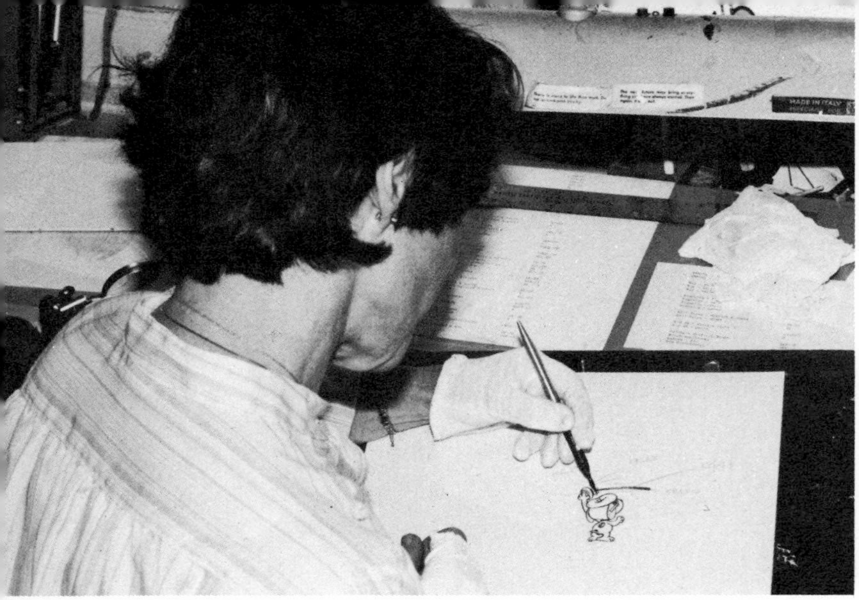

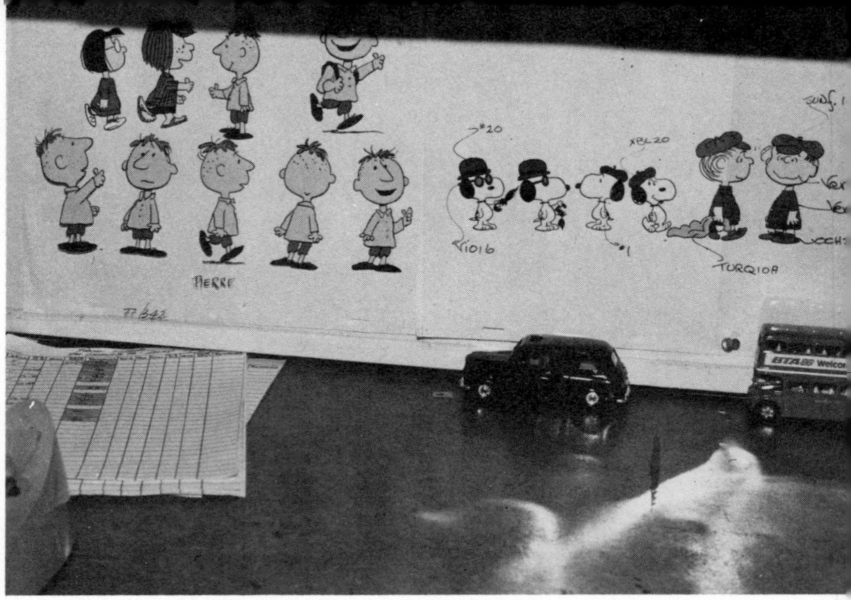

"All this work is done on what we call 'cells' which are transparent so that these drawings can eventually be placed over our scenic layouts — which are backgrounds for the action — like a set for a stage play or a movie.

"Our painters all have a color model sheet for each of the characters so that again we will have consistency throughout the film.

"Having completed the inking of a specific 'cell,' the 'cell' is turned over and the demanding task of hand-painting each of these drawings begins. It takes at least ten to fifteen minutes to complete the painting of each 'cell.'

"When the inking and painting for an entire scene have been completed, we then lay the 'cells' — one by one — over the background, and cameraman Nick Vasu starts to photograph in color what will be the final pictures.

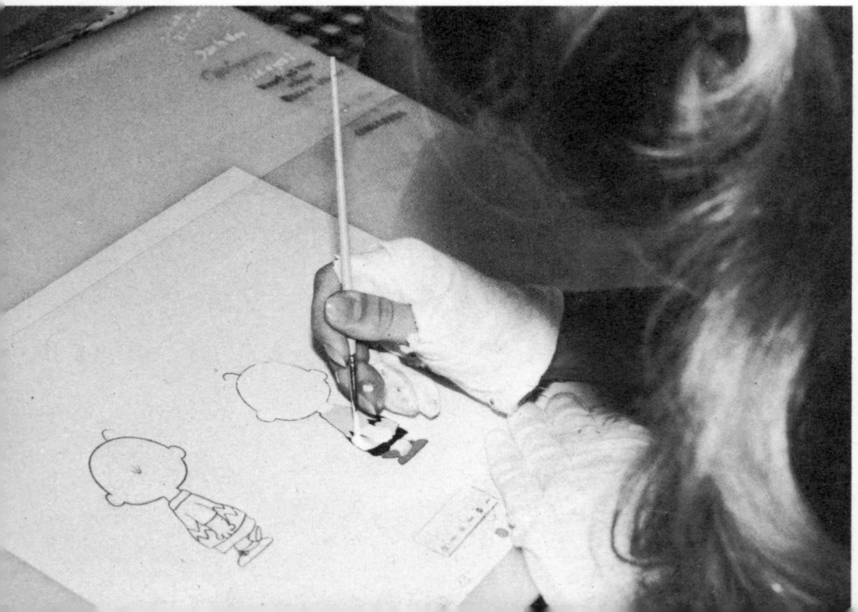

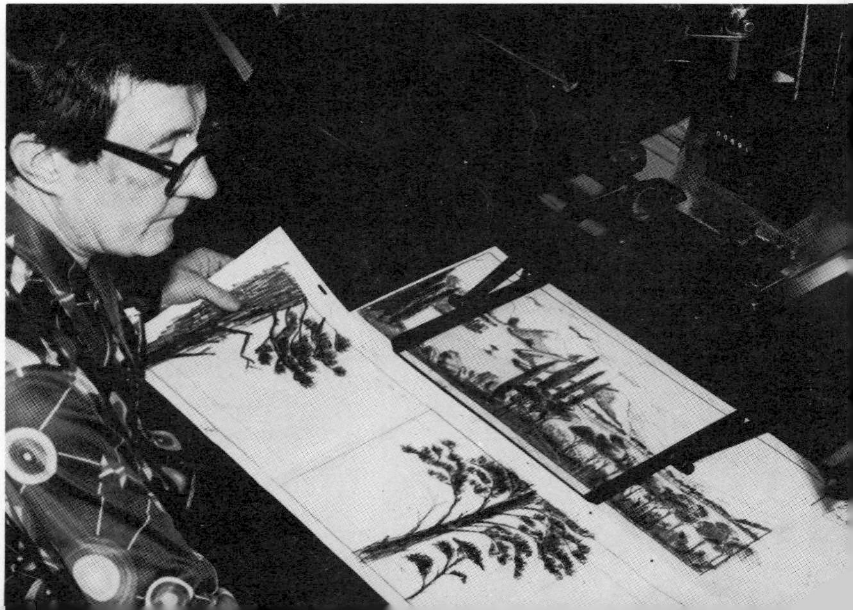

“Meanwhile, again up in northern California, our musical composers and directors (seen here with Sparky going over our storyboard — Judy Munsen, *left*, and Ed Bogas, *right*) will be creating the musical score.

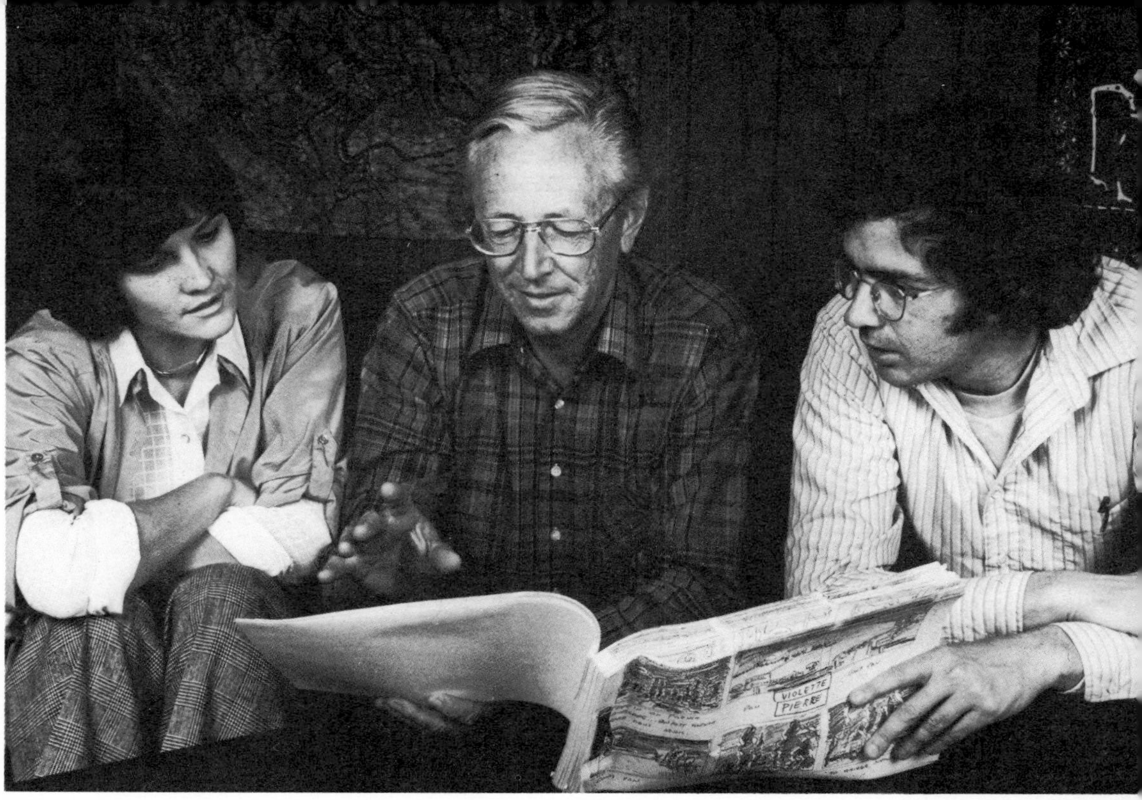
VIOLETTE
PIERRE

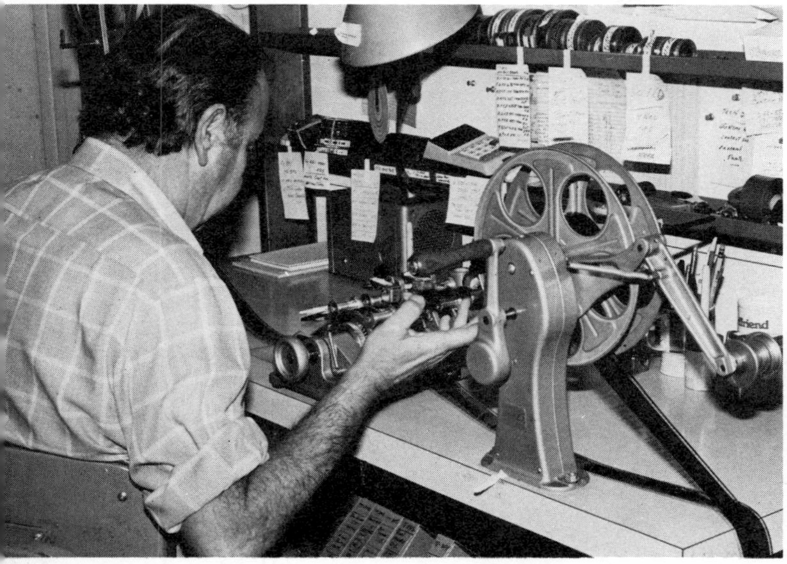

“Then our editors Chuck McCann and (here) Roger Donley take the sound track — including dialogue, sound effects, and music — and match it to the picture.

“Somehow, after about two years of this nonsense, a 75-minute film will appear miraculously in theaters all around the world.”

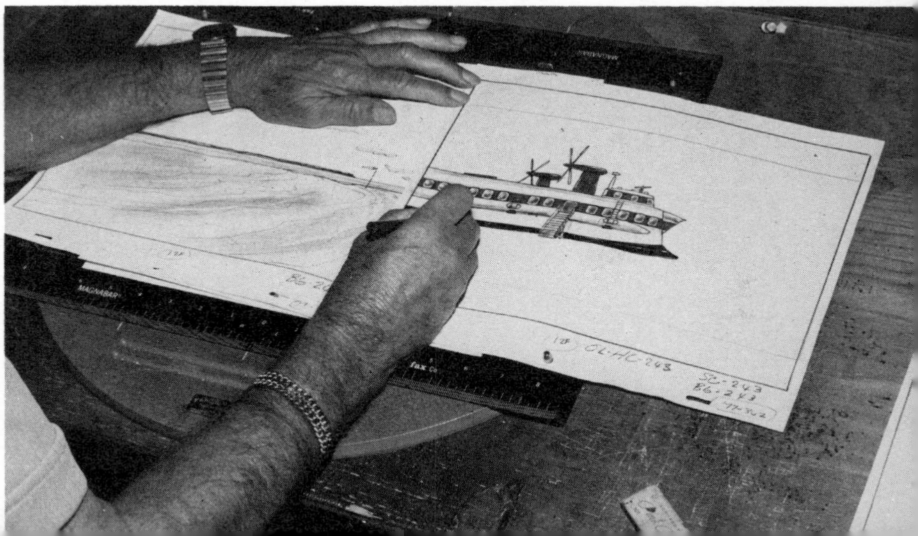

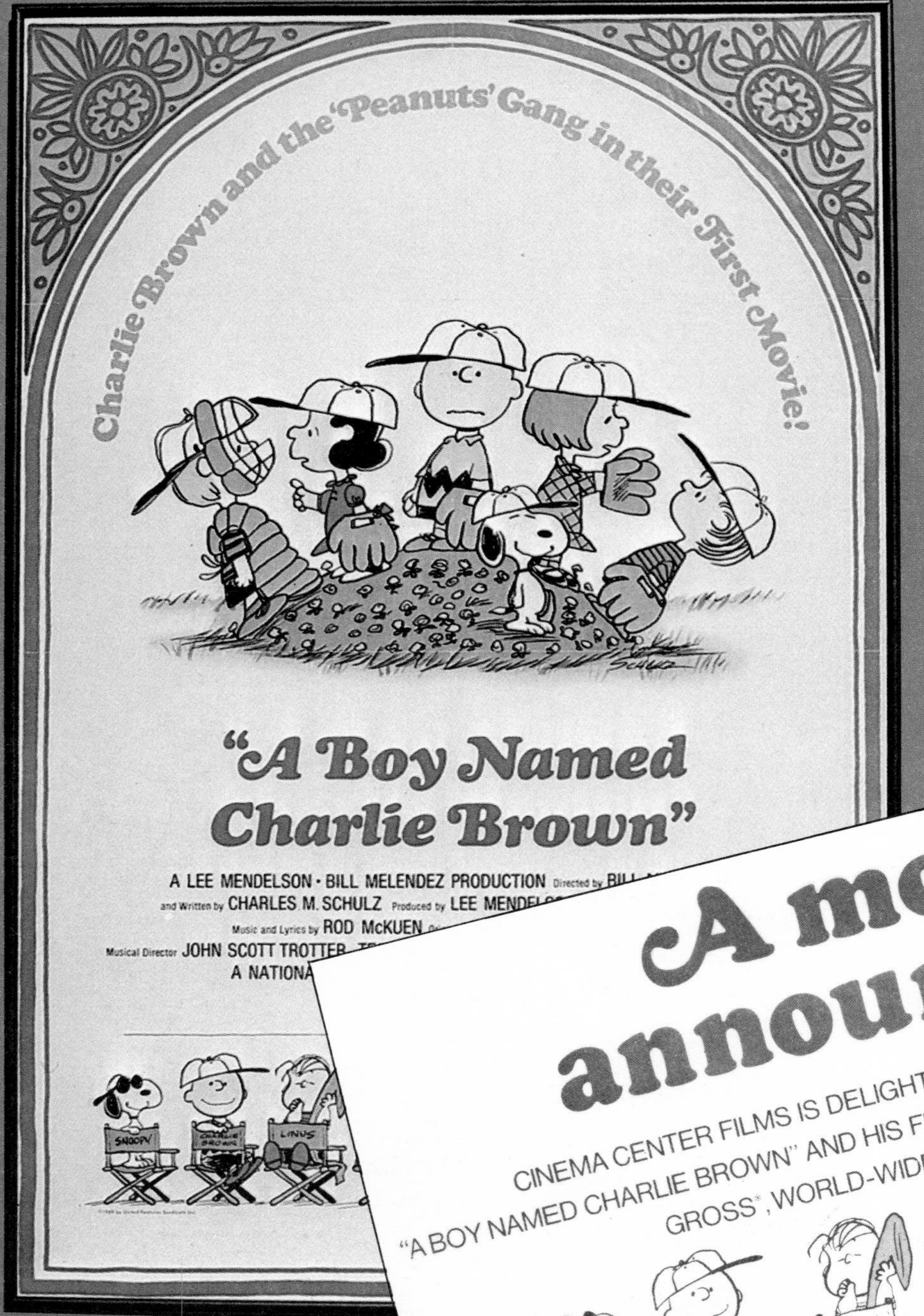
Charlie Brown and the 'Peanuts' Gang in their First Movie!
"A Boy Named Charlie Brown"
A LEE MENDELSON · BILL MELENDEZ PRODUCTION
and Written by CHARLES M. SCHULZ
Music and Lyrics by ROD McKUEN
Musical Director JOHN SCOTT TROTTER
SNOOPY
LINUS

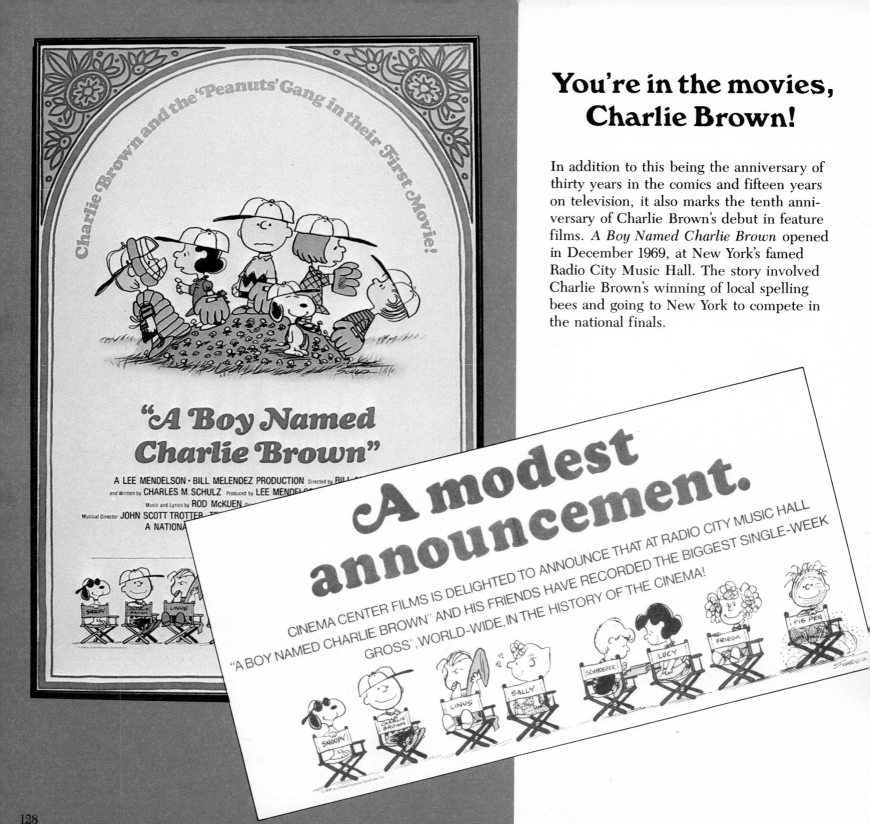

You're in the movies, Charlie Brown!

In addition to this being the anniversary of thirty years in the comics and fifteen years on television, it also marks the tenth anniversary of Charlie Brown's debut in feature films. *A Boy Named Charlie Brown* opened in December 1969, at New York's famed Radio City Music Hall. The story involved Charlie Brown's winning of local spelling bees and going to New York to compete in the national finals.

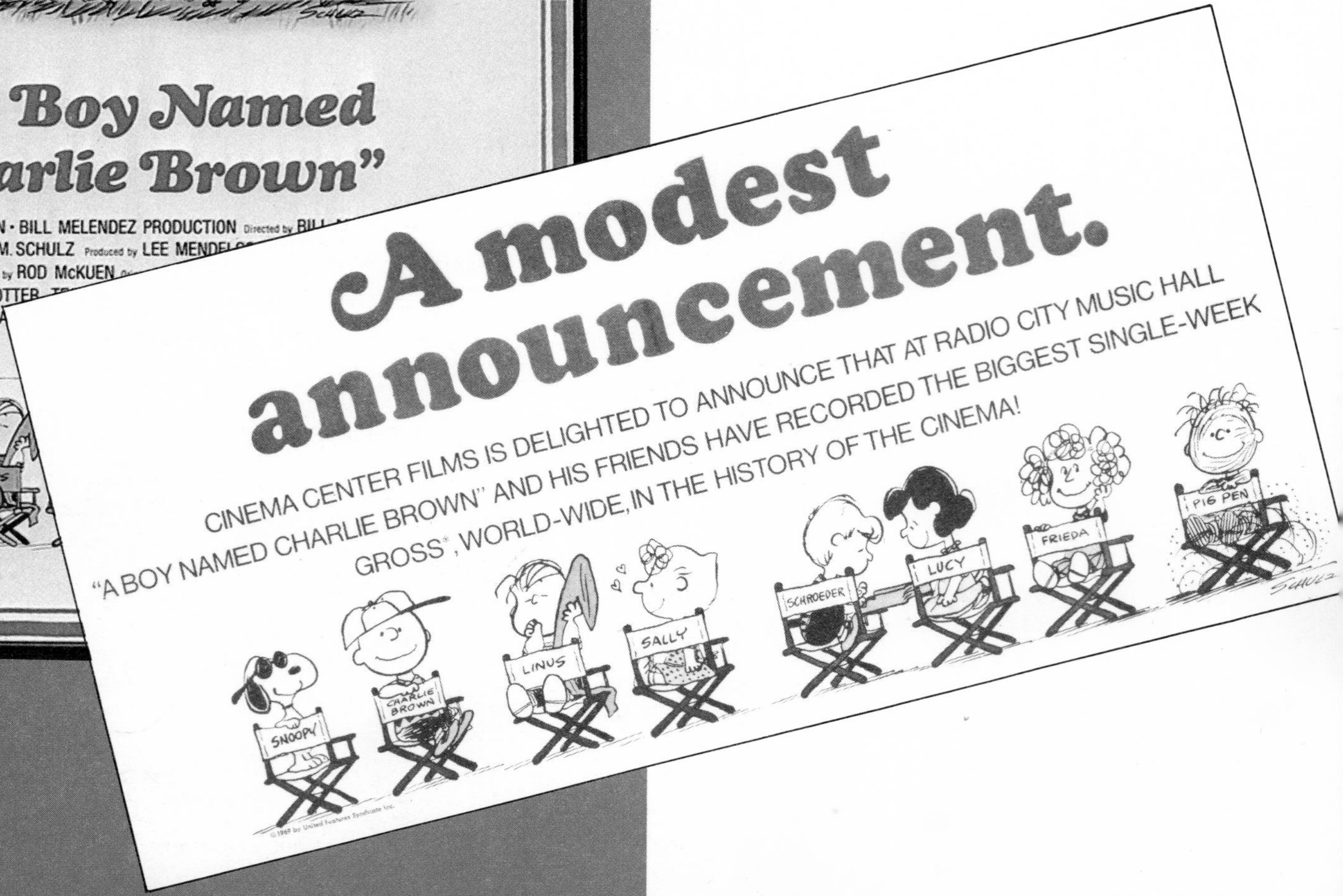
A modest announcement.
CINEMA CENTER FILMS IS DELIGHTED TO ANNOUNCE THAT AT RADIO CITY MUSIC HALL
"A BOY NAMED CHARLIE BROWN" AND HIS FRIENDS HAVE RECORDED THE BIGGEST SINGLE-WEEK
GROSS*, WORLD-WIDE, IN THE HISTORY OF THE CINEMA!
SNOOPY
CHARLIE BROWN
LINUS
SALLY
SCHROEDER
LUCY
FRIEDA
PIG PEN

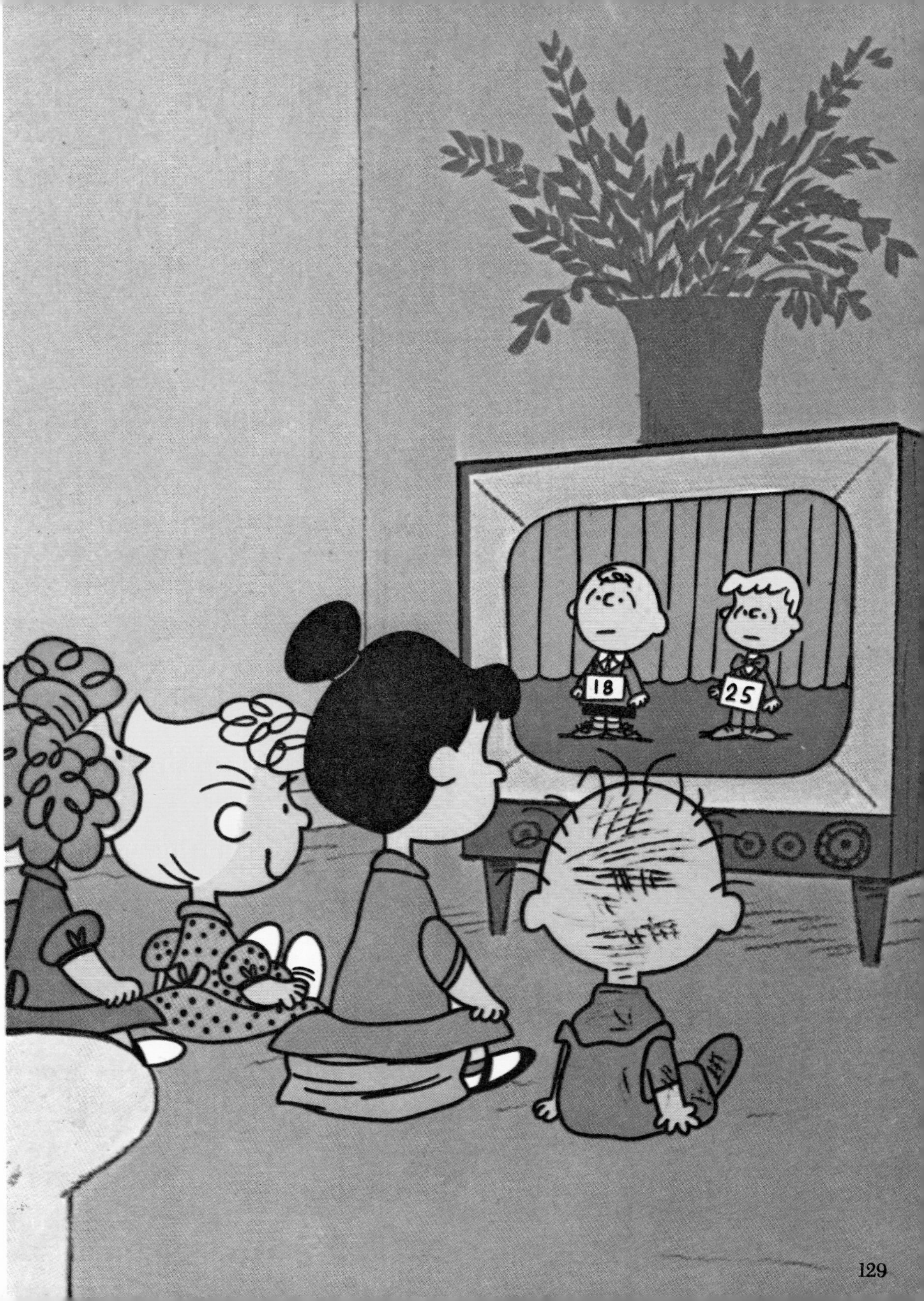
18
25

Tension is high as all of Charlie Brown's friends at home are gathered around a TV set to root him on. Finally, it's the last round and only Charlie Brown and one other contestant remain in the contest.

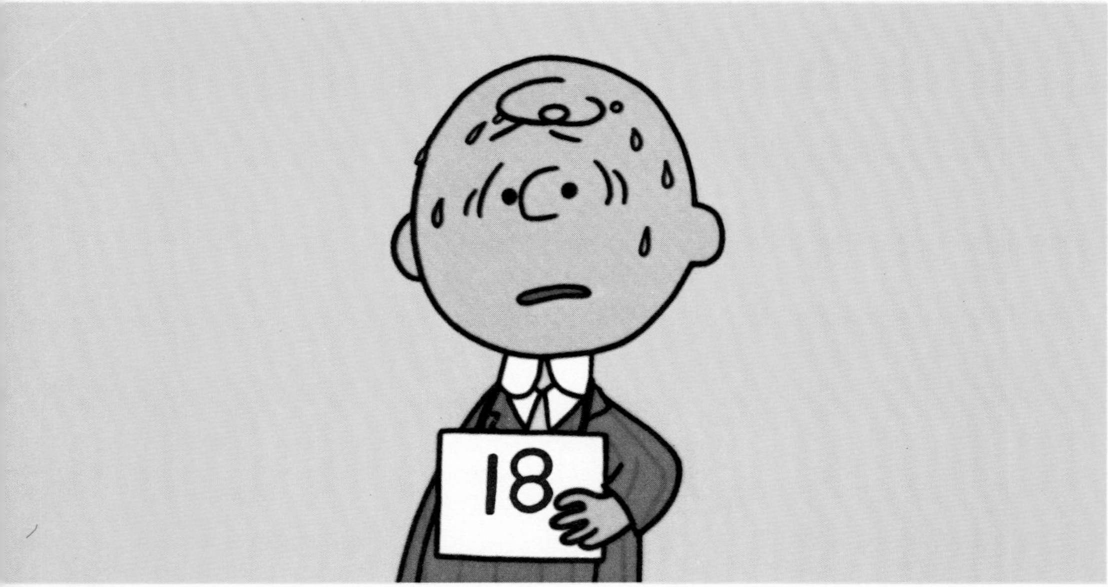
18

Then Charlie Brown needs to spell just one more word correctly to win the competition. Sweat pours down his face when he hears the final word: "beagle." Says Lucy at home: "He can't miss *that* word. That's his own dog. He's going to win. HE'S FINALLY GOING TO WIN SOMETHING!!"

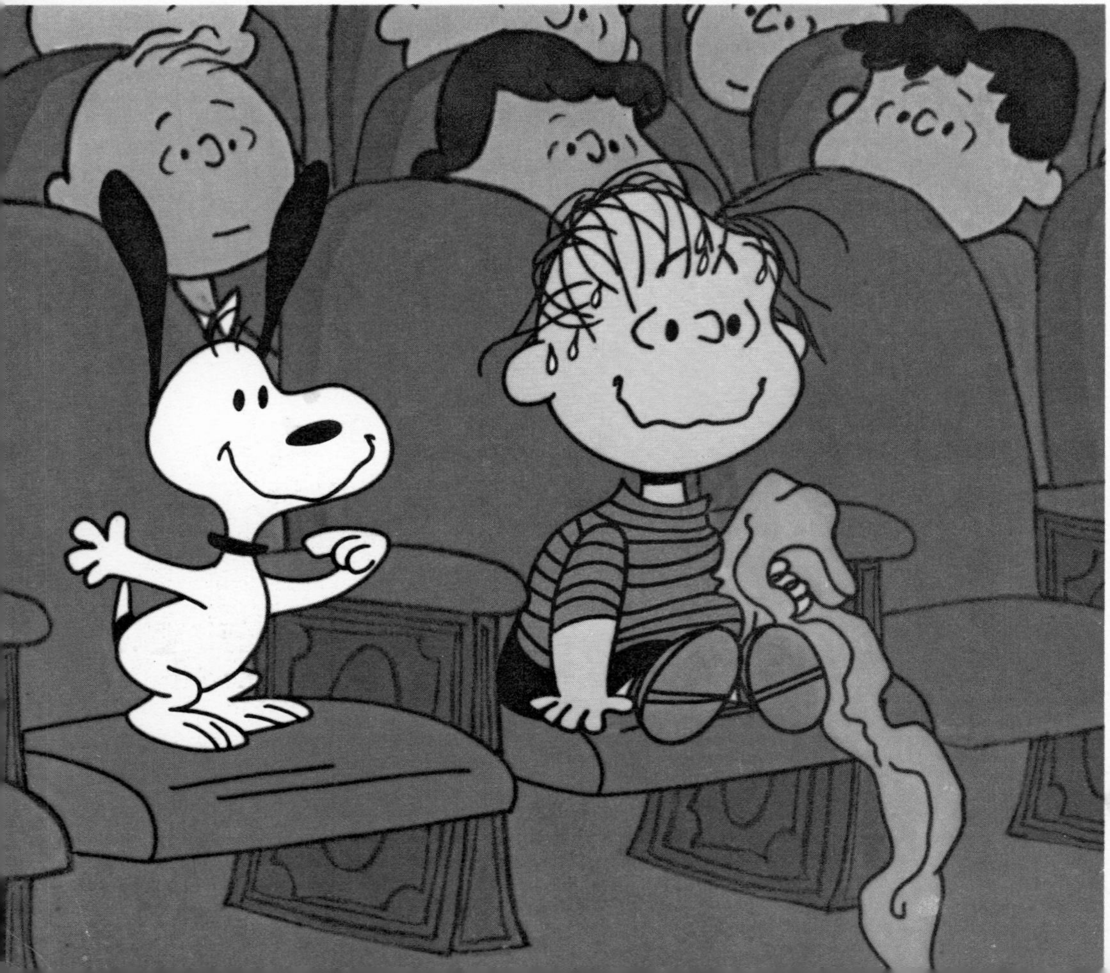

Snoopy, sitting in the front row of the competition in New York with Linus, starts gesturing to Charlie Brown on the stage to remind him that *he's* a beagle.

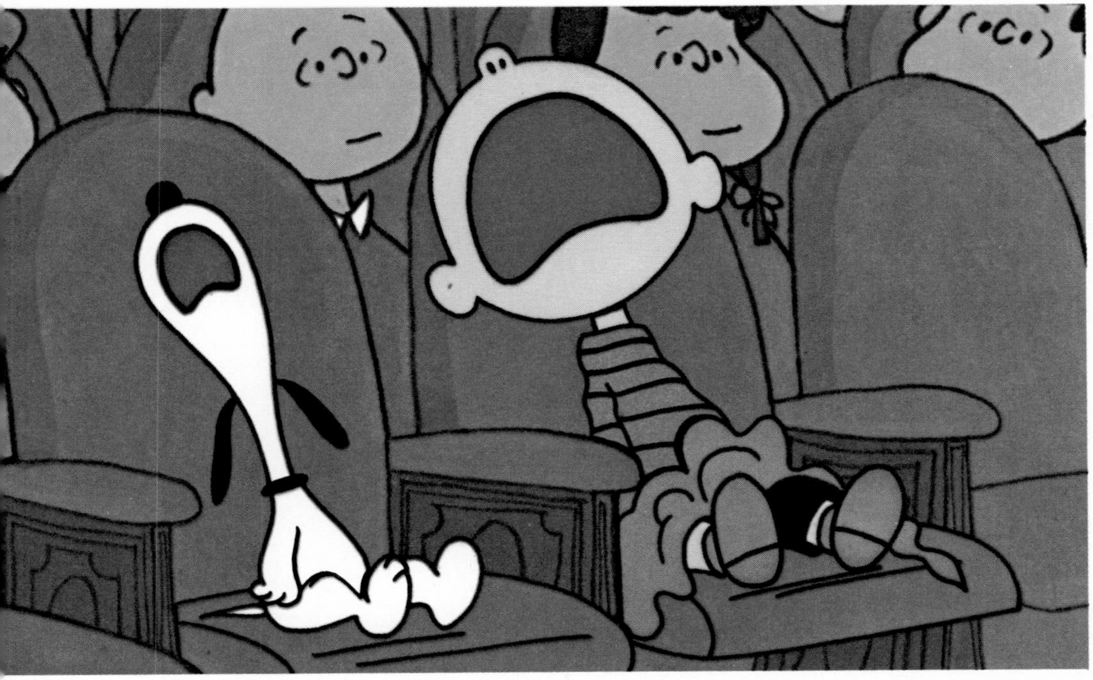

But poor Charlie Brown misspells the word — "B–E–A–G–E–L" — and a lot of crying ensues.

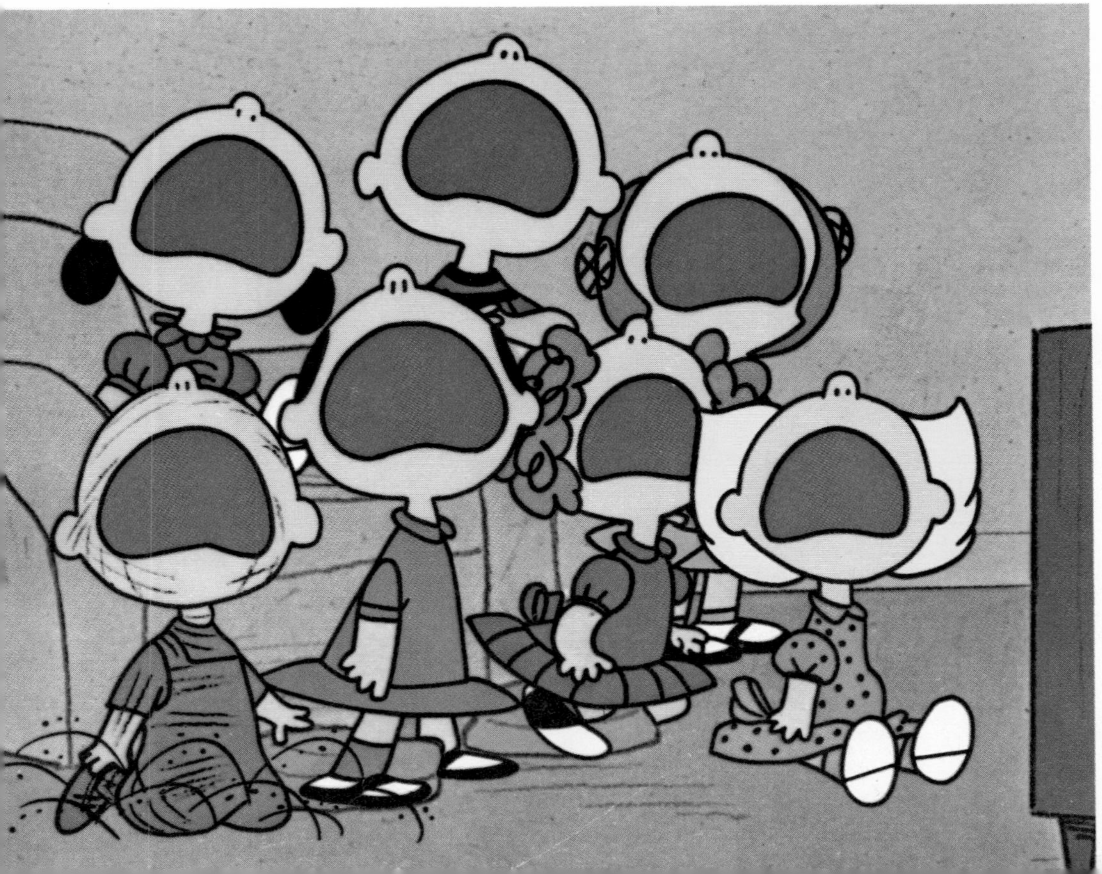

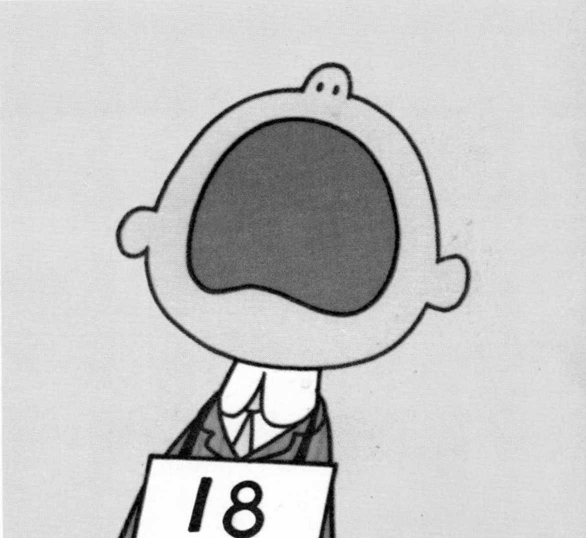
18

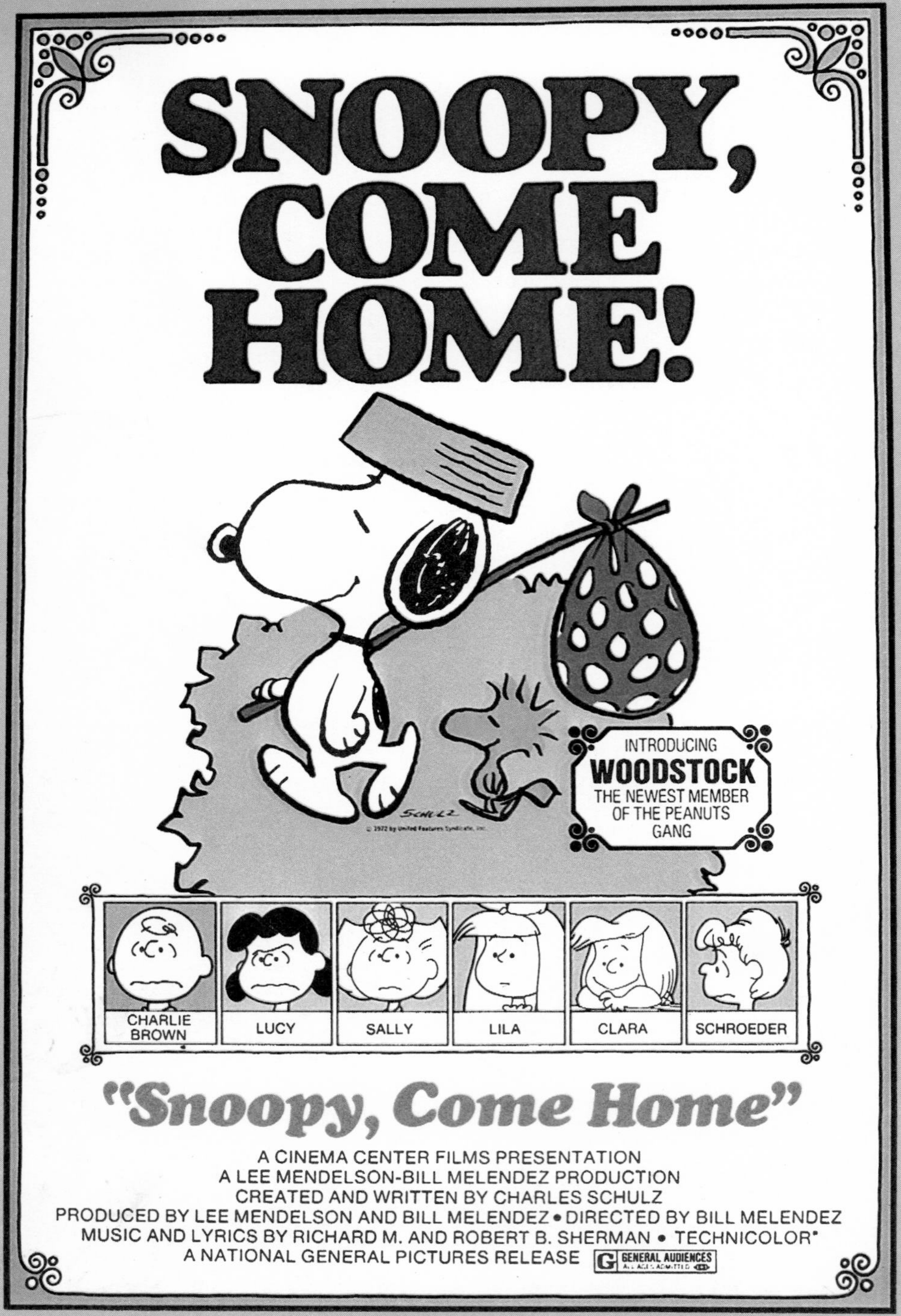
SNOOPY, COME HOME!
INTRODUCING
WOODSTOCK
THE NEWEST MEMBER OF THE PEANUTS GANG
CHARLIE BROWN
LUCY
SALLY
LILA
CLARA
SCHROEDER
"Snoopy, Come Home"
A CINEMA CENTER FILMS PRESENTATION
A LEE MENDELSON-BILL MELENDEZ PRODUCTION
CREATED AND WRITTEN BY CHARLES SCHULZ
PRODUCED BY LEE MENDELSON AND BILL MELENDEZ • DIRECTED BY BILL MELENDEZ
MUSIC AND LYRICS BY RICHARD M. AND ROBERT B. SHERMAN • TECHNICOLOR®
A NATIONAL GENERAL PICTURES RELEASE
G GENERAL AUDIENCES

Snoopy, Come Home, released in 1972, was our second movie. Snoopy discovers, much to Charlie Brown's horror, that Charlie Brown was not his original owner. That distinction belongs to a girl named Lila, and after all these years of silence, Lila writes to Snoopy and asks him to visit her in the hospital. Snoopy helps her to recover and she asks him to come and live with her. Snoopy feels that he must be loyal to his first owner, and so he tells a shocked Charlie Brown that he is leaving.

Snoopy's going-away party was surely the saddest scene we've ever created. When Snoopy said good-bye to Woodstock and then to Charlie Brown, we had a "first" at a *Peanuts* movie: an audience in tears. No one could imagine Charlie Brown and his best friend being separated.

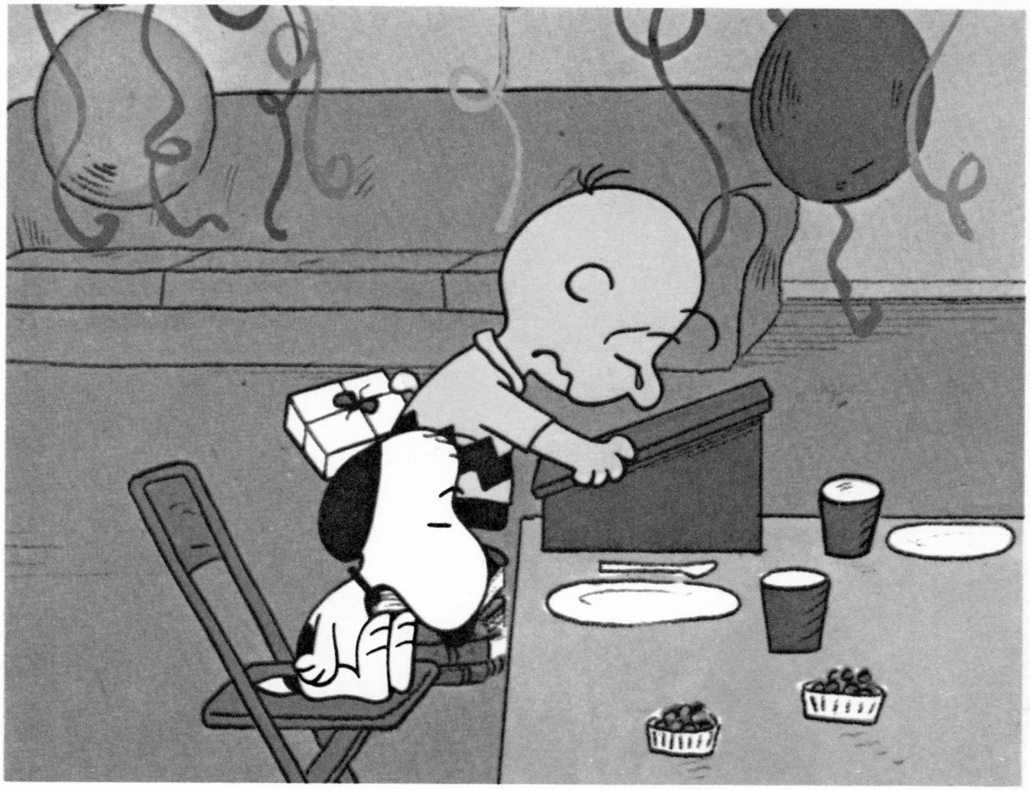

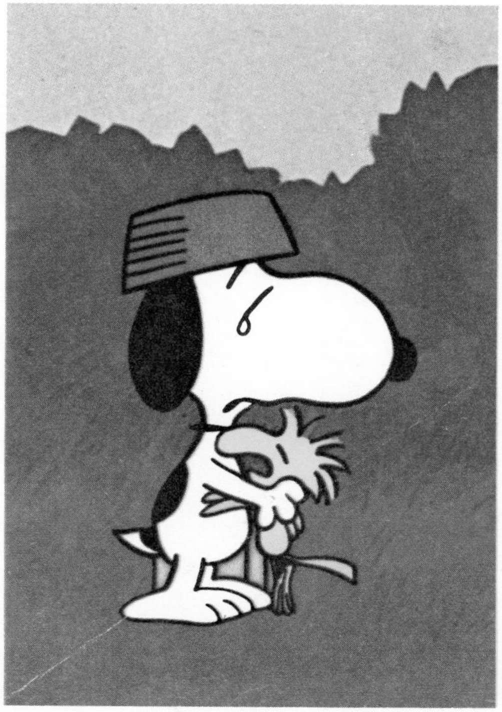

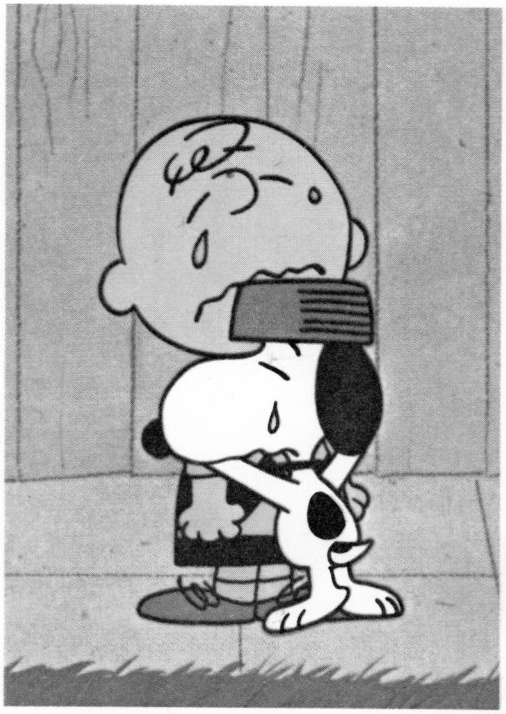

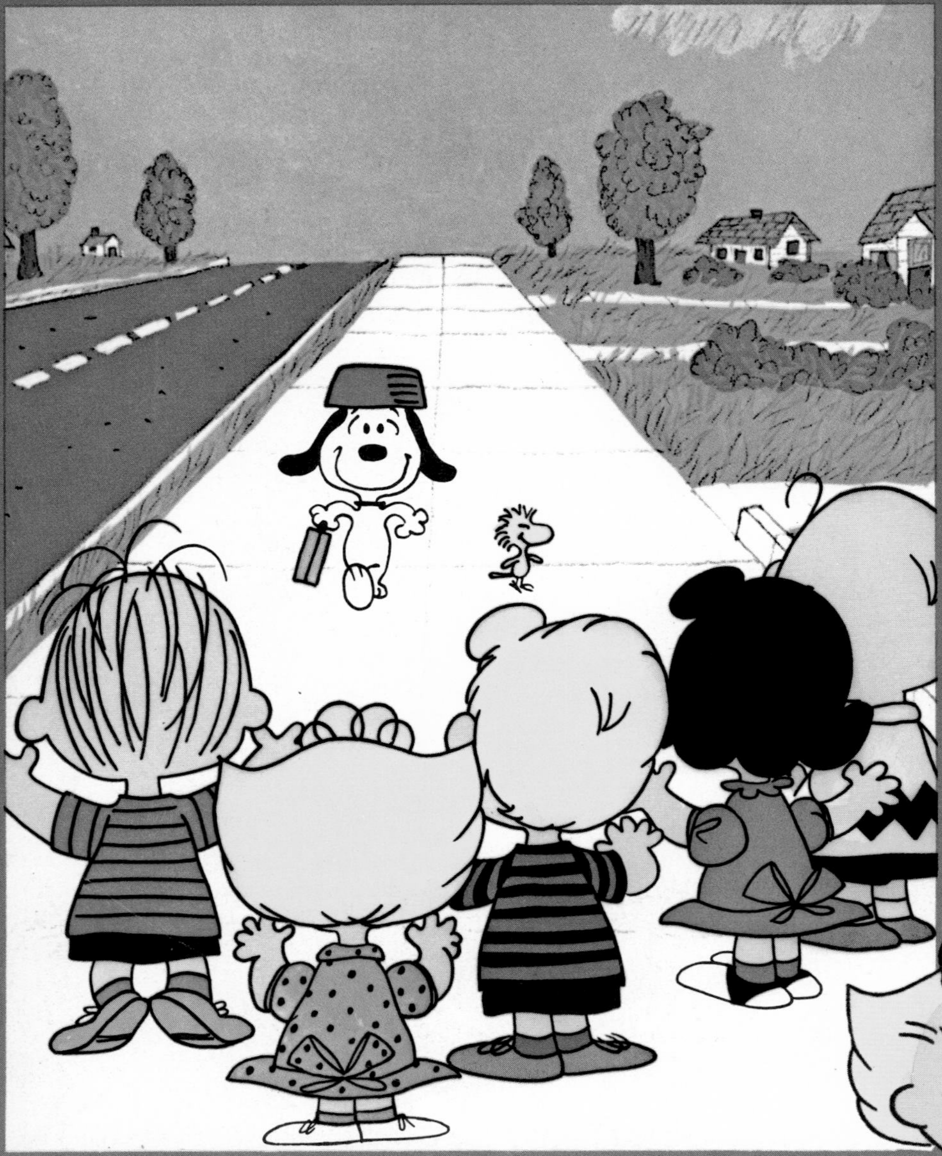

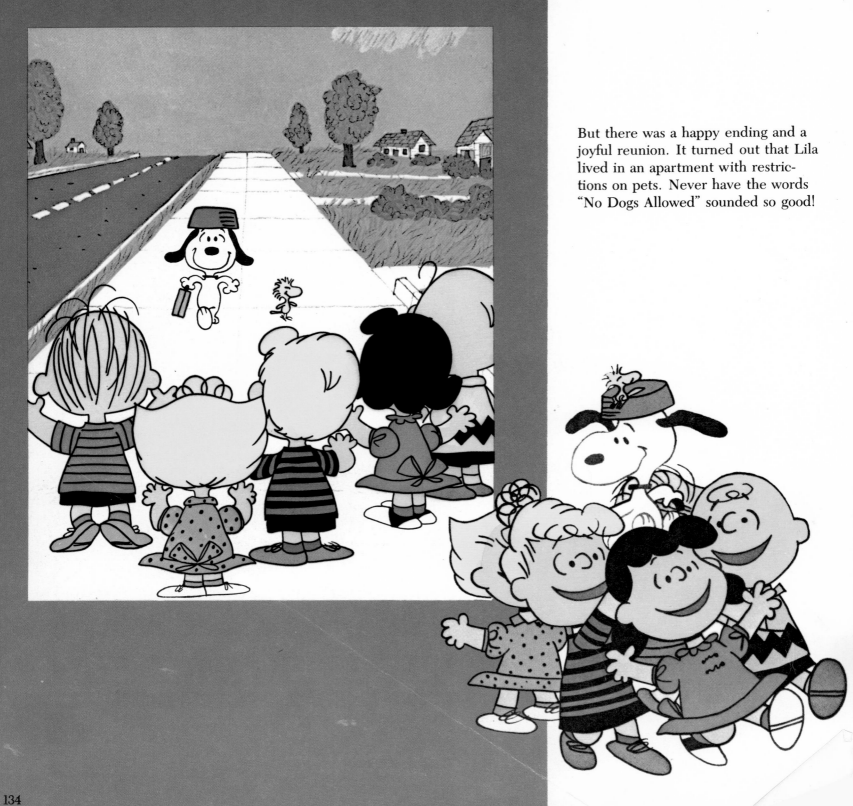

But there was a happy ending and a joyful reunion. It turned out that Lila lived in an apartment with restrictions on pets. Never have the words "No Dogs Allowed" sounded so good!

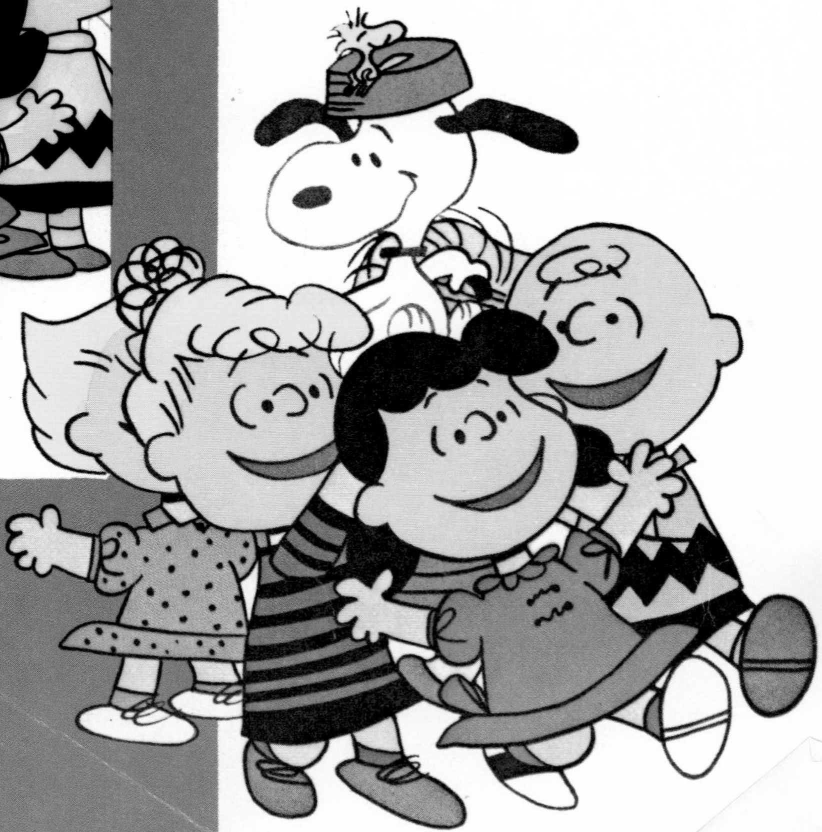

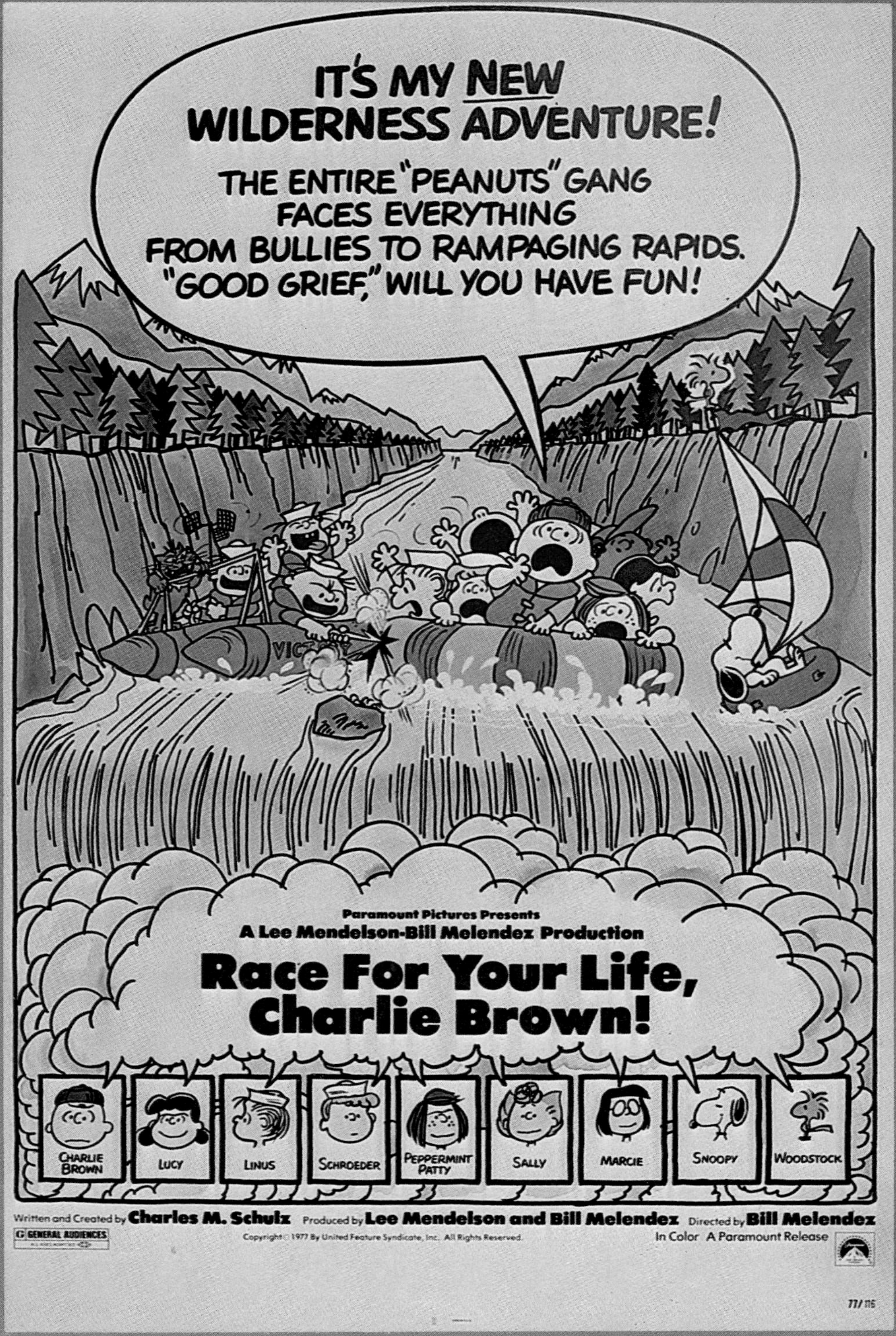
IT'S MY NEW
WILDERNESS ADVENTURE!
THE ENTIRE "PEANUTS" GANG
FACES EVERYTHING
FROM BULLIES TO RAMPAGING RAPIDS.
"GOOD GRIEF," WILL YOU HAVE FUN!
Paramount Pictures Presents
A Lee Mendelson-Bill Melendez Production
Race For Your Life,
Charlie Brown!
CHARLIE BROWN
LUCY
LINUS
SCHROEDER
PEPPERMINT PATTY
SALLY
MARCIE
SNOOPY
WOODSTOCK
Written and Created by Charles M. Schulz
Produced by Lee Mendelson and Bill Melendez
Directed by Bill Melendez
G GENERAL AUDIENCES
Copyright © 1977 By United Feature Syndicate, Inc. All Rights Reserved.
In Color A Paramount Release
77/115

Our third movie, *Race for Your Life, Charlie Brown,* was released by Paramount in 1977. It involved Charlie Brown and his friends shooting the rapids in a rafting competition.

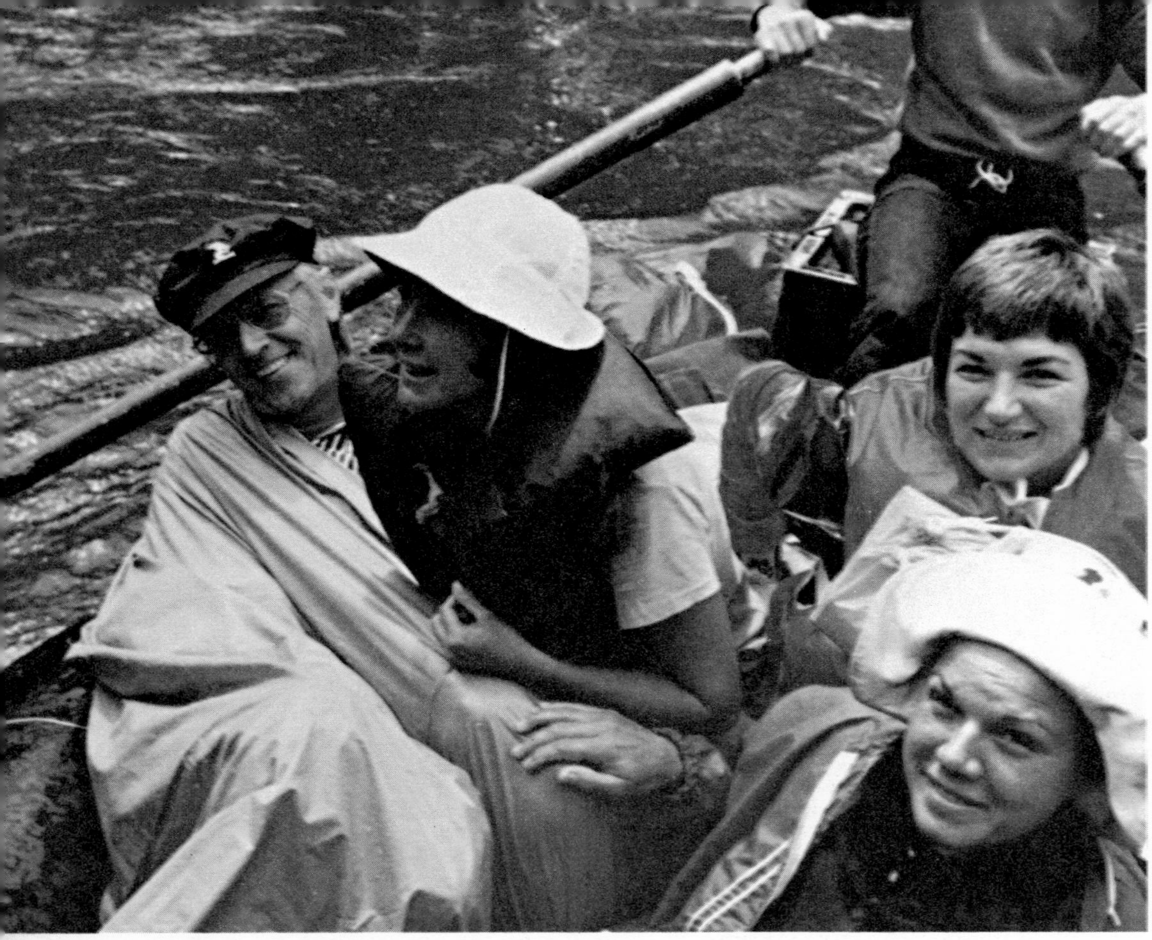

Until this time, Sparky's rule of thumb concerning travel was that he would go somewhere only if he could be home by noon. But in order to get the right mood for creating *Race for Your Life*, he and Jeannie and friends rode a rubber raft down the rapids of the Rogue River in Oregon. This research led to scenes like those on the next page.

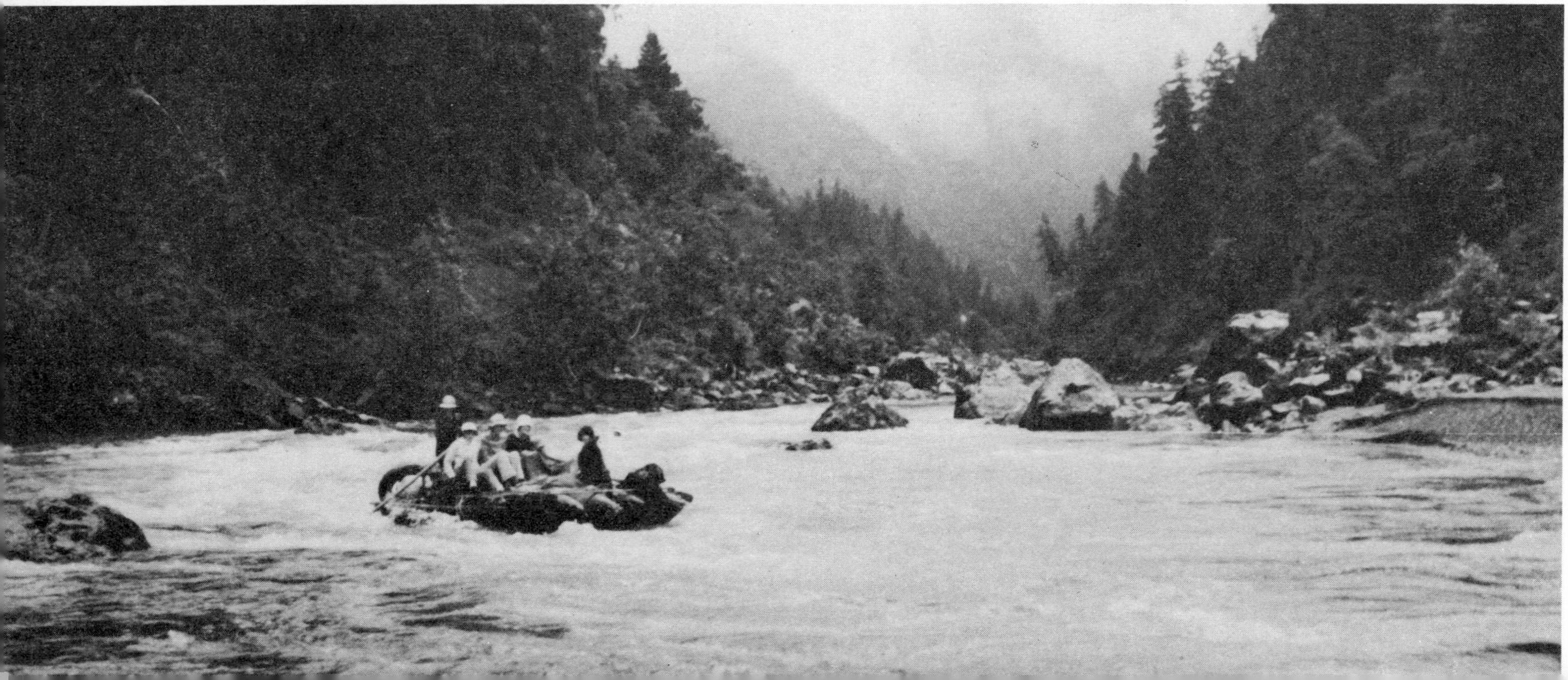

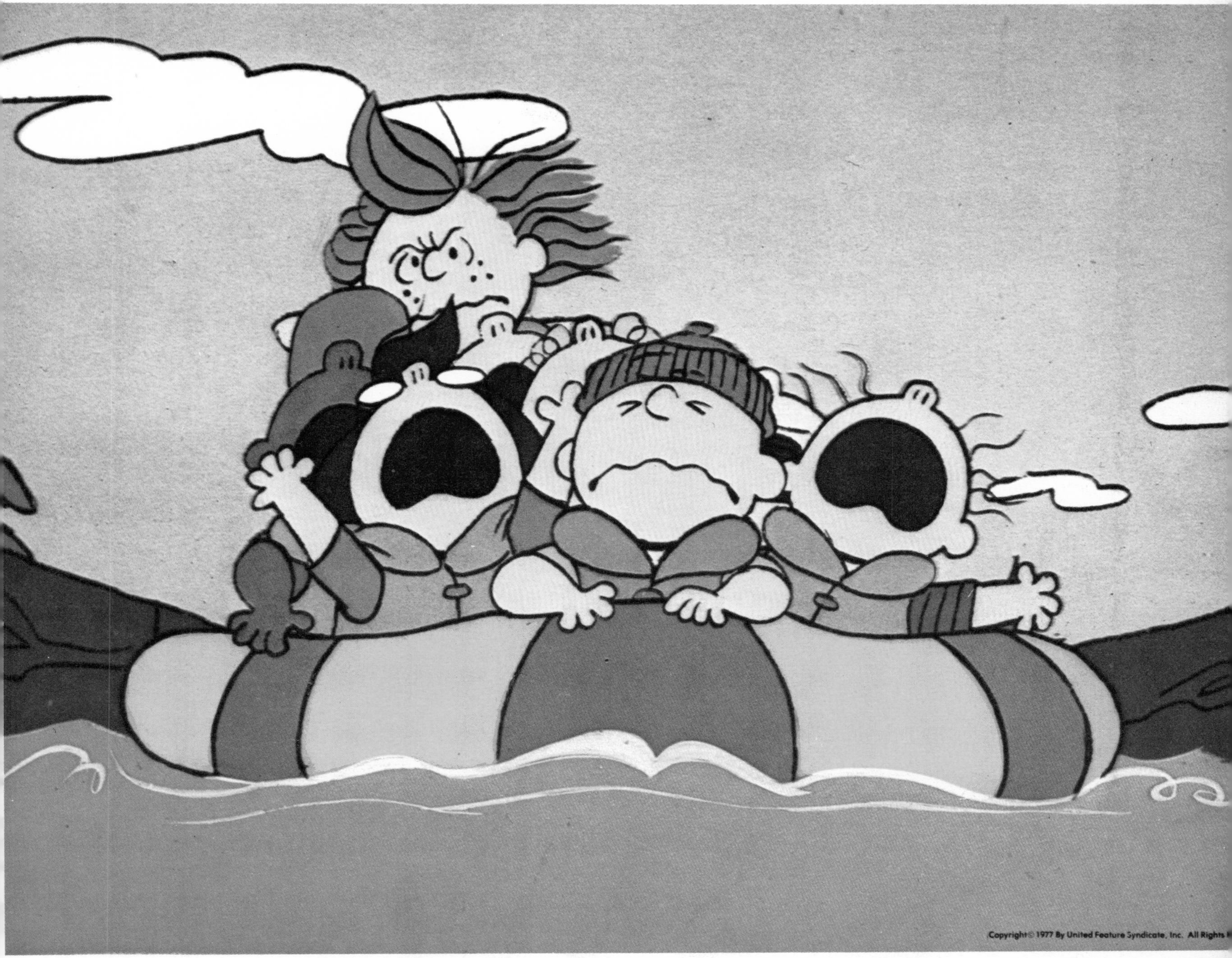

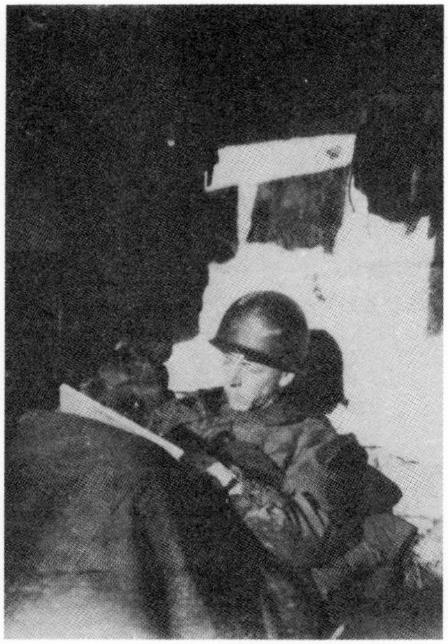

This is Sparky in 1945 where he billeted at a château in France for six weeks with his company of American soldiers.

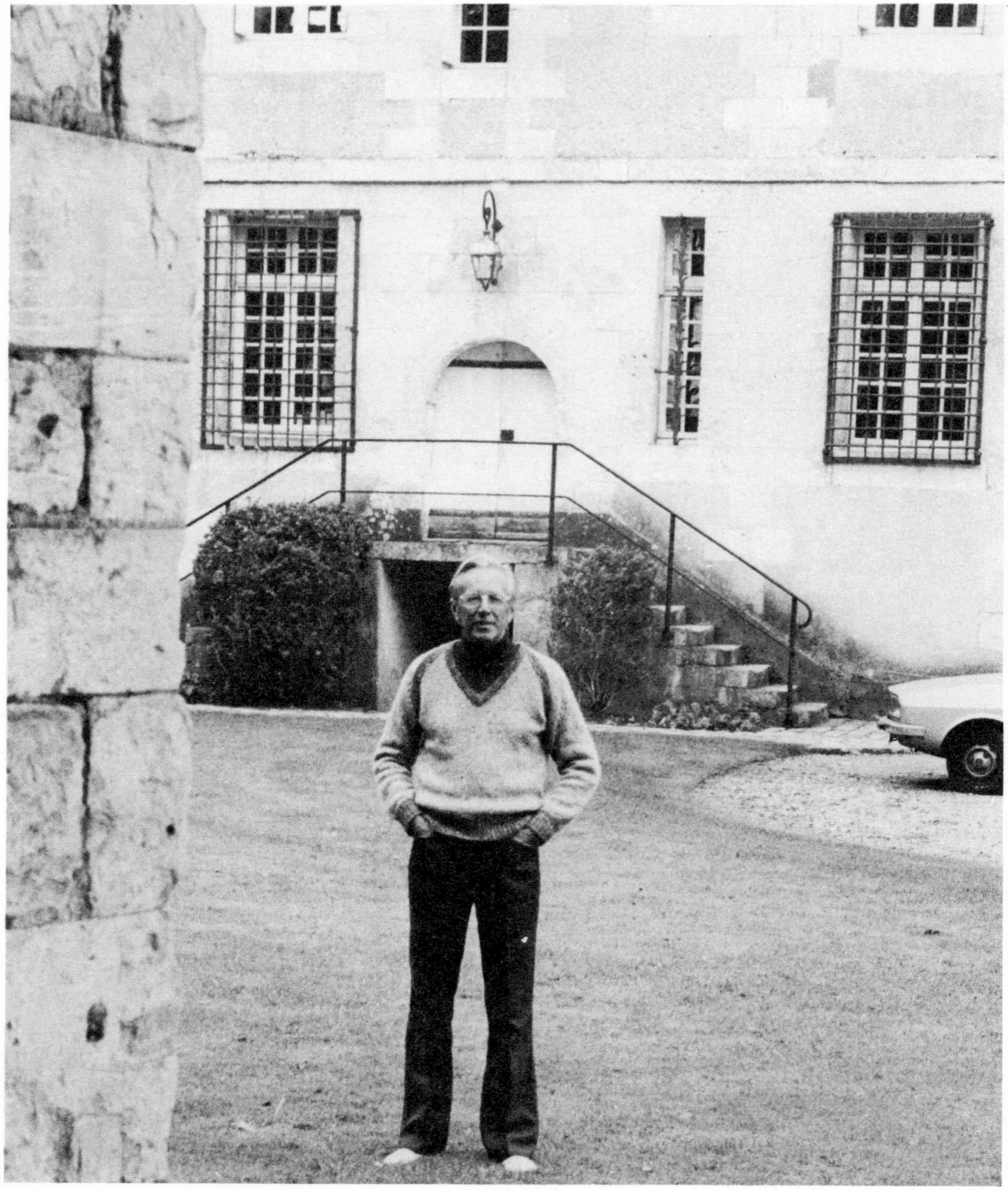

Here, thirty-four years later, Sparky revisited the château and was so inspired by this return visit that his trip became the basis of our newest movie, *Bon Voyage, Charlie Brown . . . and Don't Come Back*, a 1980 summer release by Paramount.

Sparky has called this trip perhaps the most emotional experience of his life. His years in the army and away from home were probably the most difficult of his life, and he feels that much of what goes into Charlie Brown comes from this period. He rarely sketches "just for the fun of it," but he was so moved by this experience that he made these sketches of the area near Normandy.

Le Havre

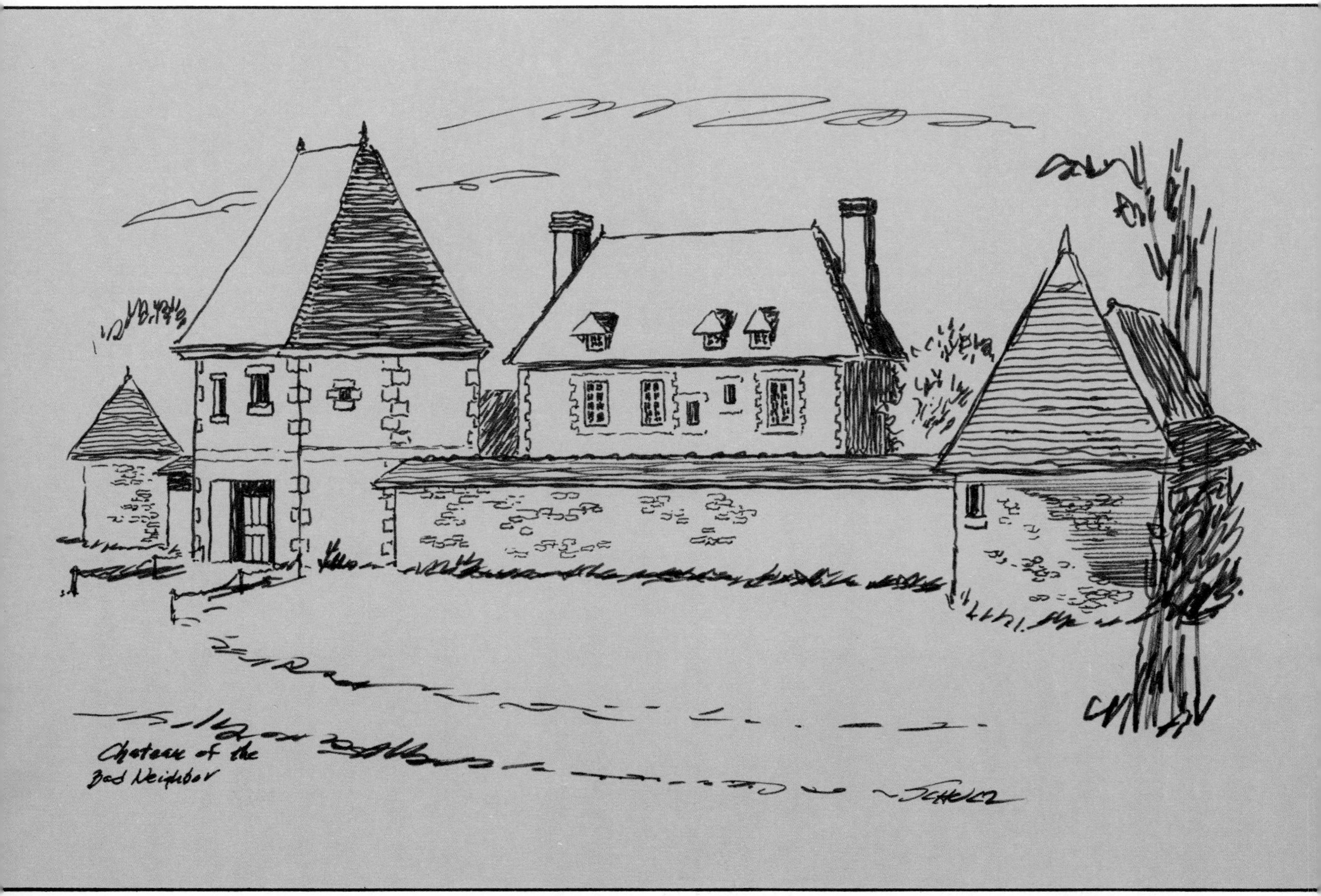
Chateau of the Bad Neighbor

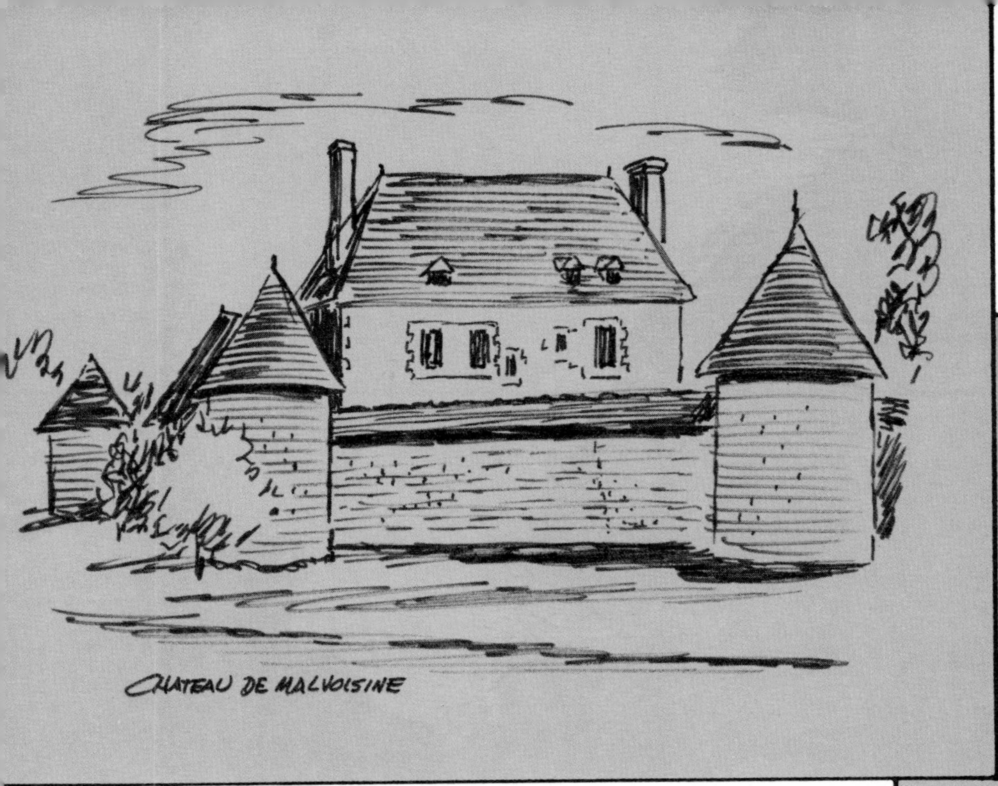
CHATEAU DE MALVOISINE

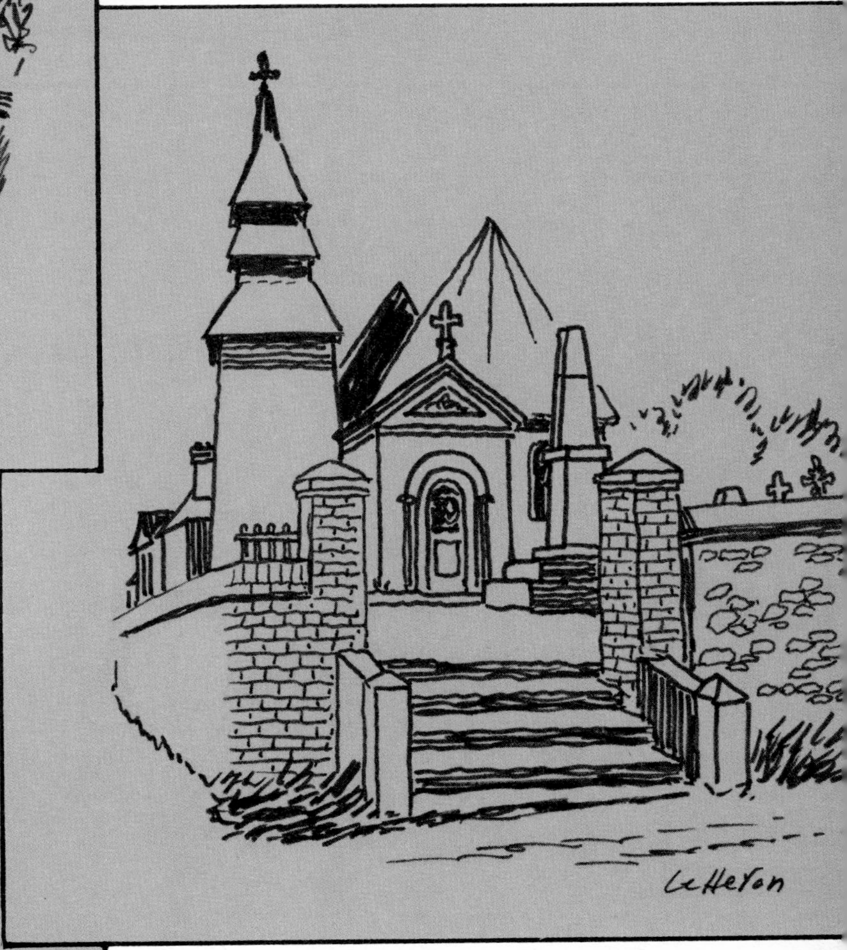
LeHeron

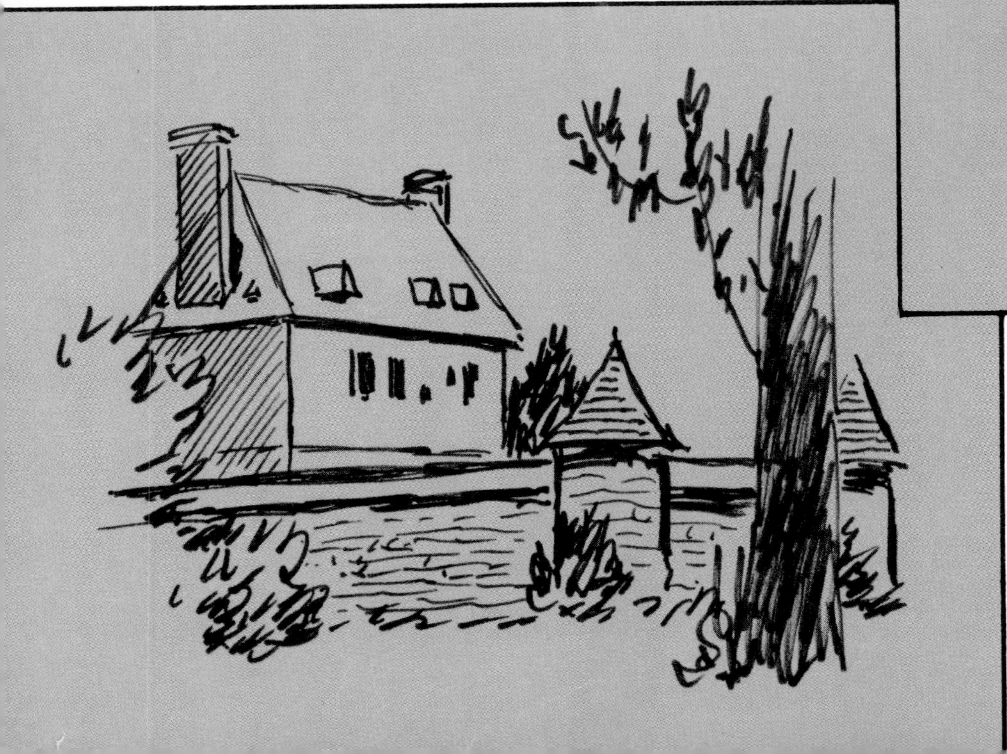

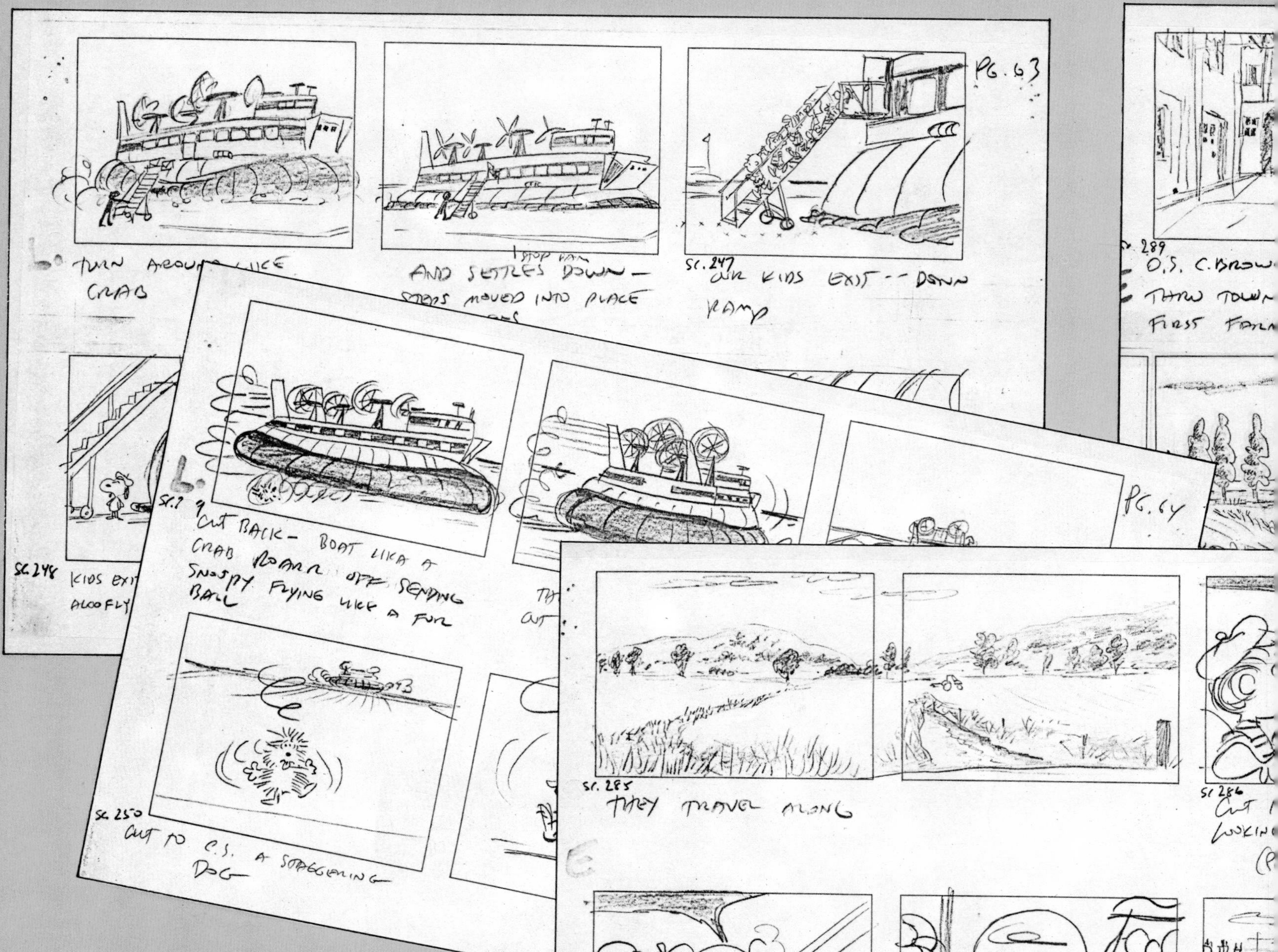
PG. 63
TURN AROUND LIKE CRAB
AND SETTLES DOWN —
STEPS MOVED INTO PLACE
SC. 247
OUR KIDS EXIT -- DOWN RAMP
SC. 289
O.S. C.BROWN
THRU TOWN
FIRST FARM
SC. 248
KIDS EXIT
PG. 64
CUT BACK — BOAT LIKE A CRAB ROARS OFF SENDING SNOOPY FLYING LIKE A FUR BALL
SC. 250
CUT TO C.S. A STAGGERING DOG

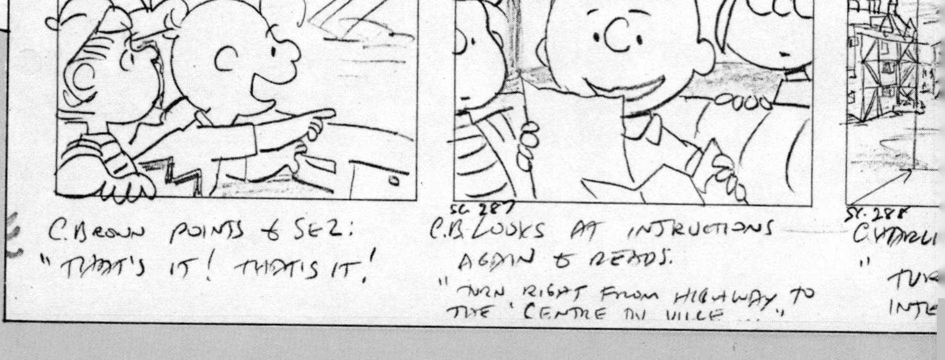
SC. 285
THEY TRAVEL ALONG
SC. 286
SC. 287
SC. 288
C.BROWN POINTS & SEZ:
"THAT'S IT! THAT'S IT!
C.B. LOOKS AT INSTRUCTIONS AGAIN & READS.
"TURN RIGHT FROM HIGHWAY TO THE 'CENTRE DU VILLE'..."

Charlie Brown and friends find themselves at a château in France for the *Bon Voyage* movie, where he, Linus, and Snoopy have some terrifying experiences. These are a few of Bill Melendez' storyboards from the movie.

SC. 290
PAN PAST OLD BLDGS
LINUS! (O.S.) "WOW! LOOK
AT THOSE OLD BLDGS!!"

PG. 70

SC.318
(C.B. (O.S.) "THIS IS THE TOWN,
THIS IS 'LE HERON'! I
SAW THE SIGN, AND, LOOK,

SC. 319
C.B: "THAT MUST BE
OUR SCHOOL!"

SC. 320
SCHOOL RECEDES

IS WAITIN
A FARM

SC. 32

PG. 69

AR- C.BROWN
... EXPECTANTLY

ND THEM VERY INDISTINCT)

N O.S. VOICE

HT AT FIRST
TION...

SNOOPY PEELS INTO
GLOOM ....

SNOOPY INTO HAPPY
TYPE - POINTING

SC.325
SEE CHATEAUX IN
MURKY GLOOM

PAN TO LEFT - ACCROSS LENGTH OF CASTLE.

SC.325A
CUT BACK TO BRIDGE-
LINUS + C.BROWN DUET
TOO ....
C.B. "THIS IS IT, LINUS, THIS IS WHE
WE'RE GOING TO STAY. "

You have great memories, Charlie Brown

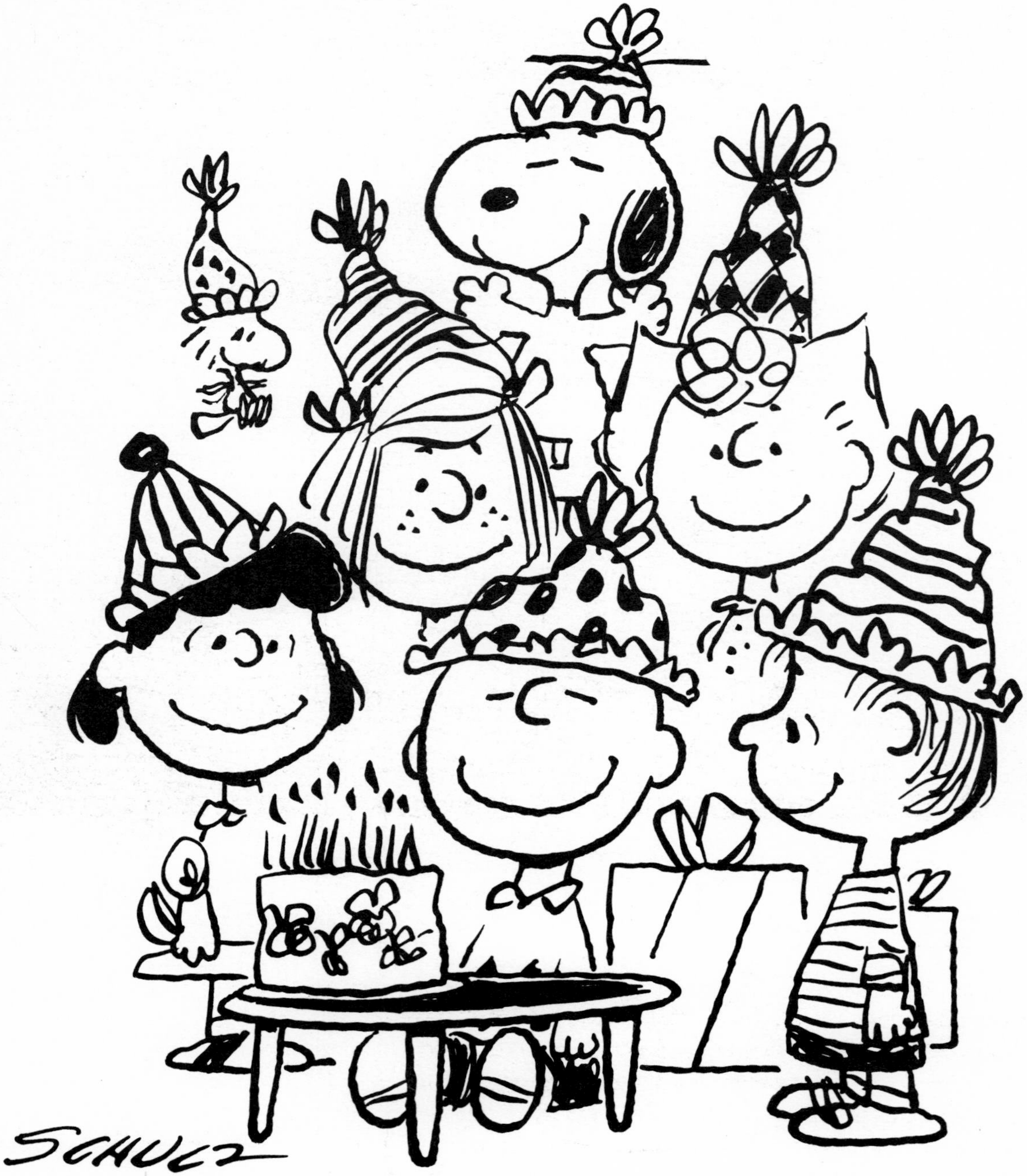
SCHULZ

Thirty years have brought many honors to Charlie Brown and Charlie Schulz:

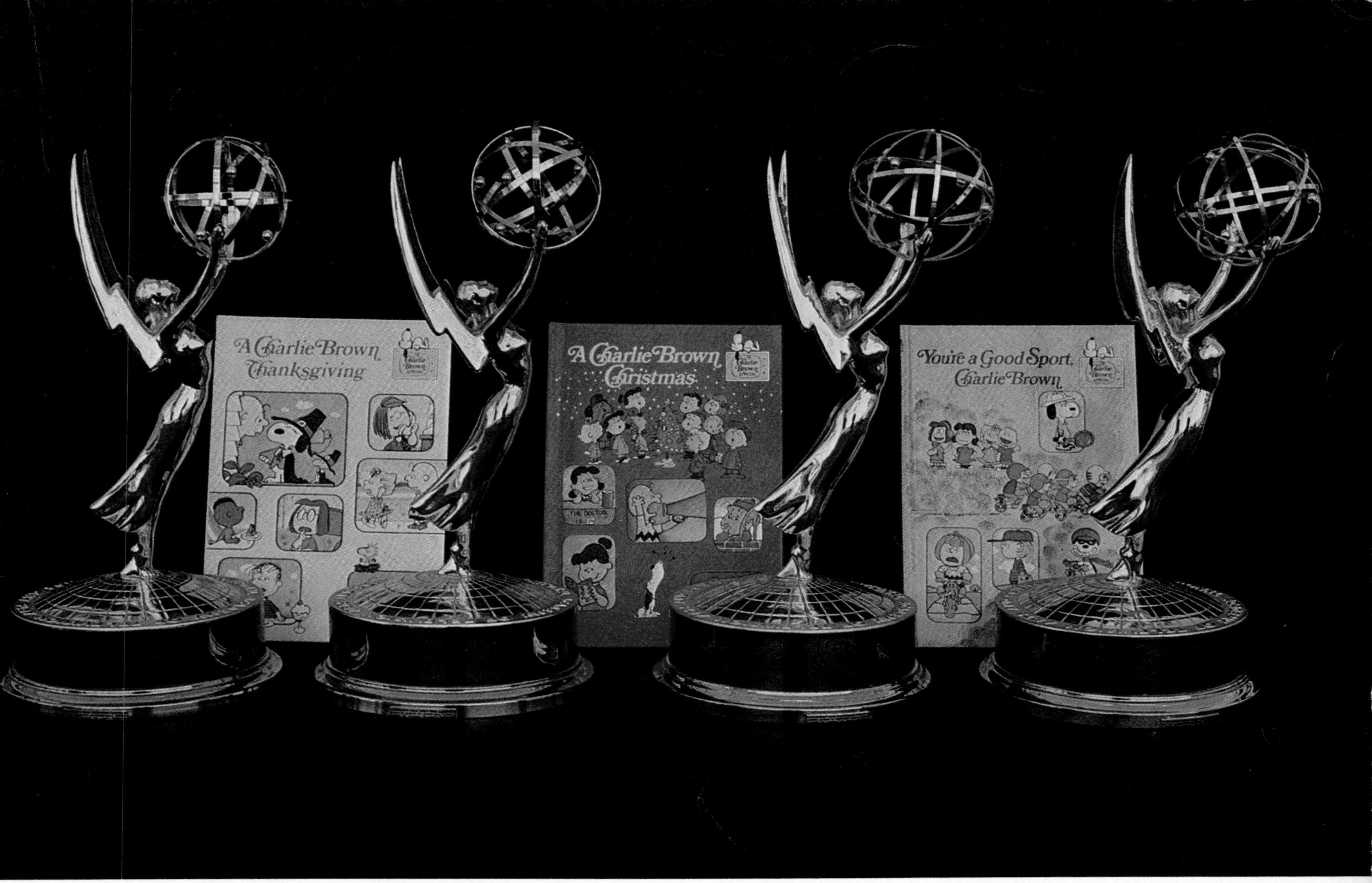
A Charlie Brown Thanksgiving
A Charlie Brown Christmas
You're a Good Sport, Charlie Brown

Twelve of the eighteen Charlie Brown animated half-hour specials received Emmy nominations, and three of those won Emmys: *A Charlie Brown Christmas*, *A Charlie Brown Thanksgiving*, and *You're a Good Sport, Charlie Brown*. We also were fortunate to win a fourth Emmy for a one-hour documentary celebrating the twenty-fifth anniversary of *Peanuts*. Somewhere between forty and fifty million people tune in to each of these shows, and the loyalty of these viewers, which is unprecedented, is deeply appreciated by all those who are involved with the productions.

"YOU'RE A GOOD MAN, CHARLIE BROWN"

Schulz

One of Sparky's greatest thrills has been the success of the musical-stage hit *You're a Good Man, Charlie Brown*. The show had a four-year run in New York and since has traveled to major cities throughout the world. When you include local theater-group performances, it is the most-performed musical in the history of the American theater.

Originally produced by Arthur Whitelaw and Gene Persson, with book and music by Clark Gesner, the show came to television as a program for the Hallmark Hall of Fame.

"YOU'RE A GOOD MAN, CHARLIE BROWN"

Side One
1. OPENING (2:17)
2. YOU'RE A GOOD MAN, CHARLIE BROWN (2:00)
3. SNOOPY (THEY LIKE ME) (3:21)
4. SCHROEDER (2:57)
5. THE KITE (2:05)
6. MY BLANKET AND ME (2:59)
7. QUICK CHANGES (0:38)
8. THE BOOK REPORT (5:26)

Side Two
1. THE BASEBALL GAME (5:08)
2. THE DOCTOR IS IN (3:06)
3. THE RED BARON (2:06)
4. LITTLE KNOWN FACTS (2:31)
5. SUPPERTIME (3:31)
6. HAPPINESS (3:37)
7. YOU'RE A GOOD MAN, CHARLIE BROWN (REPRISE) (0:48)
All selections published by Jeremy Music Inc., ASCAP.

Additional orchestrations by Ralph Burns.

Recorded at Regent Sound Studios, Inc., New York, N.Y.
Recording engineer: Bob Liftin
Photography: Gary Null
Album design: Loring Eutemey

ATLANTIC RECORDING CORPORATION
1841 BROADWAY, NEW YORK, NEW YORK 10023
℗ © 1972 Atlantic Recording Corporation Printed in U.S.A.

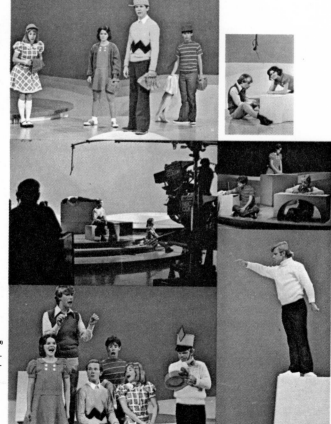

146

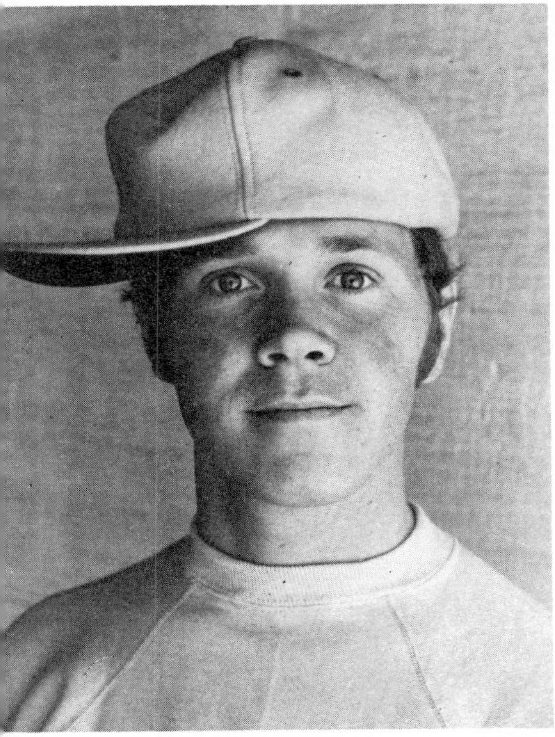

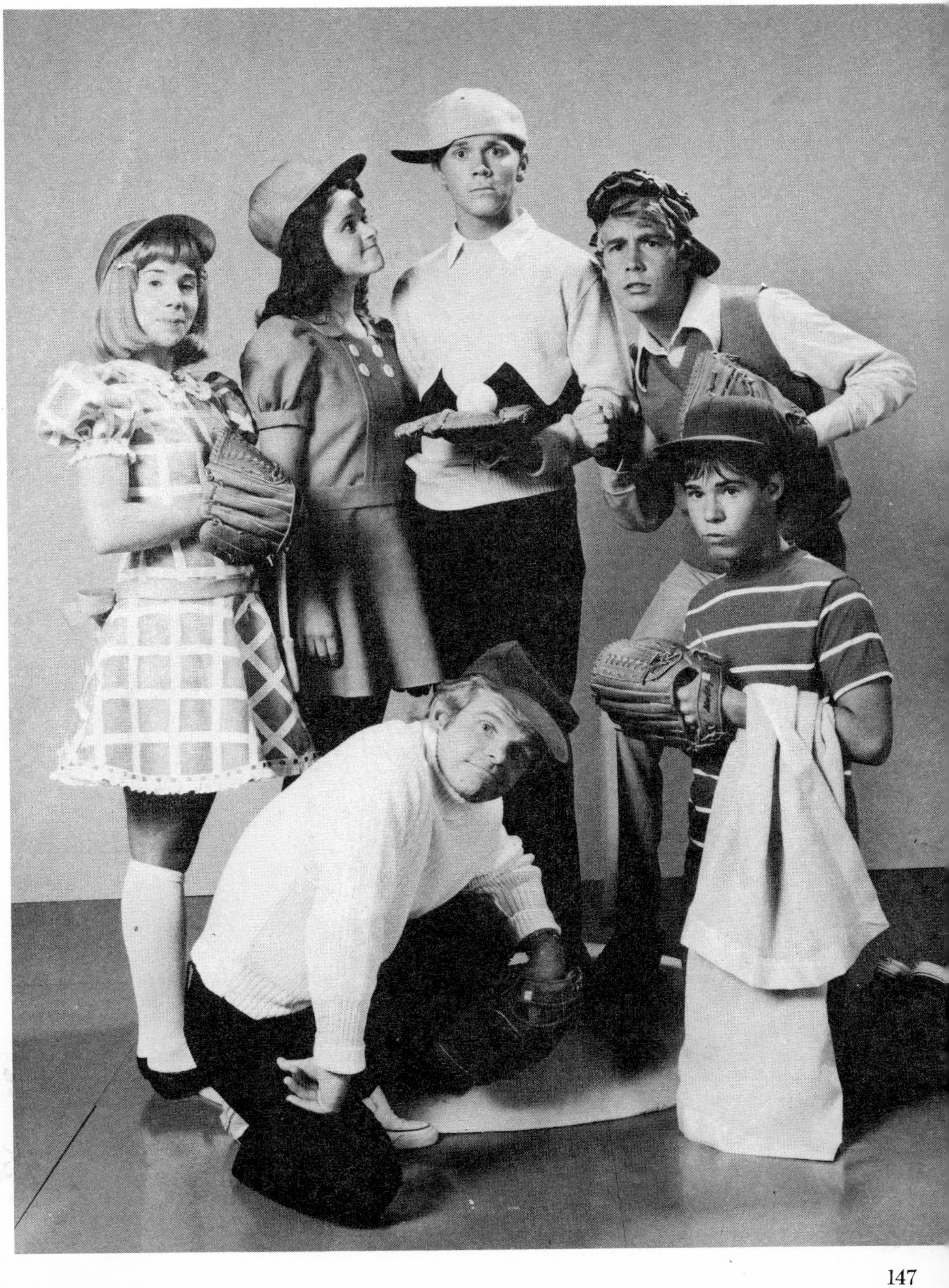

Wendell Burton (*above*) played Charlie Brown in the Hallmark presentation. The entire cast (*clockwise*) included Noelle Matlovsky (Patty), Ruby Persson (Lucy), Burton, Mark Montgomery (Schroeder), Barry Livingston (Linus), and Bill Hinnant (Snoopy).

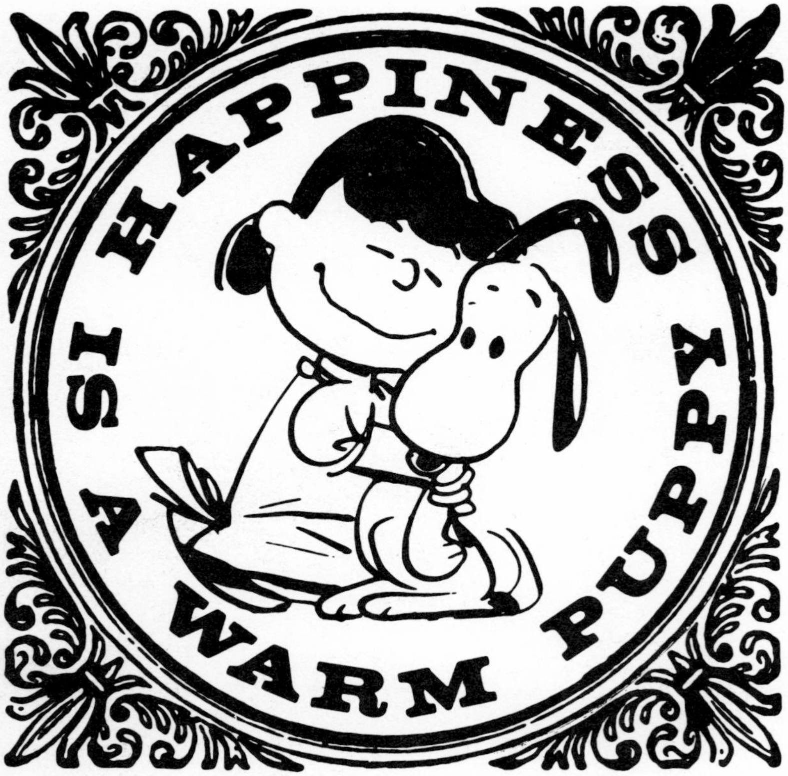
HAPPINESS IS A WARM PUPPY

Gesner's great musical score included the hit song "Happiness," which itself had been inspired by this small book (*left*) which was published in 1962. It became the number one best seller nationally on both the fiction and nonfiction lists. The idea of the book came from Connie Boucher, president of Determined Productions, whose company produces many of the *Peanuts* products. One of those products in particular—a stuffed *Snoopy* doll—has become so popular that a recent newspaper article declared that "Snoopy has replaced the teddy bear in the cribs of America." Speaking about these *Snoopy* dolls, Sparky said:

"I realized lately that, after all these years, in one sense Snoopy has gone off and is leading a life of his own in certain ways . . . especially the stuffed Snoopy. I draw the comic strip each day and of course I force Snoopy to do what I want him to do. But if a small child is playing with a stuffed *Snoopy*, Snoopy is now off in this other life doing things over which I have no control. He's out there kind of living his own life. It's kinda spooky when you think about it."

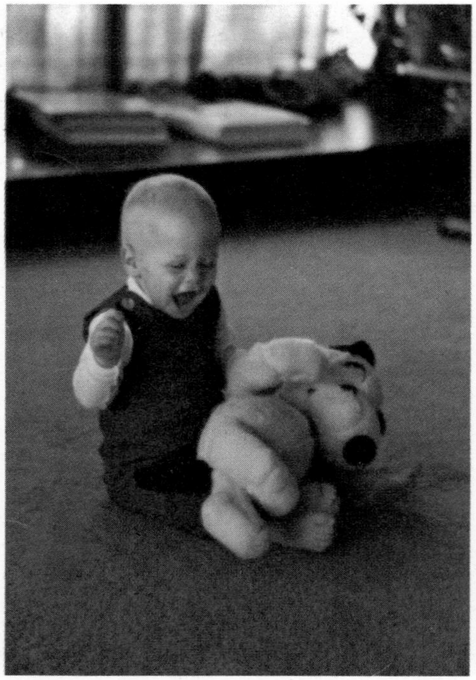

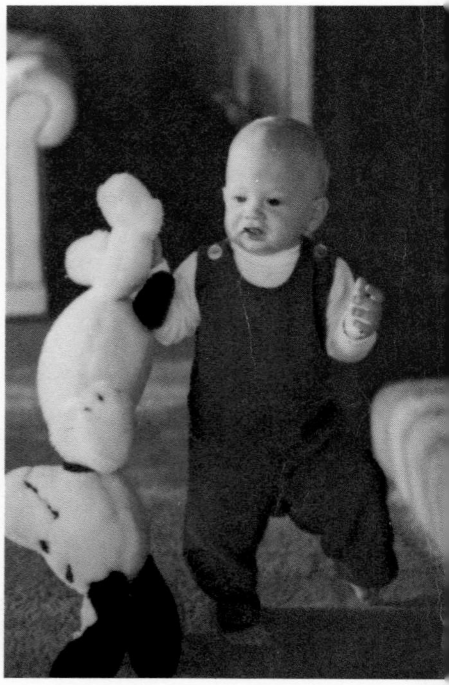

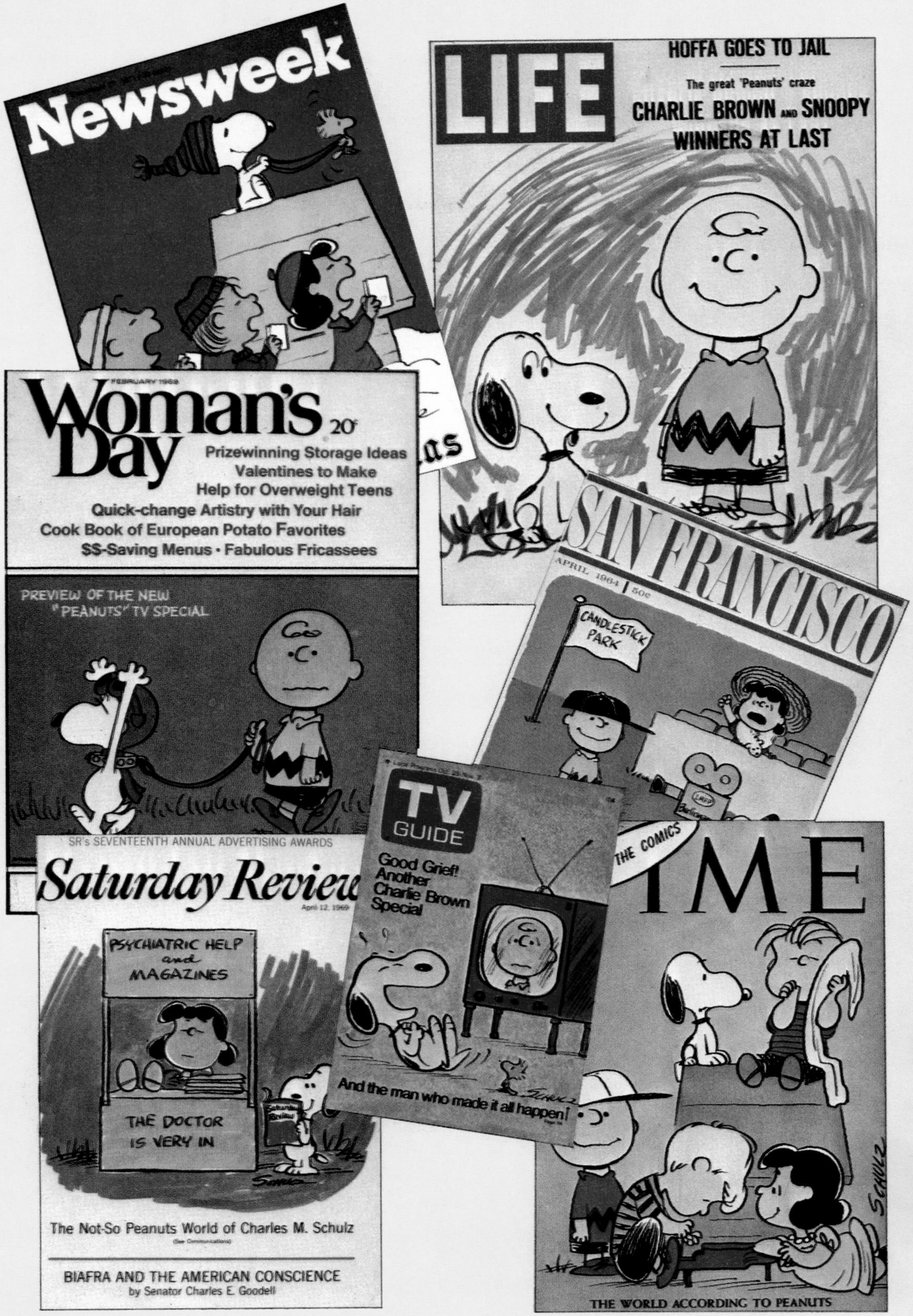
Newsweek
LIFE
HOFFA GOES TO JAIL
The great 'Peanuts' craze
CHARLIE BROWN AND SNOOPY
WINNERS AT LAST
FEBRUARY 1969
Woman's Day
20¢
Prizewinning Storage Ideas
Valentines to Make
Help for Overweight Teens
Quick-change Artistry with Your Hair
Cook Book of European Potato Favorites
$$-Saving Menus · Fabulous Fricassees
PREVIEW OF THE NEW "PEANUTS" TV SPECIAL
SAN FRANCISCO
APRIL 1964 50¢
CANDLESTICK PARK
TV GUIDE
Good Grief! Another Charlie Brown Special
And the man who made it all happen!
THE COMICS
IME
SR's SEVENTEENTH ANNUAL ADVERTISING AWARDS
Saturday Revie
April 12, 1969
PSYCHIATRIC HELP and MAGAZINES
THE DOCTOR IS VERY IN
The Not-So Peanuts World of Charles M. Schulz
BIAFRA AND THE AMERICAN CONSCIENCE
by Senator Charles E. Goodell
THE WORLD ACCORDING TO PEANUTS
SCHULZ

Sparky is an avid moviegoer, book reader, and magazine reader. Thus it has been especially pleasing to him to have seen his characters on the covers of many national magazines. I note that only one of the characters appears on *each* of these covers, and wouldn't you know that it would be Snoopy.

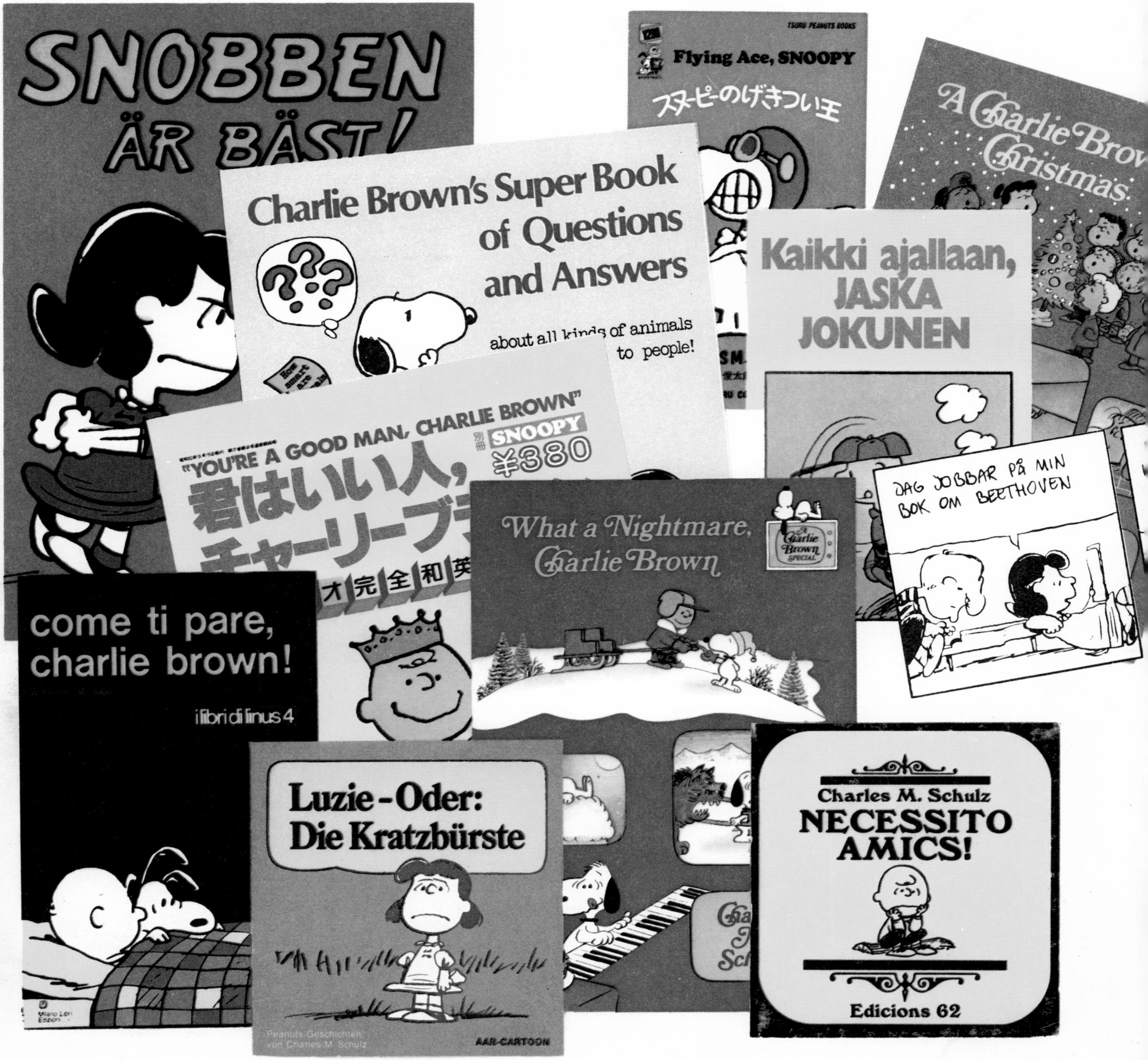
SNOBBEN ÄR BÄST!
TSURU PEANUTS BOOKS
Flying Ace, SNOOPY
スヌーピーのげきつい王
A Charlie Brown Christmas
Charlie Brown's Super Book of Questions and Answers
about all kinds of animals
to people!
Kaikki ajallaan, JASKA JOKUNEN
"YOU'RE A GOOD MAN, CHARLIE BROWN"
別冊 SNOOPY ¥380
君はいい人,
チャーリーブラ
オ完全和英
DAG JOBBAR PÅ MIN BOK OM BEETHOVEN
What a Nightmare, Charlie Brown
A Charlie Brown SPECIAL
come ti pare, charlie brown!
i libri di linus 4
Luzie - Oder: Die Kratzbürste
Peanuts-Geschichten von Charles M. Schulz
AAR-CARTOON
Charles M. Schulz
NECESSITO AMICS!
Edicions 62

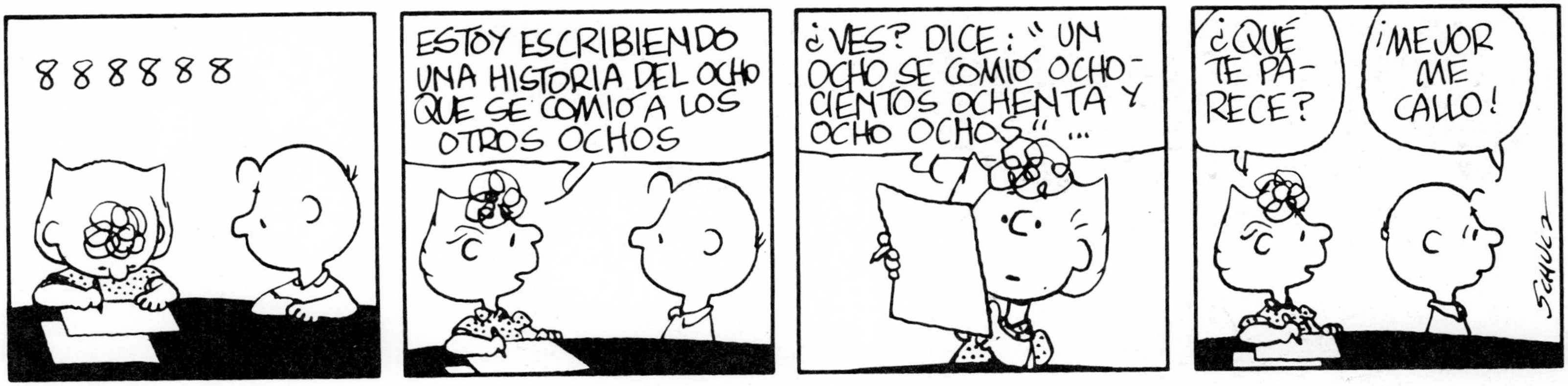
8 8 8 8 8 8
ESTOY ESCRIBIENDO UNA HISTORIA DEL OCHO QUE SE COMIÓ A LOS OTROS OCHOS
¿VES? DICE: "UN OCHO SE COMIÓ OCHO-CIENTOS OCHENTA Y OCHO OCHOS"...
¿QUÉ TE PA-RECE?
¡MEJOR ME CALLO!
SCHULZ

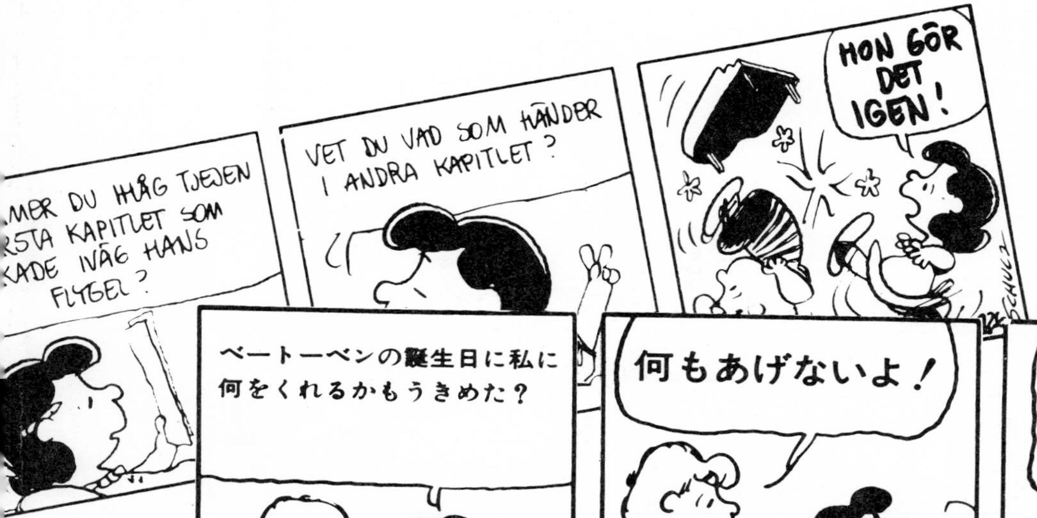
MER DU HÅG TJEJEN
RSTA KAPITLET SOM
KADE IVÄG HANS
FLYGEL?
VET DU VAD SOM HÄNDER I ANDRA KAPITLET?
HON GÖR DET IGEN!
SCHULZ

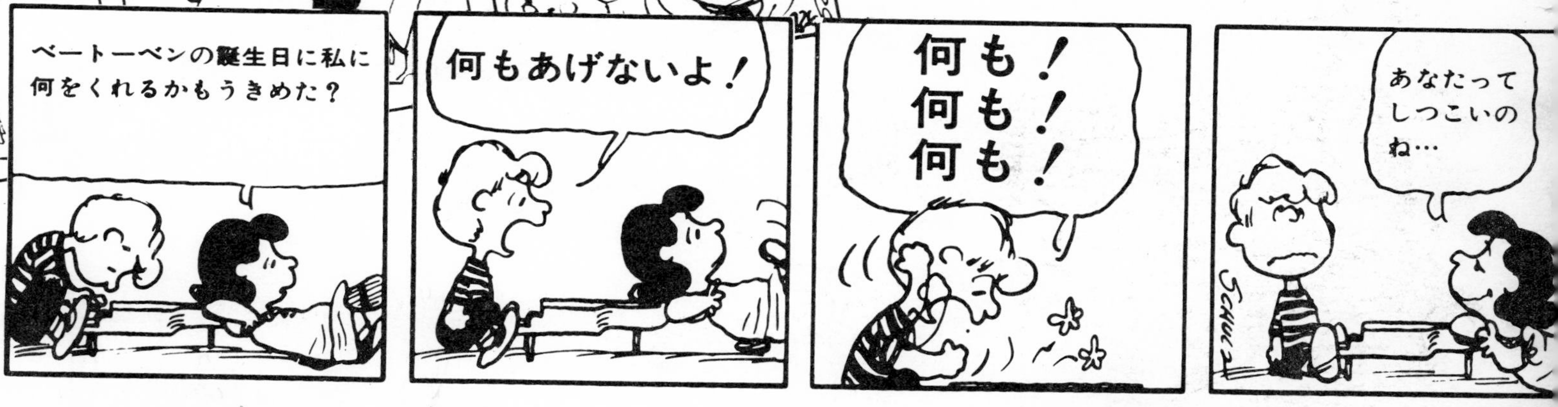
ベートーベンの誕生日に私に何をくれるかもうきめた？
何もあげないよ！
何も！何も！何も！
あなたってしつこいのね…
SCHULZ

Sparky also gets much satisfaction that his comic strip and books appear not only in the United States but in dozens of different languages around the world, as do the movies and TV shows. A recent item in *U.S. News and World Report* stated: "U.S. films make up about one third of all those shown in Poland. Twelve U.S. movies now playing in Warsaw include: *Star Wars*, *Rocky*, *Battle of Midway*, *Julia*, and *Charlie Brown and Company*." A recent animated film we made with the American Dental Association has the *Peanuts* characters showing the proper way to brush your teeth, and this film will be sent throughout the world, especially to developing countries.

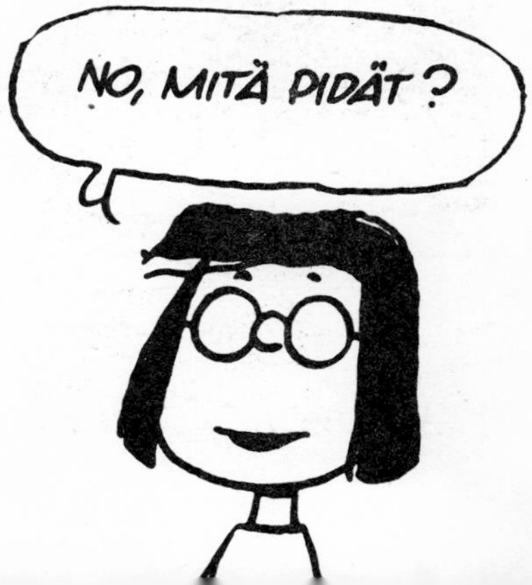
NO, MITÄ PIDÄT?

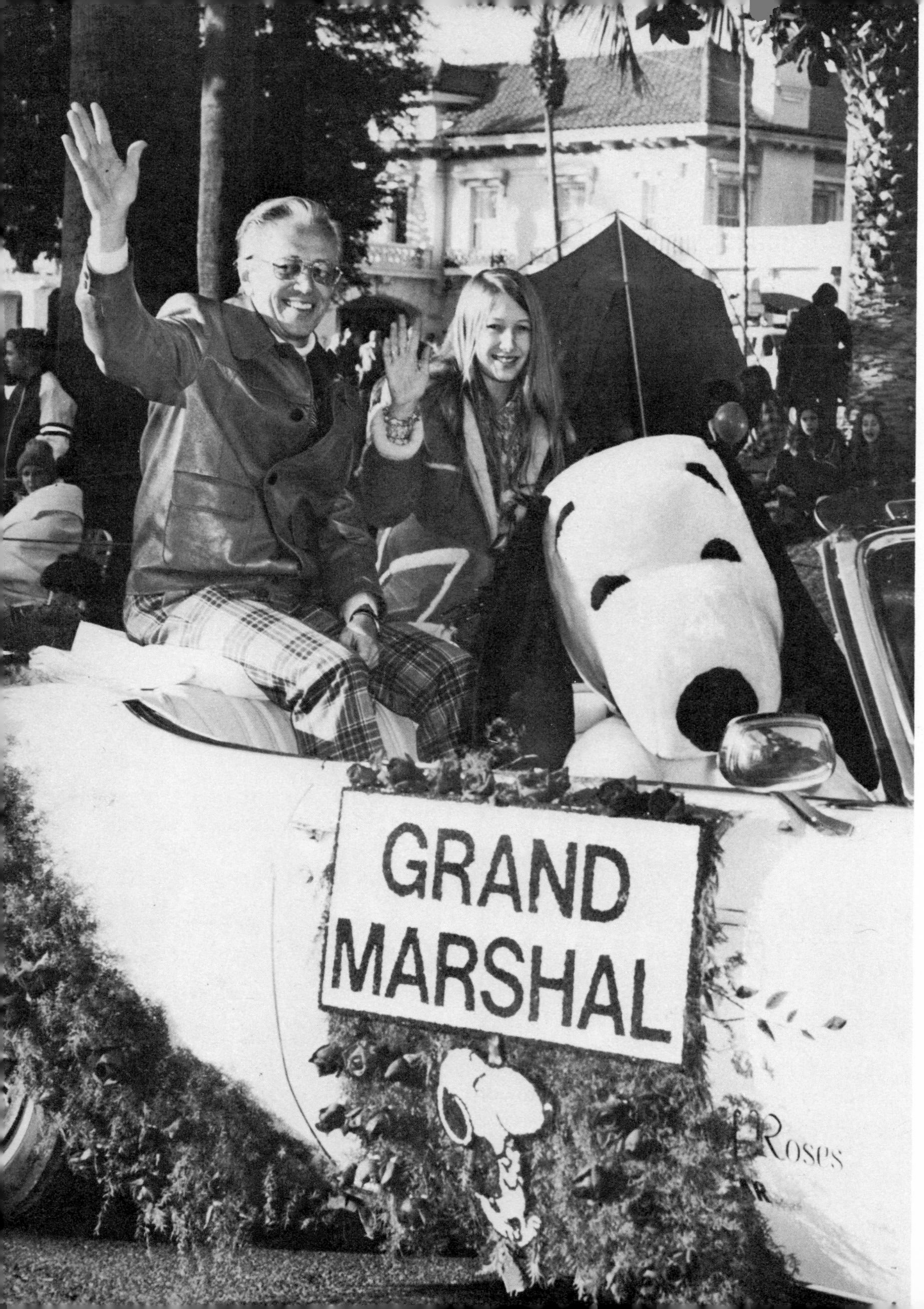
GRAND
MARSHAL

A few years ago Sparky served as Grand Marshal of the Rose Bowl Parade and was joined in the lead car by his daughter Amy.

In 1978 Sparky and Jeannie traveled to Montreal to receive the award as International Cartoonist of the Year, voted on by seven hundred comics artists from around the world.

Over these past fifteen years, Sparky, Bill Melendez, and I of course have a lot of great memories, and we've shared a lot of laughs.

We were in a men's clothing store in Hollywood a few years ago, where Sparky had just purchased a suit. The saleswoman, as she was writing up the sales slip, overheard us all talking.

She stopped writing the sales tag and asked, "Are you *the* Charles Schulz?" When Sparky nodded his head, she got very excited. "Oh . . . I've seen all your TV shows, and your movies, and I have a whole room of Snoopy things, and I never miss the comic strip and . . . oh, if you could just give me your autograph, it would make me the happiest person in the world."

Sparky is always very nice about autographs, and in fact he usually draws a character as well. He was so pleased with this lady's reaction that he proceeded to draw four or five of the characters on an 8 x 10 sheet of paper.

Well, now the lady really went "bonkers" and raced around the store showing the drawing to salespeople and customers alike.

She finally came down to earth, returned to the cash register, and started to complete the sales slip for Sparky's suit. After adding on the tax, she looked up, told Sparky the total cost, and then said, "Now, Mr. Schulz, do you have some form of identification?" We all broke up.

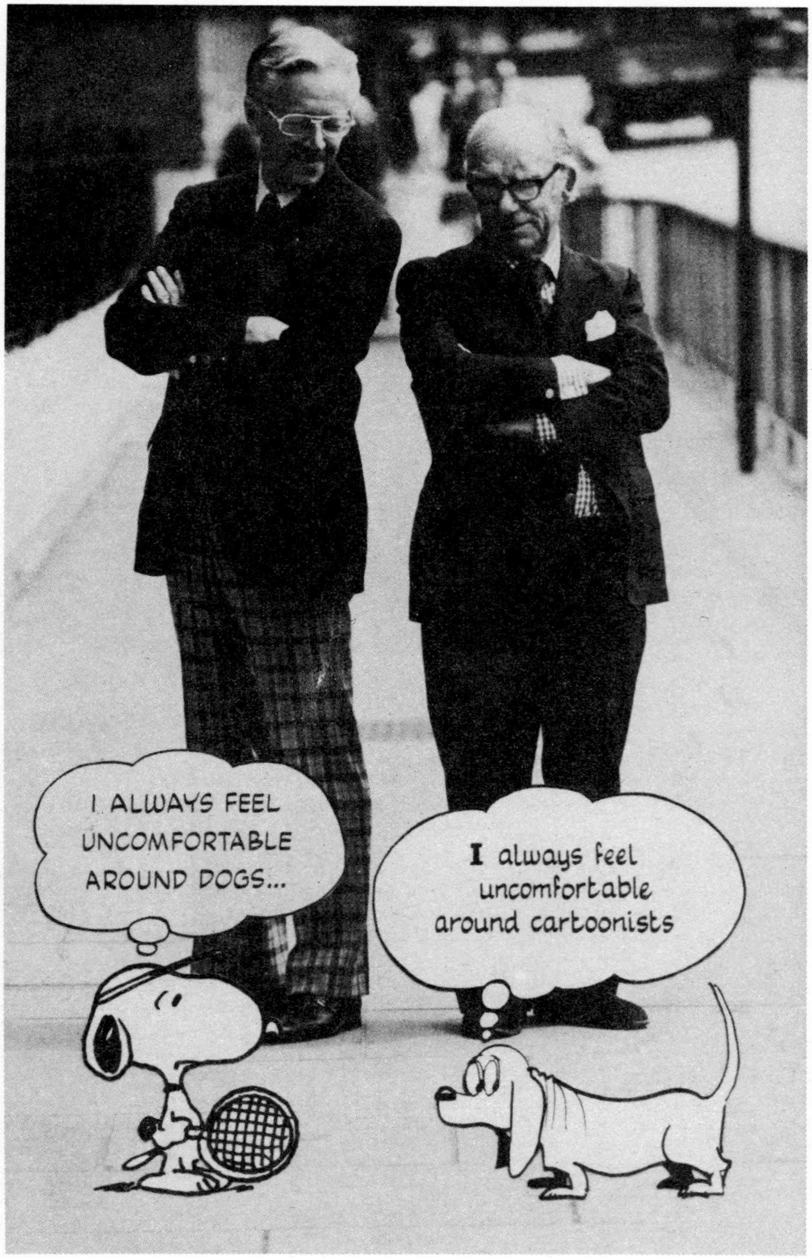
I ALWAYS FEEL UNCOMFORTABLE AROUND DOGS...
I always feel uncomfortable around cartoonists

Sparky visited Alex Graham, creator of *Fred Basset*, while attending the tournament at Wimbledon in England.

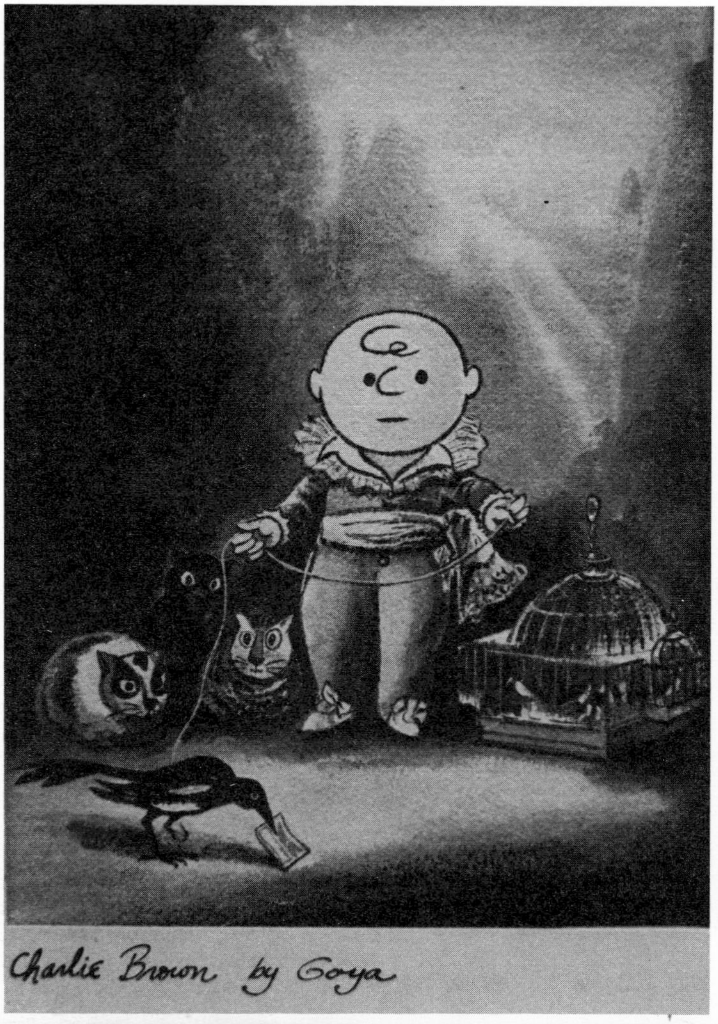
Charlie Brown by Goya

Artist Eldon Dedini sent Sparky his interpretation of how Goya might have painted Charlie Brown.

So I'm happy to report that all our trees and plants are doing very well.

And I'd like to complete my report by quoting J. Sterling Morton, founder of Arbor Day. In closing his Washington Arbor Day address of 1894 he said, "So every man, woman, and child who plants trees shall be able to say on coming as I come, toward the evening of life, in all sincerity and truth, 'If you seek my monument, look around you!'"

Many of our television specials have focused on holidays. My personal favorite is *It's Arbor Day, Charlie Brown* because we were able to talk about the beauty of nature and the importance of conservation. At the conclusion of the show Sally (*left*) read a tribute to the founder of Arbor Day. A few weeks after the broadcast Sparky received a very nice letter from the grandaughter of Mr. Morton, thanking Sparky for paying tribute to her grandfather. She said, however, that it really was Mrs. Morton — her grandmother — who was the driving force behind Mr. Morton. So we herewith set the record straight!

Thank you.

"WERE YOU IN WHEN I CALLED?" SHE ASKED
HEE HEE HEE HEE

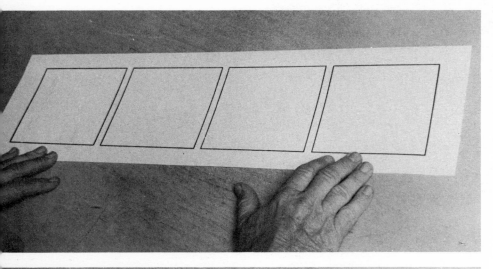

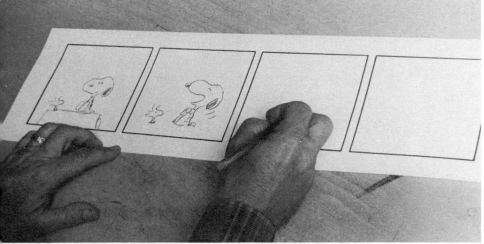

I would think that the most fitting conclusion to this book of celebration would be to go to where it all began — the drawing board.

Every day he must stare at those blank four squares and create a new, funny idea. He once described it to me "like having to do a new term paper every day." Some days the idea comes immediately, other days he may sit for hours and come up with nothing.

When he does commit himself to drawing, he'll sketch everything in pencil first. His space — these four squares — and his time — just a few seconds of the reader's attention — demand a tremendous focus from him as both artist and humorist.

After he completes the sketches and words in pencil, he will start the final process in pen and ink.

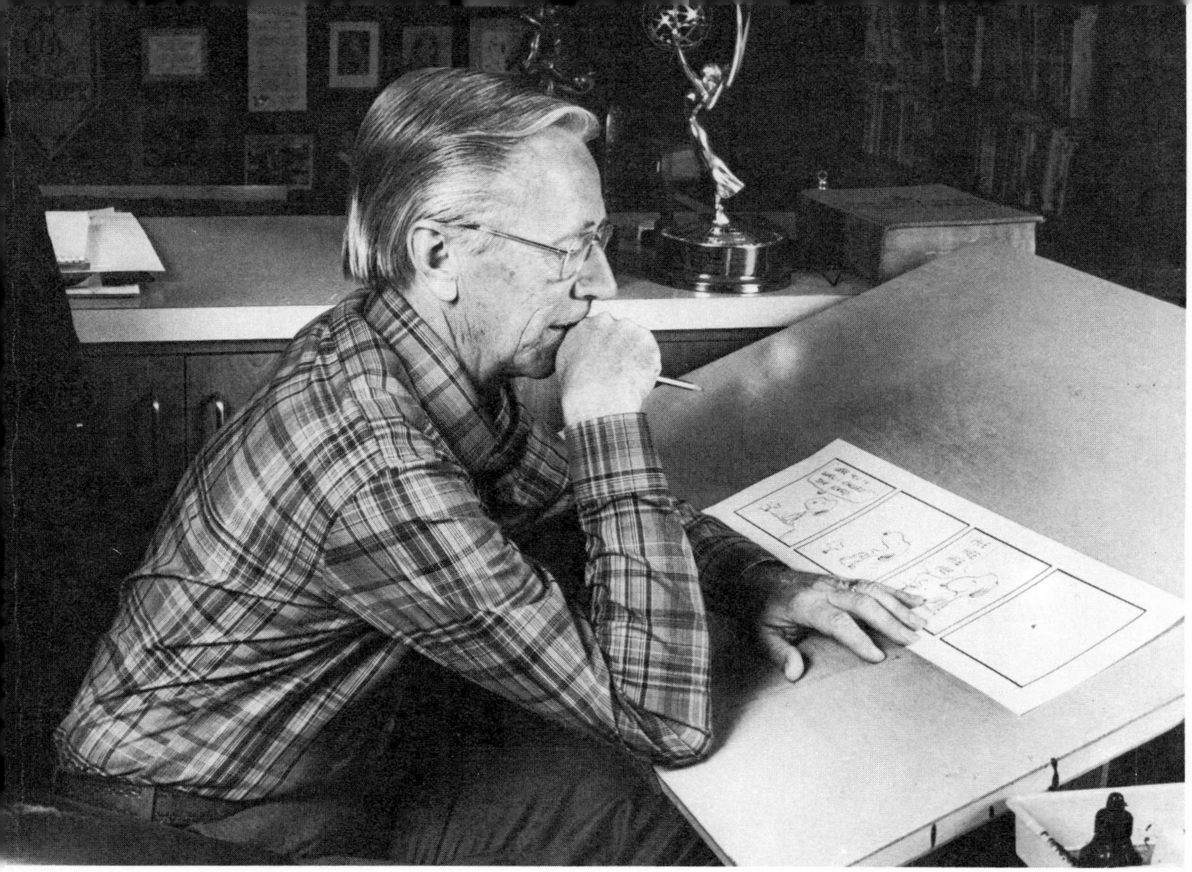

And then . . . that final square. The payoff, the punchline, that he's had to deliver over ten thousand times.

A moving poem on the following page by Monte Schulz, Sparky's son, best sums it up:

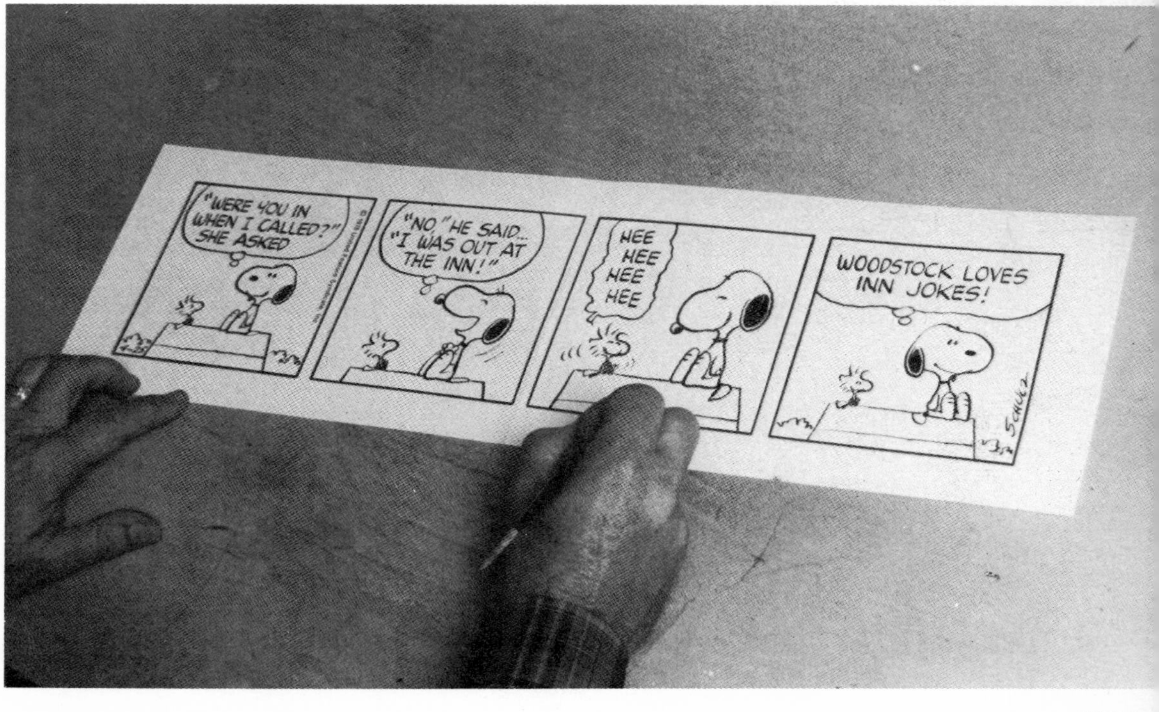
"WERE YOU IN WHEN I CALLED?" SHE ASKED
"NO," HE SAID... "I WAS OUT AT THE INN!"
HEE HEE HEE HEE
WOODSTOCK LOVES INN JOKES!
SCHULZ

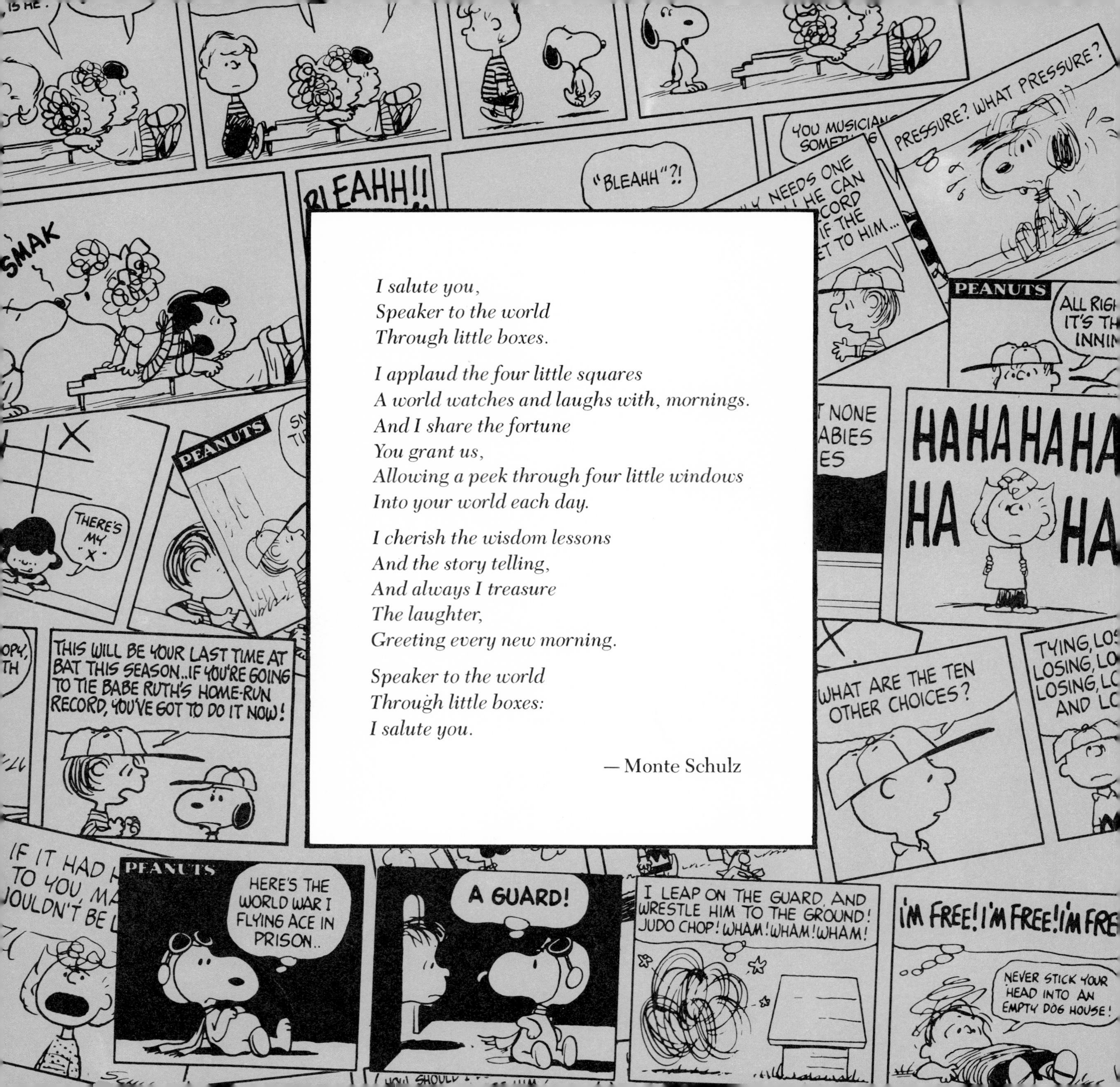
SMAK
"BLEAHH"?!
PRESSURE? WHAT PRESSURE?
PEANUTS
THERE'S MY "X"
HAHAHAHA
HA
HA
THIS WILL BE YOUR LAST TIME AT BAT THIS SEASON..IF YOU'RE GOING TO TIE BABE RUTH'S HOME-RUN RECORD, YOU'VE GOT TO DO IT NOW!
WHAT ARE THE TEN OTHER CHOICES?
PEANUTS
HERE'S THE WORLD WAR I FLYING ACE IN PRISON..
A GUARD!
I LEAP ON THE GUARD AND WRESTLE HIM TO THE GROUND! JUDO CHOP! WHAM! WHAM! WHAM!
NEVER STICK YOUR HEAD INTO AN EMPTY DOG HOUSE!

I salute you,
Speaker to the world
Through little boxes.

I applaud the four little squares
A world watches and laughs with, mornings.
And I share the fortune
You grant us,
Allowing a peek through four little windows
Into your world each day.

I cherish the wisdom lessons
And the story telling,
And always I treasure
The laughter,
Greeting every new morning.

Speaker to the world
Through little boxes:
I salute you.

— Monte Schulz

ACKNOWLEDGMENTS

We would like to thank the following people for
their contribution to the preparation of this book:
Ole Risom, our editor; Bill Melendez and his staff
for their art work; and Murray DeAtley (CBS-TV Press)
and Glenn Mendelson for their photography

CREDITS

"Linus and Lucy" © 1965 Record Specialist Inc.
and the Estate of Vince Guaraldi, by special
permission.
Photographs of Apollo 10 mission, by permission
of the National Aeronautics and Space Administration,
Houston, Texas.
Photograph of Hank Aaron, by special permission of
the Atlanta Braves.
The following covers:
Woman's Day, reprinted by permission of Woman's
Day Magazine. Copyright © 1968 by CBS
Publications, Inc.
San Francisco Magazine, reprinted by courtesy of
San Francisco Magazine. All rights reserved.
Life, reprinted by courtesy of Life Magazine,
© 1967 Time Inc.
Saturday Review, reprinted by permission of
Saturday Review Inc. © 1969.
Time, reprinted by special permission of
Time Magazine, © 1965, 1967, 1969 Time Inc.
All rights reserved.
TV Guide, reprinted with permission from TV GUIDE®
Magazine. Copyright © 1972 by Triangle Publications,
Inc., Radnor, Pa.
Ms., reprinted by special permission © 1976 Ms.
Magazine Corp. All rights reserved.
Newsweek, reprinted by special permission © 1971 by
Newsweek, Inc. All rights reserved.